A

BOOK

The Philip E. Lilienthal imprint
honors special books
in commemoration of a man whose work
at University of California Press from 1954 to 1979
was marked by dedication to young authors
and to high standards in the field of Asian Studies.
Friends, family, authors, and foundations have together
endowed the Lilienthal Fund, which enables UC Press
to publish under this imprint selected books
in a way that reflects the taste and judgment
of a great and beloved editor.

THE SCRIPTURE ON GREAT PEACE

DAOIST CLASSICS SERIES

Stephen R. Bokenkamp, Series Editor

Barbara Hendrischke

THE SCRIPTURE
ON GREAT PEACE

The *Taiping jing* and the
Beginnings of Daoism

University of California Press

Berkeley   Los Angeles   London

University of California Press, one of the most
distinguished university presses in the United States,
enriches lives around the world by advancing
scholarship in the humanities, social sciences, and
natural sciences. Its activities are supported by the UC
Press Foundation and by philanthropic contributions
from individuals and institutions. For more information,
visit www.ucpress.edu.

University of California Press
Berkeley and Los Angeles, California

University of California Press, Ltd.
London, England

Library of Congress Cataloging-in-Publication Data

Tai ping jing. English
    The scripture on great peace : the Taiping jing and
the beginnings of Daoism / [translated by] Barbara
Hendrischke.
        p.   cm—(Daoist classics series)
    Includes bibliographical references and index.
    ISBN-13: 978-0-520-28628-3 (pbk : alk. paper)
    ISBN-10: 0-520-24788-4 (cloth : alk. paper).
    1. Hendrischke, Barbara, 1940–   II. Title.
III. Title: Taiping jing and the beginning of Daoism.
BL1900.T22552E64   2007
299.5'1482—dc22   2006018986

Manufactured in the United States of America

21   20   19   18   17   16   15
10   9   8   7   6   5   4   3   2   1

This book is printed on Natures Book, which contains
50% post-consumer waste and meets the minimum
requirements of ANSI/NISO Z39.48–1992 (R 1997)
(*Permanence of Paper*).

CONTENTS

PREFACE

The *Taiping jing*, or *Scripture on Great Peace*, sets forth views on social and political organization that are exceptional. There is nothing quite like them in other texts from ancient and early medieval China. The text proclaims that the traditional gap between the status of men and of women and also between leaders and followers must be narrowed. It also questions the reliability of scholarly traditions of reasoning and demands that the belief in heaven's life-giving power be the sole principle of human action. It invites every concerned individual to enter into an ongoing dialogue with everyone else. Humankind, faced with the possibility of an imminent and violent end to the world brought about by the crimes that men have committed throughout history, is called upon to jointly mobilize its resources. There is therefore no doubt that this text has a lot to say, but it is not easy to access its message. Recent Chinese editions and Chinese-language translations of the text, however, have eliminated some of the problems inherent in accessing its message, and this translation is deeply indebted to them.

My involvement with the *Scripture on Great Peace* has been of some duration, and thanks are due to many colleagues and friends, and in particular to everyone in Daoist studies. From my perspective, Daologists across the world have shown themselves to be true followers of the *dao*, open, cooperative, and happy to share information and invite others to venture into their field. Special thanks are due to Christoph Harbsmeier for initiating this translation project. The librarians at the University of Sydney's Fisher Library and at the University of New South Wales have helped me access resources. Jon Kowallis and Lance Eccles have critically looked at passages of my work. Sue Wiles and Mary Severance have helped to improve its readability. Florian Reiter has been a source of encouragement, and Hans Hendrischke has provided generous organizational support. The comments of Gil Raz and the University of California Press's anonymous reader have been instructive and inspiring. Stephen Bokenkamp has patiently and with great wisdom made this publication possible.

CONVENTIONS

This translation of the *Taiping jing* follows the wording of the second edition of Wang Ming's text, published in Beijing in 1979. His emendations of the original text found in the Daoist canon are followed unless otherwise specified; his punctuation is occasionally replaced by that used in more recent editions.

References to the text are by section and page number. Since Wang Ming's edition is divided into chapters this might at first sight be confusing; however, this system is meant to help organize the text into meaningful units. The received text is divided into chapters *(juan)*, and each chapter is subdivided into several sections. Each section typically deals with a single topic, and the sections assembled in one chapter often have little in common. For this reason the chapter number is irrelevant for understanding and interpreting the scripture and is therefore ignored when quoting passages from the text.

In addition to section and page number, references to the text point to the layer to which a passage belongs (for more on this, see the Appendix). When no layer is mentioned the material is from layer A, that is, from those parts of the text where a Celestial Master talks to his disciples. When the passage referred to is not from the *Taiping jing* proper but from its Tang dynasty digest, the *Taiping jing chao*, this is so indicated: the word *Chao* is added to the reference, as is the respective part of the nine parts of the *Chao* that have been transmitted. There is a purpose to this rather cumbersome and space-consuming method of referring to the text. By the standards of ancient and early medieval texts the *Taiping jing* is a long scripture, and yet I have observed that its internal logic is remarkable. To locate all the passages referred to in their own environment might allow readers to share this observation and help them appreciate the text's coherence and argumentative insistence.

· Introduction

The *Taiping jing* 太平經, or *Scripture on Great Peace* (hereafter TPJ), is an outsider with respect to China's tradition of great books. It differs in content and style from the texts that helped to create, nourish, and sustain the country's central institutions and thereby became part of them. It was not until the twentieth century, when scholars began to articulate their skepticism about these institutions and search for alternative traditions, that the TPJ gained broader scholarly attention.

When Werner Eichhorn took an interest in the TPJ in the 1940s and 1950s he approached it with the suspicion that he would find something akin to an early Chinese version of the *Communist Manifesto* in terms of its dynamic impact and its call to the exploited masses of the Chinese peasantry to discard their chains.[1] Eichhorn soon realized, however, that this was not quite the case. Instead, the TPJ's authors warned people not to ignore existing hierarchies and admonished subordinates to obey and support their leaders in an orderly fashion. Nevertheless, Eichhorn remained interested in the scripture. Contrary to earlier voices, both Chinese and Western, he insisted that the authors of the TPJ were serious in their attempt to reform society, improve the lot of women, and strengthen people's belief in heaven. Their message, he argued, was coherent and of historical relevance. At the end of the Han dynasty the authors of the TPJ attempted to restore to the fading dynasty the harmony, order, and happiness of its first decades, now a memory some three centuries old.

When the Communist Party came to power in China in 1949, the TPJ received more attention from scholars and intellectuals than it had since its first publication in the sixth century C.E. Scholars like Hou Wailu and Yang Kuan as well as the wider public read the text as if it were the foundation for that alternative tradition of peasant culture, peasant uprisings, and critical, materialist thought that China's Communist intellectuals saw as their own.[2] The TPJ was hailed as the voice of the landless who in the second century C.E. had drifted through the Chinese countryside in search of a livelihood. We know that these people confronted landowners and government representatives not just by voicing slogans and reform proposals, but with arms, and before long their opposition led to the downfall of the ruling dynasty. China's twentieth-century Communist scholars and intellectuals placed the TPJ in the midst of all this. The drastic formulations of the peasants' misery struck Communist readers as a depiction of a prerevolutionary era: the people were impoverished and starving, left without protection against illness, or perished in prisons without cause. In their destitution they rid themselves of their baby girls in order to save the expense of raising them, or they abandoned all family ties and refrained from marrying. Many died young and without offspring. People did not even have the means to properly bury their dead. The authors of the TPJ called the wealthy and powerful to task for all this, and they accused the rulers of shirking their responsibility for the people's welfare.

The main interest of Chinese Communist scholars was the TPJ's message. Their attempts to investigate the text's composition and authorship were curtailed by the ideological desire to uphold its status as an authoritative formulation of early revolutionary sentiment. Free from such constraints, Japanese scholars, on the other hand, tackled the text's origin and history in earnest. Ōfuchi Ninji, Yoshioka Yoshitoyo, and others came to conclusions about the writing, editing, and publishing of the text that have been widely accepted.[3] Their work integrated the history of the TPJ in the broader context of the cultural and intellectual development of medieval China, in which religious practices and ideas played an increasingly important role. They stressed that medieval Daoism contained a powerful message of salvation. For historical as well as doctrinal reasons, the TPJ was central to this message.

In reconstructing the history of the text, Ōfuchi, Yoshioka, and others perused a wide range of medieval China's Daoist material, dating from the second to the eighth century. Max Kaltenmark's focus was narrower.[4] He firmly situated the scripture at the onset of Daoist religious thought. In his interpretation, the TPJ authors introduced their readers to the basics of a Daoist way of life, combining political ideas with elements of personal lifestyle. Men were told that in their personal lives they must concentrate their vital essence in order to remain in good health and live a long life, and in particular they must practice meditation in order to increase their energy and achieve their goals. They must also follow general rules of good behavior and be prepared to be held responsible for their earthly deeds after death. On a communal level, believers were advised to create institutions that would allow them to cooperate with and care for one another and to protect the environment in which they lived. People were expected to share whatever material goods, knowledge, or skills they possessed so that general harmony and happiness would prevail.

The TPJ is rich enough to support each of these interpretations. Historically, it throws light on the Chinese worldview during the period of late antiquity. During this era the unified empire that went back to the First Emperor of the Qin and the founders of the Han dynasty who succeeded him had lasted for several centuries and was on the verge of breaking up. During the first and second centuries C.E. new economic forces had emerged, established hierarchies had dissolved, and the empire's governance was rapidly deteriorating. This created social and economic hardships that in turn raised new concerns and fears not addressed by the prevailing philosophical and political ideas that had helped to maintain and stabilize the empire and its organs. A process of intellectual reorientation that involved academic institutions and their prominent representatives as well as the wider public thus came into play. A rapid growth of religious interest, which encompassed all social strata, is testimony to this. It may well be said that the TPJ represents a critical review of dominant Han dynasty social and moral ideas from the perspective of this newly formed religious consciousness.

Since the views of the TPJ were later incorporated into the Daoist tradition, it is tempting to call the religious views expressed in the text "Daoist." It would be more precise, however, to see the text as a link between what has been termed early China's "common religion" and the later Daoist tradition. The text deals with the relationship between man and heaven, man's sins against heaven and the resulting punishment, the approaching apocalypse, and heaven's promise of salvation. Heaven's envoy, the Celestial Master, who speaks through the TPJ, has arrived to announce this promise to the world. The book contains lists of commandments and suggests that individuals who follow these might be rewarded by health and long life, both for themselves and for their children. It explains what to expect after death and how to prepare for it. All this is addressed in the first instance to a group of believers, but it is meant to reach the men who hold political power. The Celestial Master's pledge is that if the rulers do as he bids, they will prosper as individuals and they will make their subjects happy.

Because the TPJ does not belong to China's "great tradition," Chinese philological researchers did not tackle this text until the second half of the twentieth century. This means that it has come down to us more directly than have most "great" texts. It has not been revised and smoothed by generations of editors and commentators, as so many other old Chinese texts have been. The text as it stands is poorly written, containing mistaken characters and strange words and expressions. Dogmatic variations and modifications and sometimes even inconsistencies abound. However, it is also full of unusual ideas and unique concepts. It is the aim of this translation to give a full picture of the text, that is, of its rhetoric, its argumentation, and its ideas. A consecutive part of it has therefore been translated, including sections with an intriguing and important message and others that seem to have relatively little to say.

Since the TPJ is a rather isolated text, it is not always easy to comprehend what it says. Still, the main ideas are clear and not difficult to understand, even for readers who are not acquainted with the world from which it stems. It is actually more accessible than most Daoist texts: it uses only a limited number of technical terms, and it presupposes very little education in doctrinal matters. Despite this, the notes that accompany this translation are long. They are an attempt to clarify and elaborate upon the arguments put forth by introducing material from other parts of the text. They are also an attempt to show how much the TPJ is indebted to and a part of China's mainstream intellectual history, without ever acknowledging its indebtedness by naming its sources or quoting them in detail.[5]

THE NOTION OF "GREAT PEACE"

The TPJ does not belong to any group of texts, nor does it speak for the interests of any well-defined school or faction. There is, therefore, no simple way to identify its place in history or the traditions to which it belongs. Instead, an indirect approach might be helpful for sketching its intellectual and social environment. The text deals with the arrival of "great peace" *(taiping)*. Politicians and thinkers of the Han dynasty (206 B.C.E.–220 C.E.) made much use of this term, and their understanding of *taiping* forms one of the foundations of the TPJ's social and religious teachings. At the same time, and in a contrasting social and intellectual environment, there was, moreover, a Taiping Movement that resulted in violent peasant uprisings. The program of these rebels can also serve as background for the message conveyed in the TPJ. But while the authors of the text are indebted to the ideas and ideals of both groups, that is, of politicians as well as of peasant rebels, their aims and ways of thinking cannot be identified with either.

"The Scripture on Great Peace" is an impressive title. The word "scripture" *(jing)* places the text in proximity to the classical works transmitted from a venerable past. To recite these works was said to be the beginning of all learning.[6] A scripture was expected to address a serious and universal need. The character *jing* originally signified a warp, that is, the vertical thread in weaving, and also, in a slightly different written form, a road, that is, something that is being employed to pass through things.[7] One of the first books recorded as *jing* was the *Mohist Canon*, a concise text on the art of reasoning.[8] The title "scripture" was honorary. It was attached to texts that were or were thought to be comprehensive, unique, or seminal. There are long "scriptures" among the thirteen classics, but the short *Laozi* was also called a "scripture." *Jing* was seldom applied to the works of an individual. The *Taixuan jing* by Yang Xiong (53 B.C.E.–18 C.E.) is an exception. It was characteristic of a scripture that it would invite exegesis,[9] so that a host of commentaries might develop around it. Although as the Daoist and Buddhist canons grew the number of "scriptures" increased, the word remained a sign of respect.[10]

The slogan of "great peace" referred to political stability and social harmony. The character *ping* is a pictogram of a set of scales. While "great" *(tai)* can be rendered as "universal," it also functions as a device to make another character into a noun and give it the honor and weight of a concept.[11] "Great peace" sounded attractive to everyone. It did not point to any particular philosophy or ideology, and therefore it did not alienate anybody. While there can be no doubt about the origins of the TPJ, one of China's earliest and most relevant religious texts, an interest in great peace preceded the beginnings of religious Daoism and also extended far beyond it. The following two occurrences of great peace are striking.

The First Emperor of the Qin dynasty (221–206 B.C.E.) is said to have declared:

> Previously I have collected what has been written and have expurgated from it all that was found useless. I have assembled large numbers of experts on literature and on vitality techniques. I wanted to promote great peace.[12]

In 1853, the Christian-oriented leader of one of the largest rebellions China had ever experienced established the Heavenly Kingdom of Great Peace (*Taiping tianguo* 太平天國) in Nanjing and reigned over much of eastern and central China for more than ten years. In both of the above instances, the notion was used in a programmatic sense, pointing to the direction in which society as a whole was expected to move. The mention of great peace was meant to authorize a change of power. Both historical figures were empire builders—real or potential—with a keen sense of their public image and of the power of cultural symbols.

The idea of great peace did not come into use until the period preceding the creation of the Qin dynasty empire, that is, in the third century B.C.E. It does not go back to ancient China's great philosophers, who typically formulated specific concepts of how to behave and how to govern that were meant to compete with and oppose other specific concepts. Despite their differences, however, these philosophers were all interested in the question of what sort of conduct would lead to good government, social order, and personal happiness,[13] and for some of their Han dynasty successors, "great peace" meant just that. Others, however, envisaged the need for a wider range of forces and argued that good conduct alone would not suffice to achieve great peace. A ruler who acted humanely, on the advice of Mengzi, or with general concern, as Mozi suggested, would not achieve it. Neither would rule by law in the fashion of Han Feizi. Instead, from the second century B.C.E. onward, mystical aspects of ancient thought came to the fore. The disengagement of a leader who remained distant, remote, and immobile like the pole star[14] and the strengthening of spiritual power[15] were seen as good preparation for putting the world and oneself in order, as was simplicity. The *Laozi* and other quietist works praised such conduct. With the establishment of the Han dynasty, the *Laozi* became or remained a very popular book. Certain aspects of its message were adopted by influential political thinkers. These aspects were reflected in the *Chun qiu fan lu*, for example, a text said to go back to Dong Zhongshu 董仲舒 (ca. 179–ca. 104 B.C.E.), who became famous for his promotion of Confucian ideas. The *Chun qiu fan lu* says that the ruler of a country should be like the heart, which keeps the body in order through its retirement and seclusion. The ruler should thus remain disengaged and reign the country through *wu wei* 無為, that is, through nonpurposive action, as advocated in the *Laozi*, and thereby bring about great peace.[16] It was a ruler's "virtue" or "power" (*de* 德)—a term explicated in Laozi's *Daode jing*—that was said to enable him to attain great peace.[17]

The significance of great peace and the question of how to obtain it became a focus of Han dynasty political thought. Risking oversimplification, one might say that one position stressed the ruler's spiritual perfection and emphasized minimalist administrative procedures and strong psychological control, and that the other was mainly concerned with the moral character of a ruler and his entourage and with proper and wide-ranging administrative policies. Pursuant to this division, some thinkers were interested in the changes great peace would bring to astronomical phenomena, weather conditions, and nature in general, while others thought that social order and the people's contentment alone were signs of great peace, and that there was no reason to look for other tokens. Although the two positions coexisted and often coincided, they still characterize two contrasting approaches to the issue.

He Xiu 何休(129–82) was a prominent advocate of the second position, and proper administration was for him an important issue. Following Mengzi's lead, he saw as great peace a situation in which the population praised the ruler because taxes were low.[18] For him, songs of praise as they were transmitted in the *Book of Songs* were proof of the prevalence of great peace.[19]

To consider the people's attitudes as heaven's voice was in line with pre-Qin ideas about the "mandate of heaven." The people's satisfaction was a main criterion for great peace.[20] This point was expressed in the *Han shu* chapter on ritual and music in the following manner:

> A king must rely on the rituals practiced by former kings; that is, he must take measures appropriate to the season of the year. Loss as well as benefit arises from the feelings of the people. When regulations are implemented step by step, great peace will be attained and everything will be all right.[21]

Here the stress is upon a ruler's respect for and ritual observation of the course of the agricultural year. The happiness of the people, and in consequence the arrival of great peace, depends upon it.

The ruler's respect for moral values is another issue. As Wang Chong (27–ca. 100) put it:

> The proof that government has managed to establish great peace is that the population responds to this by feeling secure and cheerful. Confucius said: "Cultivate yourself, and you will make the population feel secure. Even Yao and Shun found this difficult." That the people feel secure is proof of great peace. When someone rules over others, men must be his starting point. When the people feel secure, Yin and Yang are in harmony. When they are in harmony, the ten thousand beings and plants are being nourished.[22]

Again, the critical factor here is the mood of the population. Once the people are happy the harmony among them will improve the natural environment. A ruler is expected to look after his subjects, and thus start the process that will lead to general improvement and that will eventually also involve weather conditions and the harvest.

Perceived from this angle, political factors are responsible for the onset of great peace; however, once it has come about heaven and earth will cooperate to create a harmonious and prosperous natural environment. Rain, wind, snow, and dew will all come at the right time and place, and even thunder and lightning will no longer cause fear. The forces of Yin and Yang will be in complete balance.[23]

There was, however, an alternative approach. Since cosmic harmony was seen as resulting from natural forces, some thinkers stressed the need to directly involve nature in the process of creating great peace. Zhuangzi hinted at this need when he praised the ideal world of the past:

> When reward and punishment were clear, foolish and wise were properly placed, noble and base occupied their stations, worthy and inadequate were seen for what they were; invariably they were allotted tasks according to their abilities, invariably their tasks derived from their titles. This is how one served the man above or was pastor to the men below, put other things in order or cultivated one's own person. Cleverness and strategy were unused. Men invariably referred back to what was from heaven in them (*bi gui qi tian* 必歸 其天). It is this that is meant by great peace (*daping* 大平), the utmost in government.[24]

Jia Yi 賈誼 (201–169 B.C.E.) expounded similar ideas when he explained how the Yellow Emperor, the legendary figure whom early Han dynasty adherents of the *Laozi* set up as a model ruler, created great peace. The Yellow Emperor was said to have acted like water, that is, reaching everything without antagonizing anyone. He first established righteousness and proper human relationships, and then went on mystical journeys, for instance to distant Mount Kunlun, in the far west. "The world attained the state of great peace only because the Yellow Emperor was one with *dao*."[25]

While it is tempting to draw a line from this passage to certain ideas expressed in the TPJ, the Han dynasty discourse centered on more complicated ways of procuring the support of heaven. An apparatus of particularly elaborate and expensive imperial rituals was put in place. The creation of a Hall of Light (*ming tang* 明堂) was thought to be helpful. Its supporters argued that the Yellow Emperor had at the outset of history reigned from such a hall. For Han dynasty rulers its legendary history, architectural measurements, and cosmological correlations imbued such a building with great symbolic value. It was meant to be the place from which great peace would be installed.[26] Emperor Wu (r. 141–87 B.C.E.), who greatly expanded the Han empire, was particularly interested in this project and planned to set up a Hall of Light to aid in the proper performance of all ceremonies linked to the course of the year. He believed that the construction of the hall "would promote great peace."[27] After lengthy discussions in 109 B.C.E. the hall was built close to Mount

Tai (in contemporary Shandong),[28] and a year later the emperor visited the slopes of Mount Tai to perform in person the Feng and Shan sacrifices[29] and thus announce publicly that great peace had been achieved.[30] Court officials stressed the point that Emperor Wu had thereby achieved what the First Emperor of the Qin had attempted without success. When the First Emperor was about to perform the ritual, bad weather had prevented its completion,[31] an event his enemies often referenced. More than a century later, however, the founder of the Later Han dynasty (25–220) emulated Emperor Wu and performed the ritual successfully, thereby consolidating his reign. In each instance the ruler's own authority and that of his dynasty were at stake:

> On the day the ruler receives the [heavenly] mandate, he revises [ritual] regulations in accordance with heaven. When the world has been brought into a state of great peace, he performs the Feng and Shan sacrifices to announce great peace. Why does this have to be done at Mount Tai? Because it is the beginning of the ten thousand beings, the place for [the process of] alternation [between Yin and Yang].[32]

The notion of great peace was thus crucial to the self-representation, and presumably the impact, of a ruler. To achieve great peace meant to prove oneself worthy of heaven's mandate. It was not the *need* to achieve great peace that was contentious but rather the *method* for achieving it. The positions held by Jia Yi on the one hand and Emperor Wu's advisors on the other can be seen as reflecting an opposition between a *dao*-based and a "literature"—here documented as ritual-oriented— approach to government that, according to Mark Lewis, dominated intellectual life until the early stages of Emperor Wu's reign.[33] In changing guises, however, it probably remained in force much longer, despite all official support for the literature faction.

A major controversy developed around the question as to at which point in time the world had been in a state of great peace. There was agreement that Great Yao, one of Confucius's and Mengzi's ideal rulers of the long-distant legendary past, had reigned over a world in peace. His successors Shun and Yu were also said to have brought peace about.[34] The same was said about the Yellow Emperor. However, such praise for the past included a certain critique of the present that others repudiated. The First Emperor in the speech just cited did not claim he had achieved great peace; with some modesty, he confessed only that he aimed for it.[35] On other occasions he showed more self-confidence. In 210 B.C.E. he authorized an inscription that claimed that the people were happy to follow the unified rules he had put in place and that they felt privileged to maintain great peace.[36] Wang Chong, a realistic and independent-minded thinker of the first century C.E., argued that a state of great peace had been reached when the government was stable and the population content, and that this had certainly been achieved in recent times and was actually the case during his own lifetime. Certain cosmic manifestations might or might not accompany this situation; they were not crucial to it. There was also no need for the Yellow River and the Luo to bring forth celestial charts and texts to announce the advent of great peace or for phoenix and unicorn to be sighted. Universal peace could take place without such signs.[37] For Wang Chong, Emperor Wen (r. 180–157 B.C.E.) had created great peace at the outset of the Han dynasty through his lenient and benevolent rule. So, too, had certain Later Han rulers achieved great peace, in Wang Chong's opinion.[38] This judgment reflected Wang Chong's fairly narrow understanding of the notion of great peace, for which, in his view, good harvests and general bliss were not essential. Instead, he stressed that the people at present remained calm and honest even when harvest failures had made them destitute, and that this signified great peace. He also mentioned the much-increased size of China as an accomplishment that recent rulers had achieved and praised the civilizing impact of this on neighboring people.[39]

Scholars who opposed Wang Chong's matter-of-fact understanding of the term and attributed historical uniqueness to a period of great peace found it difficult to decide whether Confucius had managed to achieve or even promote great peace. Although his *Spring and Autumn Annals* was written with the aim of great peace in mind, as Dong Zhongshu remarked,[40] this did not necessarily have any immediate effect. In the *Annals,* Confucius is said to have covered three historical periods, that is, a period of disorder, a period of approaching peace, and a period of universal great peace "when the barbarian tribes became part of the feudal hierarchy, and the whole world, far and near, large and small, was [or would become] like one."[41] In this particular meaning and directly linked to the figure of Confucius, the term "great peace" became part of Kang Youwei's (1858–1927) speculations about "great unity" (*datong* 大同) in the early twentieth century.[42] All agreed that perfect social conditions were necessarily universal.[43] A state that deserved to be called *taiping* had to encompass the world and not be limited only to China.

From the second century B.C.E. onward there was no doubt about Confucius's exemplary lifestyle, irrefutable teachings, and decisive historical impact, but that these achievements had in fact resulted in a reign of great peace was less obvious. The depiction of Confucius's position was, in this respect, as multifaceted as becomes a spiritual leader who combines attributes of a teacher, a missionary, and a savior. As Wang Chong observed, the Master had said explicitly that the world would be at peace only one generation after the arrival of a true king.[44] Similar questions can be raised in regard to the role of the Celestial Master, who is the main speaker in much of the TPJ. His teachings were authorized by heaven and he devoted all his life to preparing humankind for the arrival of great peace. The depiction of his personal situation, his doctrine, and his historical role contains discrepancies resembling those that Han dynasty scholars created around the figure of Confucius. While the Celestial Master's influence is shown to have promoted the arrival of great peace, like Confucius, he was not in a position to bring it about. Both Confucius and the Celestial Master were depicted as teachers who tried to persuade or convert the rulers of the day to implement reforms. It was not in their power to turn into political leaders and enact reforms personally.

Clearly, great peace was desirable. It was the best situation for the empire and the world in general. Throughout the Han dynasty there was no doubt that any responsible ruler would attempt to achieve it. The writings of Wang Fu 王符 (90–165) document the term's popularity. He did not fill the word "great peace" with specific content but used it as a medium to propagate his major social and political aims. In suggesting policy, he often reached the conclusion that what had been suggested was the precondition for opening up the road to great peace:

> This is the crucial point in all government activities: nothing is better than to restrain what is superfluous (*mo* 末) and concentrate on essentials (*ben* 本), and nothing is worse than to keep a distance from what is essential, while adorning superfluous items. In building a state it is essential to make the people wealthy, and basic to rectify all that is learned. When the people are well off, they can be taught. When one learns what is correct, one can become righteous. When the people are poor, they neglect doing good. When teachings are confused, there will be deceit. Let people attend schools and there won't be any disorder (*luan* 亂). Let them be righteous, and they will be loyal and full of filial piety. This is the way an intelligent ruler proceeds: he concentrates on these two in order to create the basis for great peace and to arrive at the good fortune of receiving auspicious omens.[45]

For Wang Fu, proper and widespread education, the merit-based selection of officials, and correct work ethics[46] were the conditions for achieving great peace. There can be little doubt that the authors of the TPJ agreed with Wang Fu on several points. The following line of argumentation contained in the *Qian fu lun* is very similar to that adopted by the TPJ's Celestial Master:

> So, for this reason, if one wants to achieve great peace, one must first of all harmonize Yin and Yang. This can only be done by following the intentions of heaven. To give security to one's people is the only way of following heaven's intentions. For the sake of this security, one must examine one's men carefully. Therefore, the root of a country's success and failure and the means by which to establish control and order are an intelligent selection [of officials].[47]

The term "great peace" remained attractive even while over the course of the second century c.e. the dynasty grew increasingly removed from a state of stability, peace, and popular approbation and contemporary observers began to lament the lack of order and social cohesion. Wang Chong was rather isolated among the intellectuals of the Later Han dynasty when he found evidence of great peace not only in the generations preceding his own, but also in the world around him. Originally the rule of the Han dynasty had ushered in an era of relative stability and well-being through setting up new institutions, promoting economic growth, and enlarging Chinese territory, but problems set in toward the end of the first century b.c.e. that were followed by a period of civil war. Some consolidation was achieved when the Later Han dynasty was founded in 25 c.e., but the situation changed rapidly over the course of the second century c.e. Patricia Ebrey has suggested that one of the major Later Han innovations was the government's laissez-faire attitude toward economic processes. Government officials had widely distributed improved tools during the Former Han dynasty and had actively promoted new methods of cultivation. These developments came to a standstill in Later Han, when the concentration of land and resources such as agricultural skills in a few hands caused the impoverishment of large numbers of people.[48] There was unrest on several fronts when processes of social cooperation on which much of the political and administrative system rested came to naught. The landless fought against landowners and administrative authorities, and the administration tried in vain to rein in the big estates. Struggles between different factions of the ruling strata turned violent. The fact that basic survival became increasingly difficult added a certain utopian flavor to the idea that general harmony and welfare, that is, great peace, should prevail among men. Toward the end of the Han dynasty there was so little chance of an orderly arrival of great peace that a rebellious movement took up the slogan. Known as the Taiping Movement, it involved an uprising that resulted in the rebels controlling China's eastern provinces for several months in 184 C.E.

THE PEACE THAT WILL SAVE THE WORLD

The text of the TPJ does justice to its title and centers on the need to lead the world to great peace. The peace the TPJ's Celestial Master talked about was the same peace Han dynasty intellectuals had in mind. Once it arrived it would enable all within China and beyond to live happily and without worries. Heaven and earth would show their approbation through reliable and plentiful harvests. While auspicious portents might occur, they were not essential. The text reiterates what Han dynasty intellectuals thought about the methods of achieving great peace. The ruler and, with certain modifications, the men engaged to provide advice and implement policies must possess personal integrity. This was usually expressed as adherence to the virtues contained in Confucius's *Lun yu* and in the *Mengzi:* maintaining a certain distance from events, refraining from emotional entanglement, and performing the necessary rituals with proper devotion and concentration. The welfare of the people had to be considered, and an example set that might encourage them in good conduct. There is a high level of consensus about this in Han dynasty sources. Figures as far removed from each other as Liu An 劉安 (?179–122 B.C.E.), who believed in personal immortality and quoted the *Laozi* and the *Zhuangzi*, and the skeptic Wang Chong, who saw himself following the tradition of Confucius, deemed such behavior by the ruling class a prerequisite for great peace. Moreover, the world of nature became a major and active component of social cohesion, and Han dynasty thinkers were concerned with it when they discussed the analogy, correspondence, and interrelationship between heaven, earth, and men. Men were supposed to consider humankind as part of a trinity and to act accordingly in all their endeavors, but the practical consequences of this knowledge were largely confined to the sphere of ritual observances. It was here that a symbolic unity between the three dispensations was confirmed and maintained throughout the course of the year and in continuous response to all the developments and accidents of regular life. The emperor as well as his family and subordinates would attempt to correspond to heaven, for instance, by changing their clothes, their food, and their daily observances with the changing seasons.

The authors of the TPJ did not disagree in principle but stressed the problem that adherence to the teachings of Confucius and Mengzi had failed to make a ruler's position secure and his subjects happy. For the authors of the TPJ a process of rethinking was therefore necessary, and they went further in their search for great peace than was customary, arguing that only a major social reshuffling could bring it about. For them, great peace was no longer a state that would be achieved by administrative or ritual means. It did not originate in a ruler's benevolence, political skill, or spiritual power, but instead in heaven's concern for humankind. Heaven's cooperation was deemed essential for creating a situation in which great peace could be achieved. They stressed that their position between heaven and earth obliged men to actively promote the interest and welfare of heaven and earth. Performances of rituals and respect for heaven's symbols as documented in imperial ceremonies would not suffice.

Great peace would be achieved once humankind had become one with heaven. While the TPJ authors did not invent this formula, they gave it a radical interpretation. "Heaven" (*tian* 天) is a difficult word. While it has to be seen as one coherent concept, it also covers a wide spectrum of meanings. Its meanings extend from the physical sky to "law giver" and "supreme moral principle." It can also refer to the world of nature as opposed to the human world. Although heaven has anthropomorphic traits such as a will or a heart, it can be misleading to see heaven as a deity. It is neither almighty nor eternal. It does not speak, but one might say that it has a voice. Natural occurrences, when observed and properly analyzed, can announce its intentions. The forces of Yin and Yang in their continuous flux and the arranging and rearranging of the five phases serve as the main tools for this analysis. In contrast to some of the sources quoted earlier,[49] the TPJ does not proclaim that the people speak for heaven. They have an impact on it and they influence its "feelings," but what these feelings are must be extracted from natural events.

The authors of the TPJ proclaimed that society had to abolish all habits that prevented its naturelike functioning. They saw a particular need for the general togetherness of all, and even for a certain equality between all, in the sense that deficiency, want, and worry in one part of society would certainly have an impact on the whole. This togetherness had to be active, as was the cooperation between man, heaven, and earth in the course of the agricultural year. Thus, not to communicate and not to participate was seen as an evil, an idea that led to a number of detailed prescriptions, from the need to convey any knowledge one might have gained to the demand that wealth should be shared and that everyone should take part in productive labor. Everybody, including women and serfs, was part of this social interchange. While prescripts related to great peace are varied and comprehensive, the TPJ's reform program is best understood from its prohibitions. All blockage and rupture had to be prevented. The opposite of the search for great peace was not the disorderly approach to things, nor was it rebellion (*luan* 亂), as Liu Xiang 劉向 (79–8 B.C.E.)[50] and other Han dynasty thinkers had presumed, but rather "to interrupt" (*jue* 絕), which also meant "to bring to an end" or "to kill." The TPJ authors stressed that heaven's interest lay in creating, nourishing, and maintaining life. Thus, whatever brought life to an end was opposed to great peace.

Since great peace meant harmony between nature and men, the need to maintain the integrity of heaven and earth required social reforms. This was man's constant responsibility. There was, however, one other consideration. He Xiu and other mainstream thinkers had hinted that great peace would arrive at a certain stage of historical development. It was also generally accepted that historical development took place in cycles; Dong Zhongshu's name was linked to a complex construction of the sequence of eras and their specific rise and fall, their timing explained and prognosticated by complicated calendrical and numerological speculations.[51] Historical eras were thought to relate to each other as if they were the five phases, producing one another as fire and earth did, or overcoming each other, as in the following passage from the *Lü shi chun qiu:*

> Before the phase of water is about to replace the phase of fire, heaven is bound to make it known that qi[52] of water is growing in strength. When this is the case, one's color must be black and all activities must be geared to the phase of water. Once the phase of water has arrived and one is not aware of the [proper] figures and other preparations, things will proceed to the phase of earth [which overcomes that of water].[53]

So, in order to correspond to the cyclical change that had allowed him to ascend, a new ruler, and in particular the founder of a new dynasty, had to reestablish official life as a whole. The transition from an era that was seen as dominated by one of the five phases to a new era that was controlled by another phase brought about the need and the opportunity for a new beginning.

> When I now say that a new king must change the institutions, this does not mean that he must change the course of things or alter their principle. Since he has received a mandate from heaven, the surname is altered and the kingship renewed. As king, he does not continue [the line of] kings before him. . . . For this reason he moves to a new abode, assumes a new title, changes the beginning of the year, and alters the color of clothes. All this is only because he doesn't dare not to comply with heaven's intention and make its position known.[54]

While this view of history incorporated the possibility of decay and destruction, it also contained the promise of innovation.

The authors of the TPJ made some use of these speculations and stressed that the present circumstances favored a new beginning. But, in principle, their approach to historical development was different and radical.[55] They argued that if great peace were not achieved now, the end of the world—that is, the end of humankind, heaven, and earth—would be in sight. By envisaging the end of the world the TPJ authors transcended the discourse of the Han dynasty literati.[56] They did not depict this end in any detail,[57] but it was stated with great clarity and decisiveness that all life would cease if it were not preserved by the arrival of great peace.

Ancient society, and as a consequence the Han empire, had to fall apart before such ideas came to the fore. These ideas remained a powerful component of Daoist thought throughout the Middle Ages, although in a modified, less utopian format. The expectation of a sudden end was juxtaposed with the promise that the community of Daoist believers would be transferred at exactly that point in time to a safe place and delivered from all evils to a new life of perfect bliss.[58] For the authors of the TPJ, however, this option did not exist. For them, the only possible salvation lay in convincing everyone to mend their ways.

THE TAIPING MOVEMENT

In the main, the ideas of the TPJ's Celestial Master were in accord with the intellectual and social environment at the end of the Han dynasty. During the Han dynasty many called for reform, but the methods of achieving those reforms were subject to controversy. Certain thinkers and politicians called for a return to the old values of simplicity and integrity; others sought to strengthen the implementation of the legal code. Virtually all attempts at the implementation of reforms proved futile and did little to overcome the blatant weakness of the imperial dynasty and its administration, faced as it was with the increasing presence of independent and often ill-adjusted social groups.

Among these were large numbers of people who had been forced to give up their land and thus their livelihood. They had little to lose. The existence of such groups is well documented, including by government attempts to ameliorate the situation. Itinerant men and their families were promised tax relief when they returned to the place where they had once owned land; local officials were advised to feed them from public granaries; and restrictions on hunting, fishing, and the use of government forests were abolished.[59] Over the course of the second century C.E., however, the landless became too numerous for public support and there were frequent violent uprisings. Groups of drifting peasants were easily persuaded to risk their lives in order to get access to public granaries or other sources of food. Certain officials who were perceived as particularly severe would also meet with resistance and insubordination. At the same time, both land concentration and productivity increased. The constant division of land brought about by the rules of inheritance helped to create an ongoing need for the acquisition of new land, so that units of cultivation became larger and were worked on more efficiently through advances in agricultural tools and methods. There was therefore a decrease not only in the number of independent farmers, but also in the number of those needed to work the land.[60] The fact that the owners of large estates employed militias to protect their belongings strengthened the likelihood of armed conflicts. These remained regional, but they destabilized the political system as a whole.

There can be little doubt that the large groups of starving and destitute people who roamed the country in search of employment and food were a political force to be reckoned with. A redistribution of land might have been the answer, but this could only be implemented after the dynasty in power had been toppled. Whether these groups would also have contributed in any way to the formation of ideas is much more doubtful. Yu Xu 虞詡 (d. 136), a skillful politician who had handled several uprisings with great success, arrived at the following conclusion: "These rebels stick together like dogs or sheep. All they want is to be warm and eat their fill."[61] But if we want to do justice to the TPJ and its place in China's intellectual history, we must raise the issue of what these rebels aimed for.

The Taiping Movement, which erupted in the Yellow Turban Rebellion of 184 C.E., came as the climax of decades of uprisings. The latter inherited all of the former's instruments of initiating, organizing, and staging an armed rebellion. Rebel leaders were literate and, in principle, aware of the need to let cultural symbols work for them. While they certainly demanded tax relief and other welfare measures, they also took the trouble to define their historical and cosmic position. In this respect, their choice of a color to signify their intentions was relevant. Yellow, which in the system of five phases was the central phase, was considered the color of earth, for instance, and could be seen as being produced by and consequently following the phase of fire, which the Later Han rulers saw as their own symbol. Moreover, yellow was the color of the legendary Yellow Emperor, whom early Han dynasty thought had linked to the *Laozi*. Yellow thus became the color that late Han dynasty rebels who wanted to replace the ruling house frequently appropriated. Another option was black, which represented the phase of water. Again, this was related to the reigning dynasty's own phase of fire, which the "Black Emperor" hoped to overcome just as water can extinguish fire. Although most rebels took up traditional titles like "king" or "emperor," some chose more programmatic names. In 148 C.E. rebel leaders in eastern Henan called themselves "Sons of the Yellow Emperor" and "Perfected" (*zhen ren* 真人), a term that goes back to Zhuangzi, who heaps the following praise on the perfected:

> The perfected of old did not know how to be pleased that they were alive, did not know how to hate death, were neither glad to come forth nor reluctant to go in; they were content to leave as briskly as they came. They did not forget the source where they began, did not seek out the destination where they would end. They were pleased with the gift that they received, but forgot it as they gave it back. It is this that is called "not allowing the thinking of the heart to damage the way, not using what is of man to do the work of heaven." . . . Hence, they were one with what they liked and one with what they disliked, one when they were one and one when they were not one. When one, they were of heaven's party, when not one, they were of man's party. Someone in whom neither heaven nor man wins over the other is what is meant by "perfected."[62]

With the use of the figure of the Yellow Emperor and the title of "Perfected," the rebels entered the sphere of the supernatural. The above passage, complex and philosophical though it may be, shows that the perfected can be seen as mediating between heaven and men, and even between life and death. In this sense, the title suggests that its owner has extraordinary spiritual powers. This became of interest to the First Emperor of the Qin dynasty, who attempted to join the ranks of the perfected himself.[63]

While the expectation of superhuman support was omnipresent in Han dynasty China,[64] it must have been essential when a group of peasants ventured to take on officials and other representatives of state authority. "Shamans" (*wu* 巫), as the historians called them, were always at hand to accompany rebel leaders and offer advice. They were involved, for instance, when the Red Eyebrows staged an uprising in 18 C.E. Before the rebel leaders announced the foundation of a new empire, *wu* in their service spread it about that a local deity had demanded the installation of an emperor.[65]

Over the course of the first and second centuries C.E., spiritual concerns became more widespread and powerful. A first-century *wu*-led uprising did not end with the execution of its leader. His followers spread the message that he had not really died but lived on as a deity. Consequently, calm was restored only after these followers had also been crushed.[66] "Messenger," which meant messenger from heaven,[67] was another title that suggested that a rebel leader had divine support. This was what Zhang Bolu 張伯路 and his followers called themselves when they set out in 109 C.E. to eliminate higher officials and burn government buildings. There were many such insurrections from the 140s onward, pointing to a weakening of the authority and legitimacy of the ruling dynasty. Perhaps Mansvelt Beck has a point when he links the rebels' demands directly to the realms of the Han court, where in 144 C.E. the general-in-chief Liang Ji 梁冀 (d. 159) had fairly openly poisoned the ruling emperor in order to replace him with his younger brother.[68] It is also interesting to note that in the regions where Zhang Jue 張角 and his followers were at work, no uprisings are mentioned for the decade preceding the year 184 C.E.;[69] it was as if calmness had spread in preparation for a major effort to topple the reigning dynasty.

We know more about the background and activities of the Taiping rebels than about their predecessors. Their uprising was bigger and the dynasty's defenses were weaker. The rebels therefore posed a serious threat, not just to regional or provincial authorities, but to the administration of the empire as a whole. Consequently, the ancient historians took them seriously. Their observations are important to us since we must assume that the TPJ originated in an environment where the misery and despair of the people, as well as their beliefs and hopes, were similar to those of the late Han peasants.

Zhang Jue began recruiting followers around the year 171 C.E.[70] Wide-ranging epidemics were reported for that year, as they were for the years 173, 179, and 182.[71] Healing the sick was one of his primary activities:

Zhang Jue from Julu [in present Hebei] had recently called himself "great worthy[72] and honest teacher." He believed in the teachings of the Yellow Emperor and Laozi. He assembled disciples around him. Kneeling before him, they confessed their mistakes. With incantations and water in which talismans had been dissolved, he attempted to cure illness. Sometimes he succeeded. The people had faith in him. He sent eight disciples to the four directions in order to convert the world to his "excellent teachings" (shan dao 善道).[73] They spread lies and delusions, and in the course of more than ten years his followers numbered several hundred thousand. This involved commanderies and provinces. Everyone from Qing, Xu, You, Ji, Jing, Yang, Yan, and Yu came under this influence. Zhang Jue installed thirty-six fang 方. Fang is the same as "general." A great fang was in charge of more than ten thousand men, and a small fang more than six or seven thousand. Each of them installed his own chiefs. They then spread the message: "The blue heaven has died and the yellow heaven must be established. When the *jiazi* 甲子 year is here the world will have great joy." They wrote the characters *jiazi* everywhere with white chalk, in the capital on walls and on the gates to bureaus, and on official buildings in provinces and commanderies. In the year 184, the Great General (*da fang* 大方) Ma Yuan-yi 馬元義 and others planned for an uprising in Ye [in southern Hebei] after they had gathered tens of thousands in Jing and Yang [in the south]. Ma Yuan-yi traveled several times to and from the capital, consulting with regular palace attendants Feng Xu 封谞, Xu Feng 徐奉, and others. They agreed on the fifth day of the third month for a simultaneous uprising, inside [the capital?] and outside. Before the uprising had taken place, Zhang Jue's disciple Tang Zhou 唐周 from Jinan submitted a memorial in which he made [the plan] known.[74]

The uprising got off to a premature, but still very powerful and quite united, start before Zhang Jue could be apprehended. In 184, which was a *jiazi* year and thus the beginning of a new sixty-year cycle, the rebellion broke out simultaneously in sixteen commanderies to the south, east, and northeast of the capital, Luoyang. Local army contingents were quickly defeated, provincial governors were kidnapped, and imperial officials fled the scene.[75]

What does this account teach us about the ideas that informed the rebels and their movement? Zhang Jue found access to people through healing the sick. He is said to have called himself "great physician."[76] In this capacity, he made use of talismans addressed to the spirits that were thought to have brought forth the illness. When issuing a talisman, Zhang Jue is said to have performed the ritual of raising the staff with nine knots in accordance with shamanistic practice.[77]

Zhang Jue is called a follower of Huang-Lao 黄老; that is, of the Yellow Emperor and of Laozi, or rather of a school of thought that went under the name of these two legendary figures. This school is represented on the one hand by a set of texts dating from the early Han dynasty that deals with political thought.[78] The texts incorporate ideas from not only the *Laozi*, but also other ancient texts. The ruler is supposed to remain distant and to concentrate on his spiritual excellence, while government is expected to be limited, lenient, and welfare-oriented. Laws and regulations rather than personal morality and judgment are seen as proper and efficient guidelines. On the other hand, Huang-Lao was the label used for individuals who searched for personal health, longevity, and even immortality, a search that was popular at least from the First Emperor of the Qin onward and that remained so throughout the Han dynasty. The titles of several early medical texts also refer to the Yellow Emperor.

Zhang Jue's movement grew rapidly. He shared the leadership with his two brothers, thus creating a trinity, which was of great symbolic value in that it was seen to represent the unity of heaven, earth, and man. The three assumed the titles "General of Heaven," "General of Earth," and "General of Men."[79] Moreover, Zhang Jue emulated earlier rebels by calling himself "Yellow Heaven" and by distinguishing his followers by requiring them to wear yellow headbands, or even, according to another source, yellow clothing:

> The Yellow Turbans dressed only in plain yellow. They did not carry weapons but wore long gowns and moved comfortably as if on wings. When they arrived in a commandery or county, everyone followed them. On such a day, heaven would be all yellow.[80]

Officials tolerated the movement. While people joined rapidly, the authorities did not get involved because Zhang Jue was only "educating" his followers.[81] Certain reports described the situation as serious, however, and suggested measures of repression:

> Zhang Jue's secret plans become increasingly dangerous. The empire is full of whispers and rumors, and it is claimed that Zhang Jue and his followers have gained secret entry into the capital and have spies within the court. They twitter like birds, they have the hearts of wild beasts, and they make plots together. But in provinces and commanderies the whole question is taboo. Nobody wants to hear about it. [Officials] compare notes with one another privately, but they are reluctant to say anything in the open.[82]

Because of factional controversies, such warnings were not heeded. After the eunuchs instigated a proscription in 169 C.E., career officials were largely expelled from power and could only hope that an uproar would weaken the eunuchs' position. This hope was fulfilled when the proscription was finally lifted in the year 184 C.E. Once the central government had taken things in hand, the rebels' main forces were defeated in less than six months, but uprisings under the name of the Yellow Turbans continued for years in various locations. The government relied increasingly on local warlords and their private armies to contain the rebels.

The rapid growth of the movement is of greater relevance for us than its eventual defeat, which only tells us that at that stage the dynasty still had enough authority to make it feasible for all factions of the ruling strata to unite in its defense. Here is another description of the movement's beginnings:

> Zhang Jue and his brothers began an uprising in Ji [present-day southern Hebei], under the slogan of Yellow Heaven. There were thirty-six *fang*, who promoted cooperation everywhere. The leaders were like stars behind clouds, encircled by their rank and file, who, dragged into this by exhaustion and hunger, made the most of it.[83]

Events proved Zhang Jue's message to have been so attractive that after about ten years of proselytizing he could command the support of several hundred thousand followers:

> Some people sold up all their property and left their homes to follow him. The pilgrims blocked the roads, and those who became ill and died before they reached him numbered by the tens of thousands.[84]

The rebels must have dominated life in Han China's most populous provinces for about six months. Their message, if we are to trust the historians, consisted of the promise that illness would be healed and that welfare measures would be put in place once the reigning dynasty had been overthrown. Whether a promise of salvation and spiritual transformation was at stake, we cannot tell, but we know that the rebels' program was of some general interest. They had numerous contacts with all strata of the population. What they promulgated was said to have been noticed and read in the capital, and there is also Fan Ye's spurious note that the Yellow Turban leader made use of a text on great peace, as will be discussed later.

What did Zhang Jue and his followers believe in? They believed in a world of spirits who had the power to cause, prevent, and heal illness, and also in the arts and techniques associated with the name of the Yellow Emperor through which they hoped to increase health, energy, and power and thus to prolong their lives. They also believed in their own mission. Zhang Mancheng 張曼成, chief of a group of Yellow Turbans in Nanyang (in present-day Henan), showed great confidence when he called himself the "high spirit messenger" (*shen shang shi* 神上使).[85] Zhang Bolu had also used the title "messenger," and one can see here parallels with the use of the word "messenger" in grave-securing writs. We will come back to this in more detail. Buddhist attacks on Daoist practices made much of the fact that the early Daoists shared many of their techniques with shamanistic practitioners.[86] Buddhist sources accused Zhang Lu and his predecessors of making use of the *Huangshen Yuezhang* 黃神越章, the "Yue-type petition to the Yellow Spirit,"[87] to control demons, for instance. Similar accusations could have been made against Zhang Jue. He healed by magic techniques, in particular through talismans. We may therefore assume that his success in converting large numbers of people lay partly in providing the services they expected from the shaman, or *wu*, they trusted.

Zhang Jue had an ambitious agenda. This is documented in his attempt to associate his activities with heaven. He is said to have assumed the title of Yellow Heaven (*zi hao huang tian* 自號黃天), either for himself or for the period of his reign.[88] Another source says "he spoke of himself as 'great peace of the yellow heaven' (*huang tian taiping* 黃天泰平)."[89] Clearly, for Zhang Jue heaven was a divine power with which he felt entitled to establish direct contact as if he were heaven's son and thus, we must conclude, the emperor.[90] But the Yellow Turbans are also said to have promoted the "Grand One" (*Tai yi* 太一 or 乙), another divine entity of high standing, and in the following remind Cao Cao (155–220) that he once did likewise:

> Formerly in Jinan [in today's Shandong], when you damaged religious altars,[91] you believed like us in the Grand One of the Center and of Yellow (*zhong huang tai yi* 中黃太乙). It looked as if you had understood the correct way, but now you once more go astray. The course of the Han is completed and the yellow dynasty must be established. When heaven makes a great turn, not even someone like you can remain in place.[92]

While the Grand One figured in Warring States religious beliefs, its role was enhanced by Emperor Wu of the Han. On the advice of certain *fang shi*, that is, experts in vitality techniques, in his service, the emperor initiated sacrifices to the triad of the Grand One, heaven, and earth.[93] But the Grand One was also a popular deity to which followers of *dao* addressed hymns in the second century C.E.[94] It later became an important figure in the Daoist pantheon. For Tao Hongjing (456–536), the Grand One was in charge of all the minor deities, who enliven, protect, and control the human body. Its title "the essence of the embryo, the master of transformations" reveals that it was seen as the principle of evolution, as the oneness in the process of development.[95] When the TPJ's Celestial Master advises disciples on how to live long lives, he mentions the Celestial Grand One *(Tian tai yi):*

If you don't want to die from exhaustion, you must keep company with *qi* as if you were the mysterious female [*Laozi* 6]. You need to resemble heaven to do this. Then how can you ever die? If you can't achieve it all at once set up a room for meditation and go there to think about *dao;* by fasting you will unite with *qi*. In this way, the spirits of heaven and earth will all assemble and you will not return to ordinary life but attend the Celestial Grand One, who will receive you in audience in the central pole star (*zhongji* 中 极) and install you with talismans (*fu* 符).[96]

Judging by their choice of divine support, the rebels certainly had imperial ambitions. They meant to reinvent the whole system and its major deities, transforming heaven as well as the Grand One into promoters of yellow, that is, of their own program. They thus acknowledged the tradition of heaven's authority and of heaven-instigated cyclical change. The promotion of yellow survived the Yellow Turbans' defeat. When Cao Cao's son established his own Wei dynasty in 220 C.E., he called the first reign period "Yellow Beginning" (*huang chu* 黃 初).[97]

THE MOVEMENT OF THE CELESTIAL MASTERS

The historical importance of the Taiping Movement and Yellow Turban Rebellion is enhanced by the fact that they were not isolated events. The various peasant rebellions that preceded them have already been mentioned. Moreover, they were followed by uprisings right up until the Han dynasty was dissolved in 220 C.E. We may assume that since economic and political circumstances did not improve, the demand for alternative solutions also did not subside. Moreover, the comparative strength and vigor of these uprisings further damaged the dynasty's authority and legitimacy.

The movement of the Celestial Masters that later Daoists cherished as the beginnings of their religious community was contemporaneous with Zhang Jue's activities. Since it lasted longer and developed in a less violent fashion, we know much more about it than we do about the Taiping Movement. This knowledge is at least as important for the reading of the TPJ as what we know about Zhang Jue. Because the Celestial Masters are seen as the founders of the Daoist religion, ample research on them has been undertaken. What we need to do here, therefore, is only to throw enough light on them to help us better understand the TPJ.

Zhang Ling, who is also and more respectfully called Zhang Daoling 張 道 陵, was supposed to have created the movement of the Celestial Masters and to have been the first person who was addressed by the title of Celestial Master. What is known about this figure is sketchy, but we may well assume that he was a historical figure. He is said to have grown up in northwestern Jiangsu and then moved to Sichuan, where he set up a religious group in the Heming Mountains west of Chengdu. Hagiographic sources tell us that he studied the classics[98] when young but then became interested in longevity practices, an interest he found difficult to maintain, for financial reasons. He seems to have come from a peasant background. In Sichuan, he managed to attract disciples and financial supporters. Members of his group were expected to contribute five pecks of rice, thus leading his movement to become known as the "Way of Five Pecks of Rice." The movement was continued by his son and by his grandson, Zhang Lu 張魯 (fl. 190–215), who became associated with a certain Zhang Xiu 張修 (probably no relation). In the year 184 C.E., that is, at the time of the Yellow Turban Rebellion, Zhang Xiu staged a local uprising. In 190 C.E., both Zhang Lu and Zhang Xiu were co-opted by the provincial governor to safeguard Hanzhong, that is, the region that was their stronghold and that stretched from northwestern Sichuan to Hubei and Shaanxi. Both were appointed to official rank at a time when, as mentioned above, the central government was beginning to rely increasingly on local strongmen and their armies to subdue uprisings in the tradition of the Yellow Turbans. Moreover, Zhang Lu's access to the governor was improved through his mother, who is said to have had free access to the governor's home, thanks to her beauty as well as her expertise in longevity techniques.[99] Zhang Lu eliminated Zhang Xiu, and relations with the provincial administration soured after the death of the governor. As a consequence, Zhang Lu took further steps toward making his own territory independent from provincial interference. The central government cooperated and installed him as "Gentleman of the Household in Charge of Protecting the People," and thus governor of Hanzhong, which he renamed "Hanning." His position was strong enough that he became a party in the struggle for power that accompanied the demise of the dynasty.

From 196 C.E. onward, the role of the Han emperor was reduced to that of a puppet in the hands of Cao Cao, which gave some legitimacy to Cao Cao's quest for power. But there were other contenders: Sun Quan (182–252), south of the Yangzi, Liu Zhang (d. 223), and, later, Liu Bei (161–223), toward the west, south of Hanzhong. The Liu family had the same name as that of the ruling Han dynasty, a fact of some propagandist relevance. There were clashes between Liu Zhang and Zhang Lu.[100] While Cao Cao had been unsuccessful in his attempt to amalgamate the territory of Sun Quan and Liu Zhang—that is, the states of Wu and Shu—he managed to extend his reign toward the west, and in 215 C.E., after lengthy negotiations, Hanzhong became part of Wei, that is, of Cao Cao's territory. Zhang Lu and his sons received official titles to signify their allegiance to the Wei court and the population at large was resettled in different parts of China. Thus ended China's first, and for a long time its only, theocracy.

The movement in Sichuan lasted for more than a generation. Its success can be credited to several conflicting factors. The relative geographical isolation of Hanzhong added to the stability and duration of Zhang Lu's reign. Since his independence posed no threat to the central authority, he was left alone. Moreover, the region was so close to China's western border that non-Chinese people participated in the movement. The uprising of the year 184 C.E. as well as subsequent upheavals in the region incorporated the Qiang, whose threatening presence had replaced that of the Xiongnu toward the end of the second century C.E. Their participation swelled the numbers and increased the strength of the Celestial Master movement and might also have had an impact on the formation of certain shamanistic rituals of purification. Opponents of Daoism mentioned these "scandalous" practices in their attacks:

> The Fast of the Mud and Soot goes back to Zhang Lu. Since the Di barbarians were hard to civilize, he controlled them by this method; they rolled in the mud like asses, smeared their faces with yellow earth, and, their combs removed, let their hair hang down.[101]

On the other hand, Zhang Ling is said to have been educated in the east. We must assume that this is where the institutions and practices that the Celestial Master and Taiping movements had in common had originated. Moreover, Zhang Ling and his successors produced writings, among which might have been the *Laozi* commentary entitled *Xiang'er* 想爾.

The beliefs and practices that prevailed in Zhang Lu's community were not dissimilar from what we know of Zhang Jue's aims and methods. As was the case among the Yellow Turbans, the process of healing was important for attracting, converting, and controlling people. In treating patients, the Celestial Master movement stressed the confession of sins, as had Zhang Jue. The sick were expected to withdraw to an oratory to meditate on their wrongdoings. A libationer (*jijiu* 祭酒) put the confessions of the sick in writing, together with the patient's full name. Three copies were made: one was placed on a mountain to be sent to heaven, another was buried in the earth, and the third was immersed in water. The spirits would then, it was hoped, be reconciled and allow the patient to recover.[102] Rituals of confession became characteristic of the early Daoist movements, perhaps adapting certain Buddhist practices.[103] Not only the sick, but everyone was expected to practice what was called self-examination. People were sent to repair roads as retribution for wrongdoing. For a small offense (*guo* 過), less serious than a crime (*zui* 罪), they were expected to work on a length of one hundred feet. Only after three violations would someone be subjected to formal punishment as outlined in the Han dynasty penal code. Thus, moral standards were reinforced by involving spirits in a system of rewards and punishments. This was not new in itself. Warring States accounts of historical events contain examples of celestial or spiritual retribution that resulted in culprits suffering and the good being rewarded. The *Mozi* stresses the idea of recompense,[104] but in the main, with the exception of Han Feizi and his intellectual friends, philosophers remained aloof from the idea that men should do good because it paid. The program of the early religious movements, however, catered to a mass audience, and in this respect the authors of the TPJ were more careful, as if they were aware of the unreasonable expectations that a simple moral system based on rewards and punishment might raise. They created their own system, more complex and multilayered but still based on the promise of rewards for good deeds and thoughts.

The well-being of individuals was regarded as dependent upon that of the community. Hanzhong was divided into twenty-four "commanderies" (*zhi* 治). The character *zhi* means "to govern" as well as "to heal," and both of these activities were tasks of the libationer, who combined administrative with spiritual functions. In this way, he—or she, at least at a later stage of religious organization—was expected to "control evil" (*jian ling* 姦令). Regular recitations of the *Laozi* were central to ritual practice. Believers would withdraw to oratories or "houses of quietude" (*jing shi* 靜室) to meditate. Another institution was the "responsibility huts" (*yi she* 義舍), where provisions were kept. Travelers were permitted to eat their fill, but if more were removed, the spirits would take revenge and make the culprit ill. It seems that the administration was efficient. Chen Shou (233–97), author of the *San guo zhi,* put it in the following terms:

> They did not set up any local officials, but everything was administered by
> libationers. The people as well as the foreign tribes were quite happy with it.[105]

Does all this point to a society in a state of great peace? We must assume it does, although its appearance was not in all respects as earlier Han dynasty thinkers had imagined it. The scope of the great peace was regional. The people were happy to cooperate, and this cooperation was achieved by novel means. We hear nothing about the model behavior of their leaders or about a process of ongoing education, nor were the leaders seen to perform any rituals reminiscent of the state cult, as, for instance, the Feng and Shan sacrifices that were mentioned above. However, coordination between men and nature played a role in Zhang Lu's community, and symbols were used to promote it. All numerical figures—that is, thirty-six, twenty-four, nine, and so on—were of cosmic numerological relevance; the unity between heaven, earth, and men was acknowledged; and the standard calendrical unit of the sixty-year cycle was used. Men's needs were taken into consideration, and in return they were expected to follow the rules and become, as the Daoists put it, "good" people. Such people did not prove their worth by simply obeying their parents and superiors but were expected to concentrate all their endeavors on strengthening life, in the first instance their own. From a philosophical point of view, there is nothing new in this. The quietist chapters of the *Guanzi* and parts of the *Huainan zi* point in a similar direction. However, these texts addressed their advice to members of the elite, who hoped by these means to gain power and influence. The attempt to transform such ideas into political policy by propagating them on a mass scale was new and required strengthening belief in a world of spirits, where good deeds and good thoughts were supposed to result in good health and cosmic harmony. The word *gui* 鬼, often translated as "demon," occurs frequently when the historians report on Zhang Jue, Zhang Lu, and their followers.[106] Again, the belief in the power of demons and other spirits is well documented and was a general feature of ancient and medieval China. However, in the early Daoist community spirits were put to systematic use. The doctrine of the omnipresence and irrefutable judgment of these spirits replaced the need for the state's repressive organs, and it covered political leaders with a comfortable mantle of authority. They had less need for the traditional tools of governments. Instead, they maintained order and conveyed a sense of purpose by referring to their spiritual support. The rebels' institutions had a certain utopian quality and thus resembled the program that the TPJ's Celestial Master explained to his disciples. It involved the active, responsible participation of all human beings and of the world of spirits. The historians do not mention the promise of longevity. Whether it occupied a special place on the rebels' agenda or was subdued by concerns for health and welfare, we cannot tell.[107]

We are told that Zhang Jue was a follower of the Yellow Emperor and of Laozi. That is all we hear with regard to his belief in Laozi. Our sources are more explicit with regard to Zhang Lu. For the Hanzhong community, the recitation of the *Laozi* was a major, if not the main, ritual event. The adoption of the text and the figure of Laozi made this community special and distinct from other groups that gathered around shamanistic healers. That the *Laozi* was a text to which many people turned for basic advice about life, and about death, is clear from the fact that it was frequently used as a funeral object. Its attraction lay not only in its content but also in the magic, spirit-controlling powers associated with it. The text itself is rather short, consisting of only "five thousand characters," as the Daoist tradition has it, and is mainly composed of isolated rhymed passages. Its message is often cryptic and occasionally contradictory. The text is addressed to a ruler who seeks social and political stability, but it can also be read as proverbs or prophesies, deep in meaning but not easy to access. Without explanatory annotation, therefore, it might have been used more as an object of adoration and wonder than for practical guidance. It seems that Zhang Lu understood this problem and produced a commentary to guide believers' reading of the old text.[108] According to the *Xiang'er,* the *Laozi* is a guide for self-cultivation. Meditation, breathing exercises, and sexual practices play a role in helping believers to transcend death. Moral rules are incorporated, including both a long list of general commandments such as not to kill, but also specific advice on how always to remain flexible and never to waste *qi*, rush into action, seek fame, or delight in arms. As Stephen Bokenkamp points out, much attention is paid to the distinction between what is correct and "orthodox" (*zheng* 正), in the sense of adhering to *dao* as a religious doctrine, and what is false.[109] The term *wei*, as in the *Laozi*'s *wu wei* 無 為, is thus to be understood as "artificial" and "false" (*wei* 偽). The TPJ's Celestial Master would have approved of such advice. While the teachings of the *Xiang'er* were meant to help believers live long and happy lives, they could also be taken as a guide for a harmonious and stable society. They thus differed from the more intellectual and mystical interpretations of *Laozi* by Yan Zun (first century B.C.E.), Heshang Gong (second century C.E.), and Wang Bi (226–49).

Making the *Laozi* into a religious text was an important step in the formation of the Daoist religion, but it was eclipsed by the deification of the figure Laozi. The transformation of both text and man seem not to have originated with the Daoist mass movements but rather with aristocratic practice. King Ying of Chu was said to have established a cult for Buddha in 65 C.E. and recited "the subtle words of Huang-Lao." He received the praise of Emperor Ming (r. 57–75) for such pious and gentle conduct.[110] This points to the ritual of reciting the *Laozi*, but not necessarily to a cult for Huang-Lao or for Laozi as a deity.[111] However, Emperor Huan (r. 146–68) did initiate such rituals toward the end of his reign.[112] While different sources from the second half of the second century C.E. speak of the figure as if it were a divine being, they do not convey a uniform picture; they stress different aspects. On the one hand, we learn from the *Scripture on the Transformations of Laozi* that the Lord Lao's existence was characterized by a chain of transformations that made him appear as various personages in different periods.[113] On the other hand, in the early

Celestial Masters movement Lord Lao and *dao*, or "the one," are used interchangeably, as we find in the *Xiang'er:*

> The one disperses its form as *qi* and gathers in its form as the Most High Lord Lao, whose permanent rule is on Mount Kunlun.[114]

The Celestial Master tradition centers on the moment in 142 C.E. when Lord Lao installed Zhang Daoling as Celestial Master, an event not mentioned in the *Scripture on the Transformations of Laozi*. Such variations are relevant for our understanding of the message contained in the TPJ. We here meet many ideas in their first formulation, that is, before or during the first attempts at the establishment of doctrinal orthodoxy. For this reason, lack of uniformity must be expected. Central points, however, might well be commonly accepted. In the case of the figure of Lord Lao, the central point is the text of the *Laozi*. *Transformations* has a line that accords completely with the ritual practices of Zhang Lu's Celestial Masters community: "If you want to know where to find me [Laozi], recite the text of five thousand characters ten thousand times."[115]

THE *TAIPING* MISSIONARY PROJECT

When the Celestial Master who figures as the main speaker in the TPJ sent disciples into the world to preach the arrival of great peace he resembled the leaders of the Daoist movements of the Later Han dynasty. He taught believers they should change their lifestyle and adhere to new values, and he proclaimed the need for social and political reorganization. Some of his ideas resemble those of Yellow Turban and Celestial Master Daoism, but this does not mean that the authors of the TPJ derived their insights from those movements or that Zhang Jue and Zhang Lu learned from the TPJ. Contacts were less direct and more complex. Manifestations of the emerging Daoist religion were not uniform. When Lord Lao became a religious personage, for instance, he was equipped with various, and sometimes conflicting, qualities from the outset.[116] However, there were several important points on which there seems to have been agreement among Daoist-oriented groups.

For the TPJ's Celestial Master, as well as for the religious movements known to us from historical sources, the key to social order, health, and happiness was the personal morality of all group members. To enforce this morality, spirits who offered rewards and meted out punishment were envisaged. For the authors of the TPJ these spirits were agents of heaven. The regulations that were set down—for example, with regard to the consumption of wine and meat—differed, but they all pertained to quietist values and respect for the maintenance of vital energy. Repentance played a role, although rituals evolving around this are not reflected in the TPJ.

Human beings were expected to see themselves as agents of a superhuman power. For the TPJ's Celestial Master this power was heaven. *Dao* played a limited role and Laozi no role at all. Still, the parallels are striking. Not to follow commandments was not just a mistake or a crime; it was a sin. The use of language and the details differ: for instance, *zui*, which in the TPJ is often "sin," an offense against heaven's will and against the protection and strengthening of life, seemed for Zhang Lu's community to mean "crime," that is, an offense against clearly defined worldly rules. This difference might reflect the fact that Zhang Lu's reign was theocratic. In both contexts good and bad were redefined from a novel perspective, thus creating a community that was independent of the Han dynasty state and critical of its values.

The TPJ's Celestial Master demanded that his disciples organize and spread the good news to the whole empire. This was, in fact, what Zhang Jue and his followers did, for more than a decade and with great success. By pointing to the onset of a new sixty-year cycle, they incorporated some eschatological elements to add urgency to their message. Missionary activity also played a role in the Sichuan community, especially after it was dispersed in 215 C.E. We may assume that from the perspective of the TPJ's Celestial Master the different groups of believers who in the second century C.E. and beyond spread new religious ideas, commandments, and institutions were all participating in or competing with his own project of saving the world.

HISTORICAL STAGES OF A SCRIPTURE ON GREAT PEACE

The origin, transmission, and finally publication and dissemination of a *taiping* text are interwoven with the development and growth of the Daoist religion, and this is the background against which the following brief account of the scripture's historical stages is meant to be seen. When we consider the widespread interest in the arrival of great peace during the Han dynasty, it is not surprising that the concept appeared in the title of a text. A text on great peace can be detected at several stages, but there are no early quotations or reliable bibliographical accounts that would allow us to establish a date for the writing of that text. Since the language and content of the text point to the second century C.E., we may assume that these stages actually dealt with textual material that has been transmitted in the TPJ as we know it today. They are of interest even if they cannot be proven to represent historical fact. The received text contains important observations and conclusions, and some historical background is helpful for reading them properly. Even if we can't record this background accurately, an approximation—a picture derived from elements that fit the time and circumstances of the text in question—still might improve our understanding of what it says. One might argue that textual history is relevant to the understanding of texts only to the extent that it can be proven to be historical fact, but it is my contention that even certain stories about texts can be of help in reading them.

The first of these stages is the well-documented attempt to submit a *taiping* scripture at the Han dynasty court. Gong Chong 宮崇, who presented it to Emperor Shun (r. 125–44), came from Langye. He acknowledged Gan Ji 干吉, an "expert in vitality techniques" (*fang shi* 方士), as his teacher. This is a situation that any reader of the received text of the TPJ will immediately recognize. In terms of the received text, Gan Ji was the "Celestial Master," whose words were recorded in the TPJ. He sent his disciple, the Perfected Gong Chong, to approach the "virtuous ruler" in Luoyang, who happened to be Emperor Shun, and to personally present to him the Celestial Master's scripture. If we stay within the scenario that is outlined in the received text, Gan Ji's scripture would not be the TPJ as we have it today, but rather the material that preceded it and that is talked about throughout the received text as "the Master's writings." This was the material the disciples were expected to propagate, and with this in hand the emperor would be able to instigate the reforms that were necessary to save the world from the approaching apocalypse. The Daoist tradition has followed the historical accounts and has heaped glory upon Gan Ji, as can be seen in the tale of his meeting with Laozi.[117] However, as the *Hou Han shu* informs us, Gong Chong's mission did not succeed and, incarcerated in Luoyang, he perished.

The source of Gan Ji's great peace scripture was a school or a movement of some scope and duration. This is clear from the fact that someone else attempted to do what Gong Chong had failed to do. The well-established, erudite Xiang Kai 襄楷, also from Langye, presented the scripture in official style in the year 166 C.E. The contrast between the two submissions is striking. Xiang Kai was a mainstream bureaucrat who has been given a biography in the *Hou Han shu* but not in any Daoist collection of biographies. On the other hand, Gong Chong's only mention in non-Daoist sources is in Xiang Kai's memorial, while many collections of Daoist biographies contain the story of his life. We may conclude that between the 140s and 160s, that is, roughly from one generation to the next, the Taiping Movement in Langye had come to attract adherents among the upper strata who were known as scholars and had close contact with the central administration. In addition, Xiang

Kai was able to remind Emperor Huan of his own Daoist interests. The emperor had authorized rituals for the veneration of Laozi at the imperial court and at Laozi's supposed place of birth in Huxian (in today's Hubei, on the Han River).[118] At this stage, then, Daoist beliefs had become acceptable not just in a specific regional environment, but even in the capital.[119] When Xiang Kai's attempt failed, he was initially detained at court but was then permitted to return home safely, where he remained a public figure of some consequence.[120] He raised his voice to promote the cause of career officials against what they saw as eunuch upstarts. He was recommended for office at the beginning of the reign of Emperor Ling (r. 168–89), and again in 188 after the defeat of the Yellow Turbans, when the eunuchs' faction had fallen from power. However, in the mode of Zhuangzi, he declined both offers.

While the *taiping* scripture's next stage is more conjectural, there are good reasons to believe what we are told in the *Hou Han shu* by Fan Ye (398–446). In annotating Xiang Kai's memorials, Fan Ye mentions that Zhang Jue, leader of the Taiping Movement and of the Yellow Turban Rebellion that resulted from it, knew of Gan Ji's book.[121] It seems that Fan Ye's statement, made long after the event, reflected a generally accepted view. Zhang Jue's shamanistic paraphernalia, his acclaim for Huang-Lao ideas, and the choice of the color yellow all helped, as we have seen, to shape the program of the Yellow Turbans.[122] There are two further pieces of evidence that, in my opinion, strengthen the plausibility of Fan Ye's assertion. The first is the creation of a statelike community toward the end of the second century C.E., which tells us that at that historical stage Daoist ideas had considerable social and political impact. As shown above, the Sichuan Daoists, as if guided by the TPJ's Celestial Master, based their rule on the establishment and maintenance of moral norms and regulations that would make people healthy, safeguard their livelihood, and help them to live long lives. The second point supporting Fan Ye's statement is the existence of written material that propagated the aims of Zhang Jue's movement. We are informed that certain men of rank in the capital were reading it.[123] We know, therefore, that Zhang Jue and his friends were literate and made use of texts. Also, the *Hou Han shu*'s mention of Zhang Jue's interest in Huang-Lao points to some extent toward the *Laozi*-oriented political philosophy we find represented in the received text of the TPJ.

The next stage involves another mentioning of a text with "great peace" in its title. We must remind ourselves that not many ancient and medieval texts were made public with as much éclat as were texts on great peace. This holds true for both Gan Ji's text and a great peace text submitted to Emperor Ai (r. 7–1 B.C.E.) before the reign of Wang Mang. After some initial success, the astronomer Li Xun (fl. 17–

5 B.C.E.) and other promoters of this early *taiping* text fell from grace, but the scripture itself remained in the imperial library and continued to be consulted.[124] The text submitted in the second century C.E. by Gong Chong and again by Xiang Kai suffered a similar fate. This text had the title "Book of Great Peace with the Title Written in Blue" *(Taiping qing ling shu)* and was kept in the imperial library after it had been submitted to Emperor Shun. The text was certainly read by the court's academic specialists, if for no other reason than to criticize it:

> The officials reported that the work Gong Chong had presented was unorthodox and false, outside the canon of the classics; nevertheless, it was received and retained.[125]

The breakdown of the dynasty brought a natural end to all official presence of the scripture. What this meant for its physical existence we cannot tell. The next mention of a scripture on great peace is in the catalogue that Ge Hong (283–343) produced of the books in the library of his teacher Zheng Yin 鄭隱.[126] Zheng had, as Ge Hong explains, studied with Ge Xuan, his great-uncle.[127] Ge Hong copied and owned some of these works himself, while he only made a note of others. Among them were a *Taiping jing* 太平經 in 50 *juan* 卷 and, closely aligned, a *Jiayi jing* 甲乙經 in 170 *juan*.[128] This is the first mention we find of the title *Taiping jing*. Ge Hong's *Jiayi jing* has also been thought to indicate the TPJ, since the received text is divided into ten parts named after the ten celestial stems and into 170 chapters, but this identification remains conjectural.[129] It is by far the longest "scripture" in Ge Hong's list of books. Ge Hong says that the scriptures, reports (*ji* 紀), charts (*tu* 圖), and talismans (*fu* 符) he mentions consist for the most part of just one *juan*,[130] so he sees no need to record the number of chapters for most of them. He mentions *juan* numbers for a collection of talismans in 500 *juan*, the *Jiayi jing*, the "Book on the Nourishment of Life" *(Yang sheng shu)* in 105 *juan*, the *Taiping jing*, another collection of talismans in twenty *juan*, and several titles with ten or fewer *juan*.

This library, which we may assume contained material that was available in the early third century C.E., originated in the breakdown of the Han dynasty.[131] Judging by the titles, most of the works dealt with specific techniques, as, for instance, the alchemical work "The Essential Scripture on Yellow and White" (*Huangbai yaojing* 黃白要經), or "The Scripture on Looking inside Oneself" (*Nei shi jing* 內視經). The "Scripture on 'What Is as It Is'" (*Ziran jing* 自然經) probably dealt with breathing techniques. "The Scripture on Pacifying the People" (*Xi min jing* 息民經) was on a more political topic. Again judging by their titles, the works came from various sources. There is no reason why the TPJ in its received form should not have been among them.

On the other hand, there is not enough evidence to allow us to establish that the received TPJ is identical with the *taiping* text in Ge Hong's list of books. As the titles on this list are not accompanied by any quotations from or information about the respective books, we cannot even draw lines from one mention of a *taiping* text to another, quite apart from the problem of linking any of them to the received text. On the other hand, we have no way of excluding the possibility of a coherent transmission. The Celestial Master of the transmitted text of the TPJ mentions that his disciples had received texts, the study of which was meant to prepare them for meeting with and being instructed by him. This creates the impression that there was a movement, or one might even call it a school, with a set of texts and organized tuition. These texts were not the received text of TPJ, in which they are frequently mentioned and perhaps quoted.[132] When pressed to give them a title, the Master comes up with "Scripture that Pervades All" (*Dongji zhi jing* 洞極之經). Such a scripture might, as did many others, have had several names, among them *Taiping jing*. As I see it, we may assume that texts in the lineage of great peace beliefs existed before the sixth century, under the titles of *Taiping jing, Dongji zhi jing, Jiayi jing*, and perhaps even *Shen shu*,[133] which is how Xiang Kai had referred to the text he submitted to Emperor Huan. While it is plausible to link these titles to the received text, such a linkage cannot be proven. I find it even more difficult to connect certain titles with specific layers of the present-day text.[134]

The notion of great peace moved closer to the center of Daoist concerns when a section entitled *Taiping* was added to the religion's canon of scriptures as one of four "support" sections. These must be seen as resulting from the activity of a certain Meng, a contemporary of Emperor Wu of the Liang dynasty (r. 502–49).[135] Despite a lack of detail, the argument that a *taiping* text must have been in existence at this stage is valid. We know little of Meng's work and of the composition of the Daoist canon in the early sixth century. However, it is unlikely that Meng would have created a *Taiping* section had there been no *taiping* scripture to include in it.[136] The only figure whose interest in such a text has been recorded is Chu Boyu 褚伯玉, who is said to have died in the year 479, at eighty-six years of age. Daoist sources inform us that he read the TPJ and lived by it.[137] This is corroborated by the *Nan Qi shu*, which reports that the first emperor of the Qi dynasty set up a *taiping* monastery in Chu Boyu's honor.[138]

The next and decisive stage is Huan Kai's 桓闓 "discovery" of the text. He found it in "three lacquered boxes" and showed a sample to Tao Hongjing (456–536), who said the material was authentic. However, Huan Kai fell ill and remained ill until, on Tao Hongjing's advice, he returned the material to where he had found it.[139] This is what Daoist sources tell us. The *Mao shan zhi* account makes Huan a high-ranking disciple of Tao Hongjing.[140]

This misadventure of a first publication must be seen as dependent on Tao Hongjing's relationship to the ruling Liang dynasty. He retired from court in 492 with imperial permission and on an imperial pension. Important as they were for the fate of Daoism, his good relations with Emperor Wu were not without tension. Strickmann aptly points to the contradiction between Buddhist and certain literati reports of the emperor's reign that make him something of China's Buddhist ruler *comme il faut,* and the *Sui shu* account, which stresses Tao Hongjing's impact on the emperor. [141] The emperor's promotion of Buddhism and the consequent repression of Daoism from the year 504 onward went hand in hand with an increased support for Tao Hongjing and in particular for his alchemical experiments. However, the imperial interest in Tao Hongjing's activities did not stretch to everything the Daoist deemed important. If we wanted to pick an obvious date for Tao Hongjing's warnings against publicizing a *taiping* text, it would be the years after his southern expedition. In the year 512, after Tao had reached the Southern Peak and found a place to settle in its vicinity, the emperor demanded his return to the capital.[142] As a compromise Tao left the south but returned to the Mao shan premises instead of following the emperor's invitation to the capital.

The emperor, it must be assumed, was much more interested in his own personal immortality than in the eschatological beliefs behind Tao's pilgrimage to the south. The disappointment this caused Tao can explain why he felt skeptical about promoting the *taiping* text, which for him, as for Huan Kai and, later on, Zhou Zhixiang 周智響, must have been relevant as a document of eschatological thought. However, Tao's skepticism might also have been more general and based on a certain censorship directed against all Daoist writings. In 517 Tao presented to Emperor Wu his *Record of Master Zhou's Communications with the Invisible World.*[143] This edition of the posthumous manuscripts of his young disciple was the last work Tao Hongjing wrote. Strickmann shows that the publication of Daoist texts came almost to a standstill between 517 and 549.[144] It is possible, therefore, that Huan Kai's unsuccessful attempt to publicize a *taiping* text fell into the first decades of this period (Tao Hongjing died in the year 536). The situation changed after 549. The death of Emperor Wu and the Hou Jing interregnum led to a political breakdown, signified by a rapid succession of inadequate emperors, which created a certain amount of ideological openness in contrast to Emperor Wu's strict adherence to what he saw as Buddhist principles. Xiao Gang (503–51), who became Emperor Jianwen under Hou Jing's command, wrote commentaries on the *Laozi* and, more significantly, since this was undertaken less frequently, on the *Zhuangzi*. He had met Tao Hongjing while governor of Southern Xu.[145] The *Jinlou zi* of Emperor Yuan (508–55), who in 552 succeeded Emperor Jianwen, signified a broad interest in alternative values and also the contempt with which scholars traditionally regarded career- and wealth-oriented activities. The emperor also conducted readings of the *Laozi*.[146] There is no reason to suggest that during these decades Huan's work on the *taiping* manuscripts was discontinued. Clearly, Tao Hongjing's skepticism applied to the publication rather than the study of the scripture. Huan's personal contacts—he had entrée to the ruling house of the Liang dynasty and to Zhou Zhixiang, who finally rescued the old text[147]—make it plausible to link his work to the public interest in great peace that emerged at the end of the Liang and the beginning of the Chen dynasty.

At this final stage, the compilers of the text as well as their official promoters argued that the text had a long history of creation, transmission, neglect, and failed rediscovery: "When Huan fell ill, Tao said: 'The doctrine of Great Peace should not yet be implemented. You are ill because you obtained it by force.'"[148] In contrast, the time was said to be ripe around the year 556, during the change from the Liang to the Chen dynasty. On this occasion, the text emerged as an official enterprise under the supervision of Zhou Zhixiang. Considering the size of the sixth-century TPJ, it is easy to see that imperial support was useful, not only for propagandistic reasons but also for practical ones. The transport and editing of such a long text must have been costly. Upon the scripture's successful completion, the Monastery of Perfect Truth (Zhi zhen guan 至真觀) was set up to promote its study. These activities were aimed at increasing the authority of the Chen dynasty. "Great peace" was in 556 officially declared to be the title of the reign period, when Chen Baxian (503–59) had secured his position but had not yet declared himself emperor.[149] Historical sources do not venture an explanation for the beginning of the new reign period, but it might have signified the elimination of Wang Sengbian (d. 555), Chen Baxian's most serious rival. This would mean that from the beginnings of their dynasty the slogan of great peace was closely linked to the Chen rulers.

The received text consists of the remains of the sixth-century text. Quotations confirm this.[150] Most importantly, a Dunhuang fragment (S 4226) from the first half of the seventh century[151] with a full TPJ table of contents assures us they are one and the same. The new edition was put under the spiritual charge of the Latter Sage of the Golden Gate, who played an important role in sixth-century eschatological speculation. The inclusion of the sage signifies not only the involvement of the

Daoist pantheon in *taiping* concerns, but it also attests to an evolution of eschatological considerations. In the received text of the TPJ, it is assumed that the world will soon end since it has been worn down by the evils humankind has perpetrated. This threat is linked, however, to the promise that the cyclical patterns of heaven will provide an opportunity—the last opportunity—to turn things around and arrive at great peace. This was not the way Tao Hongjing saw it. He argued that an apocalypse was imminent and unavoidable.[152] Only Daoist believers would then be saved by the descent of the Latter Sage of the Golden Gate, who would conduct believers to a safe place where they would happily await the arrival of great peace while humankind in general would perish.[153] According to Yoshioka's brief overview of the origin and history of the Latter Sage, this figure is intimately linked to the Upper Clarity (*shangqing* 上清) tradition. The deity was prominent in the lifetime of Tao Hongjing, or may even have become prominent through Tao Hongjing. This must be kept in mind with respect to the timing of the reissue of the TPJ. Its success and the deity's prominence both signify an interest in eschatological speculation. These were not yet enough in fashion at the time of Chu Boyu in the fifth century to have paved the way for the official acknowledgment and distribution of a *taiping* scripture.

Even a cursory look at the Latter Sage makes it clear that he had different, if not contrasting, facets, all of which are relevant to the message of the TPJ. His family name was Li and he was seen as a Laozi incarnation, so that his person became intertwined with the figure of Li Hong, whose messianic promises were on several occasions adopted by the ambitious leaders of popular movements.[155] However, Daoist eschatology was put to contradictory uses.[156] Beyond his rebellious potential, the Latter Sage was a figure an emperor could invoke as evidence of the imminent arrival of great peace for all under his own reign.

THE ORIGIN OF THE TPJ

The TPJ as we have it today goes back to the sixth century, a period when the Daoist religion was canonized and systematized. Collecting, editing, and producing texts was as much a part of religious activity as were millenarian concerns and the interest in personal longevity. The production and subsequent promotion of the TPJ suited this environment. The text dealt with the threat of imminent universal destruction, proposed general political and social reforms in order to avoid this fate, and reserved an important place for techniques of meditation as a means to improve the quality and length of life not only for believers but for society as a whole.

All this was in accord with sixth-century Daoism. Other aspects of the TPJ were more problematic. A text entitled *Scripture on Great Peace* reminded the public of certain stages in the origin and growth of Daoism that were better left unremembered. In 184 C.E., the "Way of Great Peace" of the Yellow Turbans had, as shown above, become one link in a chain of events that quickly led to the downfall of the Han dynasty and in turn to the end of a unified empire. In the sixth century, there was no doubt: the TPJ the Daoists propagated was a rediscovered version of the old Han dynasty text.[157] On the one hand, this made the new TPJ one of the oldest texts of the Daoist tradition. On the other hand, it was accompanied by a touch of insurrection and disorder. However, the scripture was successfully promoted, what it said was accepted, and it was successfully transmitted. This in itself was, one could argue, a sign of Daoist strength. The position of Daoists at court and throughout society was so well established that they had little to fear from a public remembrance of their origins.[158]

When we turn to the sixth-century editors for advice on the text's origins, we are referred back to the second century and the figure of Gan Ji, of whose historical existence there is but little evidence.[159] Early quotations and other references do not exist, so our main source for identifying the text's origin can only be the text itself. Much of what it says and how it is said remind us of the movements described above. It resembles a text from the Later Han dynasty. Its worldview stresses heaven's patterns and a system of correlated entities, among them Yin and Yang. It attributes the dominant role to the phase of fire and the color red, which means that it was meant for publication in a world reigned by Han dynasty rulers; only rebellious movements would promote yellow or black. To the extent to which an administrative system is hinted at, it could be that of the Han. The main point here is that the text appears to lack elements that would necessitate attributing it to a later date, such as loans from Buddhist writings, and it seems to reflect a rather elementary stage of Daoist beliefs. The text mentions virtually no historical figures, events, or places, with the exception of the Kunlun range, the Yellow River, the Luo, Luoyang,[160] and perhaps Chang'an.

While we do not know the author or authors, the text contains some information on the background of its main speaker, its fictitious authors, and their intended audience. The TPJ authors refrain almost completely from all direct reference to written sources, except for works distributed within their own circle. They refer to the historical past only in the most general terms, not presuming that their readers have any specific knowledge of China's great texts. The authors show no personal interest in achieving an official career and do not assume such an interest of their audience. While they wish to serve a ruler and his people, they see the need to enter into such a relationship from the outside, as heaven-sent advisors with a unique message. Moreover, much of the text is written in a language that differs from standard written Chinese. To use such language and to identify with what was written in such language was to distance oneself from the world of erudition and learning. The text shows an unusual concern for the people, as opposed to the ruler and officials, and, it should be noted, a certain knowledge of the people's plight. This does not mean that the TPJ is "revolutionary," but it does suggest that its authors were not established members of the social and cultural elite. Also, when the authors discuss administrative policies they refer primarily to fairly small units and not to the empire as a whole. Reforms, it seems, must start at a local level before they can reach the wider world.

This does not mean that the Celestial Master, who acts as the main speaker throughout much of the text, is ignorant of mainstream culture. He has access to the literary tradition[161] and is fully aware of issues that dominate it. How those ruling and those ruled should coexist, how the individual is expected to juggle his—and, in the case of the TPJ, also her—conflicting responsibilities, how to find a proper hierarchical order for moral values and norms, what to make of heaven and its dominance, how to explain natural disasters, and how to make sense of historical change: these were for him the relevant topics. He takes a stand on all these points, and time-honored positions on political and moral thinking reappear in what he says. He recommends the reduction of government, stresses individual moral responsibility, sees disasters as heaven's response to human transgressions, and proposes that we live and rule in accordance with cosmic, that is, heaven's, order.

We might deduce from this that the Master was an erudite thinker who had chosen to popularize the concerns of Han dynasty moral and political thought and give them a large audience, but that is not the case. He presents himself as the founder of a religion. He propagates belief in the way of heaven and promises humankind salvation once they ascribe to this belief. He deals with the existential fears and concerns of which we are aware from imagery in poetry and the visual arts[162] but that the philosophical literature of the period did not fully appreciate. The Master knows how to control the spirits, who might cause illness and shorten life, and how to ensure an afterlife without trouble.

In other parts of the text the illustrious, otherworldly figure of a Celestial Lord and his staff instruct readers on how to deal with the celestial bureaucracy. Throughout the TPJ, the people's well-being depends on spiritual support. While there are ways to influence these spirits—such as through meditation and a quiet style of life—they are in the first instance heaven's obedient servants. Man's main concern, then, must be his own relationship to heaven. The Celestial Lord promises salvation, as does the Celestial Master. Judging by the questions raised by the Celestial Lord's disciple, health, longevity, and the final ascendancy to heaven result from "right" conduct, that is, from fulfilling certain clearly defined commandments and from demonstrating the general virtues of piety, loyalty, and sincerity.[163]

Early religious Daoism encompassed different groups of people. Within its ranks were certainly educated, well-positioned individuals. While their lifestyles and ideas were oriented toward the values expressed in texts like the *Laozi* and the *Zhuangzi*, they were not necessarily active participants in any religious movement. Xiang Kai, the second-century promoter of a great peace scripture, is a prominent example of this. The religion, however, also attracted the "masses." Their leaders, usually literate and with some formal education, created religious congregations and, when successful, as Zhang Lu was, created statelike communities that promised a better life for all through social reform, Since this was the TPJ's main topic, it is tempting to see its origins in these groups.[164] That there is not a more obvious resemblance between the doctrines of the TPJ and the ideas promoted by the Daoist movements must be because of a certain material disproportion between a long scripture and isolated bits of information. Even if district and provincial officials had been more forthcoming in their reports on these movements we cannot expect that the ancient historians, court officials that they were, would tell us much about the beliefs held by groups of discontented, if not rebellious, peasants.

Vague as all this is, we can still conclude that such a social environment was a possible birthplace for a text like the TPJ. Moreover, it seems almost impossible to imagine any other background for this text. It expresses a worldview that encompasses much of the Han dynasty discourse, expresses eschatological concerns, and is pre-Buddhist. It is tempting to say that it is also pre-Daoist. The Celestial Master's authority is heaven, for instance, rather than *dao*. This represents, we might argue, one of the points of departure of this religion.

Another point worth mentioning is the text's apparent lack of literary ambition and sophistication, evident in its use of language, its verbosity, and its repetitiveness. This does not mean the authors disregarded the rhetorical effect of their work and the need to please, impress, and persuade their readers. However, their means of doing so differed radically from those of established modes of literary production. Therefore, there are reasons to believe that the text was produced not only by men who did not share the elite's literary taste and interests, but also in a mode that was unusual. It is reasonable to assume that the rather complex scenario of an interchange of opinions between the Master and his disciples depicts a situation in which the authors actually participated. To have created it for the sake of increasing the plausibility and persuasiveness of the Master's message seems too much of a literary effort. Thus, what the received text tells us may be taken at face value: a charismatic figure who is addressed as Celestial Master tells his audience that he has been sent by heaven to instruct disciples so that they can approach the political rulers of the day, make them believe in heaven, and reform their policies. Conversations between the Master and his disciples and the Master's lectures form the main content of the TPJ.

The word *shi* 師, meaning "master" or "teacher," is the phonetic equivalent of *shi* 使, or "messenger." The title "Messenger Sent from Heaven" occurs frequently in second-century C.E. archaeological materials and in historical sources dealing with this period.[165] Several rebel leaders chose that title, among them Zhang Bolu and his followers.[166] However, Zhang Jue, the Yellow Turban commander, used "master," as did the initiators of the Celestial Master movement in Sichuan. Although the TPJ's Celestial Master was certainly not alone in the claim that heaven had chosen and authorized him, we are told more about him than about any other "master." Pressed by curious disciples, he explains that at one stage he followed other masters and thus had some schooling. However, he was disappointed in the results and thus came to regard heaven as his true teacher. He had taught other disciples before those depicted in the TPJ, but with little success, since their motivation had been insufficient. He is a transcendent, with a place in the world beyond, and will soon leave the human realm behind. He has received books from heaven and has personally written texts. He reads books. He is, for instance, aware of the *He tu*, the *Luo shu*, and other prognostic material.[167] None of this contradicts the little we know of the historical or semihistorical figures who assumed the title of "master," and it agrees with the sagas woven around them. The hagiographic account of Zhang Daoling, for instance, the supposed founder of the Sichuan Celestial Master movement, has much in common with the picture the TPJ's Celestial Master draws of himself.

The Master's disciples remain similarly anonymous. They are not beginners, but rather hold the rank of Perfected. They are literate, and they have read all the material the Master has written or recommended. Their ages and backgrounds are not known. However, we must expect them to have families and to be men. They accept the obligation to continue the missionary work the Master, or rather, as they would claim, heaven, demands of them.

The TPJ describes in detail how the Master instructs his disciples. They meet, the disciples extend some polite greeting and ask questions, and the Master responds with a fairly long explanation. At this point, he often reminds disciples to take notes. This advice is repeated at certain intervals, as if to structure the lecture, and the disciples accept this task.

All this I take as an accurate picture of how much of the TPJ originated; it consists of the notes taken by devoted students who were instructed by an individual who called himself "heaven-sent teacher." A closer look at the form of the text will reveal more details and corroborate this thesis.

LANGUAGE AND STYLE

Much of the text looks as if it consists of transcriptions. If we assume that disciples jotted down the questions they raised along with the Master's answers and admonitions in response, we can explain certain formal characteristics of the text. The first of these characteristics is its use of language, and in particular the choice of characters. The words used are generally long. There are three-character nouns, and verbal predicates often consist of two characters, with the addition of a verbal modifier and a verbal complement. The text is verbose, and without the refinement associated with "elegant" medieval prose.[168] The text's verbosity is apparent when it is compared to its Tang dynasty digest, the *Chao*, which eliminates the third character in clusters, as well as verbal complements and particles.[169] The distance between the language of much of the TPJ and the way esteemed Han dynasty writers expressed themselves suggests that the TPJ reflected the way people spoke and that what we call nonstandard elements are in fact traces of colloquial language use.[170] In this regard, the TPJ resembles early Chinese Buddhist scriptures.[171] Eric Zuercher has studied this material in some detail.[172] He sees the nonstandard language in second-century Chinese translations of Buddhist texts as deriving from the spoken language of that period. This language was perpetuated in the Buddhist tradition parallel to the way in which *wenyan*, the language used in classical scriptures, developed as a constant feature that was largely independent of the spoken language. Since the TPJ had virtually no impact on the Daoist scriptural tradition, its language did not play this role. It did not initiate a specifically Daoist style of expression.

The TPJ, and in particular the dialogues between the Celestial Master and his disciples, shares a number of characteristics with the material studied by Zuercher. Words are frequently not monosyllabic.[173] However, this is also a token of the changing language use of the Later Han dynasty; it occurs not only in early Buddhist translations, but also in Wang Chong's first-century C.E. *Lun heng*.[174] The order of characters in compounds is to some extent reversible,[175] and single characters and compounds can be interchanged without any noticeable difference.[176] Adverbial compounds are not as frequent in the TPJ as in the translations, but they exist, particularly for *fu* 復 and *gong* 共.[177] Word classes can probably be called "clearly defined," as Zuercher put it with regard to his material. But there are exceptions. While words, particularly when they are compounds, are commonly used as either noun or verb or adverb, there are isolated cases of uncommon usage, such as the use of *ping* 病 in the meaning of "to make [them] ill" and *zai* 災 as "to send [them] disasters" with a direct object.[178] This is similar to Zuercher's findings. In other respects, the TPJ uses language differently from how it is used in the Buddhist material and is much closer to classical language usage. It does not mark the plural and there is no hint of *shi* 是 functioning as copula.[179] Despite such differences it may be safely assumed that the TPJ's elements of nonstandard language stem from the language spoken at the time and the place of its origin, just as Zuercher has argued for the early Buddhist translations. For the Buddhist material this was what Zuercher called the "metropolitan area," but we have no reason to suppose that this is where the *taiping* material came from. The saga of its origin points to the region of Langye and to the early second century, about a generation or even two generations earlier than Zuercher's material, which he sees as stretching from 150 to 220 C.E. There are therefore good reasons for the difference between the two forms of language use. Zuercher adds the important caveat that the language of the early Buddhist translations was not the language the translators spoke, but was rather written language modified by the spoken. To a small degree this also holds true for the TPJ, which consists not of everyday conversations but of dialogues of instruction. Still, the text's verbosity and the use of three-character compounds give the appearance of directly recorded spoken language.

The primary evidence for the text originating in transcripts, however, is not its use of language but its composition, which in almost all respects runs counter to the general rules and constraints of writing as they can be deduced from other ancient and medieval texts. Moreover, it has almost nothing in common with other texts based on, or written as if they were based on, spoken communication.[180] Those texts were carefully edited, while the TPJ material was not. We must assume that this material was not submitted to any responsible authorial impact; at least we can state with certainty that it looks as if it consists of transcripts in raw, unedited format. We must keep in mind that the entire TPJ comes from an environment in which men followed novel rules in regard to their beliefs, their lifestyle, and also the writing and collation of texts. So, the question of whether the transcriptlike quality of much of the TPJ is the result of editorial intent or whether it represents the text's real origin is difficult to answer. Based upon my reading of the TPJ, I prefer to see the Celestial Master dialogues as the work of a number of disciples who did their best to jot down what they heard. Although no definitive evidence can be produced to support this view, this thesis still seems to be the only way to explain the stylistic characteristics of most of the text.

To see the dialogues as transcripts produced by different students provides a good explanation for certain stylistic divergences between sections. Individual sections make repeated use of specific expressions that occur hardly anywhere else in the text. The following are examples from the sections translated here. Section 50 uses the expression "to walk this way" (*xing ci dao* 行此道) for a way of doing things; in section 54 to be keen for knowledge is compared with the thirst for water; section 58 uses *daolu* 道路 for "the right way"; section 60 uses *raorao* 擾擾 for the confusion and moral laxity of this world; and section 64 continually talks about change in human activities and in nature as "advance and retreat" (*jin tui* 進退).[181]

Given the TPJ's purpose of creating a missionary movement and attracting general interest, too much space is taken up by irrelevant conversational passages, such as greetings, polite remarks about the wish for and need to enter into a discussion, repeated admonitions to the disciples to pay attention, and finally their discharge at the end. All of this detracts from the text's readability and argumentation. It reduces the amount of space available for explaining and supporting certain novel ideas. The Celestial Master's message is therefore hidden beneath a large amount of what one is tempted to call small talk. Although its rhetoric is at times persuasive, the TPJ is too long and too repetitive not to antagonize interested readers.

The way each section is composed adds to the impression that only a real meeting, an actual interchange of words, could have been its motive force. This is pointed out in some detail in the notes that accompany this translation. Section 60, for instance, contains accounts of two meetings. Both deal with the same subject, that is, with the isolation that is experienced by a person who prefers harsh and severe methods, and both give the disciple a chance to enter the discussion with a defense of severity. The section thus is rife with redundancy. From a literary point of view, it is about three times longer than it should be. The random change of topic in section 41 serves as another example. The second half of this section deals with the fate and social function of women, a quite different topic from that in the first half, which is how poverty results from political mismanagement. Both parts, however, are linked by conversational elements, as if their sequence resulted from the free flow of an informal teaching session. The meandering course of section 61, which is moved along only by the disciple's questions, is another case in point.

A characteristic element of the dialogues between the Celestial Master and his disciples is the continuous creation of the complete message. This offends principles of literary composition as well as of argumentation. Almost every meeting serves as an occasion for voicing certain basic statements: heaven has sent the Master to teach and the disciples to learn; heaven will send forth great peace; humankind must be prepared for its reception; heaven makes its will known through the Master's texts; the disciples must approach a virtuous ruler directly or indirectly with these texts in hand and let him instigate the necessary reforms. The repetition of these points attests to the independence of each section. They were not written as part of a coherent text, but rather each was a small element in an ongoing project of building a missionary movement, and their certain argumentative stubbornness might be said to equal propagandist intensity. The sequential chapters or sections resemble Sunday sermons, which continue to reproduce a narrow set of beliefs, rather than academic lectures. The unmodified written account of these sermons runs counter to the economical use of language.

The autonomy of the sections is enhanced by the fact that contrasting aspects of some basic issues are stressed in different sections, in accordance with specific needs of the argument. The sections have their own individual argumentation, as one would expect from a good lecture or sermon. So section 42 observes that Yin is represented by the figure "two" and argues against female infanticide, citing the fact that each man should have two wives, while section 44 states that Yin is "one," just as Yang is, and that only through the two of them is a third created. In section 62, the Master demands that the true scripture must be kept secret and shown only to the right person. His aim here is to make the scripture seem precious. Throughout most of the text, however, the disciples are urged to make the scripture public, as soon and as widely as possible. In general, the Master stresses that three are needed to create things and keep them going. He thus takes the family or the state, which is created through the cooperation of people, officials, and ruler, as his model. However, he also offers a dualistic approach, as if the Yin and the Yang of the natural world were enough to safeguard creation and continued existence.[182]

The argumentative role of the disciple is another case in point. Certain issues are raised only because the disciple instigates discussion of them, as for example toward the end of section 43, where he raises the important question of why heaven wants men to know what to expect. The figure of the disciple is crucial for the text's literary quality and argumentation, limited as both might be. He remains nameless but comes to life almost as vividly as the disciples of the *Lun yu*. All he says shows him to be eager and well intentioned, but at the same time of mediocre abilities and slow to understand. The reader can be expected to feel some sympathy for the disciple's intellectual misadventures. It can be argued that the invention of such a figure is in contrast with the otherwise poor literary quality of the text.

In its combination of argumentation and persuasive modes, the text is as unique stylistically as it is original and unusual. The amount of dialogue varies throughout the text and is greater in its earlier parts. Additions to *taiping* material from other sources have also been written in this style. This is obvious from the fact that the first section of the *Chao*, which is an account of the Latter Sage of the Golden Gate and was clearly written later than the bulk of the TPJ, contains a number of elements that are characteristic of the dialogues between the Celestial Master and his disciples.[183] Another point that suggests the plausibility that the text was not the explicit labor of an author or a group of authors—and, from my reading, an important point—is its argumentation and stylistic quality. The text communicates certain original and relevant ideas, presented in a quite novel and populist manner. However, when we consider the length of the text in relation to what it says, it can seem longwinded and carelessly constructed. This impression is reinforced by the fact that the selective mechanisms of cultural, scholarly, and religious traditions have permitted few, if any, ancient texts of this sort to reach us. This enhances the value of the TPJ as we have it today. It gives us a unique glimpse into the way ideas were expressed in late antiquity and how they were promoted by and among men outside established intellectual circles.

THE SCRIPTURE'S MESSAGE OF SALVATION

The received text of the TPJ is stylistically quite coherent when we consider its length, its origin, and its history. Most of it is written in one identifiable style. This, we might add, is in line with the surprising coherence of the text's message. We must assume that it had a powerful religious and intellectual impetus, as it filled the better part of 366 sections with threats of damnation, demands for imminent conversion, and the promise of the arrival of great peace. While this may be seen as a religious, if not an escapist, reaction to a world in trouble, I also see it as an attempt to reread the entire Han dynasty discourse from the perspective of providing salvation to a world in great disorder. Original as the *taiping* doctrine might be, it is built through slow and persistent reasoning on a foundation of generally accepted knowledge about nature and society.

One might argue that the size of the scripture is not accidental. To reread an established culture of the size, depth, and vitality of Han period China is in itself a formidable project. It was probably necessary to be an outsider to do this, but this fact made the project even more daunting because outsiders were not skilled in the techniques through which this culture took form. Also, the project was directed, at least in part, to outsiders, which meant that its argumentation and representation had to be geared to their backgrounds and interests.

The size of the scripture can also be seen as related to the movement or movements from which it stemmed. Its size reflects the success of second-century millenarian movements. This was a period of energetic and ongoing missionary work. The disciples' eagerness and the Master's threats and promises were real. Men did meet to discuss these matters, and they saw the need, so well established in all other aspects of their life, to spread their insights by writing them down. The TPJ reflects their numbers and their zeal.

The scripture tells us what a world in peace will be like and identifies the many changes that will have to precede and accompany this peace. The two stages—the initial movement toward great peace and its consequent arrival and reign over the world—are not always clearly separated. Elements of what the perfect world will be like can already be perceived while the process of reform is under way. In any case, the authors of the text seem to assume that everyone knows what great peace entails and for this reason concentrate on telling their readers how to get there. There remains a certain vagueness about the aim, as if to allow for the fact that a ruler's wishes and fears might differ from those of his subjects, and that the expectations of a religious professional might differ from those of lay believers. But while much about the state of great peace remains undefined, the preparatory program through which it is to become a reality contains precise prescriptions that outline radical social reform.

The following brief account of this program selects points of interest. The TPJ is long and its different sections have different argumentative goals. Some sections propose a novel approach to certain issues that are depicted in a more conservative manner in other sections. However, this does not reduce the relevance of the text's new ideas. The fact that confrontational and radical points of view are embedded in standard observations and values adds realism and practicality to the program. The authors of the scripture do not create a new world ex nihilo; they create it from and between the structures of the world their readers know. For us, the context of late Han dynasty values and behavioral guidelines is not clearly defined, and what the TPJ says can contribute to our knowledge of this context. Also, certain ideas are set forth that are not found elsewhere. That this is not accidental is confirmed by the fact that the TPJ's Celestial Master introduces these ideas as if they were novel and that his disciples react to them with hesitation and surprise. The amount of novelty, striking as it is, must, however, be seen in relation to the intellectual dynamism of early medieval China. The TPJ's unique textual tradition happens to make these ideas available, but they stem from a specific historical environment of social and philosophical concerns. We must assume that the ideas set forth in the TPJ are a token rather than a full representation of the fertility of this environment.

The program is meant to advise political leaders on how to prepare the world for great peace. In this reform process, men in power become heaven's tools. They must therefore decipher its will, which for the authors of the TPJ means attend to the Celestial Master's message as conveyed in his texts and spread by his disciples, practice ritual meditation, and closely observe and analyze astronomical phenomena. The heaven of the TPJ is somewhat closer to men than it is in the great books of China's ancient tradition. Its omniscience pertains to all individual concerns. Once a man believes in heaven there will be a solution to his problems, in this world and also after death. In this respect the two realms are not seen as being in conflict. Someone who serves heaven while alive can hope to have a reasonably good life for as long as it lasts and to avoid harassment after he has died. If he is lucky, he might even enter the celestial bureaucracy. Conversely, the man who does not serve heaven will die from illness when young and have a hard time in the world below.

Central to the image of heaven as well as to that of earth, which is its partner and supporter, is their power to give and maintain life, as is evident in the harvests men reap due to heaven's bounty. Of course, heaven is also the source of order, regularity, constancy, and reliability, and all these qualities should be understood and imitated by men in their own endeavors, but they are all minor virtues and concerns that need to be activated in the service of the protection of life, which is the main concern.

A ruler's most important concern, therefore, must be for men's livelihood. It is asking too much of individuals or families to leave them to fight for themselves. It is the ruler's responsibility to provide for their basic needs. He must look to the supply of food, enable his subjects to support a family and raise children, and also find clothes for them so they can go about their activities in decency and be protected against the cold. Social groups of special concern are the fools, the aged, and the infirm.[184]

As far as food goes, the ruler is to look after the distribution of grain and prevent hoarding. He is also to make sure that everyone helps in the production of food. But, most importantly, through his personal relations with heaven he is to ensure that harvests are sufficient and are not damaged by irregular weather conditions or natural disasters like droughts, floods, and hornets.

Procreation is a human and a cosmic need. It closely reflects the interest in life that runs through the whole reform program. Sexual relations and the birth of children make people happy and help them to re-create in their own sphere heaven's creative energy. Since sexual life is seen as central to men's well-being, the role of women is redefined. The main point is that unless there are sufficient women available, not every man can marry, and, ideally, each man should have two wives, just like a master has two servants, one to his right and the other to his left. In order to achieve this ratio, female infanticide must come to an end. This can be expected to happen naturally—no parent likes killing a child—when girls are put in a position where they are of use to their parents. At present, it costs money to raise girls, but they offer no return. It is suggested that the services a woman performs for her husband should enable her to support her own aged parents, just as sons do after they have married. Parents would then have no reason not to bring up daughters.

The role of women reflects that of earth, and maltreatment must be avoided in both cases for reasons of procreation and fertility. If Yin is not respected there will be neither children nor harvests. This means that one must not dig the earth up at random, a demand that is combined with other environmental dictates, such as the prohibition against clearing hills by fire.

The program is addressed to the ruler and his advisors. It proposes radical reforms, including a greater social responsibility for the people as a whole. Great peace will arrive only when the ruler can make the people change their attitudes. This assigns a central role to communication between different political and social strata.[185] Government and people communicate by way of writing; although there is room for an initial oral flow of news, information and instruction is seen as being spread by writing. This is stressed in the TPJ when the Celestial Master admonishes students not only to listen attentively, but also to take careful notes. The success of the reform program is therefore seen as depending on the efficiency of the written word and the proper handling of texts. Once entrusted with scriptures that have been circulated or created by the Celestial Master and his disciples, a ruler is to have his literary specialists edit them and publish them. Properly skilled and guided, these specialists will also produce florilegia of other writings, older as well as contemporary. This material will then be distributed and men will read, recite, and meditate upon it. The message that is thus conveyed documents its trustworthiness by being unambiguous and easy to comprehend. As soon as men understand its meaning they will realize the consequences of their current misbehavior and they will change. They will, for instance, allow their daughters to live, and they will treat the earth with respect.

The relationship between the people and their government is dynamic. Each is expected to make the other's existence possible. The reforms that prepare for great peace involve so many items of everyday personal life that their implementation seems to presuppose a community of believers. While administrative success depends on the people's belief, the people see the organs of government as an institution that reads, interprets, and conveys heaven's will. At this point, the people's contribution is again critical. Government policy must rely on the people's observations in that it relies on the people for reading heaven's will. The people must keep track of all irregularities in the course of nature so that heaven's feelings can be properly analyzed. Much attention is paid to the methods by which the people can make their observations known at the higher levels of government. Competition and struggle between different administrative layers and a strong tendency to intercept the flow of information from one layer to the other seem to be taken for granted. So individuals must not only be willing to do the right thing by informing their superiors, but they must also be clever enough to succeed in doing so. This point is symptomatic of much of the reform program. The TPJ authors depict society, whether of the present world or of the future world of great peace, as a community. The community is structured hierarchically, but it functions through cooperation rather than through a system involving random commands and blind obedience.

Readers will protest at this point that much of what is set forth here is well-known, and that there is nothing in this particular account of the proper relationship between ruler and people that has not been said or at least hinted at in the great texts of pre-Qin and Han times. Nevertheless, it is proposed here in new words, and problems are isolated and identified. While this brings into focus the need for active cooperation, it also problematizes it, thus creating a realistic platform for political reform. The people are expected to cooperate, with their own personal interests in mind. Their relationship with heaven is direct and personal. Although they can rely on their betters to know the details of heaven's will, persuasion alone will bring them to conform to it. This sets a new task for the ruler and his advisors. It is not—or at least not only—the example they set and the educational activities they instigate that has an impact on the people. People cannot be expected to cooperate simply because they respect their ruler and his virtue. What the government must bring about is better described as conversion than education. The people must understand that it is heaven's good will that dictates their fortune, that is, life, health, progeny, and sufficient means. Moreover, death does not end it all. Misbehavior in this world will also ruin one's fate in the netherworld.

The demand that correct information be spread and that the texts conveying what is true be made known is juxtaposed with strong warnings against producing and publicizing texts that do not conform to heaven's will. It is crucial that not just men in responsible positions but everyone be able to distinguish between these two sets of material. It is not easy to make the distinction, but there are a few clear criteria. Texts that criticize heaven and the government of the day are certainly wrong, as is material that encourages the application of penalties and that is not clear and lucid. The heterodoxy that must be opposed seems to be widespread and often remains unspecified. However, when there are specific accusations they are mainly directed against certain second-century political thought.[186]

We can only infer indirectly whom the TPJ means when it talks of "people." Clearly, responsibility for the arrival of great peace and thus for renewal and change lies with them. This shows that their social and political role is newly defined. They are seen as including a relatively wide range of groups. While the authors draw images from the cultivation of the soil and from craftsmanship, activities that would always be identified with "the people," they also mention that there are low-ranking officials, sedentary people, and itinerants, and that individuals from all three groups are, within their group's parameters, subject to the ruler as well as to heaven. Each individual is expected to assist and support both, which in the case of heaven is often phrased as the need to support the spirits in their course of action. Since many of these spirits reside in a person they can easily and directly be appeased by a life of quiet contentment and friendly concern for others. That issues are linked to each other by correlation is a well-known fixture of Han dynasty thought. However, the TPJ's Celestial Master tends to stress dependencies that are otherwise ignored. Of course, a virtuous ruler will promote virtue in those who depend on him. His entourage will try to imitate him and things will improve. But a virtuous subject can do the same: when their subordinates do the right thing, the men in charge will improve their behavior. So the way in which individuals conduct their lives is crucial. This does not abolish social hierarchy, but rather reduces its force. From a cosmic and a celestial perspective the right and wrong of each individual, independent of their rank, are of similar importance.

Good health can be seen as proof of a proper lifestyle. On an individual level the link between the two might not be directly manifest, but in principle it exists. The man or woman who pays attention to heaven's commandments will not fall ill, while someone who neglects heaven might pay for it with his life. While one's date of birth has an impact,[187] what is stressed here is personal responsibility as opposed to the material conditions of life, which to a large extent result from proper governance. A person must look after his or her own essence. While this means following heaven's commandments, it also involves dietary rules, meditation, and quietude. Longevity is also central to social relations. To be kind to others means to prolong their life, by making them happy as well as by procuring for them proper medical treatment.

An important element of personal as well as public life is the avoidance of resentment. Individuals must be careful not to become resentful, and men in a leading position must make sure that their subordinates are satisfied. Whatever causes men to bear a grudge must be avoided. That is why it is important that people do not adhere to wrong ideas. If not taught properly they might, for instance, see heaven as being responsible for their sufferings, or they might blame the government of the day for bringing misery upon them. People must learn to consider that today's rulers have inherited the wrongdoings of their predecessors and that change must not be expected to come about all of a sudden. Even well-intended and well-informed rulers need time to counteract the mistakes of the past and allow the program of great peace to proceed. On the other hand, officials and their apparatus must not cause resentment among the people by disregarding their plight or imprisoning the innocent. The need to avoid resentment also plays a role in the prohibition of infanticide, a cruelty that all women resent and that for this reason alone is bound to create cosmic upheaval. The prevention of resentment is also behind a fastidious process of selecting and supervising officials and clerks. Superiors must make sure they assign their subordinates to jobs they are well able to handle, lest they become desperate. Moreover, whistle-blowers must be protected. If they are not, their resentment will in the future obstruct the flow of information.

Prescriptions in the TPJ for the conduct of life cover a broad spectrum. They include general demands, such as the need to stress what is of "communal" interest instead of concentrating on private gain, and the need to take one's own person, or rather the process of self-cultivation, seriously. More specifically, the problem of alcohol consumption is addressed: it can do damage to family life and must be constrained. Dietary issues are also of relevance: to eat little and to attempt to live on the consumption of nothing but *qi* (vapor) will improve health and longevity. Meditation is essential for staying healthy as well as for becoming wise. Followers of great peace are always part of a family and can become full-time devotees, that is, disciples of the Celestial Master, for instance, only after the children have grown up. There is also the need to look after, and in particular to prolong the lives of, one's aged parents. On the other hand, once those parents are dead one must make sure that funeral and ancestral sacrifices are kept simple.[188] This shows that the salvation envisaged by the authors of the TPJ does not entail an extravagant way of life or one that is difficult to sustain. Men are expected to participate in the *taiping* salvation project by remaining within their social and intellectual boundaries.

At this point the grand reform project ebbs into outlining the conditions for individual salvation. The border between these two projects is at points identical with the distinction between textual layers, but there is much overlap.[189] We could say that the TPJ is traditional enough to avoid all hints at possible contradictions between society and the individual. It has advice for individuals whom society has forsaken, but there is no question that an individual's attempts to live and to live for a long time are in the interest of society at large. A complex and time-honored network of linkages is set up between the two. The individual might want to establish good personal relations with the celestial bureaucracy in order to strengthen his claim to a place in heaven and ensure his name is listed in the registers of life, but he must also lead a life of kindness and benevolence in order to live long and become a transcendent. His life expectancy depends on promoting the life of others, and the practice of meditation serves his own health as well as wider social aims. On the other hand, wide-ranging social reforms are set up and propagated as if they were the basis for individual well-being. All of this connects the TPJ to classical moral and political philosophy. The authors of the scripture have adapted it to the complex and dynamic social environment of which they were a part.

NOTES

1. See Eichhorn 1955 and 1957.
2. See Hou 1959 and Yang Kuan 1959.
3. See Ōfuchi 1940 and 1941, and Yoshioka 1970.
4. See Kaltenmark 1979.
5. The following brief introduction is meant to support the translation. It is not intended to provide an overview of TPJ scholarship (for this, see Espesset 2002a) or to present more than a limited contribution to the ongoing discussion of the text's date, authorship, and form.
6. This is how Xunzi (2.1.26) put it; cf. Lewis 1999: 118.
7. See Lewis 1999: 297f.
8. See *Zhuangzi* 91.33.29.
9. See Lewis 1999: 288.
10. See Bokenkamp 1997: 20f.
11. *Da* 大 can play the same role; *Zhuangzi* (34.13.36) said that the rulers of old created *daping*.
12. See *Shi ji* 6.258; cf. Eichhorn 1957: 115.

13. In the *Chun qiu fan lu* (chap. 21 *"Kao gong ming"* 考功名, p. 177) the results of "good government" are called "great peace":

> For this reason the brightness of sun and moon does not result from just one intensive ray and the great peace brought about by the wise does not arise from one isolated good deed.

14. Cf. *Lun yu* 2.1.

15. As suggested in the *Guanzi*, or in Mengzi's reflections on *haoran zhi qi* 浩然之氣.

16. *Chun qiu fan lu* 78 *"Tian di zhi xing"* 天地之行, p. 461.

17. *Chun qiu fan lu* 22 *"Tong guo shen"* 通國身, p. 183.

18. See Cheng 1985: 217. Here He Xiu annotates a *Gong yang zhuan* passage, which says that taxes should not exceed one-tenth of the produce (Duke Xuan, fifteenth year, 16.2287a–b.).

19. In this he followed Wang Chong 王充 (27–ca. 100); see *Lun heng* 60 *"Xu song"* 須頌, pp. 847f.

20. See *Shi ji* 23.1160. Great peace was to be achieved through "ritual correctness," but this in itself was said to undergo modifications in line with the people's changing habits and customs; cf. Eichhorn 1957: 116.

21. *Han shu* 22.1029.

22. *Lun heng* 57 *"Xuan Han"* 宣漢, p. 815; cf. Forke 1962, vol. 2, p. 192; cf. *Lun yu* 14.42.

23. This is from a doubtful citation of Dong Zhongshu, as quoted by Eichhorn (1957: 120) from Zhao Lingzhi's (Song) *Hou qing lu* (chap. 1, p. 8). In the *Chun qiu fan lu* (chap. 6 *"Wang dao"* 王道, pp. 101–5) the reign of the Five Emperors and Three Kings of the distant past is painted in similarly rosy colors. Nothing was amiss. The ruler demanded only moderate taxes and labor services, men were honest, good, and gentle, poisonous insects and wild animals did not attack others, weather conditions were perfect, prisons were empty, and the barbarians voluntarily submitted to the Chinese emperor.

24. *Zhuangzi* 34.13.34–36, translation (slightly modified) by A. C. Graham 1981: 262.

25. *Xin shu* 9 *"Xiu zheng yu"* 脩政語, p. 96.

26. As stated in *Huainan zi* 2 *"Chu zhen"* 俶真, p. 5b; the text says "Great Hall," which the commentator Gao You (ca. 168–212) understands as "Hall of Light." For the function of this building see Puett 2001: 158f.

27. *Han shu* 22.1031.

28. The Han dynasty building was set up some distance from an earlier Zhou dynasty building of the same name. Eichhorn (1973: 110f.) argues convincingly that in the second century B.C.E. there was little actual knowledge about a pre-Qin "Hall of Light" and the ceremonies performed in it. This increased the liveliness with which the topic was debated under Emperor Wu.

29. See Loewe 1974: 82.

30. As was the function of these sacrifices; see *Bai hu tong* 18 *"Feng shan"* 封禪.

31. See *Shi ji* 6.242.

32. See *Bai hu tong* 18 *"Feng shan,"* p. 278; cf. Tjan 1949/1952: 239 and Eichhorn 1957: 126.

33. Lewis 1999: 340–44.

34. See *Lun heng* 25 *"Dao xu"* 道虛, p. 316.

35. See *Shi ji* 6.258.

36. See *Shi ji* 6.262.

37. See *Lun heng* 54 *"Ziran"* 自然, p. 778; 53 *"Zhi duan"* 指瑞, pp. 746f.

38. He mentions Emperor Guangwu (r. 25–57) from the beginning of the Later Han dynasty and Emperor Zhang (r. 75–88) from his own lifetime; see *Lun heng* 57 *"Xuan Han"* 宣漢, pp. 818–22.

39. See *Lun heng* 57 *"Xuan Han,"* p. 823.

40. See *Chun qiu fan lu* 6 *"Wang dao"* 王道, p. 109.

41. See Bodde 1981: 250 and He Xiu's comments on *Gong yang zhuan*, Duke Yin, first year, 1.2200b.

42. See Fung Yu-lan 1952/1953, vol. 2, pp. 681–85; cf. Cheng 1985: 213–17.

43. See *Lun heng* 57 *"Xuan Han,"* p. 823.

44. See *Lun yu* 13.12, as quoted by Wang Chong, *Lun heng* 57 *"Xuan Han,"* p. 817.

45. *Qian fu lun* 2 *"Wu ben"* 務本, p. 14.

46. See *Qian fu lun* 18 *"Ai ri"* 愛日, p. 219.

47. *Qian fu lun* 9 *"Ben zheng"* 本政, p. 90; cf. Pearson 1989: 119.

48. See Ebrey 1986: 609 and 618. Censuses were taken in the year 2 C.E. and again in 140 C.E. Between these two dates, the population, or at least the taxable population, seems to have shrunk from 57.7 million individuals to 48 million. See Bielenstein 1986: 240.

49. Cf. Cheng 1985: 217.

50. See *Shuo yuan* 13 *"Quan mou"* 權謀, p. 125.

51. See Bokenkamp 1994.

52. *Qi* 氣 can be rendered as "breath," "pneuma," "vapor," or "energy." It is the stuff things, actions, and events are made of, their existence, or at least potential existence. It is left untranslated, as in many instances is *"dao,"* in order to prevent an undue and unnecessary curtailment of the original text.

53. *Lü shi chun qiu* 13 *"Ying tong"* 應同, p. 677; see Bokenkamp 1994: 62.

54. See *Chun qiu fan lu* 1 *"Chu Zhuang wang"* 楚莊王, pp. 17–19, and Fung 1952/1953, vol. 2, p. 62.

55. See Petersen 1990b.

56. Zuercher (1982: 3) gives the third century C.E. as the starting point for messianic speculations; he also argues that these speculations were indigenous, that is, not instigated by Buddhist influence. While this account must be somewhat revised in view of the TPJ's notion of imminent disaster, it remains a fact that even at the end of the dynasty mainstream texts seem to express full confidence in the way heaven assigns its mandate; therefore, they don't consider alternatives.

57. See Cohn 1970 and see Bokenkamp (1994: 69; 83) for later Daoist sources.

58. See, for instance, *Shangqing housheng daojun lieji* 4a–6a; Bokenkamp 1997: 347–50.

59. Ebrey 1986: 620f.

60. Ebrey 1986: 618.

61. See *Zi zhi tong jian* 49.1583; cf. Eichhorn 1955: 297.

62. As translated by Graham 1981: 85, slightly modified; the passage is in the "Inner Chapters" (15.6.7–9 and 16.6.19–20).

63. Historically speaking, then, the rebels' use of the title does not go as far back as the *Zhuangzi*. When the First Emperor wanted to become "perfected," he hoped to become full of energy and live for a long time. He tried to achieve it by following the advice of certain experts in vitality techniques, who told him, for instance, to hide his abode *(Shi ji* 6.257).

64. See Loewe 1982: 104–13.

65. See *Hou Han shu* 11.479f.

66. See *Hou Han shu* 24.838 and 18.694f.

67. See Fang 1993: 8.

68. Mansvelt Beck 1986: 337.

69. See Eichhorn 1955: 298.

70. Zhang Jue is a well-known figure, and the story of his rebellion has attracted much scholarly attention; see Maspero 1981: 373–78, Eichhorn 1955, and Bokenkamp 1997: 29–36.

71. See Eichhorn 1955: 297 and *Hou Han shu* 8.332, 334, 342, and 346.

72. For the expression *da xian* 大賢, see also *Hou Han shu* 54.1784; a "worthy person" was one approved by everyone. For the authors of the TPJ a worthy was a person of rank who was capable of political leadership.

73. This phrase has impressed historians; it can also be found *San guo zhi* 46.1094.

74. *Hou Han shu* 71.2299f.; cf. *Zi zhi tong jian* 50.1864f. and de Crespigny 1969: 7–9.

75. See Mansvelt Beck 1986: 338f.

76. *Da yi* 大醫; see *Hou Han ji* 24.290.

77. See Yu Huan's 魚豢 (of Wei: 220–64) *Dian lue,* as quoted by Pei Songzhi in the commentary to *San guo zhi* 8.264.

78. See Peerenboom 1993.

79. See *Hou Han shu* 71.2300.

80. See Yang Quan's (of Jin: 265–319) *Wu li lun,* as quoted in the commentary to Sima Biao's (240–306) *Treatises;* see *Hou Han shu, zhi* 17.3346.

81. See *Zi zhi tong jian* 58.1864.

82. See *Zi zhi tong jian* 58.1865; translation by de Crespigny 1969: 8, modified.

83. In Sima Biao's *Treatises,* which were written before Fan Ye's (398–446) *Hou Han shu;* see *Hou Han shu, zhi* 17.3346.

84. See *Zi zhi tong jian* 58.1864; translation by de Crespigny 1969: 7.

85. See *Hou Han shu* 71.2309 and cf. Fang 1995: 147.

86. See *Xiao dao lun* (*Hong ming ji*, p. 149b) and cf. Kohn 1995: 115.

87. "Yellow Spirit" can be used as another term for "Yellow Emperor," as Liu Shaorui has suggested. My translation follows Liu Shaorui 1992, Wu Rongzeng 1981, and Eichhorn 1955: 313. Fang Shiming's (1995 and 1993) "Yellow God Yuezhang" is difficult to reconcile with Ge Hong's (*Baopu zi neipian* 17.89; cf. Ware 1966: 298) use of the term. *Huangshen Yuezhang* occurs on inscriptions that are meant to make graves secure, that is, to protect the living from the spirits of the dead, and on other objects of demon control, such as on talismans worn by travelers for their protection.

88. See *Hou Han shu, zhi* 17.3346.

89. See *San guo zhi* 46.1094.

90. The *Hou Han shu* (71.2300) also informs us that Zhang Jue sacrificed human beings to heaven. This is difficult to reconcile with the rest of his program and has not been accepted into the *Zi zhi tong jian* account of his activities.

91. Around the year 184; see Wang Shen's (of Jin: 265–319) *Wei shu*, as quoted in the commentary to *San guo zhi* 1.4.

92. See *Wei shu*, as quoted in the commentary to *San guo zhi* 1.10. This is from a letter that Yellow Turbans active in Qing (today's Shandong) addressed to Cao Cao in 192 C.E., probably with the aim of reaching an understanding with the emperor's most influential servant. He attacked and overpowered them, however.

93. See Robinet 1997: 43.

94. See Seidel 1969: 59.

95. See Robinet 1997: 135.

96. See TPJ 160.450.

97. See *San guo zhi* 2.62.

98. See *Shenxian zhuan* 4.16a–17b.

99. See *Hou Han shu* 75.2432.

100. See Mansvelt Beck 1986: 351.

101. See *Bian huo lun* (*Hong ming ji*, p. 49a), translation by Maspero 1981: 384; cf. Eichhorn 1955: 319f.

102. See *Dian lue*, as quoted *San guo zhi* 8.264.

103. See Zuercher 1980: 135f.

104. The *Mozi* chapters on heaven's will (*tian zhi* 天 志) and on spirits (*ming gui* 明 鬼) provide many examples. The concept of recompense pervades the encounters between the last emperors of an old and the founders of a new dynasty; see Schaberg 2001, chapter 6. Compare also the fate of King Ling of Chu as told in the *Zuo zhuan* (Duke Zhao, thirteenth year, 46.2069b) and the figure of Du Bo (*Guo yu*, Zhou, 1.10).

105. *San guo zhi* 8.263.

106. Newly converted followers were "demon soldiers" (*gui zui* 鬼 卒), as if they owed corvée service to the demons; Zhang Lu was said to teach *gui dao*, "demons' *dao*," and

his mother was seen as an expert in it (*San guo zhi* 8.263 and *Hou Han shu* 75.2432). Zhang Jue was said to have trusted in *shen* 神 and *ling* 靈 spirits.

107. The historians' general account of the early Celestial Master community is remarkably positive. Its institutions bear a certain resemblance to descriptions of Da Qin, the "Roman Empire," where the figure of thirty-six and the "houses of responsibility" can be found. "Da Qin" was said to be a mysterious place in the far west, which no one had seen with his own eyes but which writers of the third and fourth centuries talked about when they described a state as they thought it should be (see Stein 1963).

108. For the date and author of the *Xiang'er*, see Bokenkamp 1997: 58–62.

109. See Bokenkamp 1997: 40–53.

110. See *Hou Han shu* 42.1428f.; cf. Zuercher 1959: 26 and Seidel 1969: 48f.

111. On the meaning of Huang-Lao and Huang-Lao jun, cf. Seidel 1969: 48–55. The *Hou Han shu* (50.1669) establishes an indirect link between the Yellow Turbans and Huang-Lao jun: when accused of conspiracy, worshipers of the deity and their friends—who did not support the Yellow Turbans—needed to claim that they addressed the deity only to gain long life and personal benefits, and certainly not with any political aim in mind. However, the fact that Zhang Jue was called an adherent of "Huang-Lao teachings" (see *Hou Han shu* 71.2299) may have been a reference to his worldview rather than to his religious practice.

112. First mentioned for the year 165 (*Hou Han shu* 7.313), the rituals took place so often that they are mentioned in the final appraisal of the emperor's career (7.320); cf. de Crespigny 1976: 82f.

113. See Seidel 1969 on the *Laozi bianhua jing (Scripture on the Transformations of Laozi)*, written between 185 C.E. and the breakdown of the dynasty, and the *Laozi ming (Inscription for Laozi)*, written 165 C.E. The representation of the figure of the Laozi in both texts is not identical.

114. See *Xiang'er*, p. 3 (*Laozi* 10) as translated by Bokenkamp 1997: 89, slightly modified; cf. also Puett 2004.

115. See Seidel 1969: 70.

116. As above, cf. Seidel 1969: 45f. and passim.

117. See Petersen 1990a: 182–89.

118. See Seidel 1969: 36f.

119. See de Crespigny 1975: 34–42.

120. See de Crespigny 1976: 31.

121. See *Dian lue*, as quoted in the commentary to *San guo zhi* 8.264, which is taken up in *Zi zhi tong jian* 58.1864. See also *Hou Han shu* 30B.1084.

122. See *Hou Han shu* 71.2299.

123. For both points, see *Zhi zhi tong jian* 58.1864 and 1868.

124. See Petersen 1992 and cf. Loewe 1974: 276–82.

125. De Crespigny 1976: 31f., translating *Hou Han shu* 30B.1084.

126. *Baopu zi neipian* 19 *"Xia lan"* 遐覽.

127. See *Baopu zi neipian* 4 *"Jin dan"* 金丹, p. 12.

128. See Yoshioka 1966: 51.

129. As Petersen (1990a: 199) points out.

130. As Ge Hong expressly states: see *Neipian* 19, p. 96.

131. Ge Hong (*Neipian* 4, p. 12) informs us that Ge Xuan's library goes back to Zuo Ci 左慈, whose Ulenspiegel-like encounters with dignitaries of the late Han and early Three Kingdoms period are related in the *fang shi* chapter of the *Hou Han shu* (82B. 2747f.) and in the *Shenxian zhuan* (5.19b–20b).

132. See TPJ section 50, below.

133. A *Shen shu* 神書 in 170 *juan* is mentioned in the *Mouzi* (see *Hong ming ji*, p. 6a). It is said to deal with Wang Qiao (that is, Wangzi Qiao: see Kaltenmark 1987: 109f.), Chi Song (that is, Chisong zi: see Kaltenmark 1987: 35), the eight transcendents, and longevity. There is no need to identify this "spirit scripture" with the book mentioned by Xiang Kai. *Shen shu* as used in Xiang Kai's memorial is probably not meant to be a title but rather a respectful reference to the work entitled *Taiping qing ling shu* (but cf. Keenan 1994: 147f. for an alternative view).

134. Among those who have introduced schemes for such identification, Petersen (1990a), Ōfuchi (1997), and Yamada (1999) deserve special attention since they not only attempt specific identifications but also provide an introduction to the earlier debate. See the Appendix for more details.

135. Maeda (1994) argues that the *Zhengyi jing* played a crucial role in the process of setting up the "four support sections." Therefore, the fact that the *Zhengyi jing* refers to a 144-*juan* version of the text, rather than to the 170-*juan* edition that the received text resembles, makes it likely that a certain Meng in the early sixth century (see Ōfuchi 1997: 290f.) knew only the 144-*juan* text and that the new 170-*juan* edition was not available during his lifetime. A similar point is made by Yamada (1999: 143–44) when he mentions that the creator of the *taiping* "support section" must have been in possession of a fragmentary version of the old Han text to have created a supplement of this name, since the new 170-*juan* version was not available at that time.

136. It is noteworthy that the concept of great peace did not enter the organization of the Daoist canon until this stage, that is, no earlier than the lifetime of Tao Hongjing. There seems to be no simple answer to why this was so. Yamada (1999: 140) reconsiders some of the frequently raised speculation on this point, and he mentions in particular Lu Xiujing's (406–77) selective approach to Celestial Master material and Kou Qianzhi's (d. 448) mainstream outlook. There also remains the question of why the *taiping* section was set up as the supplement to the section or cavern of the Daoist canon that focused on Lingbao (Numinous Treasure) writings. Yamada (1999: 148–51) argues that there were doctrinal reasons for this in that both groups of texts aimed at saving the world; in other words, they dealt with social and even political issues.

137. See *Shangqing daolei shixiang* 1.11b–12a; cf. Reiter 1992:30–32. Chen Guofu (1963: 465) and Bumbacher (2000: 199–201f.) both accept the passage as a proper *Daoxue zhuan* quotation.

138. *Nan Qi shu* 54.927.

139. See Mansvelt Beck 1980: 163.

140. See *Mao shan zhi* 15.2b–3a. The attribution of such high rank is enhanced by a *Taiping yulan* (666.2972a) quotation from the *Zhen'gao*, which Bumbacher (2000: 341) identifies as part of the *Daoxue zhuan*. It deals with the life of Sun Tao, a disciple of Tao Hongjing. In Bumbacher's translation the last two sentences read:

> Tao Hongjing held fast in his hand the secret instructions, so that his disciples were seldom able to see them. He only handed them down to the two persons Sun Tao and Huan Kai.

The *Mao shan zhi* account of Huan's life does not mention the TPJ episode. It was perhaps not important enough to deserve much notice and must have taken place when Huan was still quite young and within the precinct of Tao Hongjing's school. However, there seems to be no reason to question either his historical identity or his TPJ-related activity.

141. See Strickmann 1978: 468.

142. See *Huayang Tao yinju neizhuan* 2.11b; Strickmann 1979: 155.

143. See Bokenkamp 1996.

144. See Strickmann 1978: 472.

145. See *Nan shi* 76.1899 and *Liang shu* 4.103 and 109; cf. Marney 1976: 119f.

146. After the demise of Hou Jing, Xiao Yi, prince of Xiangdong, ruled for just two years as Emperor Yuan, from 552 until his execution in 554. Much of the received text of the *Jinlou zi* consists of quotations of passages from similar earlier collections of wise sayings and meaningful anecdotes; see, for instance, the episode about the rich and the poor (6.112) and about Gong She of Chu (6.110); for the emperor's interest in the *Laozi*, see *Liang shu* 5.134.

147. Huan is said to have been employed as head of the Qingyuan zhi guan (Monastery of Far-Reaching Clarity) by Xiao Wei (476–533), Liang emperor Wu's brother, who became prince of Nanping in 517 and played a role in Liang dynasty literary salons (see *Liang shu* 22.348, *Nan shi* 52.1291f.; cf. Marney 1976: 62). Huan's stay in the Monastery of Far-Reaching Clarity is also documented on a stela, whose inscription is given in *Mao shan zhi* 21.1a–b; in Bumbacher's translation (2000: 460) it reads, "There is also Qingyuan's monastery, which the Prince of Nanping, Xiao Wei, had set up. This was where Tao Hongjing's disciple Huan Qingyuan dwelled. Huan's teacher-name was Fakai." Moreover, Huan is said to have set up a Daoist oratory, here called Jing she 精舍 (Cottage of the Essential), on the right-hand side of Fragrant Hill (Yugang; impossible to locate), for which "the retired scholar Zhou" wrote an inscription (*Mao shan zhi* 15.2a–b). Fukui Kojun (1952: 227) and others believe "the retired scholar Zhou" to

have been the Daoist Zhou Zhixiang, who "discovered" a *taiping* text for Emperor Xuan (r. 569–82) of the Chen dynasty.

148. See *Preface to the Double Character Talismans of the Scripture on Great Peace*, TPJ p. 745.

149. See *Liang shu* 6.144f.

150. Quotations are frequent in Tang dynasty material. The text is quoted in the *San-dong zhunang* (1.21a–23a; cf. Reiter 1990: 29–31) and in the *Daodian lun* (TPJ p. 54, 58, 59, 78, 100, 102, 132, 136, 158, 512, 699, 719), for instance, both from the seventh century. The *Yunji qiqian* (6.15b–16a) account of the seven Daoist canon divisions dealt with earlier is another example; it argues that the "unity of the three" *(sanyi)* was the *taiping* division's main idea, which is a quite adequate characterization of the content of the TPJ. The passage includes a set of quotations documenting the socio-political aims of the text, particularly the interplay between heaven, doctrine, and government. The quotations in Li Xian's (651–84) commentary to Xiang Kai's biography in the *Hou Han shu* show that the new TPJ had reached beyond Daoist circles. Although only two of these quotations can be verified in the received *taiping* material (for 30B.1081, see TPJ p. 18, *Chao;* for *Hou Han shu* 30B.1084, see TPJ p. 219, *Chao*), they are all relevant to the message of the old text. They deal with the need to perceive the threefold structure of the world, and to keep in mind the methods of population increase, as well as the origin of natural disasters and the methods for controlling them. Li Xian's (*Hou Han shu* 30B.1080) own words provide further evidence of the role played by the new TPJ in the discourse of the early Tang. He states:

> This sacred book (*shen shu*, the term used in Xiang Kai's memorial) is the TPJ of the Daoists of today. The scripture is divided into ten divisions in line with the heavenly stems, and each division has seventeen chapters *(juan)*.

It must also be kept in mind that the concept of great peace was put to political use during the early Tang period. The message was conveyed in mysterious ways to Tang Gaozu (r. 618–26) that great peace would prevail if he officially promoted Daoism. Also, the auspicious prophecy of Wang Yuanzhi (d. 635) in regard to the future Taizong said that he would be "Son of Heaven of Great Peace" (see Wechsler 1985: 70–73).

151. On the basis of taboo characters, Espesset (2002a) plausibly dates the fragment to between 626 and 657. Giles (1957: 219) dates it to the late sixth century and is supported in this by Ōfuchi (1979a: 509; 549–50), whose argument is based on the similarity of the features of S 4226 with other, dated, manuscripts. For a reproduction of the original manuscript, see Zhang 1992, vol. 6.

152. See Bokenkamp 1994: 69–70; cf. also Nickerson 2000: 264.

153. In the *Zhen'gao* it is claimed that if you are to become an official of the Latter Sage (*hou sheng zhi chen* 後聖之臣) and let the people be in great peace *(taiping min)*, you need to "keep all twenty-four spirits within you"; see *Zhen'gao* 9.104, quoting a *Baoyuan yulu bai jian qing jing* 苞元玉籙白簡青經.

154. The Latter Sage who figures in the publication of the TPJ combines aspects of several deities: he has contact with Green Lad, appears in a *renchen* year, and has the family name Li; see Yoshioka 1970: 72–88. The deity is first mentioned in the *Shenxian zhuan* (1.1b) biography of Laozi as the saint's incarnation after the period of the Three Majestic Rulers. Given the status of Laozi, the origin of the wording of this particular biography is even more problematic than for the *Shenxian zhuan* as a whole (Penny 1996: 186). The inclusion of the Latter Sage might therefore result from a later addition. But the Sage became well established with Tao Hongjing if we are to trust the frequent mentions in the *Zhen'gao*, in particular in chapter 9 in the context of an approaching universal cataclysm. In Tao Hongjing's *Dongxuan lingbao zhen ling weiye tu* a figure whose name includes "Golden Gate" occurs in various places (p. 3b; 5a). He is expected to descend in a *renchen* year as Imperial Lord of the Golden Gate of Great Ultimate named Li (Taiji jin que dijun xing Li; p. 8a) to instruct the Ruler of Great Peace *(taiping zhu)*.

155. See Seidel 1969/1970; cf. Yoshioka 1970: 89.

156. See Nickerson 2000: 274.

157. See Li Xian's commentary to Xiang Kai's *Hou Han shu* biography (TPJ p. 747); see also the textual history recorded in S 4226 and in the *Preface to the Double Character Talismans of the Scripture on Great Peace* (TPJ p. 744).

158. The details of the saga of the TPJ's discovery strengthen this point. Tao Hongjing's hesitant attitude is testament to his political acumen. For a "Scripture on Great Peace" to be published and promoted, the time had to be right.

159. See Petersen 1990a: 182–87 on Gan Ji.

160. Called "the capital Luo" (*jing Luo* 京洛) (TPJ 198.611, layer B), as was customary during the Later Han period; for Chang'an see below, section 50.

161. An educated reader was often reminded in what the Master said of passages in the *Laozi* and also the *Lun yu*, as pointed out in the notes that accompany this translation.

162. See, for instance, certain *yue fu* poems, as collected by Anne Birrel 1988: 78–93, or the anxiety manifest in tomb building and burial ritual (see Powers 1991: 50–58).

163. Takahashi (1988) gives a good account of the Celestial Lord's arguments, that is, of layer B. However, Takahashi's high expectations of a text's coherence and unity led him to see too many discrepancies within this material to define it as one layer.

164. See Seidel 1969/1970. The argument that the TPJ's Celestial Master does not endorse rebellious conduct is as irrelevant to the question as the fact that he promotes the Han dynasty's color, red. While the dynasty was in power there were necessarily constraints on public utterances.

165. Fang Shiming (1995 and1993, the latter in Chinese, quoting the original sources) shows that the title "messenger from the Celestial Emperor" (*tian di shi* 天帝使, and *tian di shen shi shi zhe* 天帝神師使者) (1993: 8) occurs on grave-securing writs, suggesting that this prompted rebel leaders to use the title.

166. See *Hou Han shu* 28.1277 (Biography of Fa Xiong): *shi zhe* 使者. See also *Hou*

Han shu 71.2309 (Biography of Zhu Jun): the Yellow Turban Zhang Mancheng called himself *shen shang shi* 神上使.

167. See TPJ 55.85; 59.100; 63.140; 65.152; 129.331; 132.348; 165.461; the material is also mentioned in layer B, TPJ 185.566.

168. Ornamental particles abound, particularly *fu* 復 (again). Directional verbal complements such as *qu* 去, *lai* 來, *chu* 出, *shang* 上, and *xia* 下 are also in use.

169. Some examples of this are referred to in the notes accompanying the translation. In the first lines of section 132 (pp. 348f.) the *Chao* omits *zhi shu* 之 屬 (the like of) and cuts out the Perfected's answer *bu ye* 不 也 (This is not so). It also cuts out the three-character verb *wei zuo qiu* 為 作 求 (to search), reduces *qu zhong* 取 中 to *qu* (here used as *ba* 把 as in later Chinese), and replaces the phrase *fu yu shang* 付 於 上 (to submit) with *xian* 獻.

170. The choice of unorthodox forms of characters points in the same direction. See Yu 1997.

171. The use of *qu* 取 in disposal constructions is one point that brings the wording of the TPJ into proximity with the language used in early sutra translations; see TPJ 100.229: *qu qi zhong da shan zhe ji zhi yi wei tian jing* 取 其 中 大 善 者 集 之 以 為 天 經, where *qu* 取 is used as *ba* 把 as in later Chinese; see also TPJ 78.190 *dan qu wei yan huan yi ni kao* 但 取 微 言 還 以 逆 考 (investigate again the subtle words) and *Qu qi zhong da shan zhi shi you yi yu di wang zheng zhi zhe liu zhi* 取 其 中 大 善 之 事 有 益 於 帝 王 正 治 者 留 之 (Retain in this those events of great excellence that are of use to emperors and kings when they attempt to reign properly) (TPJ 129. 334). Cao and Yu (2000) argue that the disposal structure originated in Later Han dynasty Buddhist translations.

172. See Zuercher 1977.

173. The formation of trisyllabic words by joining synonyms occurs often in layer A: *zeishashang* 賊 殺 傷 (to injure) (TPJ 41.36; 59.99); for several similar word formations with the component *zei* see Liu Dianjue's TPJ concordance (Liu 2000: 1752); *yu'anbi* 愚 闇 蔽 (foolish) (TPJ 110.295 and *yubi'an* TPJ 165.461); *julijie* 疽 癘 疥 (skin disease) (TPJ 127.319 and 320). "Natural calamities" (*zaibiankuai* 災 變 怪) occurs frequently (TPJ 55.86; 59.100 and 102; 61.114; 127.322).

174. See Hu Chirui 2002: 280–85.

175. *Shu wen* 書 文 and *wen shu* are used interchangeably (TPJ 55. 85), as are *le yu* 樂 欲 (e.g., TPJ 78.190; 204.646; 208.661) and *yu le* (TPJ 176.515; 204.639 and 640). However, most disyllabic concepts used in the TPJ occur only in a standard sequence, such as *cheng fu* 承 負, *di wang* 帝 王, *junwang* 君 王, and *zaibian* 災 變.

176. Nouns are more often monosyllabic when used as an object than when used as the subject. *Zai* (disaster) occurs on its own mainly when used as an object (see, for instance, *jie zai* 解 災, TPJ 63.134, and *zeng zai* 增 災, TPJ 65.152). However, disyllabic objects are also frequent. Isolated characters tend to be enlarged when they serve as subjects. So *ping* (peace) becomes *taiping* or *pingqi* 平 氣. In other words, the use of *zaibian* in-

stead of *zai*, *junwang* instead of *wang*, or *wenshu* instead of *shu* seems to be for rhetorical rather than semantic reasons.

177. See Zuercher 1977: 181. For *xiang yu* 相與, see TPJ 41.35 and 59.100; for *yu gong* 與共 see TPJ 61.113 and 122. In addition to the compounds *yifu* 亦復 (TPJ 55.85; 217.328; 186.569, layer B) and *haifu* 還復 (TPJ 50.65) mentioned by Zuercher, *fanfu* 反復, *fuzhong* 復重, *zhongfu* 重復, and *fugeng* 復更 are often used as adverbial compounds, in layer A as well as in layer B.

Inclusive adverbial compounds are used frequently. Zuercher lists *xidou* 悉都 (TPJ 132.356), *xijin* 悉盡 (TPJ 165.460), and *jinxi* 盡悉 (TPJ 204.632). *Xi* is the most frequently used inclusive adverbial and occurs in a large variety of compounds. Moreover, the TPJ makes frequent use of *ju*, as in *xiju* 悉具 (TPJ 188.577). It is characteristic of the TPJ to have trisyllabic inclusive adverbial compounds, as in *xijudou* 悉具都 (TPJ 55.86; *qie* 且 is corrected to *ju*) and *xidouhe* 悉都合 (TPJ 78.191).

Zhe 者 is used as final particle, as described by Zuercher for his material. Although in much of the text its occurrence agrees with classical usage, it can also serve as a final element in a conditional subordinate clause, as, for instance, in TPJ 42.38: *Ling shi tu di you bu hua sheng zhe* 令使土地有不化生者.

The number of interrogative pronouns and adverbs is limited. The particle *he* 何 and combinations with *he* abound; *yunhe* 云何 is used frequently as an interrogative in all layers of the text.

178. See TPJ 166.462; 176.515.

179. There are more examples of the TPJ's relative conservatism: *yu* 於 is mainly used in a postverbal position to express direction, and *zuo* 作 is used only rarely and only as the full verb "to act, to do, to make." There is, however, at least one instance of an enclitic *zi* 子 (TPJ 65.148), as opposed to the Buddhist translations and classical usage. Enclitic *gu* 故 occurs, but only in classical form as far as I can see (for instance, the use of *bu de hui guo fan gu ye* 不得悔過反故也, TPJ 66.160).

180. See, for instance, passages in Yang Xiong's (53 B.C.E.–18 C.E.) *Fa yan* or Ge Hong's (283–343) *Baopu zi*.

181. See below, notes to TPJ 50.64; 54.82; 60.104; 64.144; 58.94.

182. See section 177, which uses the image of the two hands that are necessary to get things done. Harada Jirō (1984) argues that Dong Zhongshu's ideas form the background for the TPJ's stress on three and, as one would expect, he points to the *Yi jing* for the twofold approach.

183. See TPJ pp. 1–8, *Chao*.

184. See TPJ pp. 694f., *Chao*, part 8. In the following, references will be provided only for topics not mentioned in more detail in the subsequent translation and notes.

185. This topic has for good reasons attracted a large amount of scholarly attention; see Hachiya 1983, Hendrischke 1992, and Espesset 2002c.

186. When Cui Shi (d. 170 C.E.) and Wang Fu demand a stricter application of the penal code they go into a direction opposite to that suggested by the TPJ's Celestial Master.

187. The authors of the text reflect the contradiction this entails and stress that a virtuous life is the overriding cause of health and longevity (TPJ, layer B, sections 181; 186; and 188, in particular p. 578).

188. Since the quality of the soil where the deceased are put matters, geomancy plays a certain role; see TPJ 76.182f.

189. See the Appendix, below, for details on this point.

· How to Distinguish
between Poor and Rich

This section is one of the most practice-oriented in the text.[1] It consists of two parts, one analyzing relations of property and the other the lot of women. The first is too short to be a separate section of its own, and there is no other material in the received text to which it could belong. The second part is linked closely to the following section, section 42, an indication that here, at least, the sequence of sections is not haphazard.

The first half of the section discusses the stages of wealth and poverty and how they are achieved. I have found no parallel in Han dynasty or earlier material of these different stages. Rhetorical as this account might be, the enumeration of the different types of poverty stresses the severity of social conditions and the prevalence of misery. Poverty is depicted as an element of the apocalyptic scenario. Its rapid increase is supposed to persuade men that there is an urgent need to change their ways. An almost theological need to tie different levels of being into one unified structure induces the Master to juxtapose men's poverty with that of the earth. However, heaven's position is too exalted to allow the idea of celestial poverty.

Once the Master has defined the stages of poverty and environmental destruction, as we might understand the expression "earth's poverty," he moves toward an analysis of what causes them. He points out that the plight of individual families stems from outside factors. Both poverty and wealth have a cosmic dimension. Since men are children of heaven and earth, they thrive only when their parents thrive. Thus an individual and his family cannot prosper in a community that is in misery.

Even the royal house is not exempt from this nexus. Individual wealth is said to be a fake; only a self-sufficient community can be called wealthy. In line with the *Laozi*'s image of ideal communal life, wealth is seen as created exclusively by agricultural production. The possession of valuables becomes relevant only when basic necessities are in short supply.

The prevention of poverty and the achievement of wealth, then, are the same thing, and both are said to result from proper political action. Here the Master assembles lines of thought common in quietist political philosophy, for instance in the *Huainan zi*.[2] Impoverishment is the result of poor politics. It came into being when *dao* was replaced by *wen* (culture) and by military rule. The Master does not seriously pursue these thoughts, referring to them only in passing before he arrives at his own message: a community will be wealthy when its government takes the triad of heaven, earth, and men into proper account. The government must establish a direct relationship between the agricultural producer and the cosmic, natural sources of fertility and growth. This precludes other, more prominent, ancient approaches to the problem: neither individual industriousness nor proper economic policy will create wealth.[3]

The second half of the section is possibly premodern China's most outspoken attack on female infanticide. The argument is characteristic of the way the Celestial Master sets forth his doctrine. He argues on cosmic rather than on moral grounds. The main evil in infanticide is the distress and resentment it provokes in females. Their protests reach heaven and earth, which react by causing harvest failures. Another evil resulting from it is a shortage of women, which makes it difficult for each man to have two wives and thus ensure his progeny. But the problem is too fundamental to be solved by decree. Parents don't kill girls because they want to. They feel they can't afford to bring up children from whom they will get no return. The Master thus suggests that girls should be made more valuable by permitting them to earn their keep, just as boys do. They should be to their husbands what an official is to his lord. This would enable a daughter to support her own parents in exchange for the trouble they took to raise her. In this situation a wife would be happy and not of "two hearts," as the Master puts it. She would no longer serve her in-laws at the cost of forsaking her own parents.

It is remarkable that the position of the TPJ in this matter is as isolated as it is. Clearly, infant mortality was such that newborn children were in general not yet seen as human beings, so that Confucian arguments for humane behavior were not applicable to them. As a consequence, the Master does not apply moral considerations, but rather points to the "resentment" created by such killings and its destabilizing cosmic effect. The Master's program for changing the situation amounts to premodern China's only attempt to allocate to women the full measure of human responsibility. Their filial piety, which to those in the second century C.E. was roughly equivalent to their morality, was to be equated with that of men.

·   ·   ·

(41.29) Step forward, Perfected! You have been coming to study the doctrine *(dao)* for such a long time. You have really learned it all by now, don't you think?

If you had not again spoken to me, I might have thought so. But as soon as I hear your words, I know it is not so. Now I would like to reach the end but I can't think of another question. If the Celestial Master would only reveal my shortcomings once again!

All right, come here. What do we mean by "rich" and "poor"?

Well, those who own a lot are rich and those who own little are poor.

What you have said appears to be true but is in fact false.

What do you mean?

Take someone who often cheats, deceives, flatters, steals, and robs. How could we call him "rich"? Or take a situation where the people in general own a lot while the sovereign owns but little. How could we call him "poor"?[4] (41.30)

Foolish and stupid as I am, I felt I had to speak up when the Celestial Master set out to instruct me. I am not good enough; I am at fault.

If *you* say you are not good enough, how shall the common people know the meaning of poor and rich?

If only you would think of my ignorance as being as that of a small child[5] who must be instructed by its father and mother before it gains understanding.[6]

True. Modest as you are, you don't go amiss.

Yes.

Collect your thoughts. I will tell you all.[7] We speak of "rich" when there is sufficient supply. By making everything grow, heaven provides enough wealth. Thus we say that there is enough wealth when supreme majestic qi[8] arises and all twelve thousand plants and beings[9] are brought to life. Under the influence of medium majestic qi, plants and beings are slightly deficient in that it cannot provide for all twelve thousand of them. This causes small poverty. When under the influence of lower majestic qi, plants and beings are again fewer than under the influence of medium majestic *qi*, and this causes great poverty. When there are no auspicious portents[10] [signifying the approach of majestic *qi*] at all, the crops[11] won't grow, which is extreme poverty. Take a look at a peasant family if you wish to know what this amounts to. Should they not possess any rare and valuable objects, they are considered a poor family.[12] Should they not be supplied with what they need, they must be seen as an extremely poor family.

The problem lies in the poverty of heaven and earth. Once all twelve thousand plants and beings come forth and are nurtured by earth without detriment, earth becomes rich. If it can't nurture them well,[13] it becomes slightly poor as long as injuries remain small, and quite poor should they be large. If crops were to shy away from being seen and fail to grow, injured by earth's body, this would lead to extreme poverty. Without jade and other valuables and with half the yields damaged, great distress and poverty would come about. Such complete damage would eradicate a poor family.

Now think of heaven as father and earth as mother. Should father and mother be in such extreme poverty all their children would suffer from poverty. The king's government is a replica of this. Thus the wise kings of antiquity, whose reign reached out to all twelve thousand plants and beings, became lords of great wealth. Harvests that reach two-thirds of their potential provide a lord with medium wealth. When they amount to only one-third, he has but little wealth. With neither valuables nor crops, he becomes a lord of great poverty.[14] Once half of his harvests are damaged, his house is in decline. If all are damaged, he becomes a man of great poverty.

The wise and worthy of antiquity reflected deep in their dark chamber[15] on the question of how poverty and wealth were achieved through [adhering to] *dao* and virtue. Why should anyone ask about this? Through meditation, men will find out for themselves.[16] (41.31)

Excellent! If the Celestial Master would only show kindness to emperors and kings! They have suffered bitterly and for a long time,[17] and have been frustrated in their ambition. Whereby does one achieve such poverty and such wealth?[18]

Yes, fine! Your question touches upon the crucial point of certain subtle sayings.[19] Well, how they are put into practice brings about gain or loss. Once someone follows the true doctrine *(dao)* with all his might, heaven's life-giving spirits[20] will help his mission. So spirits sent by heaven and good harvests will be plenty. If a man enacts virtue, earth's nourishing spirits will come forth[21] to assist his conduct of affairs. Thus, he will gain half of his potential wealth. Once someone enacts humaneness, the humane spirits of the harmony that prevails in the realm between heaven and earth[22] will step forward to help him conduct his affairs and achieve a small measure of wealth. Someone who attempts cultural refinement is on the way to intrigues and deceit, so that deceitful spirits will come forth to help him. Thus his conduct will be in some disorder. (41.32) But if he were to undertake military action, bandit spirits would be bound to appear in his support. Government would thus be directed against the will of heaven. It would injure and harm even good men.[23]

Dao sets the rule for heaven's conduct.[24] Since heaven is the highest of all spirits (*zui shen* 最神), true spirits come forth to assist its mission. Since earth nurtures, virtuous spirits step forward to assist its mission. Humane spirits come forth to help a man's mission if he is humane. Cultured men are preoccupied with deceiving each other by means of culture. They have lost their root. Thus deceitful spirits appear to assist them. Once superiors and inferiors deal with each other by means of culture, their affairs are in disorder. Soldiers subdue others through punishment, murder, and injury. Bandits do the same. Any man who in subduing others is guided by anger, joy, violence, and severity is a bandit. So, large numbers of bandits step forth to threaten his reign. Since they often damage people's belongings, such a way of government entails a loss of property.[25]

Thus antiquity's supreme lords, who subdued others through *dao*, largely accorded with the will of heaven. They governed as if they were spirits. They subdued others through true *dao* without causing distress. Lords of middle rank exert control through virtue, and lords of lower rank through humaneness. Lords of chaos subdue others through cultural refinement, and those of disaster and defeat rule by punishing, murdering, and injuring others. Thus the supreme lords of antiquity ruled over others through *dao*, virtue, and humaneness instead of inflicting injuries by means of culture or through punishing and murdering others. Since this is the case, the use of such means is despicable.[26]

However, a supreme lord resembles heaven and earth. Since heaven is prone to giving life rather than to inflicting injuries, we call it lord and father. Since earth likes to nurture the ten thousand plants and beings, we call it honest official and mother. Since man thinks in a humane manner and shows the same concern and care as heaven and earth do, we call him humane. Through their goodness these three manage to govern and to lead the ten thousand plants and beings. But one cannot govern by deceiving and punishing, [for then] disasters grow in number and make it impossible for emperors and kings to achieve great peace. So this must stop.

Now if you, Perfected, were to give my book to a lord in possession of *dao* and virtue and he implemented what it says energetically, he would reach a position that would correspond to that of heaven. Thus he would achieve great peace. There is no doubt that we would call his house rich. In this case nothing would cause emperors and kings to suffer distress. In the opposite case we would speak of a poor house.

Nowadays people sometimes call each other "rich families." Why is this so?[27]

This is what they do, but the common people talk nonsense. When we use the word "rich" we mean that everything is provided for. (41.33) If one single item is lacking, [supplies] are incomplete. For this reason the wise and worthy of old did not demand perfection from individuals, since they did not see them fit for it.[28] Today goods are in short and incomplete supply in all eighty-one territories.[29] It is impossible to achieve any long-term sufficiency, so goods are obtained from other territories. Now to what degree can one individual family be rich? Would you like to go along with the nonsense that common people put forth?

No, I would not dare to.

You have learned to watch your words, so don't utter nonsense, or you might bring disorder to the standard patterns (*zheng wen* 正文) of heaven and earth and they won't serve as a model for men.[30] Be careful.

Yes, I will. Now the Celestial Master has shown himself to be merciful and loving. He has a kind regard for emperors and kings who on their thrones suffer distress and fail to be in favor with heaven.

Since it has all been explained to them they should be able to find the path that leads to the great peace of supreme majesty.[31]

Foolish as I am, I have received a large amount of writings. I feel dizzy and confused as if I was a youngster and I don't know what to ask next. Since you are heaven's enlightened teacher, do convey all its warnings![32]

Yes, fine. Well, according to the model set by heaven, Yang's cipher is one and that of Yin two.[33] So Yang is single and Yin is a pair. Therefore, lords are few and subordinates are many. Since Yang is honored and Yin is humble, two Yin must jointly serve one Yang. Since heaven's cipher is one and that of earth is two, two women must jointly serve one man.

Why should it be necessary that two persons care for one?

The place next to someone in an honored position must never be left empty. When one is employed the other must remain standing or sitting next to the person in the center to look after his needs. So the one resembles heaven while the two are similar to earth. (41.34) Since men are children of heaven and earth, they must imitate both. The world has nowadays lost *dao,* so girls are often despised and even maltreated and murdered, which has caused there to be fewer girls than boys. So Yin's *qi* is reduced, which does not agree with the model of heaven and earth. Heaven's way establishes the model that a solitary Yang without a partner will bring drought and cause heaven not to rain when it should. Women correspond to earth: Should one single woman be despised, it is as if all in the world despise their true mother. Should they maltreat, hurt, or murder[34] earth's *qi*, it will be cut off and cease to give life. In great anger the earth would then turn hostile, so that a plethora of disasters would make it impossible for the king's government to achieve peace.

Why?

The male is heaven's vital spirit; the female is earth's. Things (*wu* 物) influence each other within their own kind. It is not only the king's fault that his government is not at peace. Instead, men have in general lost *dao* and become negligent. They are all wrong. Since there is not just one mistake but ten thousand, it is difficult to conduct government affairs peacefully and they tend to go wrong. It is the nature of heaven and earth that among all twelve thousand plants and beings human life is the most important.[35] Thus maltreating and murdering women brings profound disorder to a king's government. This is a great offense.[36]

Now the Celestial Master has opened to kings the ascent to great peace. The true scripture on great peace has appeared. Thus they need only at their leisure to go on long spiritual journeys. How can it be that to violate women entails so much calamity for them?

This is a good question. You understand what heaven wants. Truly, the whole world despises and hates women because they condemn their conduct.

What do you mean? I wish to hear it. I will try to take notes on bamboo and silk so that for ten thousand times ten thousand generations no one will dare to depart from it.

Fine. Now that you can put it down in writing, the world will in the future never again murder women.[38]

Yes, I want to write it down in order to free emperors and kings from calamities. I take pleasure in saving the lives of women [stricken with] grief.

Good. Now you have gained points in the accounts kept by heaven.

What do you mean?

Indeed, to give life to others means giving life to oneself, and to kill others means to kill oneself. Heaven's concern for you may already have increased your account with heaven. So the Controller of Fate[39] will make alterations in your personal records.

This I would never dare to accept.

One must not turn this down; it lies within the model of heaven being the way it is (*ziran* 自然). Well, women are murdered all over the world [for the following reason]: A father and mother suffer distress as long as a human being is young and small. They skimp on their own clothes and food in order to rear it. It is not only human beings who behave like this; all things that crawl and run behave like this. Everyone, big or small, must when grown up put all their energy into the search for clothes and food. (41.35) Thus the ten thousand beings all leave their father and mother to clothe and feed themselves. If they are worthy they meet with happiness; if they are not they are in distress. Furthermore, when young, a child gains daily more strength until it has ample, while its father and mother are daily more wasted by old age. Their strength diminishes until it no longer suffices. But, with its surplus of knowledge, worthiness, and strength, a child, whether male or female, must nourish its father and mother in return for their exertion and kindness on its behalf. So its father and mother must no longer clothe and feed it or we say "the weak is nourishing the strong." We speak about "adverse policy" should someone with insufficient muscle power nourish those who have more than they need. This is the reason young ones who are bound to bring distress to those who are older without providing any gains for their father and mother are often killed by them. Now their father and mother murder them because clothes and food are scarce. Wouldn't it be better to rear them and let everyone find their own clothes and food? Perfected, this is really a grievous interruption of earth's dispensation.[40] People are so foolish!

Now that I have heard this, I feel sad and alarmed. I understand that there are many grievances. What should be done?

Well, someone who likes to study but does not get clothes and food is stopped on his way *(dao)* since his studies are interrupted. But if he gets clothes and food, the worthy does not cease to learn. We should let everyone be of some use. If not they would instead cause distress and misery.

What do you mean?

Now a woman has no abode. She must get clothes and food by attending to her husband as a man does by attending to his office.[41] When a woman attends to her husband's house, they must support each other and lead their life in unison. Together they continue the dispensation of heaven and earth, until in death their bones and flesh are returned to the same place. They get clothes and food from supporting each other. If they are worthy, they will be happy; if not, they will suffer. Take soil as an example: heaven will add its share to the rich produce of fertile soil. It does exactly the same for the poor produce of meager soil. It certainly does not deprive soil of giving growth. Heaven and earth would never deprive a woman[42] of her achievement. How much more so should this be men's axiom! If it were, men would never again kill their women!

Excellent indeed! As soon as this one great and severe damage has been averted, great peace will come about for emperors and kings.

How do you know, Perfected?

Well, the affection a father and mother feel for their child is the most solid there is in this world. If the child did not make them miserable and distressed, there would be no reason to kill it. They must not kill it or else their qi *becomes that of bandits and in their great contrariness they are thoroughly devoid of* dao.[43] *For this reason it throws the reign of emperors and kings into deep disorder. (41.36) Now if women were to live without being maltreated, murdered, and violated, there would be great joy.*

Yes, what you have said is true. We may assume that you have understood. Now if one family kills one female: how many hundreds of thousands of families are there all over the world? Sometimes one family kills dozens of females[44] or a fetus is injured before birth. Grief-stricken qi[45] rises up to move heaven. How can these acts not be disorderly (*wu dao li* 無道理)? So I truly want you to know more about it.[46]

Should every human being through her own effort provide her own clothes and food, no wife would be of two hearts. She would concentrate on her activities and never again harbor any doubts. Those who lack achievement are forever deprived of a balance of mind.

So much for the methods that nature, being as it is (*tian xing ziran* 天性自然), suggests. Pay attention, Perfected, that you don't lay this book aside, but give it to a lord who is humane and worthy, so that he can free [men] from all the grief they are stricken with and from the calamities that injure them. Pay attention to what my book says so that you can explain it to everyone. It must never again be permissible to do away with females.[47]

Furthermore, this rule agrees with the model (*fa* 法) of heaven and earth according to which one man should have two wives because heaven has arranged that Yang is single and Yin is a pair. Since the height of middle antiquity men have forgotten what heaven's way intends and have often maltreated and murdered females, which has in turn caused men to be numerous and women to be so few that there are not enough. This is grossly opposed to heaven's way. By making the killing of females a common practice, men have caused even more [evil] to be inherited and passed on.[48] Later generations have multiplied the world's trespasses, so that it has become completely devoid of *dao*.

Man is heir to heaven's dispensation and woman to that of earth. If we were to cut off earth's dispensation we would no longer be able to reproduce ourselves, and then many of us would die without progeny. What an awful crime![49] Thus all must reproduce themselves and continue their kind. But if we were to interrupt earth's dispensation and exterminate humankind, heaven would forever put an end to the species populating this world.[50]

Moreover, when human beings come to life, heaven's *qi* shines forth in all of them: their head is round like heaven, their feet are square like earth, the four limbs resemble the four seasons, the five internal organs the five phases, while ears and eyes, mouth and nose are like the seven regents[51] or three luminaries. I cannot explain to you all of this, but wise men[52] know about it. The life of human beings is all Yin and Yang. Once the number of days and months is completed, they open the womb and step outside. In sight of heaven and earth, they grow up. Together they continue the dispensation of their ancestors. They assist heaven in giving life to plants and beings (*wu* 物) and assist earth in nourishing what has taken shape.

Since the spirits of heaven and earth put their trust in a certain family, their dispensation comes to live in a certain human being. That men damage it, heaven sees as a grave misdeed. But men won't keep each other in check. (41.37) Therefore heaven has sent me to make this book known to the generations to come. Although these matters are quite manifest, they are still continued, consciously. We must say that this is to consciously act against the model set by heaven. It is a crime of many layers and will no doubt put an end to humankind. Beware, Perfected, be on your guard.

Yes, I will.

Now that you have understood these issues, you and not others will be put on trial should you neglect these writings.

I would not dare to do so!

You may go now, and may each of you follow your own device.

Yes, we will.[53]

NOTES

1. The title of this section points to the topic of distinction or differentiation (*fen bie* 分別) that is found throughout the TPJ and has been aptly expressed by the text's sixth-century editors in their section titles. See section 4, "The method of differentiating harm done to the body . . . " (TPJ p. 723, *Chao*, part 1); section 24, "The method of distinguishing between good and evil in men" (only in the Dunhuang list of contents, Yoshioka 1970: 23); section 79, "The method of distinguishing the four types of govern-

ment" (Yoshioka 1970: 29; for section "80," TPJ p. 195); and section 97, "Instructions on how to distinguish the nine types of men" (Yoshioka 1970: 31, cf. TPJ p. 221, *Chao*, part 4). Poverty and wealth figure also in the title of section 349, "How to achieve poverty and wealth" (Yoshioka 1970: 57); the original text of this is lost, as is the corresponding section of the *Chao*.

2. See, for instance, *Huainan zi* 8, "*Ben jing*" 本經, p. 4b and passim.

3. Compare the *Shi ji* biographies of the wealthy (chap. 129) for the first approach and the economic material in the *Guanzi* for the second.

4. The Master here makes use of the fact that the character *fu* 富, which, while adequately translated as "wealth" or "rich," can be used interchangeably with *fu* 福, "happiness"; cf. Morohashi 1985: no. 7230, which quotes a *Shi jing* passage.

5. I read *nian* 念 for *ling* 令, with Yu 2001a: 41.

6. It is not only the Master who guides as a father and mother. The model established by heaven (*tian fa* 天法; TPJ 100.228) does as well, and so does the wise man with respect to his neighbors (TPJ 103.246).

7. This ends the introduction of the discussants and their topic. The tone of the conversation is, on both sides, polite. The topic is chosen by the Master at the request of the student. In the following, the Master gives wealth a utopian quality by insisting on its completeness: only when nothing is missing will there be real wealth. Wealth thus becomes a sociopolitical rather than an individual aim and can best be observed in the personal poverty of a king who reigns over a populous and therefore wealthy country:

> Great Yang is afraid of great Yin. . . . For this reason it is important in governing a country to see that there is wealth where the population is large and poverty and misery where it is small. (TPJ 105.264)

What is here meant by wealth is the best of several types of wealth mentioned in the *Shi ji*:

> Hence riches of the fundamentals (*ben* 本, that is, agriculture) are the best, riches from the secondary sector (*mo* 末) come next and riches gained through criminal acts are the very lowest (129.3272; trans. by Swann 1950: 451).

The source of some of this wealth can be morally doubtful:

> Neither poverty nor riches as a way of life can be taken or given; the clever have a surplus, the stupid have not enough (129.3255; trans. by Swann 1950: 422).

The *Shi ji* elucidates this statement through biographical sketches of rich persons.

The TPJ's definition of *fu*, however, is not uniform, not even within layer A material. Although in the passage under consideration moral aspects are seen as essential, this is not true for most of the text, which follows the common understanding of the word:

> Some men have obtained good, rich soil as well as the produce of heaven, earth, and the harmony between them simply by chance. They pile up millions and millions of all sorts of grain and a vast amount of jade, gold, and silver. (TPJ 103.246)

This is similar to the naïve way in which the *Guanzi*, in one of its economic rather than philosophical sections, regards the reasons for individual poverty and wealth:

> If a man is lazy and extravagant, he will become poor; if he is industrious and frugal, he will become rich. (Chap. 64 *"Xing shi jie"* 形勢解, p. 325; trans. by Rickett 1985: 66)

Although this directly contradicts section 41, it is repeated elsewhere in the TPJ:

> Should a gentleman persist in working hard, then he would become great in collecting valuables and his house would be rich and lack nothing. (TPJ 103.251)

When the Master chooses to ignore the moral aspect of the acquisition of wealth, he tends to stress the moral aspect of its distribution, as, for instance, in section 103, where it is argued that you offend *taiping* morality not by being wealthy, but by not allowing others to share your wealth.

8. For "supreme majestic *qi*," see below, section 65. The passage attributes four different degrees to heaven's influence on the growth of harvests. If this influence amounted to bad portents it would not be called *huang* 皇, since this term is reserved for items of some positive value.

9. The figure twelve thousand *(wan er qian)*, as in *wan er qian wu* 萬二千物, is characteristic of the TPJ. The whole world, for instance, is called "twelve thousand countries": "In the world there are eighty-one territories (*yu* 域) and twelve thousand countries" (TPJ p. 709, *Chao*, part 9). This is explained thus:

> Why are there twelve thousand countries? The figures of heaven start with one and end with ten. Ten is multiplied by itself. Since the way of heaven turns around when it reaches five, this amounts to ten thousand countries. The "two thousand" are added in correspondence to Yin and Yang. Look at the following example: Just as the figure ten should be the end, the months of the year are only twelve. However, in five years repeated intercalary months are inserted among them. This corresponds to heaven and earth basically originating in heaven, in that the outside and the inside of heaven's hollow grotto unite in corresponding fashion the figures of heaven and earth. Therefore, twelve months can in turn be one year only because of the intercalary month amidst them. (TPJ 139.390)

The starting point is one. It takes five steps—as explained by the figure five mentioned above—to get to ten thousand:

> The figures of heaven start with one and end with ten. One multiplied by ten is ten. Each ten multiplied by ten amounts to one hundred. One hundred multiplied by ten amounts to one thousand, one thousand multiplied by ten is ten thousand. (TPJ 139.391)

In another attempt, the figure twelve thousand is explained thus:

> This combined figure of twelve thousand countries is the same as the twelve months of one year, which make up one part, and the occasional thirteenth intercalary month interspersed among them. This is what it means. (TPJ 139.397)

The *Bai hu tong* explains that two intercalary months were interspersed in five years (chap. 9 *"Si shi"* 四時, p. 428; cf. Tjan 1949/1952: 595–96). The TPJ's explanation seems to be a subtle improvement on speculations put forward in the *Bai hu tong*, which argues that twelve thousand soldiers are needed instead of ten thousand because the number of months in a year is twelve (chap. 5 *"San jun"* 三軍, p. 200; cf. Tjan 1949/1952: 447). For the TPJ, the two thousand are that extra bit that creates a real correspondence between parallel items of different kinds. The two added to the common ten thousand "things" turns these things into an all-inclusive totality, just as the thirteenth month guarantees that the number of months makes up the whole of the year, or as thirteen (instead of the factual ten or twelve) provinces make up the country (TPJ 139.396f.). In the *Qian er bai guan yi* (Protocols of the one thousand and two hundred officials), which Tao Hongjing quotes in *Dengzhen yinjue* (Concealed instructions for ascent to perfection), "two hundred" plays a similar role (see Cedzich 1993: 33; Bokenkamp 1997: 254).

However, the use of figures starting with twelve rather than ten is perhaps mainly a stylistic peculiarity and does not convey much meaning. The *Da zhong song zhang* (Great petition for sepulchral plaints) is another text that uses this figure. On p. 22b it mentions a "Supreme Lord of Celestial Mystery and his army of twelve thousand" (*bingshi yi wan er qian ren* 兵士一萬二千人, in Nickerson's [1997: 269] translation), and smaller groups consist of 120 men.

10.   For the Celestial Master of the TPJ, as for his Han dynasty contemporaries, prognostication was an important tool of orientation in all matters of private and public life (see Seidel 1983: 303f.). Thus he must be expected to argue that heaven signifies its satisfaction through portents. The "linguistic" sections give a roundabout "definition" of *rui* 瑞:

> *Rui* is *qing* 清 (pure), *jing* 靜 (quiet), *duan* 端 (righteous), *zheng* 正 (upright), *zhuan* 專 (attentive) and *yi* 一; (one). [A *rui* is issued at a time] when the human mind (*xin* 心) is with, rather than against, heaven and earth.
>
> *I would like to know how you know that it is pure, quiet, righteous, upright, attentive, and one.*
>
> This is a good question. Now from antiquity until today it has been the nature of heaven and earth that someone who was good would achieve what was good, while someone who was bad would achieve what was bad, and that someone who was upright would achieve what was upright, while someone who was false would achieve what was false. This is the art of letting things be as they are (*ziran* 自然), and should not give any cause for surprise. So when a man's heart is righteous, upright, pure, and quiet his perfect sincerity (*zheng* 誠) moves heaven to be without bad intentions. Because of this, lucky portents and good harvests (*rui ying shan wu* 瑞應善物) will make their appearance. (TPJ 174.512f.)

This explains how lucky portents are caused by certain moral ("upright," "correct") and religious ("pure," "quiet") attitudes. This assumption is basic for the sociopolitical function of prognostication theory.

11.   The term *shan wu* 善物 (crops) is used differently in the TPJ from how dictionaries and classical texts define it (cf. *Zuo zhuan*, Duke Zhao, twenty-fifth year, 51.2110a;

Legge 1960: 711, "it is a good thing in propriety . . . "), where *wu* has the meaning of *shi* (action). *Wu* in the TPJ term *shan wu* means "products" or "produce"; see below, section 65. *Shan wu* are sent by heaven, as are portents, with which they can be linked, as in the expression *rui ying shan wu;* see the note above, and below, section 53.

12. The following layer B passage, which discusses the illness and loss of life that result from offenses against heaven's commandments, gives a vivid account of poverty:

> At this point [of a terminal illness] the parts of the body, which are in bad shape, become short of *qi* and food is not digested. Family members keeping watch might call the situation "life threatening" (*nan huo* 難活). A family in possession of some money and valuables will have something laid aside. A family without money and valuables, whose possessions are exhausted and where relatives on both sides of the family are poor, will have nothing to put forth: so when someone dies [with Long (2000: 1251) I read *yi* 已 (already) for *yi* 以 (with)] he will be buried in the ground without being given a wooden coffin. Should they later on through their toils come into some money or valuables they must then remove him from the ground. But in a family where everyone is poor, what is valuable will be lost and men will go away. When would they ever be reunited? When family members become separated, they can't support each other. So someone without a wooden coffin will turn into a demon *(gui)* without an inner and outer coffin and will roam about without a home. Moreover, he won't get any food. After death, as a demon, he will in his hunger beg for food without end. (TPJ 200.617)

This passage concludes that a person must make sure to lead a proper life so that he won't fall ill and suffer the fate just described. What it adds to section 41 is the observation that the suffering that comes from poverty reaches beyond death.

Thus the TPJ depicts poverty as an all-encompassing misery. Literary sources, however, tend to define poverty from a more upper-class perspective as a lack of valuables (see *Shuo wen jie zi* [p. 542b]: *cai fen shao* 財分少) and also as a lack of refinement, characterized by poor clothes, the lack of servants, and the need to walk rather than to travel by carriage. In a similar vein, the *Yan tie lun* chapter on wealth and poverty describes as "poor" the simple lifestyle of an official who is too honest to make commercial use of his position. While the TPJ defines poverty with more precision than as simply the absence of wealth, there is no touch of the sentimental attitude to social polarization that prevails in late Han social criticism, as put forward, for instance, by Wang Fu in his *Qian fu lun* when he accusingly lists the manifestations of wealth and argues with Confucius that "poverty is born of wealth" (*Qian fu lun* 12 *"Fu yi"* 浮侈, p. 127), as if distribution were the only economic problem.

13. As Luo (1996: 57) rightly suggests, *er* 而 must be understood here as *neng* 能, as it is often in the TPJ.

14. This is connected to what was said earlier on the relationship between a country's wealth and that of its "king," whom we must imagine as a Han dynasty prince, that is, as ruler over a commandery.

15. *You shi* 幽室 here is the place of meditation, a meaning that also occurs in nonreli-

gious texts (cf. *Hou Han shu* 27.928). Elsewhere the TPJ uses the word in a broader sense to designate the remote, well-hidden rooms where the wealthy unjustly store their goods (TPJ 103.246). The room for meditation is also called *xu wu zhi shi* 虛無之室 (chamber of void and nothingness) (TPJ 168.470, layer C), *an zuo you shi* 安坐幽室 (dark chamber of quiet sitting) (TPJ 127.322), or *xian shi* 閑室 (separate room) (e.g., TPJ 208.666). Later *taiping* material describes it as a separate, locked room behind double external and thick partition walls that ensure sounds from the outside will not reach inside (*Secret Advice by the Wise Lord of the Scripture on Great Peace;* see TPJ p. 740). This room is not supposed to be away from one's family:

> *From now on, wherein should we search* dao?
>
> We should all search it in the locked room not far from father and mother and not away from wife and children. (TPJ 208.666)

Takahashi (1986: 258) argues convincingly that the Master stresses the *taiping* believer's family links, unlike other religious groups, which praise solitude and celibacy.

16. This remark attests to the TPJ's coherence. Meditation, which is here termed *zuo* 坐 (to sit), is seen throughout as the most basic *dao*-inspired activity; see below, section 48, on "guarding the one."

17. Such suffering is often expressed by the character *chou* 愁, particularly in these first sections of the received text. It is also used in this section on p. 30 (line 11) for the plight of children of very poor parents. In this instance, the *Chao* replaces *chou* with *ri* (daily) for good reason, in that the character *chou* is more often applied to the political worries of the ruling strata than to their subjects' suffering (see Qi 1992).

18. The disciple's question redirects the discussion toward a reformist and missionary agenda. It now becomes clear that defining wealth and poverty is done to prepare for the promise that communal wealth will be achieved once *taiping*-type reforms have been implemented.

19. "Subtle sayings" are the most sacred utterances: see TPJ 78.190, and see the *Han shu yi wen zhi* (*Han shu* 30.1701), where Confucius is called an originator of *wei yan* 微言. The term is also used for material distributed by the Celestial Master (TPJ 65.146). In Han dynasty commentatorial writings, "subtle sayings" referred to the classics' supposed hidden meaning, which commentators accessed by reading between the lines, often with prognostic results (Hsiao 1979: 129–32).

20. *Sheng shen* 生神 (life-giving spirits) are most welcome:

> Men with knowledge and willpower will never lose sight of the art of life. It is their desire to act jointly together with life-giving spirits and to think in accord with heaven. (TPJ p. 711, *Chao,* part 9)

The term is more prominent in layer B. The above quotation is from a speech addressed by the Celestial Lord (*tian jun* 天君) to the Great Spirit (*da shen* 大神). There is also another mention—"This is what the life-giving spirits want"—in layer B that follows the description of well-ordered social relations (TPJ 199.614).

21. The text reads "earth's Yang and nourishing spirits" (*di zhi yang yang shen* 地之陽養神). Yu 2001a: 42 argues for correcting Yang to Yin. Yang does not belong here. Perhaps it first entered the text as a mistake for *yang*, meaning "to nourish," and when this character was correctly added the editors forgot to take out the first, mistaken, "Yang."

22. The term *zhonghe* 中和 (harmony between) occurs frequently in the TPJ. In a nonspecific way it is used as *zhong* (medium) might be used. It is stated, for instance, that for the study of *dao*, humanity is the beginning, virtue is of medium *(zhonghe)* rank, and *dao* is supreme (TPJ 163.456). It also takes the place of *zhong* in the meaning "in the middle between" (TPJ 212.676). In a more specific way it is used throughout the text to transform pairs of terms into a trinity, in particular Yin and Yang and heaven and earth, and as a consequence defines the place of man. Man is the third that Yin and Yang result in, being physically located between heaven and earth, and is also their child, their guarantor and their future. Thus, *he* is also a cosmic force. This point is stressed by Lai Chi Tim (2000: 66) when he interprets *zhonghe* as a method of ordering the cosmos. As the TPJ puts it:

> Primordial *qi* has three names: great Yang, great Yin, and the relationship between them. . . . This relationship between the two is in charge of making the ten thousand beings agree (*tiao he* 調和) with each other. It is [like] a newly born child. Children come to life through their father and mother, their mandate (*ming* 命) is derived from their father, their dispensation is derived from above, and they are entrusted with life (*sheng* 生) by their mother. So when grieved they turn to their lord, their father. . . . Harmony *(zhonghe)* must prevail between Yin and Yang. It makes the ten thousand plants and beings grow. When the people live in harmony and concord *(he tiao)*, the king's rule is in great peace. . . . The harmony between [Yin and Yang] gives accord to the reign of emperors and kings. With mutual agreement (*tiao* 調) between the ten thousand beings, each will be well governed. (TPJ pp. 19f., *Chao*, part 2)

The term has slightly different facets depending on what it is associated with and the argument it figures in. The above passage shows that Yin and Yang become effective through *zhonghe*. The term is used for what they produce, the "child," and also for their intercourse. In section 65 this trinity, as opposed to a dualistic model, is assigned cosmogonic power: Yin and Yang through their intercourse bring forth all plants and beings. This view explains the frequent usage of the phrase "Yin, Yang, and the harmony between them" instead of the simple "Yin and Yang." The trinity is always seen as a positive entity, as is the family. The single character *he* can replace *zhonghe*, but the reverse does not often hold true. In the following, more complex, image it might not be appropriate to use *zhonghe:*

> There are always the three *qi* that heaven's way consists of. The first one likes to bring to life. It is called Yang. The second enjoys letting things grow. It is called harmony *(he)*. The third loves to kill. It is called Yin. Heaven is appointed to give life. Man is in charge of nurture and growth. What has grown mature is meant to be killed. What has been killed is stored. Heaven, earth, and men combine their efforts; their activities rely

on each other. Without Yang there is no life, without harmony no growth, without Yin no killing. These three rely on each other to form one family and to let all twelve thousand plants and beings grow. (TPJ 212.675f.)

In this case, the recurrence of the image of the family is not as convincing as in other examples quoted below. The passage shows the text's characteristic ambiguity, or, rather, a certain integration of different cosmological images. Since the Celestial Master's interest does not lie in these images as such but in the moral message they convey he uses them as it suits his argument.

Zhonghe also forms a trinity with heaven and earth. Since the two are manifestations of Yang and Yin this is but another facet of the meaning just dealt with. The three are, as pointed out in section 61 (p. 113), one family:

Heaven's *dao* also forms a family, where the father resembles heaven, the mother earth, and the child the harmony between them. (TPJ 139.395)

So in order to make the cosmos resemble family life, *zhonghe* is an essential component. While it is clear that in this respect man corresponds to *zhonghe*, details differ:

The harmony in between is under the charge of man. With its help, he controls the four seasons and five phases. He must let them proceed harmoniously. (TPJ 134.371)

From what has been said so far it does not seem possible to argue that one specific meaning of the term is reserved for certain parts of the text. There is, however, one more meaning that is frequently although not exclusively used in layer B material. *Zhonghe* is not only a third force, which complements that of heaven and earth, but also the space between them, the world we live in:

Heaven's light shines downward beneath the Yellow Springs, earth's light shines upward into heaven, the light of the space between [heaven and earth] shines both upward and downward in the same manner (*he tong* 合同). So the three lights become effective through cooperation (*he he* 合和). Heaven with its own three lights—that is, sun, moon, and stars—shines downward on the space between [heaven and earth] and on earth. (TPJ 190.584, layer B)

This is the place where men live:

It was explained to the spirits that they must not at random oppose the children of the space in between, [who live] below heaven and above earth. (TPJ 187.571, layer B)

This is also the place where food grows: "All twelve thousand plants grow in the soil of the harmony between heaven and earth" (TPJ 200.615, layer B). Or, in other words:

Heaven likes to share its *dao* with men, earth enjoys letting men participate in its virtue; the harmony between them likes to feed its goods to men. (TPJ 103.248, layer A)

In the passage at hand, harmony forms a triad with heaven and earth. Its position is, as it should be, in third place and in correspondence with man and with humanity.

23. "Good men" (*shan ren* 善人) are not wicked:

The actions of good men bring about wealth; the actions of wicked men result in calamities. (TPJ p. 732, *Chao*, part 1)

The term is used in the *Xiang'er* in the same sense (10.26–29, *Laozi* 27; Bokenkamp 1997: 124). So *shan ren* are average law-abiding subjects, ranking between serfs and "worthy [officials]" (TPJ p. 222, *Chao,* part 4). In this sense, they are also the opposite of robbers and bandits (TPJ 103.250 and section 43, passim).

Up to this point, the TPJ follows common language use. The term is, however, also used in a more specific sense. The "good men" follow the moral rules proclaimed by the Celestial Master and may thus be selected by heaven to fulfill specific tasks (TPJ 207.653; 208.659; and below, 56.90). Thus the term precedes the "seed people" (cf. Bokenkamp 1997: 3), who are chosen to be exempted from the apocalypse. As Petersen (1990b: 34) points out, the term is particularly frequent in layer B material, which introduces the concept of a "supreme good man" (*shang shan ren* 上善人). The disciple whom the Great Spirit presents to the Celestial Lord (TPJ 182.551) is said to deserve this epithet:

> The supreme good man acts in such a way that he knows in advance about the external and internal [movements of] heaven and earth, appears and withdraws as Yin and Yang do, takes their [practice] as his guideline (*dao qi gang ji* 道其綱紀), ponders over them in his thoughts and does not put aside the order they provide. (TPJ 182.549, layer B)

This is a subtle way of action. The less advanced "good man" does not have the same level of sophistication: he obeys heaven's rules and is rewarded by longevity (section 203 passim, layer B).

As opposed to terms like *dongji* 洞極 and *cheng fu* 承負, which were newly created for the purposes of *taiping* missionary work, *shan ren* goes back to the *Lun yu* (7.26), where commentators equate it with "gentleman" (*junzi* 君子), that is, with the man of excellent moral bearing. While throughout layer A it occurs with this meaning, that is, pointing to an excellent follower of the *taiping* doctrine and a believer in heaven, it also refers to a regular good person who has done no harm. As the usage of the term in section 43 attests, the two meanings are not meant to be kept apart.

24. This is the correct hierarchical relationship between *dao* and heaven, although this use of the term *dao* is rare in the TPJ, which does not stress the point that heaven gets its rules from elsewhere. The order at the cosmos's top is thus: "heaven stands in awe of *dao, dao* stands in awe of what is as it is (*ziran* 自然)" (TPJ p. 701, *Chao,* part 9). This order is based on cosmogonic sequence (TPJ 139.392; p. 305, *Chao,* part 5). Since heaven is often one of two, that is, part of "heaven and earth," cosmogonic lists rarely place it at the top. What heaven and *dao* have in common is the power to give and to preserve life: "heaven likes to give life and so does *dao.* Thus *dao* is heaven's principle (*tian jing* 天經)" (TPJ p. 308, in a *Yaoxiu keyi jielü chao*—an eighth-century Daoist ritual compendium—quotation). What is, however, of more interest to the Celestial Master than such ontological concerns is the following practice-oriented relationship between *dao,* as principle of action, and "heaven," as the sky above us: "In the past as well as today every man who practices *dao* takes his model from majestic heaven" (TPJ 208.654).

25. Governments are commonly listed in a certain hierarchical or chronological order

according to their moral value. Chronological order entails hierarchical structuring, as, for instance, in the *Laozi* (38) and in *Huainan zi* 8 *"Ben jing"* 本 經, pp. 4b–5b, where government by *dao* and virtue, by benevolence, by propriety, and so on are described, the intention being to stress the major distinction between government by action and that by nonaction and to define improvement as the gradual returning to a previous stage.

The text contains another, more detailed, list of ten methods of governing (TPJ 103.253f.). These ten methods (indicated in italics) are shown below in juxtaposition with the section 41 list:

1. *dao*—sufficient wealth—heaven—superior ruler
   1. *primordial* qi—*heaven*—*prognostic writings*
   2. *what is as it is* (ziran)—*earth*—*prognostic writings*

2. virtue—half-sized wealth—earth—medium ruler
   3. dao—*men*—*prognostic writings*
   4. *virtue*—*chapter and verse commentaries*

3. benevolence—small wealth—men—ruler of lower rank
   5. *benevolence*—*chapter and verse commentaries*
   6. *propriety*—*distorted writings*

4. culture—small disorder—deceit—ruler over disorder
   7. *ritual*—*distorted writings*
   8. *culture*—*distorted writings*

5. military—lawlessness—punishments—ill-omened ruler
   9. *law* (fa)—*distorted writings*
   10. *military*—*distorted writings*

The two lists have in common a contempt for *wen* 文, here "ceremonial, decorum" in Max Kaltenmark's (1979: 30) understanding, and for *wu* 武, "military endeavors," which resembles the traditional quietist outlook presented in the *Huainan zi* (8.3b–4a). The second list stresses *yuan qi*, the primordial vapor, which ranks first from a cosmogonic point of view (cf. Asano 1982: 7, based on TPJ 139.392; 212.676) and is thus given a higher metaphysical and moral ranking than *dao*. The passage in section 103 ranks texts highly (cf. Hachiya 1983), arguing that good Daoist government, which is concerned with life, is characterized by the prevalence of sacred prognostic text, that medium-style government stresses the commentatorial tradition (*zhang ju* 章 句), and that with all other government writings become distorted.

For the passage at hand, the list of governments enhances the social and communal definition of wealth in that wealth is said to accompany a well-ordered society. The Han dynasty state in its ideal form is positioned at stage three. It is said to be dominated by the value of humanity, the creation of commentaries, and a man-centered reign.

26. The repetitiveness in this passage stems from the attempt to provide some exem-

plification, which can hardly be done in the TPJ style of writing, that is, without giving names of rulers and other historical details.

27. The disciple attempts to present an argument against the Master's narrow definition of "rich." Wang Ming does not signify a change of speakers.

28. This observation is repeated (TPJ 43.39) and goes back at least to *Huainan zi* 13 *"Fan lun"* 氾論, p. 20a, where it is argued that even Yao and Shun were not perfect in moral respects and that for this reason moral perfection was impossible to achieve.

29. For the TPJ, the world's central region consists of eighty-one territories (*yu* 域). The division into nine continents (*jiu zhou* 九州) is mentioned only once in the TPJ (TPJ 127.317), while the *Lun heng*, for instance, stresses that China is one of nine, not eighty-one, territories (chap. 31 *"Tan tian"* 談天, p. 480), as Zou Yan had supposedly argued (see *Shi ji* 74.2344; see also Needham 1956: 236). The following passages seem to suggest that Chinese influence reached all these territories and that China itself, being more than a "country," consisted of more than one "territory":

> When the good, worthy, and wise among the four barbarian tribes and in the eighty-one territories hear that China (*zhongguo* 中國) has a ruler of great virtue who governs like this, they will all wish to come to submit themselves. (TPJ 129.333)

The following passage outlines the world's size in order to explain that at different places the sky's phenomena are seen differently, just as the observers' moral condition differs:

> The world has sun, moon, and the pole star in common. It consists altogether of twelve thousand countries. The central part (*zhong bu* 中部) has eighty-one territories, divided into small parts that each make up one country. Those with plenty of virtue and excellence are twelve thousand miles (*li* 里) in size, the next is ten thousand miles from east to west and from north to south, the next is nine thousand, and so on, to one thousand and then five hundred and one hundred miles. (TPJ 134.368)

The intention of this passage is to stress the independence of countries in order to show that their fates differ in accordance with the morality of their respective governments. This world is large, considering that the thirteen figures given for countries of different moral rectitude alone would amount to 67,600 *li* and that there has to be room for 12,000 countries. The *Huainan zi* (4.2b), for instance, gives a figure of 233,500 *li* plus 75 "paces" (*bu* 步) as the size of the world (cf. Major's 1993: 147–49 discussion of the issue). Through wrong computation, as Forke argues (1962, vol. 1, p. 256), Wang Chong (*Lun heng* 31 *"Tan tian"* 談天, p. 480–82) arrives at a figure of one million *li*.

However, the Celestial Master is not concerned with these details. What matters is the fact that countries are the place where *taiping* reforms must be introduced:

> *I would like to know how many countries there are all together in the world. . . .*

> All right. The central part has eighty-one territories; beyond this there is again one circle (*zhou* 周). The world has ten thousand countries, but in the distance it runs into the void grotto, which has no exterior. The three areas [the eighty-one territories, the circle around them, and the rest] together are the twelve thousand countries. (TPJ 139.389f.)

This modifies the account given in section 134, as quoted above, but does not contradict it. Again, as pointed out with regard to the "twelve thousand plants, beings, and things," the extra two thousand are meant to define the total, including countries beyond the inner and perhaps even the outer circle.

The administrative division of these "countries" (*guo* 國) resembles that of an idealized Han dynasty empire judging by the following passage, which deals with the similarity between a family and a large state:

> The father acts as the ruler, the mother as an official, the children as the people. What they own they share with each other and make it grow, as, for instance, their crops. In such a family, all share the same major concern. Although there are ten thousand households in one county (*xian* 縣; this is its official size; see Bielenstein 1980: 101), they also constitute one family and share the same major concern. The same holds true for the ten counties, which make up one commandery (*jun* 郡), the ten commanderies, which make up one big province (*da zhou* 大州), and the ten provinces, which together form one big country (*da guo* 大國) but still constitute one big family, which shares the same concern. It is all surrounded by one identical border (*jie* 界). Should their emperor or king have virtue, his concern would reach the twelve provinces, and if this concern were great, it would reach all thirteen provinces, and yet they would all constitute one big family and share one major concern. The distant regions outside the border do not belong to the countries of men (*ren guo* 人國). When the countries of men possess *dao* and virtue, the good who live in those distant regions will come. When this is not the case, they will not come. Should virtue be lacking among men, the people from the outside regions would come to harm them. This is all one coherent area with only the one border that is the dividing line between heaven and earth. . . . One county, one commandery, one province, one country, they all mean the same: they share the same major concern. That I now report on all twelve thousand countries as [if they were] one big area is to let you know, Perfected, that they are cause for one identical concern and have one identical border in common. The rest is like these twelve thousand countries and too much for detailed reporting. For this reason the wise men of old wrote only about one small part.

> *Why did they not report on the larger area as a whole?*

> Heaven's emissary (*tian shi* 天使) had not spoken; the great mission (*da hua* 大化) had not begun. Men differed in their actions. They did not have one identical model. Therefore, they did not report [on the world as a whole]. Since today the great mission has started, all twelve thousand countries are linked together. (TPJ 139.395f.; for the additional occurrence of commune [*ting* 亭] and hamlet [*li* 里], see TPJ 127.314; for *xiang* 鄉 [district], see section 61)

So the TPJ takes into account an administrative division into hamlets, communes, counties, commanderies, and provinces (both commanderies and provinces were *guo* [country] when an imperial relative was in charge; cf. Bielenstein 1986: 506ff.) but surpasses this division toward a worldwide missionary approach. The layout of the world resembles the generally accepted *gai tian* theory (cf. Needham 1959: 210f.), but what is striking is that the aspect of surrounding water is completely missing. Zou Yan, for instance, knew of a "great ocean" (*Shi ji* 74.2344). Instead, there is only the horizon and beyond that the "void grotto" (TPJ 139.390) as the external limit.

For the passage at hand, the mention of all countries ("eighty-one territories") acts as a reminder that *taiping* concerns were global.

30.   This usage of *wen* 文 is more common in the TPJ than is the pejorative "decorum." *Wen* means "pattern," "constellation," and "text":

> *On meeting a worthy, why should one grant him texts [as one grants food to the hungry and clothes to a person who is cold]?*

Consider the reason for granting texts *(wen)*. *Wen* (patterns) originate in the east and shine in the south. So through celestial patterns (*tian wen* 天文) that originate in the northeast—and a book (*shu* 書) that has come out in the northeast—heaven makes its designs known. "Tiger" [this is, the white tiger taking up the western sky] is a pattern (*wen* 文) with its home in *yin* 寅 [the third earthly branch]. "Dragon" [the green dragon of the eastern sky] is a pattern, with its home in *chen* 辰 [the fifth branch]. Turning its back, it moves up into the sky and brightness *li* 離, the thirtieth hexagram] decorates the south. Of the three heavenly bodies that create patterns *(wen)*, the sun gives most light. So patterns originate in the east and become mature in the south, as the sun rises in the east and becomes mature in the south. Heaven demands of emperors and kings that they set up a model in imitation (*xiang* 象) of heaven. So they must grant texts in order to promote the great Yang, that is, the phase of fire (with Luo 1996: 390) and intensively promote fire in order to distinguish between what texts call right and wrong. What texts report is indeed what is right and what is wrong in this world. (TPJ 100.228f.)

The disciple also raises the question as to which texts the worthies should be granted. The Master responds that it should be the celestial scripture (*tian jing* 天經), created by the Perfected through collating the best (*da shan* 大善) texts on true *dao* from old, middle, and lower antiquity. The gist of this passage, if I read it correctly, is interesting: texts are for the sovereign what astronomical phenomena are for heaven, that is, the main tool of instruction.

Moreover, texts are also the main channel of communication between heaven and men. This is stressed in the following passage:

> When heaven wants prosperity, it provides lucky portents, patterned stones (*wen qi* 文琦), and books, and it makes sure that they are generally understood and received. When it wants decay, it conceals these texts or arranges that nobody wants to look for them. (TPJ 79.198)

So texts are a means, if not *the* means, of salvation. As soon as all false texts have been exterminated, the evil that has been inherited and passed on through the ages will vanish and great peace will arrive (TPJ 152.416).

31.   The Master "analyzes" the phrase *shang huang taiping* 上皇太平 in section 65.

32.	This passage prepares for the start of a new subject. However, poverty and the necessities of life remain issues of discussion.

33.	This is generally accepted; see, for instance, *Huainan zi* 3 *"Tian wen"* 天文, pp. 15b–16a. In this section, speculation on the lines of Yin–Yang correlation takes the place of concrete argumentation, while this correlation is not itself a topic for discussion. That the world is divided into the two forces (cf. TPJ p. 728, *Chao,* part 1) is the background for the passage at hand. However, when this division is evaluated, Yin is usually seen as covering the less desirable areas: punishment as opposed to virtue (TPJ 101.231 or 60.110f.) and death as opposed to life (TPJ p. 12, *Chao,* part 2, or section 60 as above). Yin is also identified with those in inferior positions, such as the moon and stars, as opposed to the sun, and the official as opposed to the ruler (TPJ p. 220, *Chao,* part 4). This view of the two entities of Yin and Yang leads to the pragmatic, but cosmologically doubtful, conclusion that Yin must be kept in check because its increase would be detrimental: subjects would not be loyal (TPJ 101.231) and disease might occur (TPJ 135.378). Various activities understood to increase Yin are therefore called obnoxious, including the drinking of alcohol (TPJ 105.270) and luxurious burial rites (TPJ 46.49). The contradiction between the first and second views attests to the argumentative position of the "Yin–Yang correlation." It is a rhetorical tool; it helps to market and defend a supposition, but suppositions are not founded upon it. Instead, a supposition might be founded on the contradiction between life and death, for instance, leading in consequence to the demand for reducing burials as well as abolishing female infanticide. That the first must be called "reducing the Yin" and the second "increasing it" does not seem to cause a problem for the Celestial Master.

34.	*Zei hai sha* 賊害殺 occurs only here; other combinations of these characters abound, in particular *zei hai* and *zei sha; zei sha shang* 傷 is another option. The difference lies in rhetorical effect, not in meaning.

35.	This accords with Confucius's point of view, at least according to one way in which the *Lun yu* (10.12) passage about the Master's inquiry after the burning of stables can be read. His main concern is the loss of human life.

36.	*Jiu* 咎 is often an offense involving heaven (TPJ 60.111), as opposed to *yang* 殃, which means the same in regard to earth (TPJ 58.95). This accords with the use of *yang* for offenses committed by or in regard to the dead (see Seidel 1985: 168).

37.	Cf. *Laozi* 57: "When I [that is, the sage] don't have any business, the people will of themselves become rich."

38.	These introductory remarks are long, and their gravity adds weight to the ensuing discussion. Only here is it mentioned that the students' note taking will prolong the student' lives. We may assume that the note taking actually took place. The Master reminds students about taking notes as if to suggest that a lecture is about to begin. Sections 43, 55, 63, 67, 105, 107, 108, and 156 include such a warning toward their beginning; other sections include it in the middle, as here, to signal a change of topic (63.138; 65.148; 139.391 and 393); and others still (65, 78, 133, 139, and 152) include it at the end, in a hortatory function.

39. In the TPJ, the "Controller of Fate" (*si ming* 司命) is in the first place a deity residing in a person's body and supervising the moral behavior of his charge:

> Therefore, it is said that the Controller of Fate is in the chest next to the heart. In close proximity, he observes (*si* 司) the right and the wrong things that a person does. When there is a fault he abruptly retires—why should he waste time?—and thereby abruptly reduces the years of a man's life. (TPJ 195.600, layer B)

All corporeal deities endanger a man by leaving him (TPJ pp. 27f., in a TPJ citation of the *Sandong zhunang* 1 "*Jiao dao pin*" 教道品, giving "TPJ 33" as its source; cf. Tanaka 1984: 292). The Controller of Fate is also depicted as an independent deity who keeps accounts and offers reports on them when asked to do so by the Celestial Lord (*tian jun* 天君), who then passes his verdict (TPJ p. 214, *Chao*, part 4). This second image is not necessarily distinct from the corporeal presence of the deity. The deity is well known enough to also appear in a figurative sense: man is said to be the Controller of Fate for the domestic animals (TPJ 137.383; cf. Espesset 2002b: 16), and the county head is seen as Controller of Fate for the people (TPJ p. 699, *Chao*, part 8). The deity's function is closely related to that of the "Controller of Time" (*si hou* 司候) in the text's layer B astronomical chapters (see Penny 1990; cf. Espesset 2002b: 27f.), whose accounts determine the length of one's life. He is said to reside in the Constellation Room (*fang* 房), which was supposed to act as the heavenly equivalent of the Hall of Light (*ming tang* 明堂) and to keep lists of a man's essential data, in particular the time of birth, which was thought to predetermine the course and length of someone's life (TPJ 181.547). Thus *si hou*'s bookkeeping differs from the moral supervision exercised by *si ming*.

40. TPJ p. 707, *Chao*, part 9 discusses the *san tong* 三統 (three dispensations) in a form close to the calendrical speculations about the "three orders" in the *Bai hu tong* 8 "*San zheng*" 三正, pp. 360–64; cf. Tjan 1949/1952: 548–52. However, most of the time the term *tong* is used in a less specific sense, just as if using *tian tong* instead of *tian* would remind readers of the fact that heaven is a cosmological entity. This is similar to the use of *qi*, which is added to abstract terms such as *taiping* for the sake of clarity; whether the character *qi* is added or not, peace can be imagined only in the form of *qi*. However, nonabstract terms can thus be made abstract, as, for instance, in the term *wang qi* 王氣, which could be rendered as "kingliness" (TPJ p. 304, *Chao*, part 5). Thus terms are attributed their full argumentative value by adjuncts like *qi* or *tong:*

> Primordial *qi* (*yuan qi* 元氣), the obscure (*huang hu* 恍惚), and what is as it is (*ziran* 自然) froze into one, which was called heaven. It split and on giving life to Yin produced earth, which was called two. Based on heaven above and earth below, Yin and Yang expanding into each other gave life to man, who was called three. These three dis-

pensations jointly gave life to and raised all plants and beings, which were all called goods (*cai* 財). (TPJ p. 305, *Chao*, part 5)

Discussion of the interrelationship of the three *tong* pervades much of the TPJ:

> Now the three dispensations of heaven, earth, and man are set up dependent on each other and reach perfection by shaping each other's appearance (cf. *Laozi* 2). A man, for instance, has a head, feet, and a belly. If one dispensation were in distress, all three would come to ruin. This is just as if a man were without head or feet or belly: with one gone all three would be doomed. So when man in grand fashion (*da dao* 大道) opposes heaven and earth, all three will perish. (TPJ 134.373)

However, often enough the plain terms heaven, earth, and men seem to suffice to express the full cosmological meaning.

The issue of political legitimacy, and in consequence historiographic reasoning, which often accompanies the use of the term *tong*, is not thematized in the TPJ.

41. The comparisons are striking: for a woman marriage is equivalent to the office held by a scholar. It also means that a man cannot manage any better without the support of a wife than a ruler can without the help of his officials.

42. *Ru* 汝 (you) is erroneous and must be replaced by *nü* 女 (woman).

43. *Da ni* 大逆 and *wu dao* 無道 are Han dynasty legal terms (cf. Wakae 1982); *wu dao* can be used as *bu dao* 無道. Both terms point to antigovernment activities; see below, section 63.

44. This is not a common topic in Chinese literature and thought. An exception is the moving description of infanticide given by Yan Zhitui (531–91) in his *Yan shi jia xun* 5 "*Zhi jia*" 治家, p. 51 (cf. Teng 1968: 20).

45. *Yuan jie* 冤結 (grief-stricken) seems to occur first in the *Chu ci* ("*Jiu zhang*" 九章 4.38a, trans. Hawkes 1959: 77), where it describes a woman's undefined sadness. Throughout the text the character *yuan* (冤 grievance) is also used in the meaning of *yuan* (怨 resentment). *Yuan jie* as well as *yuan* (冤 and 怨) often indicate the resentment felt by those who see themselves as maltreated and as suffering without cause. This resentment, which reaches beyond death, amounts to a major cosmic force because it stimulates heaven to cause disaster. The term is used in arguments against the severity of punishments, as, for instance, in Xiang Kai's memorial, where it occurs several times (*Hou Han shu* 30B.1077 [*yuan* 冤 only], pp. 1078 and 1081). The Celestial Master contrasts such grief and resentment with a correct understanding of the true origins of suffering, which lie, as he explains, in evil inherited from previous generations (see also sections 48 and 65, below).

46. Two characters are missing here, and the text is difficult to reconstruct. One might suspect that more than two characters have been lost, since the paragraph that follows seems disconnected. The phrase *zhong zhi* 重知 is often preceded by *zi yu* 欲子 (If you want to know more about it, [I am telling you . . .]), a phrase that usually introduces another point in the argumentation (TPJ 99.226; 134.369 [twice]; 134.373 and 375; 139.393;

152.414; 155.435; 160.450; 174.513). I have added *yu zi* 欲 子 (I want you . . .), but there is no parallel for this phrase. Yu 2001a: 46 reads the two missing characters as *fan fu* 反復 (again).

47. To kill one's child was against the law in Han times; see Hulsewe 1955: 88f. and Kinney 1993: 108–13. Nevertheless, infanticide was widely practiced, often by abandonment. There are so few known instances of criticism of infanticide that it seems appealing to link these instances, all from the Western Han dynasty, with the theory put forward in the TPJ. The best-known opponent of infanticide was the antieunuch partisan Jia Biao 賈彪. He was from Yingchuan 潁川 commandery (in the center of present-day Henan) and is said to have taken as his model the famous politician and intellectual Xun Shuang (128–90), whose home was in the same commandery. After several minor postings, Jia became prefect of Xinxi 新息 in Runan 汝南 commandery (in the southeast of present-day Henan). He died, probably in 168 C.E., because he refused to go into hiding when the anti-Party prosecutions broke out. His biography includes the following report on his rule over Xinxi:

> The small folk were miserable and poor. Many did not bring up their children. Jia Biao strictly ruled this to be the same crime as murder. South of the town there were outlaws who caused harm to people, and north of the town there was a woman who had killed her child. When Jia Biao announced an investigation and the officials all wished to turn to the south, he said angrily: "When outlaws damage people, this follows a constant principle. When mother and children injure each other this opposes heaven and runs counter to the way *(dao)*." Therefore, he drove his carriage northward to investigate the crime. When the robbers south of the town heard about it, they came to accuse themselves, their hands fastened at their backs. Over the course of some years, men thus raised thousands of children. They all said: "We were brought up by father Jia." Newborn males were named "sons of Jia," and newborn females were named "daughters of Jia." (*Hou Han shu* 67.2216)

The explanation given by Jia for his interference seems to have been moral rather than cosmological, but the usage of the terms heaven and *dao* is nevertheless the same as in the TPJ.

For two other instances of legislation against infanticide we have no explanation of the official's motive. Wang Ji 王吉, adopted son of the eunuch leader Wang Fu 王甫, became chancellor of the state of Pei 沛 (in the northern half of present-day Anhui) when he was only twenty years old. In 179, he ended up in prison due to his father's political fall and death. He is considered to have been a harsh official. His biography states, "When someone gave birth to children and did not raise them he had father and mother beheaded" (*Hou Han shu* 77.2501). In the third instance nothing seems to be known about the official except for his name, and the event cannot be dated:

> Zong Qing 宗慶 was governor (*tai shou* 太守) of Changsha 長沙 [a commandery in central Hunan]. Since people often did not have sufficient clothing and food, they did

not raise those they had borne. Qing urgently pressed the local thrice venerable (*san lao* 三老) to prevent the people from killing their children. Over the course of these years, more than three thousand children were reared by the people. Boys and girls alike all bore the name Zong. (See the citation of Xie Cheng's 謝承 lost text *Hou Han shu* by Yu Shinan 虞世南 [early Tang] in his *Bei tang shu chao* 北堂書鈔, ed. *Qi jia Hou Han shu* 7.6a, on pp. 205f.)

Since the author of this report served as commandant of Changsha in the Sanguo state of Wu, this information might have come from quite reliable local sources.

There is only one other mention of the issue in the TPJ. This is the seventeenth of nineteen commandments:

> If you want to prevent men from killing and maltreating women, you must make sure that each of them in her place works for clothes and food as well as she can. Don't allow her to be so perverse (*da ni* 大逆) as to make her parents suffer (*chou* 愁). (TPJ 108.512)

In her account of infanticide, Kinney (1993: 116f.) stresses the point that economic hardship was often seen as the main obstacle in raising a child. The *Han shi wai zhuan* (3.6a) stated that in times of great peace infants would not be abandoned.

48. The world's misery is the result not only of present-day trespassing but also of man's continuing misdemeanors ever since he was created. *Cheng fu* 承負 (to inherit and to transmit) is the term for the measure of evil that humankind is thus burdened with (see below, section 48).

49. Not to have children was considered a serious crime; see below, section 42.

50. The term *shi lei* 世類 (worldlings) for humankind (as used in *Han shu* 41.2089) is specific to the TPJ; see, for instance, TPJ 42.37; 134.373. Yü Ying-shih (1964: 86) quotes this passage to illustrate the esteem with which early Daoist believers held life, manifested in particular, as he sees it, in the TPJ and the *Xiang'er*.

51. The "seven regents" and "three luminaries" refer to almost the same objects: the sun, moon, and five planets (seven), or the sun, moon, and stars (three). The second, better-known expression could be a gloss inserted in the text to explain the first.

52. So the "wise men" (*sheng ren* 聖人) are experts on microcosmic-macrocosmic relations:

> Therefore, the wise man teaches not to rely on bridle and whip but establishes his doctrine by following the nature of what is as it is. (TPJ p. 725, *Chao*, part 1)

In earlier texts, such as the *Huainan zi*, the *sheng ren* is a personage of highest wisdom, but the figure underwent a certain devaluation. In a highly formalistic TPJ passage, *sheng ren* comes only fifth in a list of nine ranks. He is said to model himself after the harmonious cooperation between Yin and Yang and all the plants and creatures (TPJ p. 221, *Chao*, part 4). The sphere of Yin and Yang is often seen as his field: "Therefore the wise man knows how to assemble Yin and Yang, and the worthy organizes what is crooked and what is straight" (TPJ 179.525). We must expect, then, that the *sheng ren* is expert in sexual matters. He is capable of serving in government ("to rule over the one hundred surnames"), assisted by the worthy (*xian ren* 賢 人; TPJ 108.289), who fills the sixth rank. The wise and the worthy are often mentioned together (cf. Takahashi 1984: 308f.).

53. The summary says:

> This section distinguishes and explains poverty and wealth, and how the conduct of lords and kings creates auspicious conditions. It warns men not to cut off earth's dispensation. By making both men and women thrive, the king's reign is at peace.

This short section deals with sexual conduct. The need to have children is asserted despite the contemporary trend to avoid it. This need is seen as rooted not in the demands of filial piety or other family-oriented considerations, but rather as rooted in nature. The benefits of having children are said to override any benefit individuals might hope to gain from sexual abstinence or from sexual techniques preventing the flow of semen (benefit that is, in any case, described as imaginary). What is at stake is the order of nature, and in particular weather conditions and the growth of plants, which are directly influenced by individual behavior. This dynamic creates a situation in which everybody must strive to achieve exemplary conduct, which entails imitating nature as closely as possible. The term "model" *(fa)* is reserved for the conduct of heaven. Human beings are expected to take heaven's exemplary conduct as a model for their own actions. However, the section shows clearly that heaven imitates human conduct in the same way that human beings are expected to imitate heaven. Imitation is the rule according to which the entire system functions. The active element in this system is man. If he chooses to ignore what is natural, nature will follow suit. Or, as the Master puts it, if human beings don't produce children, heaven and earth will stop the growth of plants.

This section's progeny-oriented attitude toward sexual intercourse accords with the concern for social renewal evident in much of what the Celestial Master declares. However, sexual activity is said to have other functions as well. It is fun and rejuvenates men, it says in section 62, and it is what human beings want (see section 52).

That it helps to "nourish the vital principle"[1] is not a topic of the TPJ, or at least not of those parts that have been transmitted.

Returning to the proposition introduced in section 41 that "one man is the equivalent of two women," the Master stresses another aspect of the creation of life: it can happen only if it is in accord with patterns established in the trans-human world. Any relationship between man and woman must resemble Yin and Yang's numerical pattern, which is the relationship between even and odd or between two and one.[2]

The last passage adds a marginal point. Here the king is expected to represent heaven in its relationship to earth directly, and for this reason he is to have intercourse with a woman from each province of his realm.

· · ·

(42.37) Perfected, step forward. If heaven's *qi* of great harmony and peace (*tai he ping qi* 太和平氣) had just arrived, and the king's government was about to be at great peace,[3] should men be chaste[4] or not? Why should they be chaste?

The chaste reduce their desires and don't act at random.[5]

Oh, what you say, Perfected, is naïve.[6] From the height of middle antiquity, the common people have been misled. Their teachers were jealous of the truth and taught them lies.

What do you mean?

A chaste man does not beget, a chaste woman does not become pregnant. Thus Yin and Yang are not exchanged, which completely annihilates the world's population.[7] So two human beings join forces to cut off the dispensation of heaven and earth because they wish to obtain a little empty and false fame. Through their lack of progeny they lose their internal substance and cause great damage to the world. How would you have come to exist had a father and mother not brought you to life? But both heaven and earth hate human beings who cause ruptures. They are known as "men of great contrariness who disrupt order."[8] In response, such action brings forth a separation between heaven and earth so that heaven won't assent to let it rain and earth won't give birth to anything. (42.38)

Why is this so?[9]

When heaven does not give rain, this means that it does not beget because it is chaste. When earth does not let the ten thousand plants grow, this means that it does not become pregnant because it is chaste. Without rain from heaven, earth has no means to give growth, which is a great disaster for the whole world. How can one deem this to be good? Judging by what you have said you don't follow the teachings of heaven and earth, but go against heaven's way and are not inclined to assist heaven and earth in making things grow. Instead, you wish to cause ruptures. How could the words you have uttered not offend majestic heaven and august earth?[10]

My mind is weak, I am not good enough; I am mistaken. Now that I have heard what you have said I myself know that this crime is serious.

Don't [say that]. Let me tell you that actions must not run counter to heaven's way and that you won't comply with heaven's will should you heed the words of the common people. The cause for the frequent ruptures [in the relationship] between Yin and Yang lies in a lack of harmony between man and woman. These two are at the root of Yin and Yang. How could it be auspicious for the conduct of affairs to lose the root?[11]

I completely agree with the Celestial Master. What can I say?

Well, when *qi* of great majestic heaven's supreme peace is about to arrive we must faithfully take heaven as our model. For this reason we order one man to have two wives so that they resemble Yin and Yang. Yang's cipher is single, that of Yin is a pair. Thus *qi* of great harmony will arrive. Should there be too many women, the Yin *qi* would prosper; if there were too many men, the Yang *qi* would have no partner, which would go against the model [set by heaven][12] and certainly lead to disaster.

Why?

Ciphers for the human realm must agree with heaven and earth. If they don't, human energy will not suffice and we will encounter disastrous damage.[13]

What is the meaning of "The spouses of emperors and kings correspond to the soil of the earth"?[14]

What you have just said supports my words. If woman is vital spirit (*jing shen* 精 神) of the earth's soil, the king is vital spirit of heaven. The main fear is that the soil of the earth does not obtain Yang's vital spirit because the king's *qi* is not received in intercourse. This prevents earth's soil from giving birth. Thus in each province[15] the king must choose one wife to let his *qi* penetrate. Intent on giving life he fears that his begetting might not succeed because the kingly semen is not well received. Therefore, he chooses [a wife] as one would choose soil.[16] Once he begets, heaven's *qi* penetrates so that rain falls at the right time and earth gives growth to the ten thousand plants and beings. One must not honor chaste men and women or *qi* of great peace will not arrive. To remain alone in one's internal chambers is a profound mistake, which deprives the king's government of harmony and honesty.

Even the common people must not trespass against this rule. So let one man have two wives.

Yes, indeed.[17]

NOTES

1. See Harper 1987: 541 and 548.

2. The TPJ's method of argumentation generally entails following a single line of reasoning and almost always precludes historical references. If this were not true the TPJ might have mentioned the two daughters of Yao whom Shun married and thus reminded readers that its content is more conservative than its novel presentation would suggest.

3. The mood is hypothetical. Great peace is about to arrive, as the Master asserts in the second half of this section, but it has not yet done so. However, the dialogues between Master and disciples take place in a state of excited expectation. When they hear the Master speak the disciples show their appreciation by exclaiming that they feel that great peace has already arrived (TPJ 63.134; 109.291; 152.416), and the Master suggests that he feels the same way when a disciple makes a correct response (TPJ 79.196). The imminence of the arrival of great peace is the reason behind the disciples' eagerness (TPJ 61.125). They raise questions to allow the truth to come out and men to be prepared. The arrival of *shang huang taiping qi* 上皇太平氣 is said to be a most joyful occasion (TPJ 50.68). A condition for this arrival is "using both hands," or the cooperation between different actors, such as between sovereign and official, husband and wife, or master and disciple (TPJ 177.519). The promise of great peace's imminent arrival is a major component of the missionary agenda. Once it has come:

> one must join forces with the virtuous lord and not be so irresponsible as to cause damage and injury, or else *qi* of great peace will be in disarray and the reign in trouble. (TPJ 137.385)

The arrival of the Master, the teaching sessions, and the reform program are all geared toward preparing the world for the advent of heaven-sent great peace:

> Once *qi* of great peace has arrived, peace will reign forever, and never again will men be lead into death and ruin. (TPJ 134.373)

The text stresses different aspects of this process depending on the occasion. The preparations for the arrival of great peace, the effects of its presence, and how to ensure them are all thematized. One passage stands out because of the uncommon precision with which it addresses these issues and the inclusion of a subjacent promotion of spirit worship:

I would like to ask something.

Go ahead.

If heaven were about to [send] great peace, would we be able to have advance knowledge of it?

Well, from the fact that *qi* [, which represents] heaven's five imperial spirits, is in great peace, one can know in advance that this particular year is about to enjoy peace.

What do you mean? I would like to know.

Well, in spring, *qi* of the blue emperor's spirit should be in great peace, in summer that of the red emperor's spirit; in the sixth month it is the yellow emperor's spirit, in autumn the white emperor's spirit, and in winter the black emperor's.

The Master explains that this means there is neither injury nor damage to the growth of plants. He concludes:

The supreme wise men of the past clearly saw whether *qi* [representing] the five imperial spirits was at peace. So they knew instantly whether a reign was to be successful or a failure and whether peace was imminent. Perhaps you don't think so?

I would like to be instructed about "peace."

Well, that everything comes to life in spring without injury is the blue emperor's great peace, that it grows in summer without any fault is the red emperor's great peace, and that it is nourished without fail in the sixth month is due to the great peace that the yellow emperor provides. The white emperor's peace ensures that everything is harvested in autumn without damage, and the black emperor's great peace means that the harvest is safely stored in winter. After the five emperors have been in great peace for one year, men happily try to do good (*shun shan* 順善). After two years like this, there is great joy on earth. After three years, mercy and generosity fill heaven. After four years, the winds (*feng qi* 風氣) are advantageous. After five years, the nine spirits don't contend, so natural calamities and other evils are subdued. After six years the six relationships [I understand *liu gang* 六綱 with the *Chao* as *liu ji* 六紀] are seen everywhere in their correct form. After seven years, the three luminaries shine more brightly. After eight years, mercy spreads to the eight directions. After nine years Yin and Yang are fond of each other. And after ten years the ten thousand plants and beings are in place. [In the figure ten] all figures come to a certain conclusion.

In objects three is combined with ten, and if heaven, earth, and men are prepared, there will be great peace in thirty years. Should highest majestic *qi* come forth and the true doctrine *(dao)* be implemented, great peace could be achieved in fifteen years. If one doesn't work hard following the true doctrine, how can one ever dream of achieving great peace? When we say that great peace may come in fifteen years we suppose that from emperor and kings down to great and small officials everyone follows the true doctrine and does away with evil and deceit. In this way will peace come after fifteen years. Do you understand?

So if you want to know whether great peace is about to arrive or not you must merely observe whether the five emperors' spirits are at peace or not. This is clear enough. It should enable you to find out for yourself. In this way, all symptoms can first be detected in celestial spirits. Should these spirits not be at peace, how will men be able to find peace? . . . Now since heaven's first-ranking supreme *qi* of peace is about to arrive I advise you to honor the four seasons and five phases and to let everybody, great and small, promote the affairs of these spirits. In the past, men respectfully observed only the four seasons and five elements to make great peace arrive. Therefore, it moved slowly and would take thirty years to come. Since nowadays we also serve these spirits, peace will come fast, in fifteen years. Do you understand? (TPJ 140.398–400)

The time frame established in this passage agrees with the Master's promises. The whole process, through the combined efforts of heaven and men, is expected to take thirty years, or one generation, which would thus allow the children of the current generation of believers to reap the benefits. There is, moreover, the promise that proper ritual attention to certain spirits, probably the nine spirits (that is, those linked to the five phases and another four representing the four elements; see also TPJ 105.262), would reduce the whole reform process to fifteen years, which was perhaps, if we follow historical sources, the average length of large Han dynasty mass movements. It brings enjoyment of the good times within reach of the believers who initiated the movement.

See also sections 63 and 66, below, on the relationship between *qi* of peace and the actual establishment of a *taiping* reign.

4. The word *zhen* 貞 (chaste) is used by the Master and disciples to mean lifelong sexual abstinence. This is a specific use of the word, and it is surprising that the disciple doesn't need to ascertain what the Master means but instead understands right away. In general, *zhen* means "chaste" or "modest" (it is also adequately rendered as "persistent" by Wilhelm 1972: 130; hexagram 32) and is considered a female virtue. It relates to a woman's bearing, and particularly to the way she behaves toward men; the *Yijing* (hexagram 32, p. 21) says *zhen* is lucky in a woman and unlucky in a man. The character is rendered as "chaste" by most interpreters of the *Yijing*'s third hexagram (pp. 4f.; Wilhelm 1972: 37), as in "The girl is chaste, does not promise herself. Ten years, then she promises herself," but even here "persistent" is a reasonable rendering. The "chaste and obedient" women of the *Lie nü zhuan* (chap. 4) are not so much concerned with their chastity as with propriety and etiquette. This can also be seen in the *Gu liang zhuan*'s respectful rendering of the fate of Duke Gong's 共 公 widow, who died in the flames for the sake of *zhen* (Duke Xiang, thirtieth year, 16.2432b). In this sense, the word was a legal term. See *Han shu* 12.351 and 356, and cf. Dubs 1938/1955, vol. 3: 70 and 78; one chaste woman in each district *(xiang)* was to be chosen to be made exempt from taxes. The word can be used for male behavior without any sexual connotations. A certain He 和 (*Han Feizi* 13, "He shi" 和氏 750.1), for instance, who tried to present the king with a piece of jade, called himself *zhen shi* 貞士 (an honest man). With a similar meaning, and joined with *zhong* 忠 (loyalty), it also occurs in the TPJ (185.563).

The TPJ rarely calls sexual abstinence "chaste"—the character occurs in only three places—but it always criticizes abstinence, as in the section at hand. Retirement and eremitism are also seen as opposed to the belief in the arrival of great peace (cf. Takahashi 1986: 258). Sexual activity is said to be a basic human need, as documented below, in section 52. To refrain from it upsets cosmological order and risks the survival of humankind (for instance, TPJ 208.655). Not to have progeny is evil:

Now men who study *dao* must take heaven as their model in all respects. But they often give it up [絕 for *chun* 純, with Long 2000: 1344], remain without progeny, and thus let heaven's dispensation be ruined. Some are chaste [*zhen,* here "impotent," as Luo (1996: 1109) correctly translates] by nature (*tian xing* 天性), in that their *qi* is not adequate. Some are not so, but work hard to make it stop. Then Yin and Yang don't find their way and these men spread their semen on uncultivated ground. Some might even destroy their females or just go away and leave them in poverty. They are all great villains who have lost track of *dao.* . . . The wise men and great worthies of old, who knew [heaven's] prohibitions, were not willing to have any dealings with men who had no progeny, as if to rule together with them would offend the will of heaven [this could also be directed against eunuchs in government]. For this reason, the wise and worthy, who are as messengers from heaven, esteem men with progeny and despise those without. Since wise men have thorough knowledge of heaven's will they always strive to achieve it, down to the finest detail. So should not heaven itself do likewise? Now since heaven for quite a while has been devoid of good people (*shan ren* 善人), it has sent me down here to talk to everybody, advise the latter-born, and bring insight to foolish men. If heaven were to employ such men wouldn't this mean that it assembles around it men without progeny? Should men who behave in this way rise up to heaven, wouldn't this mean that heaven favors men who have no children and dislike life? So they will in fact all die on barren ground, on soil where nothing grows, in a desert without people. They will all be sent back to their own kind. Were you to disregard life [and thus] oppose heaven you would be put where there isn't any life. If you were to prefer that nobody existed then heaven would put you in a desert, where there is nobody. Since common men are too dull to see this, they say that they are redeeming themselves (*du shi* 度世), which is truly not the case. (TPJ 208.658f.)

This passage opposes all men who don't practice uninterrupted heterosexual intercourse but who instead proclaim that heaven will reward them for their abstention by inviting them up to heaven. Its basic meaning is close to that of the passage at hand. That in this case the details of "heaven's will" are ascertained through the observation of ancient social practice is interesting.

It is not clear against which group these attacks are directed. There has been detailed discussion in the People's Republic about whether the creed that made men and women leave their homes was Buddhism. This discussion was dominated by the political prominence of the TPJ in the 1950s and early 1960s and has been conveniently and sufficiently summarized by Yoshioka (1970: 136). Some arguments were based on the work of Tang Yongtong (1938: 73–80), who detected in the TPJ terms and ideas that he regarded as having been borrowed from Buddhism or as referring to Buddhism. He cited as evidence the TPJ's attacks on lack of piety, lack of procreation, the eating of excrement, the drinking of urine, and begging (TPJ 208.655f.). In 1962, the Buddhist Ju Zan (1995: 287–94) replied to this that with the exception of eating excrement, which was neither a Buddhist nor a Chinese custom and had been introduced for purely polemical purposes, the customs mentioned had Chinese roots. In 1963, Tang (Ju 1995: 296) continued the discussion by dutifully acknowledging that Buddhist practices did not play a role; for overriding ideological reasons the whole of the TPJ had to be a text from the early second century C.E., and in the 1960s there was less evidence available for the impact of first- and second-century Buddhism than there is today. But since we are free to admit that the received text has reached us in an edited version and we have more reason to take Xiang Kai's 襄楷 knowledge of Buddhism seriously (see *Hou Han shu* 30B.1082), we may say that the TPJ is a second-century text, stating at the same time that it reveals some familiarity with certain Buddhist points of view and practices.

But the Celestial Master might also have directed his attacks toward time-honored Chinese practices. Within the circles in which early Daoism originated, there was a certain tradition of antifamilism. Some practitioners left home to pursue otherworldly aims, as did, for instance, Qiu Sheng 仇生, Ping Changsheng 平常生 (Kaltenmark 1987: 81 and 91–93), and Fei Changfang 費長房 (*Hou Han shu* 82B.2743–45; DeWoskin 1983: 77–81), although the ideal of celibacy or chastity hardly played a role in this. It did in later events, such as Chu Boyu's 褚伯玉 (fifth century) escape from marriage (*Nan Qi shu* 54.926), which it is difficult to imagine occurring in pre-Buddhist times.

The issue was certainly a subject of debate within Daoist circles. The *Xiang'er's* comments on *Laozi* 6 are puzzling. It condemns sexual techniques, and particularly the technique of withholding semen, arguing very much along the lines of the TPJ that *dao* wants men to procreate. But it also observes that avoiding sexual intercourse is a shortcut to a higher form of existence:

> Men [or "human beings"] of supreme virtue with a hard and strong will are capable of not having intercourse and producing offspring. When they give this up while they are still young, good spirit (*shan shen* 善神) will be developed within them from early on. We then speak of *dao*'s vitality [or "*dao*'s semen" (*dao jing* 道精)]. This is the reason why heaven and earth have no ancestral temples, dragons no children, transcendents no wives, and jade girls no husbands. This is an important point of belief. (*Xiang'er* 2.6; Bokenkamp 1997: 84)

This belief in the benefit of chastity fits the accusations made in the TPJ. When the TPJ attacks sexual abstinence it thus attacks a rival group from within its own circle.

5. As demanded by *Laozi* 1 and 16.

6. The word for "naïve" is *chun* 純. Since Chun is also the name of one disciple (see TPJ 65.146; 67.168; 78.187; 79.195; 99.224) this might be a pun.

7. The *Chao* omits *wu* (to annul) and thereby avoids the TPJ's awkward three-character verb *jue mie wu* 絕滅無.

8. For "great contrariness" (*da ni* 大逆) see below, section 63. *Jue* 絕 (to cause rupture), here *jue li* 絕理, is the TPJ's definition of wrong conduct:

> Now rupture occurs when a man forgets the commands of *dao*. Only when he knows *dao*'s meaning can he lead his life. (TPJ p. 26, *Chao*, part 2)

Thus "to interrupt *qi*" (*jue qi* 絕氣) is the opposite of "maintaining *qi*" (*shou qi* 守氣), that is, maintaining the activity that safeguards vitality:

> Well, the *dao* of heaven and earth can last for a long time through safeguarding *qi* and not allowing it to be interrupted (*shou qi er bu jue* 守氣而不絕). Thus heaven creates good and bad fortune only through *qi*. The ten thousand beings do likewise. Without *qi* they die. (TPJ 160.450)

Jue qi can serve as a gloss for death, as in "dead, that is, their *qi* ruptured" (*si jue qi* 死絕氣, TPJ 105.272). The Master also warns against an interruption of heaven's way (TPJ 103.242), of the dispensation of heaven and earth (54.80; section 41), of the flow of information (see below, section 43), of the true *dao* (TPJ 154.431), or of food and drink (section 44). In all these cases, rupture can have deadly results. Moreover, all these instances are interconnected. Not to have progeny is particularly egregious since it causes the rupture of all three dispensations and thus of life itself. Warnings against it therefore abound (TPJ p. 22, *Chao,* part 2; pp. 214 and 218, *Chao,* part 4; 65.150f.; 134.373f.).

9. Wang Ming has here a change of speakers rather than an isolated question, but the following sentences are too important to have been uttered by a disciple.

10. These honorific terms go back to the *Shu jing* ("*Wu cheng*" 武成, p. 184c). King Wu, the founder of the Zhou dynasty, is said to have announced to "majestic heaven and august earth" the approaching battle against the Shang.

11. The expression "to maintain the root" indicates concern for the creation and protection of life in all its manifestations (see section 53, below). In the passage at hand the proper relationship between man and woman is seen as the root of cosmic order. Once it is lost, life on earth is said to be at risk.

Woman and her role are the topic of sections 41 and 42 only. However, throughout the text the believer can be female or male. This is clear from the specific observation that a woman will envisage spirits as female (TPJ 109.292), from the expression "the people, men and women" (*ren min nan nü* 人民男女) (TPJ 152.415 and 420), and from the short section 159, on sexual technique (which states "Men and woman reverse their bodies," and thus treats Yin and Yang as equal). Throughout the text, as one would expect in a nature-oriented world of thought, the togetherness of male and female is seen as the origin of everything (TPJ 65.149; p. 648, *Chao,* part 7). The *Laozi*'s "mysterious female" is mentioned as an example of how to maintain *qi* (TPJ 160.450).

12. *Fa* is used throughout the text for *tian fa* 天法, which is the manifest order of nature and men's major guideline.

13. Fundamental as this observation is, it is difficult to find other places where it is expressed in such simple terms. It points to the practical necessity of the study of correlations, without which human endeavors cannot succeed.

14. It is not clear where this quotation comes from.

15. This refers to the *zhou* 州 into which China was supposedly divided from the time of Shun onward. The TPJ mentions that there are twelve (as arranged by Shun; see *Shu*

jing, "Shun dian" 舜典, p. 128c) or perhaps thirteen (139.396), which roughly accords with the situation during Han times (Bielenstein 1980: 90–91).

16. While it is known that Daoist sexual techniques include criteria for the selection of females, the transmitted text of the TPJ does not deal with this topic. Li Xian's 李賢 *Hou Han shu* annotation, however, quotes the following passage:

> The Perfected had another question: "Why are so few children born nowadays?" The Celestial Master answered: "It's good that you have raised this. The reason is that the act of begetting does not reach its aim. If someone has intercourse with a woman (*ren* 人) in order to have children, he will open the jade gate and spread semen inside. This is just as in spring you put seeds into the soil that will grow if there is complete mutual harmony. Should you spread these seeds at the wrong time, as you would if you were, for instance, to put something into the soil in the tenth month, they would all perish and none at all would live. If you want to examine this matter further: a woman who is unable to have children (*wu zi zhi nü* 無子之女) will not give birth even if she were to receive semen a hundred times a day. This means that [the semen] does not find a place in which life can be brought forth. For this reason, the wise and worthy of old did not carelessly put their semen in ground that was not fertile. We call this to lose seeds and waste *qi*. It achieves nothing. Now the *qi* of great peace is about to arrive. But some men are perhaps without children and have thus interrupted the dispensation of heaven and earth, so that the country's population is small. It is the way of governing that countries with a large population are rich and those with a small population are poor. Now that *qi* of heaven's supreme majesty has arrived it will let things grow ten thousand times better than they did at the beginning of heaven and earth." (TPJ p. 733, from *Hou Han shu* 30B.1081)

If this translation is adequate, the argument put forth in this passage lacks cohesion, as if parts were missing, but not uncommonly so. There are fewer particles and clusters of characters, as if the original wording of the TPJ as we know it had been improved by editing. We may accept the passage as authentic. It informs us that the time at which sexual intercourse takes place and the woman's fertility are important for intercourse to be successful and lead to procreation.

17. The summary says:

> This section says: Comply with the model of heaven and earth, bring Yin and Yang together, and deliver [both] men and women from grief—then rain will fall in time to make earth fertile, and the king's reign will be peaceful.

This section is short. It lacks the background information about heaven, the missionary project, and the role of Master and disciples that is a standard feature of most sections. It also lacks the set of admonitions that usually concludes a section. The last passage connects it closely with section 41, which is also unusual.

SECTION 43 · How to Promote the Good
and Halt the Wicked

This section provides a concrete example of "heaven-guided" political administration. A general hearing is organized that is meant to unite the local population and government organs in order to isolate any unruly elements that have become active in a neighborhood. It can succeed only if it follows a ritual that corresponds to cosmic patterns. Thus the participants are divided into groups, each of which represents a cosmic force. The groups are seated in a way that reflects cosmic order. This is what we might call a worldly or participant-oriented use of ritual and is in itself an interesting phenomenon. The Celestial Master does not suggest that rituals are a necessary vehicle for understanding or influencing the will of heaven. However, a cosmos-oriented social arrangement is deemed helpful in order to convey heaven's will to men.

This arrangement is enhanced by certain supportive measures, which are dictated by psychological considerations. The measures include the use of wine, the physical isolation of the official in charge, and, most importantly, mechanisms to protect the informant and enhance his status.

The procedures described here come under the heading of communication and flow of information, and they are thus central to the arrival of great peace. Communication, in this case between a low-ranking official and a group of commoners, cannot be taken for granted. It is for cosmic reasons a positive, desirable event, and thus the Master does not hesitate to go into great detail about how to promote it. This account provides an apparently unique insight into the conduct of local government. It proves that certain points of the *taiping* program were rooted in the practical needs of centrally appointed officials of lower rank. For most of their undertakings these officials relied on local individuals willing to cooperate, and thus they could not afford to create a rift between those willing to help and those who were not.

Almost as an afterthought, this section includes an instructive passage on how we may envisage the arrival of great peace and how it is related to the Master's reform program. The arrival of great peace goes through the following stages: for numerological reasons, *qi* of great peace is about to arrive; heaven sends texts with information about this arrival and about the appropriate reform program (at this stage the Master and his disciples are at work); men implement these reforms; the arrival of the *qi* of great peace brings great peace itself. The Celestial Master continues to remind his audience of the difference between the potential of a situation, usually described as a heaven-derived chance for salvation, and its realization through human action.

.   .   .

(43.39) Perfected, step forward. Now if *qi* of great peace were about to arrive, we would wish diligent and good men to prosper and the wicked to become fewer. Thus, what should the administration do if murderers and bandits were to appear?

What do you mean?

Let's say one knows they are in the neighborhood and that the lord who is in charge has become suspicious. Since it is the lord's intention that the good prosper and the wicked become fewer he will try to lay hold of bandits as soon as they step forth.

So what should the administration do?

Now that is what you must tell us.

If the Celestial Master would allow me, I would rather not speak. Not a single word I could say would match the model that you put forth.

Why speak so modestly? Since ancient times the great wise men have not expected perfection in individuals.[1] Even if your words were not appropriate, why be so modest about it?

Yes, I will speak. But what the lord must do is reward the good and punish the wicked. If he clearly defines rewards and punishment,[2] the good will prosper from day to day and the wicked will become fewer.[3]

What you have said is correct. But do we have the names of those to be rewarded or punished?

Although I am not good enough, I have managed to speak once and would rather not speak again. If only the Celestial Master would explain it all! (43.40)

Well, you will be in charge of writing it down and I will tell you everything. The county head[4] proceeds toward the place in question, where he assembles all the villagers.[5] Former officials of higher and lower rank are seated facing east.[6] Men who understand the classics and are of virtuous conduct are seated facing north.[7] Those known to be filial sons or fraternal younger brothers are seated facing west. Diligent farmers[8] are seated in the southeast corner facing northwest. Wicked young men are seated in the southwest facing northeast.[9] The lord himself faces south.

Why must they sit exactly like this?

With each person put in his group, heaven's way is on its proper course, just as men's seating arrangement is appropriate (*shan* 善). Thus it should be easy to lay hold of the bandits.

What do you mean?

Former officials of higher and lower rank represent propriety (*yi* 義).[10] Having retired from office, for reasons of propriety they delight in giving support. Men who understand the classics and are of virtuous conduct (*dao de* 道得) represent understanding (*ming* 明). They hope that their understanding of classical education[11] will help in the detection of wicked elements. Filial sons and fraternal younger brothers represent their home district.[12] The very filial appeal to feelings [of sympathy] to make bandits return home. The filial and fraternal are inclined to constant diligence and respect, as shown during a morning audience. Once plants and beings come to life in the east,[13] they are likely to continue to move forward. The diligent are fit to be in the southeast, since this is the district of prolonging life. Never neglectful, they happily manage all plants and beings. Wicked young men are fit to be in the southwest, which is the district where Yang is decreasing and Yin increasing.[14] So should any wicked person wish to play tricks, punishment for his crimes would be at hand. Since the wicked person is as dexterous as an ape, he is put in a region of decline.

Men facing east, west, and north sit down first, while the diligent[15] and the wicked sit down afterward. Should there be wine, let each man have a cup. Otherwise, good words must be delivered to muster support for the investigation. Once everything is ready, the lord sits down in the space in between, behind locked doors. Called upon one after the other in order of social rank men begin to inform. Each tells his story and reports the name of the gang leader. What is told and reported must, in the end, be coherent.[16] If it is not, the informant is declared guilty. Those who speak incoherently are great liars and will be made known as such. Men who speak coherently will eventually be rewarded and promoted, but not immediately.

Why is this so?

Because it might cause resentment. Should a lord or a father make subordinates or sons resentful, he is neither a merciful father nor a worthy lord. In this way, he eventually drives good men away and the wicked young men who will help local officials to pursue bandits will not be able to capture them and bring their activities to a halt.

Perfected, give these writings to a virtuous lord to show to all men, so that everyone will know what they teach. (43.41) Then the good will go on to prosper, the wicked will become fewer, and bandits and evil plotters will be apprehended.

Excellent, indeed. But why show these writings in advance?

When heaven is about to let it rain, there will certainly first be wind and clouds to let men know. Heaven does this because it wants men to harvest a lot. Since we want to let the good prosper and bring the wicked to a halt, we must show these writings in advance. Now that *qi* of great peace is bound to arrive, there is a fear that by doing evil men might bring their government into disorder. Thus we must create awareness [about the arrival] in advance. The administration must imitate heaven. Heaven does not cover up men's shortcomings, nor did the wise men from early antiquity. We would have to call an administration that did this confused and stupid. It would lead to disaster, in opposition to the intentions of heaven and earth. So we must let men know in advance.

Very well. But why must the lord lock himself behind doors and let those who speak remain outside?

Well, a man about to tell secrets must not himself know his opposite number. If their heads were close together, people on the right and left would know about it, which might cause problems for the speaker. But should the lord and head of a county obtain others' intelligence and allow them to run into problems afterward, we would have to say that he was injuring loyal, faithful, worthy, and honest assistants. No one would be willing to speak up again in the future. The administration is in danger of disorder when intelligence is blocked.[17] Moreover, a lord resembles Yang that lives in Yin, while a subordinate resembles Yin that stays in Yang. When Yin and Yang understand each other, men will be happy to talk, which is bound to bring forth complete trust. This is the model of heaven being as it is.[18] Do you understand a little better?

Yes, I do.

You may go now. Watch your words. This is what is said in the writings that lead to great peace.

Yes.[19]

NOTES

1. This is almost the same wording as at TPJ 41.33.

2. The two missing characters are read as *shang fa* 賞 罰 (rewards and punishment).

3. As often, the disciple's answer here is a commonsense reply, in this case resembling the dominant, Legalist-oriented policy.

4. *Zhang* (chief) or *zhang li* 長 吏 (see *Han shu* 19A *"Bai guan gong qing biao"* 百 官 公 卿 表, p. 742; Loewe 1967, vol. 2, p. 57) is the title of the head of a county, that is, the lowest centrally installed official (Bielenstein 1980: 100). The term can also be used as a general designation for the leader of a hamlet (*tian zhai* 田 宅) or suburb (*cheng guo* 城 郭), as elsewhere in the TPJ (p. 699, *Chao,* part 8), but the proceedings described in the passage at hand strike me as being a little too formal for such a person. Also, it is mentioned that the official travels to the neighborhood, which means that he does not reside there.

5. Throughout the TPJ, the relationship between government and population is one of mutual dependency, quite in line with general political theory, although the TPJ deals with the needs of the population in more detail than the needs of the ruler. Taxes, the fighting of wars, and labor service, which originate with the ruler and play a big role in the classical thinkers' list of complaints, are not mentioned, while poverty, epidemics, violence, poor harvests, and untimely death are mentioned. These are problems that cannot be tackled by traditional political reform, and mentioning them thus opens the way for measures oriented toward great peace. The ruler is expected to give wealth to the people and to look after their needs (cf. section 41, above, and 44, below; see also TPJ 100.228), but this is not done simply through a reduction of taxes. On the other hand, the people's loyalty is also expected to be quite intensive in that they must search for drugs and recipes to help their ruler live a long time (TPJ 63.133).

Since the achievement of great peace is a joint project, communication between different political strata is an important issue. The flow of information in person described in this section is exceptional, necessitated by an emergency. The regular channel for such communication is writings (see Kaltenmark 1979: 27–29). The main difficulty in both cases is how to distinguish between true and false information. Truth, as the Celestial Master argues, can be gathered from quantity: "One cannot trust the words of one man" (TPJ 106.279; cf. Kaltenmark 1979: 27). Thus there is a formalistic way of establishing how much truth a report contains: a report handed in by one person is not true at all (TPJ 127.326), while a report handed in by ten people is most trustworthy (TPJ

127.327). The "wait-and-see" method is another option for determining truth. Individuals whose report has not been proven false over a period of three years must be rewarded with office (TPJ 65.152; 81.206; cf. Hachiya 1983: 53). This method also plays a role in section 43, where it is argued that information should be rewarded only after a certain period of time has elapsed. Since a larger number of reports guarantees more truth, the Celestial Master demands there be a network throughout the country for the official collection of written material; this should include the border regions, thus allowing barbarians to contribute as well (TPJ 129.333). At this point the demands of the scripture seem to be in agreement with the historical reality of early Daoist movements (cf. Stein 1963). The material thus collected is to be officially sorted out and compiled into a single document, which will then be distributed among the people. The individual contributors will in this case be known by name and can be rewarded.

Another major problem in all communication between officials and ordinary subjects is the need to protect informants. This difficulty is addressed in clear terms with regard to written communication. Informants are advised to leave their own hamlet, district (*xiang ting* 鄉亭), county, commandery, and even province and deliver their reports elsewhere in order to avoid the threats and intervention of local officials, notwithstanding that heavy punishments are to be applied against such officials should they interfere (TPJ 127.317).

Takahashi (1986: 259 and 263f.) has argued that the social issues the TPJ deals with are always, as in this section, related to a small rural community, while the institutions and policies of central government are ignored. There is certainly a contrast between a missionary doctrine that links in true chiliastic style the fate of humankind to worldwide socio-religious reforms and the concrete implementation of these reforms, which a devoted group of adepts can best initiate locally. The regionally enforced interdiction of infanticide (see section 42) attests to the limited range to which administrative constraints confined such reforms.

6. Officials who had retired from central government positions did in fact play a role in local affairs, judging by their sponsorship of certain local projects; see Ebrey 1980: 351f.

7. The virtue of "understanding" (*ming* 明) is associated with the south: "In the south is the great Yang; it [resembles] the ruler's full understanding" (TPJ 105.264).

8. The two groups mentioned here correspond to groups in the Han social structure. "Filial sons" and "fraternal brothers" were on various occasions locally selected, presented with bales of silk, and exempted from taxes and labor service. They were a group from whom local government representatives would recommend candidates for office in the central government. *Tian jia jin zi* 佃家僮子 is another name for the *li tian* 力田 (outstanding farmers), who were of a slightly lower rank than the "filial and fraternal" but who enjoyed similar privileges; see Hsu 1980: 24–25; 170–71. For an alternative understanding see Kaltenmark 1979: 32, where a rendering of the whole passage on which much of what is presented here relies can also be found.

9. Several groups in a list of ten that has been transmitted in the *Chao* resemble groups in the passage at hand. The purpose of organizing the population into ten groups is said to be social order and coherence, which is similar to the purpose behind the formation of groups in the passage at hand:

> "Ten groups" *(lü)* is the method of the worthy and wise of the past, who wanted men to be good and prevent them from robbing and injuring each other, so that they could fulfill their natural life span. (TPJ p. 302, *Chao*, part 5)

The first is the "group of great kindness, piety, and obedience," who excel in the art of what is as it is (*ziran zhi shu* 自然之術), which they have understood without having learned it:

> They act in agreement with heaven's intentions and further earth's wishes. Above they benefit emperors and kings; below they make the people prosperous. (TPJ p. 301, *Chao*, part 5)

The second group are "the great learned [*rou* 柔 (weak) meaning *ru* 儒] who understand morality" (*ming dao de da ru* 明道德大儒). This group resembles the second group in section 43. The third is the "group of the filial and fraternal who are starting to learn how to become better men" (*xiao di shi xue hua shan* 孝第始學化善): they avoid what is wrong and manage to be "upright" and "humane" (*zheng* 正; *ren* 仁); this group is equal to the "filial and fraternal" of section 43. The fourth are the "group of diligent farmers," that is, *tian jia jin li zi* 佃家僅力子, similar to group 4 in the section at hand:

> They are at work by sunrise, and with sunset they rest. They don't shun hard labor, which has continuous returns. They are courteous at home, nurture their father and mother, obtain the products of their soil, conform to the way of heaven, do not dare to do evil, and are of benefit to the county office. (TPJ p. 302, *Chao*, part 5)

The fifth is "the group of people largely without benevolence, young folk without propriety, who like to use weapons and devise schemes," resembling the last group of section 43. The other five groups have nothing at all to recommend them.

10. The former officials sit in the west, the position of small Yang:

> Small Yang is a subordinate, who is brought into shape [*qu zhe* 屈折 (bent)] by propriety. Since small Yang obeys the great Yang, it is formed as metal is by fire before men find it useful. The subordinate is always brought into shape by propriety before a lord sees him as a useful assistant. (See TPJ 105.264 and cf. Luo 1996: 473 for the rendering of this passage)

11. *Jing dao* 經道 serves as an acronym for *ming jing dao de* 明經道德, used previously.

12. The east is where the sun and all beings come from: "So the east is small Yang. It is the place where a ruler begins his life. Thus the sun rises in the east" (TPJ 105.263f.). Yu (2001a: 49) wants to replace *ben* 本 with *mu* 木 (wood), which would put more stress than intended on cosmic order.

13. "Therefore the east likes to give life" (TPJ 105.262). For the sequence of the four directions, see below, section 53.

14. "So the southeast is Yang and the northwest Yin" (TPJ 105.271). Section 105 refers to the *Yi jing* for detailed explanations (TPJ 105.272–74).

15. The text reads *bu jin* 不僅 (not diligent), which is the opposite of the *jin zi* 僅子 mentioned earlier. The creation of yet another social group, not mentioned earlier in the general setup, is not plausible. Therefore, *bu* is emended to *fu* 夫. The error might be based on content. For the "diligent" and the "wicked" to receive equal treatment does not look right.

16. If "coherent" is the correct understanding of *xiang ying* 相應, what is described here would be a more sophisticated way of establishing the truth than the methods mentioned above. The passage could, of course, also mean nothing more than that the outcome proves a certain informant right. Long (2000: 92) argues that the coherence between a person's words and his acts is at stake. This ignores the fact that the issue is reporting a crime committed by others.

17. This is a frequently expressed worry: "Cut emperors and kings off from the flow of intelligence and you make them suffer bitterly" (TPJ 127.318). They are thus deprived of their chance of receiving vital information:

> When majestic heaven sends calamities, anomalies, and disasters, they don't necessarily always happen in the palaces of emperors and kings, on the premises of the county office, or in front of its head. Calamities, disasters, and other irregular events are always first noticed by the people, who live in the wide, open land. But, out of respect for their magistrate, the lowly and dejected who know about them first do not dare say anything. The magistrate, out of respect for his lord, doesn't dare speak. As a result, they interrupt what heaven and earth have to tell. Since all these men wish to praise the county head and give him an excellent name, they make his achievements look great and his removal despicable. So they lose sight of proper conduct (*wu dao* 無道), conceal the calamities, anomalies, disasters, and other irregular events in heaven and on earth, and don't let news of them reach emperors and kings, who, through no fault of their own, are cut off, lack intelligence and don't understand what heaven and earth want. Their reign is then at risk of disorder. Stability is difficult to achieve. They suffer bitterly because of this. (TPJ 127.320f.)

18. When the Celestial Master uses the expression *tian ziran* 天自然, he means that a particular statement is not grounded in anything else; in the passage at hand it means that the relationship between Yang and Yin is not derived from any other cosmic entity; see also below, section 53.

19. The summary says:

> This section explains how to promote the good and to bring the wicked to a halt; to gain intelligence; to apprehend robbers and bandits; to obtain men who are loyal and trustworthy.

The translation here is more tentative than usual.

· How to Preserve
the Three Essentials

This section reads like an exegesis of Laozi's political thought. In proclaiming that there are only three human needs, it follows the fundamentalist approach of *Laozi* 81.[1] To fulfill these needs means to preserve life. Should men ignore them the world would come to an end. This position was not as unrefuted as one might suppose. It contradicts outright Confucius's dictum about the respective importance of food, weapons, and ethics. He thought food irrelevant because men die anyway. Although these needs play a role in deciding government policy and evaluating its outcome— the people, of course, have to be fed, clothed, and enabled to raise a family—they were of little concern for political philosophy. The needs that were mentioned in ancient sources—for instance, food in the *Hong fan* 's "eight government objectives" (*ba zheng* 八 政), and agriculture and sericulture in Xun Yue's "five administrative tasks"[2]—did not include the specifically Daoist item of sexual relations.

Following what is said in the Laozi, the TPJ authors argue that to concentrate properly on these needs means to exclude and give up all activities not directly linked to them. The demand to fulfill the three needs is phrased as a prohibition of the search for everything else. Such a search would result in moral depravity—called "deception" and "jealousy"—which is bound to create social and political chaos. The Master argues that the disciple is thus deceived when he thinks that we need everything that is of some use.

What is not basic, and is therefore evil, includes luxurious garments (Confucius joined in condemning these), luxury items in general, and, in particular, all policies and regulations. Concern for the three needs thus becomes synonymous with government through nonaction by a ruler not involved in administrative routine. It is also synonymous with the process of return and reversal, which is promoted in the *Laozi* as the only way to practice *dao*.

•   •   •

(44.42) Perfected, step forward.

Yes.

How many big needs are there in what men do in this world? How many small needs? And how many conditions, although not needs, have an impact on the growth of misfortune and disaster? Collect your thoughts, Perfected, to tell all.

Yes, I will. Truly, what is on one's mind one must not dare to hide.

Speak up.

In all affairs of this world what is of use is needed and what is not of use is not needed.

What you have said sounds all right but is quite wrong. I want to hear what is forever needed and must not be done away with; something without which the men who live in this world would be annihilated and the patterns of heaven turn into a cluster (*bing he* 并合) so that nothing to be named would be left.[3] Something such as this can be considered a great need. What you have just mentioned agrees somehow with what people want for the present but that will in the long run lead to a point from which misfortune and disaster develop.

Step forward, Perfected.[4] I would like to know from you what is always needed and must never be put aside.[5]

If only the Celestial Master were to speak in detail and give us his analysis and explanation. I am foolish and my efforts have failed. I have said the wrong thing once. I don't dare speak again.

Well, it is as you say. Let someone who knows do the talking. If we were to force someone who doesn't know to talk, he might find it exhausting. You cannot force men to know what they don't grasp, be it big or small. (44.43) There is no problem once they have grasped it, but it's not easy if they haven't.

This is the reason why you must please enlighten this shallow, ignorant, and incapable pupil. Please introduce me to the basics!

Yes, I will. Listen. The world has two big needs and one that is smaller. None of the rest is needed since it serves only to oppress[6] men's ears and eyes, being good for the moment but inviting misfortune in the long term. It exhausts men and makes them dejected.

What do you mean?

How foolish you are! Well, when man first came to life in this world he was part of heaven and earth. He embraced primordial *qi* in a state of being as he was *(ziran).*[7] Thus he neither drank nor ate but stayed alive through exhaling and inhaling the *qi* of Yin and Yang. He did not know hunger and thirst. In the course of time, man distanced himself from the way of the spirits[8] and gradually lost direction. So the latter-born never reached understanding. The true doctrine *(dao)* was hollowed out and became more and more deceptive. This brought about hunger and thirst. Men would die unless they drank and ate. This is the first great need. Since heaven and earth felt friendly concern, they made drink and food for them. So men drank and ate.

Heaven's dispensation consists of Yin and Yang. It must be continued. One must not interrupt the dispensation of heaven and earth. To make them continue one must imitate heaven and earth in being Yin as well as Yang. (44.44) For this reason heaven put forth one male and one female, who then produced offspring after having loved each other.

Why exactly one Yin and one Yang?

Yang at its high point begins to give rise to Yin, and Yin at its high point begins to give rise to Yang. Thus the two procreate each other, just as something that is extremely cold turns into something hot, and something that is extremely hot becomes cold. This is the technique of what is as it is.[9] Therefore, they can over a long period give birth to each other and for generations avoid any interruption to the dispensations of heaven and earth. Should male and female not get hold of each other, reproduction would immediately be interrupted. In a world without men, how could there be man and wife, father and son, lord and subordinate, teacher and student?[10] How could one bring forth and govern the other? If there were no males and females between heaven and earth, how could there be procreation? From being alone comes emptiness *(kong* 空 *)*. This is the second great need.

Thus, it is through Yin and Yang that we carry on the dispensation of heaven and of earth and don't let them become completely exhausted. [Only through Yin and Yang] can lord and subordinate control the disorder in their realms and can wise teachers and their disciples preside over the promulgation of heaven's teachings and thus assist emperors and kings in reforming *(hua* 化 *)* the world. Since all this depends on drink and food and the love between man and woman, both are great needs.

Through cold and heat, heaven's way would kill half of all men if they did not cover themselves. Thus, heaven has created the ten thousand plants and beings for men to use as clothes. But without clothes, they would live in caves and hidden grottoes where desolation would strike half of them dead. They would not be completely wiped out. This is what we call half a need.

The "great needs" that heaven's way has set up concern extinction and death. No other need is more urgent. But without clothes, men cannot drink and eat, make love, and do good deeds. Thus clothes promote worthiness, while their lack furthers bad conduct. So clothes are meant only to protect against harm. This is why the wise and worthy of old were not keen on precious garments made of dark and yellow silk.

Drinking, eating, and the mixing of Yin and Yang must not be interrupted. If they are, the world will inevitably be without men. All you need to do in order to fulfill your natural life span and continue heaven's dispensation is to safeguard these three, so that when one dies another will begin, without end. This is why the wise men of antiquity reigned with these three in mind. They did not see the rest as a need and thus they abolished all causes for disaster and misfortune.

What do you mean?

These three needs correspond to the course of nature (*tian xing* 天行): man resembles heaven, woman earth, and clothes are a means of support.[11] If we look at heaven and earth as father and mother, they support and nourish man's body. All other man-made things are superfluous, not necessary for maintaining life and procreating the species. (44.45) Instead, they lead to much deception and jealousy. They prevent the reign of peace and the arrival of majestic *qi*. They disorder heaven's way and leave the lord deeply worried. Each man takes delight in what his feelings[12] approve of. Quite unrestrained, he is intent only on continuing the fun. This is the reason why men meet with misfortune: the lord loses political authority and the small man turns to robbery and other misconduct. All this happens because things for which there is no need are in demand.

Thus the world experiences poverty and distress, and becomes desolate and wretched. Calamities and mutations occur all the time. Subordinates are eager[13] to deceive their superiors. Everyone considers this harmful. (44.46) It began a long time ago and is not just the fault of men, who live nowadays in the times of late antiquity.[14] When men inherit and transmit these evils, they forget their original and true state.[15] By indulging in what is frivolous and superficial they bring desolation and harm upon themselves and can't finish the years heaven has designed for them. The many activities latter-born men are involved in are needless and risky. So men are always in a rush, unable to come to a halt.[16]

By conducting affairs through nonaction, men understood *dao*'s meaning in early antiquity.[17] They safeguarded the root and never neglected the three needs. Thus did they achieve heaven's intentions. In middle antiquity, there were slightly too many activities and embellishments.[18] In late antiquity, men [began to] worry far too much. Much embellishment has brought forth corruption and fraud. Furthermore, men cause distress by trying to outdo each other, and they let corruption and jealousy arise in their midst. Within, they have lost their true state (*shi* 實) and departed from their root, which in turn has become damaged, leaving men confused and disorderly. A lord might feel desolate and wish to put it right, but the many hundreds of thousands of embellishments can't be overcome and they [continue] to bring disorder to his reign. Perfected, you must thoroughly consider what this means.

Yes, indeed, I will![19]

NOTES

1. In the title to this section, *ji* 急 (need) is replaced by *shi* 實 (essential), probably because of the unusual meaning attached to *ji* in this section.

2. See *Shen jian* 1 "*Zheng ti*" 政體, p. 2.

3. For this use of *ming zi* 名字 see TPJ 131.340. The passage must be seen in relation to what is said later in this section on the need to maintain life before one can maintain order.

4. This second invitation to participate in the talk seems to be superfluous. Elsewhere the phrase is of some structural relevance, when it is used in the course of a section rather than at the start. It then introduces a new question (TPJ 103.253 and 254; 129.334) or a summary of the preceding talk (TPJ 46.52; 103.252). It is a stylistic device occurring in some parts of the text—section 103 is three times thus interrupted—and rarely used in others.

5. This use of the interrogative *shui* 誰 as "what" is rare.

6. The term *yan* 厭 (to oppress) is used in Buddhist terminology for the aspect of the world that wearies the believer and from which he seeks deliverance. The deadly risk created by too much sense stimulation is well expressed in the section "Give importance to life" (*gui sheng* 貴生) in the *Lü shi chun qiu*.

7. In the TPJ, *ziran* 自然 (what is as it is) is of very high rank, as in *Laozi* 25. Here the text agrees with Yan Zun's (first-century B.C.E.) understanding of the *Laozi*'s ontological stratification (see Robinet 1977: 14; Jin 1997: 417–21), for instance, as opposed to the *Xiang'er*, which in annotating *Laozi* 25 raises *dao* to equal rank with *ziran*. This indicates that the Celestial Master sees little need to stress *dao*'s role as a cosmic force. For

him, *dao* seems to work in the more indirect way of providing the explanation for correlations and thus social and cosmic coherence.

In cosmogonic order, *ziran* follows directly after primordial *qi* (*yuan qi* 元氣):

> Primordial *qi* is Yang and in control of giving life. What is as it is causes change (*hua* 化); it is Yin and is in charge of nourishing all beings and things. (TPJ p. 220, *Chao,* part 4)

> When primordial *qi* and what is as it is are pleased they will together bring forth heaven and earth, and when these two are happy Yin and Yang will be in harmony and wind and rain will cooperate. When this is the case, they will let the twelve thousand plants and beings grow. (TPJ pp. 647f., *Chao,* part 7; cf. Li 1984).

This order is implied rather than explained or expressed in detail:

> When primordial *qi* is pleased, it brings forth great prosperity. When what is as it is is joyful, beings and objects are strong. When heaven is happy, the three luminaries are bright. When earth is pleased, harvest results (*cheng* 成) are constant. (TPJ p. 13, *Chao,* part 2)

These passages show that *ziran*'s cosmogonic rank manifests itself when it helps to order the cosmos:

> Once you have completed the *dao* of what is as it is, what would not be complete? What would not have been converted *(hua)*? Everyone welcomes it. Isn't this [like] the generosity of heaven's being what it is *(tian ziran)*? (TPJ 195.602, layer B)

Hence the need to safeguard and enact (TPJ 179.533, layer B) *ziran* and not to lose it (TPJ 168.472, layer C). It can be brought about through perfecting *dao* (TPJ 83.211). With its help, the people rule over themselves (TPJ p. 25, *Chao,* part 2) and gain longevity (TPJ p. 728, *Chao,* part 1). Nothing is superior to it (TPJ p. 193, *Chao,* part 4). When the different species are what they are, they are satisfied (TPJ 72.175). People knew this in the past (TPJ 73.178). This is the sense in which the term is used in this section. Emulating *ziran* was the lifestyle of humankind when it was young. In the days of outgoing antiquity, however, only certain individuals can achieve it, through study.

What happens through *ziran* 自然 happens of its own accord, "spontaneously," independently of outside stimuli. This is the meaning of "the method (*shu* 術; or the "model" or "example" [*fa* 法]) of what is as it is," a term that abounds in the text in reference to what is naturally so. It always carries a positive value. Wang Chong uses the term to arrive at a clear distinction between what we might call natural processes and men's actions (*Lun heng* 54 "*Ziran*"). He argues that heaven produces food spontaneously, not from benevolent concern for mankind, since benevolence is a human quality. This is in contrast to the Celestial Master's understanding of *ziran*, whereby this "method" does not exclude family relations between heaven, earth, and men.

8. The *Yi jing* (hexagram 20, p. 14) defines *shen dao* 神道 as a way of government by which the ruler relies on instructions deriving from the course of nature.

9. Joseph Needham (1962: 63) shows that the reasons behind the development of heat

and cold were unknown anywhere in the world before modern science. The explanation given here is quite systematic.

10. These four relations are indeed basic for the social life envisaged by the Celestial Master. It is no accident that they differ from the five relations introduced in the *Mengzi* (3A.4), where the relationship between husband and wife is relegated to third place, after that between father and son and ruler and subordinate, and where the relationship between teacher and disciple is not mentioned.

11. This passage uses the similarity between *yi* (clothes) and *yi* with the radical for "man" 依, meaning "to support."

12. The *liu qing* 六情 (six feelings, or conditions) are love, anger, hatred, pleasure, joy, and sadness; see *Han shu* 75.3168 (Yi Feng's 翼奉 biography).

13. With Yu 2001a: 53, *ji* 極 (ridgepole) is corrected to *ji* 亟 (hastily).

14. The present in which the Master and disciples live is the period of outgoing antiquity. *Xia gu* or *jin xia gu* 今下古 is used in this sense throughout the text's layer A, that is, throughout the dialogues between Master and disciples. The disciples are expected to show the Celestial Master's works to the "men of outgoing antiquity" (TPJ 63.141; pp. 646 and 691, *Chao*, part 7 and 8) to make them think about it (TPJ 131.347; 191.589) and understand heaven's *dao* (TPJ 212.676); the men of outgoing antiquity must remember what the Celestial Master has said (TPJ 66.167). These men are in greater need of instruction because they are worse off than were their predecessors, whose evil deeds they have inherited (TPJ 153.427 and section 48). They are therefore foolish (TPJ 131.359; 191.589), find fault with true *dao* (TPJ 141.401; 155.436), and are difficult to govern (TPJ 152.419).

This use of early, middle, and, in particular, late antiquity is not that of the *Li ji* and the *Han shu* as quoted Morohashi (1985) no. 12.494, where early antiquity is represented by Fu Xi, middle antiquity by Shen Nong or King Wen, and late antiquity by the Five Emperors or Confucius. This usage in the TPJ runs counter to the standard use of *gu* for the past as opposed to the present, *jin*. It adds an anachronistic touch to the dialogues in that it seems to incorporate the perspective of a later observer. However, if interpreted from within the Celestial Master's view of history the term refers to the expectation that the old world will come to an end with the arrival of great peace. This approach is similar to the Yellow Turbans' announcement that in future heaven, which used to be blue, would turn yellow (see the Introduction, above).

15. This resembles what is said in the *Mengzi* (6A.8) about Ox Mountain.

16. To run is an image of urgency:

> Heaven on its way *(dao)* can be at leisure or in an urgent hurry (*ji* 急), just as man in his actions can be. When heaven is in a hurry wind, rain, thunder, and lightning come all at once, and when it is urgent men on their way *(dao)* will run and get there in no time. (TPJ p. 687, *Chao*, part 8)

17. Early antiquity is said to have been the period of the Three Majestic Rulers (TPJ 63.139; 167.468), also called *shang* ("supreme," or perhaps "earliest") *san huang* 上三皇

(TPJ 78.192; 155.435). In one instance, the Three Majestic Rulers are said to have been of middle antiquity, while in early antiquity, men were ruled without the use of texts (TPJ 81.205f.). The Three Majestic Rulers were followed by the Five Emperors, Three Kings, and Five Hegemons (TPJ 63.140; 102.237). However, these figures don't occur often, and names are never attributed to them. The common *taiping* way of viewing history is to distinguish early, middle, and late antiquity. The following observation is one way to characterize the three ages:

> The wise and worthy of early antiquity (*shang gu sheng xian* 上 古 聖 賢) resided in palaces, the scholars of middle antiquity (*zhong shi* 中 士) reached transcendence in the mountains, and the scholars of late antiquity (*xia shi* 下 士) are dying among the people as if they were insects. (TPJ p. 309, *Chao*, part 5)

A return to early antiquity is equated with a conversion to *taiping* principles, as pointed out in full detail by Kamitsuka (1999: 303–8). The appearance of evil practices was a historical process in all fields: it can be seen in government policies regarding the use of punishment (TPJ 63.139; 64.143; 81.206), and it can be seen in patterns of behavior (TPJ 48.61; 101.232; 105.268). It can also be seen in the spread of heresies (TPJ p. 650, *Chao*, part 7), the corruption of texts (TPJ 47.56), the practice of infanticide (TPJ 41.36), the promotion of chastity (TPJ 42.37), and the shortening of life (TPJ 155.436f.). The length of this process points to the difficulties ahead. There was a deterioration from early and middle antiquity onward (TPJ 42.37; 110.295, layer B). The continued effort of Master and disciples is thus required to reverse attitudes that have taken so long to mature.

18. "Embellishments" (*duan* 端) (see also sections 45 and 53) stand in the way of safeguarding the one:

> It is possible to know ten thousand embellishments. But with knowing so much, one can't know the one. Only through guarding the one can one transcend the world (*du shi* 度 世). (From *Secret Advice by the Wise Lord of the Scripture on Great Peace;* see TPJ p. 743)

19. The summary says:

> This section says: If you safeguard three essentials, the *qi* of peace arrives, deception and fraud go away, and villainy and knavery are cut off.

This does not touch on the central issue of the section, which is the need to cut out what is not essential.

· The Three Needs and the
Method of [Dealing with]
Auspicious and Ominous Events

The Master argues that the lives and growth of animals and plants might be at risk
should what is necessary be neglected and accessories become overbearing. The fact
that human beings are in the same situation as the fauna and flora around them lends
strength to the warning issued in section 44: disaster beckons should human endeavors go beyond what men need to stay alive.

It is argued that the damage—that is, the promotion of superfluous objects and
activities—has already been done. Safeguarding the three needs requires reversing
this tendency. This is, as the Master put it, an issue of understanding: concern for
what is superfluous impinges on proper understanding. Understanding must thus
be restored through a definitive move from one polar entity to its opposite. This is
expressed through the metaphor of turning from the branches to the root, a move
that is seen as leading in a backward direction. The Master's words resemble the advice given by *Laozi* when it talks about turning back, for instance to childhood, in
order to restore one's energy. Going backwards also has a chronological aspect and
involves a departure from the decadence of the present, called "late antiquity," and
a return to the attitudes of early antiquity.

No proper insight can be expected when understanding is impeded, so when ob-
sessed with the "branches" men are bound to make the wrong decisions. This point
must have been of particular importance for the TPJ editors. The title of the section points to the problem of deciding what to do and what to avoid, although little space is reserved for it in the text.

(45.46) Perfected, step forward. How many big and how many small needs do animals have? How much is there that is not a need?

Well, each has its own needs, as if there were a thousand branches and ten thousand ramifications. (45.47)

What do we call these needs?

Each animal has its own aim; we can't give them names.

It is a shame you are so stupid! You were foolish before, but it has become worse!

I am no good.

If *you* call yourself no good, what are we supposed to say when common men go astray? This is *really* being no good!

If the Celestial Master would only explain things to me, foolish and dumb as I am!

Well, all animals live as men do, in the dispensation of heaven and earth and Yin and Yang. They also share the same needs—two big ones and one that is smaller.

What do you mean?

When animals first received the dispensation of Yin and Yang, they all exhaled and inhaled, took in the *qi* of what is as it is, and did not yet know eating and drinking. In the course of time, when they moved away from their root, great *dao* began to shrink and heaven's *qi* could no longer watch over them, so they became hungry and thirsty. Thus, heaven provided them with drink and food. It also became necessary to continue the dispensation of Yin and Yang. So there are male and female animals, and generation after generation they continue to bring forth offspring. If one cut off their food and drink, and if they were to not reproduce by mixing Yin and Yang, then the world would be without animals. These are the two big needs.

There is one small need. Animals have hair, feathers, or scales, but certain naked worms also survive. However, with hair or feathers animals are much more attractive (*ke ai* 可愛) and can withstand cold and heat. With scales, they withstand all injury. Since they are not necessary for maintaining life, hair, feathers, and scales amount to a small need. All other elements invite misfortune.[1] It is senseless and unreasonable not to preserve these three roots. Those who do so will die from it. That this is so (*ziran* 自然) is proclaimed by the model set up by heaven and earth. You must think about what it means and maintain these three original activities so that you will be where harmony (*zhonghe* 中和) prevails between heaven and earth.

Should there be much embellishment instead of these three [activities], we would all suffer disaster.

Excellent! I would beg to ask one question about what you have just said.

Go ahead.

Now, things that spread roots[2] and suspend branches do not eat, drink, or wear clothes. What then?

Oh no! Instead of learning more each day, you know less and less.[3]

Why do you say that?

[Plants] also have two big needs and one that is smaller.

What do you mean?

Listen carefully.

Yes, I will.

The ten thousand plants (*wan wu* 萬物) need rain to live. This is what they drink and eat. They must have day and night and they must be in the sun and in the shade. During the day, Yang's *qi* warms them; at night, Yin's *qi* gives them moisture. Thus they can grow by just staying where they are. This is how they unite Yin and Yang. They suspend their branches and spread out their leaves—these are their clothes. Some plants grow with many leaves, others with few. Here lies for them [the difference between] substance and decoration.[4] (45.48) Should rain not fall at the right time, the world's ten thousand plants would not grow. It would be a great disaster if the world were without one of its plants. So [rain] is a great need. Should [plants] not have the alternation between day and night to unite the *qi* of Yin and Yang, nothing would ripen. It would be a great disaster if the world were without the produce of plants. This is another great need. Plants with sparse foliage bear fruit, and so do plants with dense foliage. Since they all bear fruit, having many leaves is not a necessity. So [leaves] are a small need, while produce is the main thing.

Therefore, the wise men of old who preserved the three essentials (*san shi* 三實) brought great peace to their reign, found favor with heaven, and lived long and happily until they completed the years heaven had destined for them. Substance is enough; embellishments and the use of precious garments of dark and yellow silk are not necessary. For this reason, should you be intrigued by the branches, turn back to the center. Should you be intrigued by the center, then turn back to the root. Should decorum (*wen* 文) fascinate you, turn back to substance. Should substance interest you, turn back to the basis. What is basic has the same origin as heaven and earth. Should someone's vision while conducting affairs become confused by [the situation] in late antiquity, let him return his thoughts to middle antiquity. If this confuses him, he should think of early antiquity. Should this irritate him, let him think back to the rules and models proclaimed by heaven and earth. If he doubts their [validity] he will have to go as far back as the shape of what is as it is. If what is as it is gives rise to doubt, one must let one's thoughts return to supreme, primordial, numinous *qi*.[5]

Thus, in antiquity the wise and worthy reigned by drinking and eating *qi*, sat deep in the dark chamber[6] to think of *dao*, took note of the symptoms of gain and loss,[7] and did not dare depart by as much as the space taken up by a small silver coin from the models set up by heaven. Remaining pure and quiet sufficed to fulfill their intention. Their reign set up peace, just like heaven and earth. If you would only ponder the words I teach! You know, don't you?

Splendid!

All right, now that you have understood, adapt my writings to the quelling of disorder. Try them out at once, without delay. Don't hide this text; let all men see for themselves that substance and decoration have lost their proper place. Let men ponder the text's meaning. They must return to the Three Perfected [residing in their body],[8] so that they will not suffer bitterly from wicked fabrications (*xie wei* 邪 偽). Keep this in mind.

Yes, I will.[9]

NOTES

1. Here the Celestial Master, aiming for the creation of and adherence to structural parallelism, puts forth an absurd statement.

2. This expression is also used to refer to plants in TPJ 209.669.

3. This does not follow the *Laozi*'s (48) understanding of the growth of knowledge.

4. *Zhi wen* 質 文 (substance and decorum) are *Lun yu* terms (6.18 and 12.8); it is Confucius's point of view that a person needs both. "Decorum" is here used in the sense of an inferior quality, as explained below. The "substance" in plants is the produce.

5. This is as close as the TPJ gets to discussing the conditions of knowledge. The problem is approached from several angles, working with modified opposites. The first supposition uses the image of a plant and says that the root explains the center and the center the branches. The second is structured in a parallel mode reaching from basis (*gen* 根) to substance and then decorum. The third arranges historical periods as early, middle, and late antiquity, for the sake of proper government. The last and most abstract approach involves the ontological entities primordial *qi*, *ziran*, and the models set up by heaven and earth. Throughout the text, as in the paragraph that follows, this last ap-

proach is seen as the most accurate way of understanding, as is the case in much of the *Zhuangzi* (in particular chap. 4 *"Ren xian shi"* 仁 聞 世; see Graham 1989: 198).

Shang yuan ling qi 上 元 靈 氣 is used here as another, more decorative, and perhaps also more practice-oriented word for *yuan qi*. The expression *shang yuan* is used for "first," as, for instance, for the first of three sexagenary cycles. *Ling qi* occurs in the quietist chapters of the *Guanzi* (chap. 49 *"Nei ye"* 內 業, p. 272; cf. Rickett 1965: 168: "the subtle breath of life") and is used in this sense in Daoist material. See, for example, quotations from the *Zi xu yuan jun neizhuan* 紫 虛 元 君 內 傳 (*Yunji qiqian* 41.1b), which state that *ling qi* can be obtained through external and internal purification ("washing"). An identical statement can be found in *Yunji qiqian* 33.7a, quoting Sun Simiao's 孫 思 邈 (581–682?) *She yang zhen zhong fang* 攝 養 枕 中 方.

6. To do this properly amounts to good government; see above, section 41.

7. "Using such ways of thinking [as analyzing seasonal changes] the wise kings of old carefully examined symptoms of gain and loss" (TPJ p. 17, *Chao*, part 2). They were, in other words, expert practitioners of prognostics. As the *Jing fa* (p. 1) puts it:

> Misfortune and good luck arrive in the same way. We don't know where from. The only way to know this lies in emptiness and nothingness (*xu wu* 虛 無).

8. The *san zhen* 三 真 are body deities, perhaps among the most high ranking: see Andersen 1980: 5, translating the *Ziyang zhenren neizhuan* (p. 6a), which was "revealed" to Hua Qiao in 399 C.E. There, the three are said to be the infant (*chi zi* 赤 子), the perfected (*zhen ren* 真 人), and the child (*ying er* 嬰 兒). The expression *san zhen* is common in later material on meditation; cf. *Yunji qiqian*, chapters 42–44. I have not been able to find it in earlier material. This has probably tempted Luo (1996: 84) and Long (2000: 106) to replace *zhen* with *shi* (essential) as used in the preceding paragraph. Since textual criticism applied now can only hope to restore the sixth-century original, there does not seem to be a need to correct the wording. We may accept it as one of the few examples where the sixth-century editors' own usage of terms entered into their work on the old text.

9. The summary says:

> This section explains how the ten thousands plants and beings safeguard the root, and how they are happy when obtaining the three needs and come to harm when they lose them.

This section deals with funerary rituals and the ancestral cult. It argues that men suffer from the increasing presence of demons brought about by lavish sacrifices. Such a presence bodes evil because daytime and the walkways of life belong to the living. Should demons be about, their deadly qualities will cause illness and early death. The Master gives cosmological reasons for this: Life, Yang, and the sun must not be overpowered by death, Yin, and the night sky. Men must not be misled by filial piety to trespass against this rule and allow the love they feel for their parents to upset the cosmic balance. This is expressed in the rule that parents must not be served with more care when they are deceased than while they were alive.

While arguing his point, the Celestial Master conveys what knowledge there is about life after death. The two dialogues combined in this section introduce conflicting models. One depicts the dead as continuing to exist and as influencing and being influenced by their progeny. The dead are said to be responsible for their deeds still, to face interrogations, and to be in a state of happiness or anxiety. This model is used throughout the TPJ to enforce allegiance to moral rules, as one's deeds in life are expected to throw a shadow over the existence to come. Another model, which is consistent with Wang Chong's view, regards demons as fictitious. These models are contradictory, but they are both well within the framework of Han dynasty opinions about death. The aim of this section is not to determine the truth about the existence of demons, but rather to persuade men to focus on life and the living rather than on serving the dead. Both models provide good arguments for a reduction in the scope of rituals and offerings.

The gist of this argument follows mainstream Han dynasty concerns. Emperors were known to be advocates for thriftiness. Guangwu (r. 26–57), for example, claimed, "All the world thinks that rich burials are honorable and thrifty funerals disgraceful. Thus the rich vie with each other in their extravagance, whereas the poor spend their entire fortune."[1] However, it was as fashionable to ignore such complaints as it was to lament funeral expenses. Liang Shang 梁商, the father-in-law of Emperor Shun (r. 125–44), demanded that no special food should be used for the sacrifices when he died.[2] His wish was not granted. Cui Shi 崔寔 (fl. 145–67) condemned lavish funerals in his writings yet laid waste his own fortune when burying his father.[3] Most arguments centered on economic issues, which were apparently put aside when filial piety demanded it. The TPJ includes economic considerations, but it also transcends them with its principled emphasis on the value of life. What is remarkable in this section is not the message as such, but rather the line of argumentation. For cosmic reasons, the living and their concerns demand such attention that their interests must be upheld even in the face of family obligations, the observation of filial piety, and other well-established moral norms.

.   .   .

(46.49) Step forward, Perfected.

Yes.

A filial son serves his parents. After they have died, he continues this service. Should it be what it was while they were alive?

No. The son must serve his parents more than he did while they were alive.

Why is this so?

Man was brought to life and raised by his parents. When he sees them depart, never to return, in his heart he won't be able to forget them, even for a moment. In life, they saw each other daily so that he would receive their instruction and announce his comings and goings. After death, they cannot see each other. He thinks of them with a deep sigh. Thus he should serve them more than he did while they were alive.[4]

So this is what you are saying, Perfected. It completely and utterly ignores the true essentials of heaven's way. It is far, far distant from it. And yet, if you talk like this, it is clear that the common people, dull as they are, must ignore the model set by heaven (*tian fa* 天法).

What do you mean? If the Celestial Master would only . . .

Well, when alive, men resemble heaven and belong to heaven. After death, they resemble earth and belong to earth. While heaven is father, earth is mother. One should not serve one's mother more than one's father. Men are Yang when they are alive, and after death they are Yin. One should not serve Yin more than Yang. Yang is in charge; Yin is the subordinate. One should not serve the subordinate more than the person in charge. Serving Yin more than Yang brings about adverse *qi*. Serve Yin a little more and some adverse matters will arise. Serve it much more and there will be much that is adverse. We call this adverse *qi* and adverse administration. The harm that results from it makes Yin *qi* overcome Yang, inferiors cheat their superiors, and demonic spirits and other evil creatures expand their activities. They take possession of the ways of men and often walk around in broad daylight unafraid of men. So illness and disease don't come to a halt, nor does the lineup of demons come to a standstill. Do you really comprehend what a great crime this is?

I am inadequate. I have made a mistake, haven't I?[5] *Now that I have heard what you have said this is painfully clear to me. The Master is good enough to pity my tireless search and explain to me what I can't grasp. But now this mistake is minute; how can it have such consequences?*

To serve Yin more than Yang and to serve a subordinate more than someone who is superior is a big mistake. How can you call it minute when things have gone that far? Once again, you prove to be not good enough.

Besides, when men are alive they are Yang, while demonic spirits are Yin. While alive, men belong to the day, and when dead they belong to the night. You must know that the issue is roughly the following. When the day is greatly extended, the night is shortened, and when the night is made long, the day becomes short. (46.50) When Yang expands, it overcomes its Yin. Yin then goes into hiding and does not dare to appear at random.[6] Thus demonic spirits of the dead are kept down. When Yin expands, it overcomes its Yang. Yang goes into hiding. Thus demonic spirits are seen in daylight. But living men are allied with the sun, while malignant demonic beings are allied with the stars. The sun is Yang; the stars are Yin. Therefore, when the sun appears, stars take flight, and when stars appear, the sun sets. So when Yin is overpowering, demonic beings cause harm that is too grave to be described in detail. This is called expanding Yin and reducing Yang. It makes government lose control and injures the living. You must keep in mind that this is a very serious mistake.

Yes, I will. (46.51)

Thus according to the regulations (*zhi fa* 制法) of heaven's way the position of Yin should always be weaker than that of Yang. A subordinate, for instance, serves his lord obediently since he is the weaker of the two. As long as a son is weaker than his parents, he serves them with great filial piety. Should someone have become stronger without adapting to the situation he would cause much damage.[7] Thus, although he is full of compassion and love and cannot forget his parents, the filial son must not serve them more than he did when they were alive. Do you now understand a little better?

Yes, I do.

Keep it in mind. You must under no circumstances act at random by simply indulging your own wishes.[8]

Yes, I understand.

Should you wish to serve the dead more than the living you would trespass against heaven.[9]

Why is this so?

This is because you would be honoring Yin instead of Yang. We call this turning one's back on those above and showing one's face to those below. So it is an offense against heaven.

I am very guilty. If the Celestial Master could only forgive me!

Never mind. But in what you write down everything must agree with the model [set up by heaven].[10]

Yes. Now that the Celestial Master has begun to explain things, I would like to know the full meaning of "the service must not go further than it did while parents were alive."

Funeral ritual, garments, and accessories must not surpass what were used while parents were alive or else it would be considered an adverse arrangement and would inflict penalties on the dead. If you do not bury parents in line with the status under which they are registered in the records kept down below, such pretense is investigated. Since it is viewed as deceitful conduct still heavier punishment is inflicted on the dead.[11] Showing too much respect for such ominous activities brings about disaster and ruin. Ghostly demons (*shi gui* 尸鬼) thrive, epidemics plague men, and there is an upsurge in strange and irregular events.

How can one prove this?

Very good, your question! The wise men of old were involved only with their heart when attending to funerals and would never have dared to expand them. For them, burials were the world's most ominous and hideous activity.[12] They saw expanding an ominous activity as harmful. So, only their hearts were involved. They did not deem it wrong to provide the same food and drink for the dead as they had enjoyed during their lifetime. Therefore, in those times men happily and in good health completed the years destined for them by heaven.

In middle antiquity, sons who arranged their parents' funeral deviated slightly from the proper model and measure. Since they could not put all their heart into it, they forgot what it meant. Instead, showing a certain respect [for these ominous activities], they came to indulge in frivolous and superficial [habits], meant to oppress the living. (46.52) They thought of the dead only halfheartedly, and only half of them came to partake in the food. Funeral arrangements moved away slightly from what they should have been. Once sacrificial offerings were expanded, things got worse. Demons and spiritlike creatures—who knows who they were—arrived on the scene to partake of the food and remained there to pester men. This is why men fell ill more often.[13]

In late antiquity, men have inherited and passed on (cheng fu 承負) the small deviations of middle antiquity. They carry these on and add further big deviations. They don't mourn their parents from the heart. Instead, they wish to greatly oppress the living. They produce splendor with spectators[14] in mind.[15] They act without consideration for the model [established by heaven] and contrive deceptions. But this can't influence heaven. As for the dead, as demons they can't come to meals regularly. Yet sacrificial offerings are greatly expanded, in excess of the proper measure. Once a particular Yin is thus expanded, it will in turn forcefully shrink its Yang. Demons and spiritlike creatures—nobody knows who they are—who assemble for these meals tend to become reckless and to act like pernicious bandits. Murders are rife. When they have killed a person they see that their service is expanded, while nobody asks them to account for their crimes. So why shouldn't they carry on, with all their might? Therefore, evil *qi* increases from day to day until it turns around to attack the person who conducts the funeral sacrifice. There will be no end to this [as long as spirits] regularly obtain food and then follow the living in their walkways of life.

When Yin is strong Yang is weak, which is oppressive to the living. [It makes] subordinates and inferiors deceive their superiors, sons deceive their fathers, and it deprives the king's reign of peace. But the people don't comprehend. So evil grows from day to day, out of control. This is why the wise and worthy of old, with their clear understanding of [heaven's] prohibitions, did not dare to serve the dead better than they had served the living. Perfected, are you really aware of this?

How frightening! If you had not told me, being the fool I am, I would have had no way of knowing.

Step forward, Perfected![16] You and I, we both share the same concern. Heaven must have sent you to pose questions. We should not make light of it. So I will tell you all, for the following reason: when *qi* of honesty and peace is about to arrive, all activities must be in compliance. *Qi* of honesty and peace would turn away if one single *qi* were adverse.[17]

What do you mean?

Now we comply with heaven's way by expanding Yang and reducing Yin. It is adverse to do the opposite.[18] Showing respect for ominous activities brings forth *qi* that is prone to disaster. It causes government (*zhi luan* 治 亂) to lose authority (*zheng wei* 政 位). This is no small mistake. (46.53)

You must not hide these writings but must make them known and let every man see for himself their merits and shortcomings. But it is not just the mistake of heaven, earth, or the sovereign[19] if the conduct of affairs is not well coordinated. Blame lies also with the hundred families. Every individual (*renren* 人 人) has committed errors, which are increasing as they are inherited and passed on. It all comes from not sticking to what is essential. Turn away from what is essential, distance yourself from the root, and you will turn to fraud and thus become ignorant of yourself.

What do you mean?

Life is man's root; death is the subject of false reports.[20]

Why "false reports"?

Essentially, we don't have a clue as to what the deceased might want. In order to gain some knowledge, the living paint images of their appearance at random, going far beyond what they were in life. We behold these lies rather than what is essential and crucial. Once men die, their *hun* spirit returns to heaven while their bones and flesh, which belong to earth, rot to dust.[21] How can we imagine that a vital spirit should be able to eat something if we can't even imagine that it can make an appearance?[22] Bones and flesh no longer exist, they return to earth, man's true mother. Men's life takes place between heaven and earth; why should their root be different from what it was during their lifetime, involving tasks that nobody knows? Thus the filial son serves his parents as is proper in regard to their root, and will thus do what is essential. What they did not enjoy while alive they will not be able to experience in death. So offerings must not go beyond their style of life, or else[23] many strange and irregular events will occur. Do you understand? Heed my words!

Yes. I will do so. Excellent! The truth has come out.

We may say that you know. You may go.

Yes.[24]

1. *Hou Han shu* 1.51, trans. by Poo 1990: 42.
2. *Hou Han shu* 34.1177; see Poo 1990: 50.
3. Cf. Hsu 1980: 59 and Poo 1990: 55.
4. That this was a commonly held view is evidenced by the splendor of graves from the third century B.C.E. onward. Lavish funerary rites were widely and severely criticized (see Loewe 1982: 115; Wang Fu, *Qian fu lun* 12 *"Fu yi"*), but hardly with argumentative rigidity. The critique raised in *Yan tie lun* 25 *"Xiao yang"* 孝養 stresses the need for emotional involvement, as opposed to external splendor, in line with Confucius's (*Lun yu* 2.7) dictum that a person who unfeelingly nourishes parents resembles an animal. Only Wang Chong's critique is based on philosophical grounds when he argues (*Lun heng* 67 *"Bo zang"* 薄葬) that demons don't exist and that funerary services are therefore irrelevant.
5. The phrase *bu ye* 不也 here expresses a rhetorical question, in colloquial style; see Yu 2001b: 467.
6. This is dealt with in detail in section 60. It is a good example of Yin/Yang–based moral argumentation.
7. A change in social rank due to personal change is a consequence of Yin/Yang–based fluctuation. It can arise through learning (TPJ 42.96), when individuals move upward in line with their education. Here such fluctuation is seen as overriding family hierarchy in that the living son is said to be surpassing his deceased father.
8. The Master attempts to discredit a generally accepted moral norm as nothing but personal preference. In opposition to it, he sets up the preservation of life as the only valid norm. However, filial piety is depicted as a basic virtue throughout the scripture. In layer B it is seen as the most obvious manifestation of a man's goodness, in particular throughout section 195: "Among the activities of this world, filial piety is supreme and of first rank" (TPJ 195.593). It is also used in a *Chao* passage in the sense of general goodness: it is paired with longevity *(shou)*, and the filial are said to cooperate with heaven and earth, and in particular with earth, since they obey their superiors (TPJ p. 310, *Chao*, part 5; the layer is not clear).

However, throughout most of layer A the term is used in a more narrow sense. To be filial is to obey one's parents as a subordinate obeys his lord. Thus the term is paired with "loyalty" (*zhong* 忠) (TPJ 175.513) and also with a student's "obedience" (*shun* 順):

While alive, a man must be filial as a son, loyal as a subordinate, and obedient as a student. If he does not give up these three virtues his *hun* and *bo* spirit will not face any interrogation once he has died. (TPJ 96.408)

The passage at hand, then, must be seen as an attempt to rewrite the meaning of the norm of filial piety rather than as an attempt to deprive it of its rank in moral thought. To be filial means to prolong the lives of one's parents, not to bury them in splendor.

9. The short passage down to " . . . must agree with the model set up by heaven" repeats in concise form what has been said before. It seems to wind up as well as strengthen the argument by directly involving heaven in the issue: undue respect for the dead is said to be an offense against heaven.

10. *Ying fa* 應法 is one of the rare instances of a seemingly Buddhist expression (Soothill 1972: 458: "in harmony with the dharma") occurring in the text. However, *fa* here means *tian fa* 天法. The full expression *ying tian fa* 應天法 is used TPJ 65.150: "Lord, officials, and the people must all match the model [set up by] heaven."

11. We must assume that the punishment would be more severe than the routine interrogations almost everyone is subjected to at the end of a month or a year. As spirit a man is still a subject, just as he was while alive:

> In order to earn a living, all spirits and vital beings between heaven and earth must help heaven to nourish the twelve thousand plants and beings and let them grow properly, in the same way as officials and worthies live by helping emperors and kings to raise the people and the ten thousand beings. Spirits and vital beings take heaven as their model: they make themselves available for a short interrogation on the fifteenth of each month, for one of medium size at the end of the month, and for a full one at the end of the year. In this way those who deserve promotion will get it and those who don't will be asked to retire or will be punished. (TPJ 151.407f.)

12. Called *xiong e zhi shi* 凶惡之事. As the *Zuo zhuan* puts it, "Life is a good thing and death is a bad thing" (Duke Zhao, twenty-fifth year, 51.2108c; translated by Legge 1960: 709).

13. The Master does not produce a demonological handbook in the manner of the *Nüqing guilü*. He doesn't name demons, but he controls them. A rather simplistic *Chao* passage puts it like this:

> The wise men of antiquity were able to guard *dao*. When they were pure and tranquil at the time of the morning meal they called forth all the spirits (*shen* 神) to talk to them, as men today might summon their guests. The hundred spirits spoke of themselves as heaven's servants and its messengers, the group of vital beings (*jing* 精) were earth's servants and its messengers, and the hundred demons (*gui* 鬼) were messengers of the space between heaven and earth. These three were the messengers of Yin, Yang, and the harmony between them (*zhonghe*). They supported the order established by heaven and earth, and greatly benefited emperors and kings. (TPJ p. 15, part 2)

The linkage between the living and the dead is a spiritual matter, which is effected through spiritual concentration, that is, through meditation (that is, "guarding *dao*"). The background for what is said in this passage can also be seen in Confucius's demand that spirits must be kept at a distance; see *Lun yu* 6.22 and cf. Puett 2002: 97.

14. With Yu (2001a: 58), I change *gu* 古 (old) to *zhan* 占 (to predict, to examine) and understand *guan zhan* 觀占 as "to observe."

15. Luo (1996: 87) argues that the phrase *wei guan gu zhe zuo rong* 為觀古者作榮 is

taken from *Laoʒi*'s (26; see Henricks 1990: 238) phrase *rong guan* 榮 觀 (magnificent scenes). In both Mawangdui texts, this reads *huan guan* 環 官 (walled-in hostel), which makes much more sense. No interpretation of the *Laoʒi* sees *guan* as a verb, but for syntactical reasons the TPJ passage seems to force us to see *guan* as functioning verbally.

16. This starts a new dialogue, which contains a new line of argumentation. The topic is identical to the first, but the message is different. What is said here is close to Wang Chong's argument against the existence of ghosts:

> A man's death resembles the extinction of fire. Once extinguished its flame does not shine. Once a man is dead, his understanding is no longer at work. (*Lun heng* 62 "*Lun si*" 論 死, p. 877)

17. Preparation for great peace must be as inclusive as the state of great peace is expected to be: "With one *qi* interrupted, all activities go wrong" (TPJ p. 18, *Chao*, part 2), or "Should one *qi* not succeed, harmony will not be achieved" (TPJ p. 20, *Chao*, part 2). Section 56 repeats this point.

18. Yu (2001a: 58) points out that Wang Ming's attempt to correct *ling* 令 (to let) to *jin* 今 (now) is superfluous.

19. The expression *tian di ren jun* occurs once again in the TPJ in a context similar to the one at hand; the question is the attribution of responsibility for the present state of affairs and for the actions necessary to change things:

> When the reign continues to lack peace this is not because of heaven, earth, or the sovereign. The fault lies basically and in general with men. For a long time they themselves have committed severe crimes against majestic heaven and august earth. All this reaches back to the individual human being (皆 由 一 人). (TPJ 103.255, layer A; punctuation by Yu 2001a: 215; see also Luo 1996: 429f.)

20. *Si wei* 死 偽 is the title of *Lun heng* chapter 63, in Forke's (1962, vol. 1, p. 202) translation: "False reports about the dead." The preceding paragraph is a summary, the second preliminary summary of this section.

21. This is a commonly held view of death, expressed, for instance, in the *Li ji* ("*Yu ʒao*" 玉 藻, p. 1457a): "The *hun* spirit's *qi* (*hun qi* 魂 氣) returns to heaven; the *bo* spirit, which has form (*xing bo* 形 魄), returns to earth." As stated in TPJ 179.528, layer B, what continues to exist after death is *hun*, while bones and flesh are returned to earth. Thus *hun* can be held responsible for deeds done by a person while alive. It is interrogated (see above) and examined (*kao* 考) (TPJ 188.579, layer B; 195.600, probably layer B) in the world below. It is in contact with sons and grandsons:

> "Grave" is a mound where one's ancestors live. It is called "the original seed, laid out at the very beginning." "Dwelling place" (*ʒhai* 宅) is the soil, to which *hun* spirits must return in order to nourish sons and grandsons. If the soil is good, *hun* will return to nourish; if it is bad, it will come back to cause damage. After five generations, the ancestral *qi* will come to an end and again become human. (TPJ 76.182, layer not clear)

This passage is characteristic of the sections assembled in chapter 50, some of which show characteristics of layer A. They advocate the proper use of techniques, in this case *fengshui* practices, and show little interest in the message of general salvation. K. E. Brashier's (1996) careful account of "Han thanatology" shows that the Celestial Master's ideas on death, as presented in the passage at hand, belong to the broad spectrum of Han views on the human "soul" or "souls" in life and death.

22. This is Wang Chong's view; see *Lun heng* 77 *"Ji yi"* 祭意, pp. 1067f.

23. As Yu (2001a: 59) points out, the text would read more smoothly if a second *guo sheng* 過生 were added after the first.

24. The summary says:

> This section instructs: the living must be served until death; root and branches must agree with each other.

This is uncommonly short and has little to do with the content of the section.

How to Verify the
Trustworthiness of
Texts and Writings

This section promotes the nourishing of the vital principle as the basis for all social
and political reform.[1] This point lies within the core tradition of the *Laozi*'s political philosophy and has repercussions throughout ancient thought, for instance, in
Mengzi's interest in *haoran zhi qi* 浩 然 之 氣. Moreover, as Huan Tan (ca. 43 B.C.E.–
28 C.E.) informs us, this was the technique that men who studied the *Laozi* expected
to learn.[2] However, this section does not define or discuss the term, but merely establishes it as central.

Disciple and Master discuss two objections that can be made to *taiping* beliefs.
One is related to the apparent contradiction that texts, which are produced with the
aim of redeeming the world, deal with issues of lifestyle, personal discipline, and
longevity techniques, that is, with nourishing the vital principle. The Master explains
that someone who can't properly look after his own person can't take care of the
world. Another objection concerns the way heaven handles the world's wrongdoings. It is argued that heaven does not know about these wrongdoings, does not care,
and does not retaliate. The Master explains that natural disasters pronounce heaven's
judgment and that it is man's fault when these are not properly interpreted. *Taiping*-
related writings, if read carefully, can make men aware of these issues.

·　　·　　·

(47.54) *This ignorant pupil's blindness is getting worse from day to day. I bow twice before you. Now there is another question that I would like to ask the Celestial Master, the spiritlike man of supreme majesty.*

What is it?

I would like to ask about these writings. In general terms, why have they been created, why have they been published?

Good! We may say that by the way you ask you show some understanding for what majestic heaven thinks. The gist of these writings is to provide redemption.[3] Since the origin of heaven and earth, emperors, kings, and their people have both received and transmitted evil. It is for this reason that these writings have been published.

But if they have been published for this reason, why do they first of all teach how to nourish the vital principle?[4]

Yes, you have always been truly foolish and dumb, your vision blurred and your understanding hampered. Otherwise a listener might take what you have just said for modesty. But are you really and truly blind and dumb? Are you?

Yes, I am.

Perfected, you must open your ears and listen carefully. Now the people are to blame because they are not good at nourishing their own person. They are punished by the reception and transmission [of evil] because they have all lost direction. Compare this to the case of a father and mother who, in neglect of moral obligations, have trespassed against their neighbors and whose sons and grandsons will later on be injured by those same neighbors. This indicates the punishment involved in receiving and transmitting [evil]. If the former kings in their government did not match the thoughts and intentions of heaven and earth, it was not because a single individual would have upset heaven. (47.55) Since heaven was annoyed and angry, plagues, diseases, and natural calamities occurred in ten thousand different forms. Those who later came to the throne continued to receive and transmit [evil]. Should this not be brought to a halt? So the book has been published precisely for this purpose. Thus it says: The great worthies of antiquity originally all knew the way of nourishing their own person. So they understood the purpose of government and suffered hardly any loss from the reception and transmission [of evil]. In the generations that followed, masters who instructed others would often hide texts on the true and essential teachings. They transmitted instead frivolous and superficial teachings. Thus men trespassed against the essential aim of the way of heaven, which caused later generations to become more frivolous and shallow until they were unable to nourish and cherish their own person. Since this went on for a long period, they moved away from *dao*. That is to say that the world lost the art by which men retain their person safe and complete. This gave rise to a neglect of affairs, a fight for income and position, and thus the calamity of receiving and transmitting [evil]. How can you be [un]aware of what it means "to provide redemption"? (47.56)

Excellent! To hear the Celestial Master speak is like the appearance of the sun when the clouds open up—it is in no way different.

Fine, let us assume that you have now grasped what the doctrine *(dao)* means.

This foolish pupil is grateful for your kindness and has already learned a lot. If my questions do not suffice, would the Celestial Master please continue to reprimand and to warn me?

Yes. A man can only nourish others when he can thoroughly nourish his own person. A man can only cherish others when he can truly cherish himself.[5] If someone having a body[6] were to neglect it, how should he, unable to nourish his own person, be capable of nourishing someone else well? If he were not able to keep his own body intact by truly cherishing it in order to carefully safeguard the ancestral line, how could he take care of others and keep them intact?

How foolish I am.

Don't you think that you should better comprehend it more fully?

Yes, very well.

Fine. You propose that my writings cannot be trusted. Imagine you checked from beginning to end all the texts that in early antiquity were seen to match the thoughts of heaven and prolong happiness. Imagine that you also checked the texts written on bamboo slips that in middle antiquity were judged to match the thoughts of heaven, and the texts that in late antiquity are considered important for complying with the will of heaven and prolonging self-preservation. You would find them all adhering to the same universal standards. As your blindness dissolves, you will have great trust in the words of my book.

Now that heaven is angry with men, these later generations have become more careless and easygoing every day. They risk their lives to test their talents. Some very foolish people say that heaven is without knowledge and claim that it does not retaliate. But earth does not deceive men. If you sow millet, you will harvest millet, and if you sow wheat, you will harvest wheat. If you work hard, your harvest will be good. How much more so for heaven! These very foolish people do not know that heaven is filled with strong resentment. They go on teaching each other to take things easy and act foolishly. In later generations this increases from day to day. It brings about large numbers of calamities, irregular events, disasters, and anomalies.[7] These are, in fact, the profound favors that heaven bestows on a ruler, in the same way that father and son instructing each other is a sign of kindness between them. When a foolish person observes such disasters, he will not announce them to the ruler in good time but will instead keep them hidden. Thus he will cut off a path to heaven, which will increase heaven's rage. After this, any increase in the reception and transmission of evil can no longer be influenced. Even an emperor or king who had the moral goodness of ten thousand men would continue to suffer from it, for no particular reason. Thus, one might be led to presume that to do good is unreasonable, as it does not bring any benefit. This enables the very foolish to say that heaven is without knowledge. Truly, how could there be any grounds for such a claim!

When I hear the words of the Celestial Master my heart is enlightened as if I had been born again. Excellent, indeed! Although this has often caused the Celestial Master trouble, I have at all costs asked questions. (47.57) If I was mistaken to start with I have now, after all the questioning, understood the meaning of "redemption." I feel happy and without regret. Not to ask about what one does not know means that one has no way of getting there.

What you have said is right. You may go. The writings are in all respects ready; from head to foot, from belly to back, and from outside to inside they are complete, and they will on their own inform all worthy people. There is no need for further questions.

Yes.[8]

NOTES

1.   The translation of sections 47 and 48 here is taken, in slightly modified form, with kind permission from *Hawai'i Reader in Traditional Chinese Culture*, ed. V. H. Mair, N. S. Steinhardt, and P. R. Goldin, Honolulu: University of Hawai'i Press, 2005: 225–30.

2.   See Pokora 1975: 76, as quoted in the *Hong ming ji*.

3.   *Jie* 解 means "to explain," "to dissolve," and "to redeem," an ambiguity that is relevant to the wording of this section and is reflected in the student's bewilderment.

4.   Students are attracted to the Celestial Master's knowledge of *yang xing* 養性, and this knowledge is linked to the practice of meditation, and in particular to the technique called "guarding the one":

> Originally, I was interested in all three hundred methods of guarding the one and nourishing the vital principle. But now that I hear the Celestial Master speak without restraint, I would like to ask how the body can be made to last long. (TPJ 165.459)

Maspero (1981, book 9) has explained in detail the techniques involved in "nourishing the vital principle" *(yang xing)*. The assumption that the *taiping* text deals only with such techniques is not to be verified by the *textus receptus*, but the protection of life and concern with nature can be seen as the guiding principles behind many arguments. *Yang xing* is derived from living in unity with heaven:

> The pulse is in unison with heaven, earth, and the ten thousand beings; it moves forward with *qi*, and when the cycle is finished it returns to the beginning. On obtaining its cipher one nourishes the vital principle by knowing when it is time for *qi* to come and when not. (TPJ 74.180)

When editing material the Perfected is advised to:

> Assign one *juan* 卷 to each good technique (*shan fang* 善方); begin with the method of how to nourish the vital principle well, put it at the end of the book [where the reader starts to unroll it], and let all worthy gentlemen recite it. This is the centerpiece of the "Scripture that Pervades All" (*dongji zhi jing* 洞極之經). (TPJ 129.337; cf. Luo 1996: 590 and Long 2000: 680)

It is a ruler's task to distribute texts that teach this method, just as it is his task to distribute food and clothes to the needy. In contrast to this, the following material should not be distributed:

> Such books [the established classical texts] don't deal with the standard doctrine (*zheng dao* 正道), lead the worthy and the educated astray, are of no use for administrative affairs, and don't nourish the vital principle. (TPJ 100.230)

5. *Laozi* 72 raises the issue of cherishing oneself and argues that the sage can and may do so, in moderation.

6. *Laozi* 13 stresses that to have a body is a cause for worry.

7. Here the full term *zai yi bian guai* 災異變怪 is given to mention all the warnings that can be sent by heaven to make rulers change their ways; these four characters, and in particular *zai*, can occur alone or in various combinations without any visible change in meaning. A good account of the politico-moral function of aberrations from the regular course of nature is in *Bai hu tong* 6 *"Zai bian"* 災變. The TPJ insists that the inherited and transmitted evil is increased when minor officials block reports on such aberrations so that they don't reach the ruler (cf. the long discussion at TPJ 127.315f. and below, section 59).

8. The summary says:

> This section instructs on the question of how the Celestial Master's writings have been published from beginning to end.

· An Explanation of the
Reception and Transmission
[of Evil] in Five Situations

The term "reception and transmission [of evil]" (*cheng fu* 承 負), used only in the
TPJ, is central to its doctrine. It points to evil deeds, which in *taiping* terminology
are violations of heaven committed in the past and inherited by the present. These
violations have resulted in a continuous chain of evil that reaches far into the past
and is continuously carried on and reinforced, with no end in sight. Humankind is
doomed once these evil deeds have accumulated to a certain extent. This concept
contributes greatly to the text's millenarian message and is one of the two reasons
given for the need to initiate a *taiping* movement (the other reason was that calculations of cosmic cycles suggested that a new beginning, a great peace, was possible).

That there will be an end to the process of inheriting evil is the message of salvation the Celestial Master has come to proclaim. This section argues that a proper
understanding of *cheng fu* is in itself a means to halt at least reinforcement of the
chain. If people aren't aware that the world's troubles stem from the faults of their
ancestors, they might unjustly accuse their contemporaries. This would cause resentment, which in itself enlarges the load of evil. Much of the text dwells on the
fact that *jie*, "to analyze," also means "to abolish," and, as in the preceding section,
it is not always clear whether the analysis of *cheng fu* or its abolition is thematized.

The origin of the term "reception and transmission [of evil]" lies in the belief
that the good and bad deeds of ancestors influence the fate of their descendants.
This is hinted at in the *Book of Changes*.[1] But while the term's origin lies in the family tradition, the TPJ transforms it into something of concern to humankind, at least

in its layer A material.[2] The abolition of the evils inherited from the past and thus the avoidance of an apocalyptic end is the main aim of the Celestial Master's missionary activities. His presence, the disciples' study, their subsequent promotion of the doctrine, and finally the policy reforms that can be expected to result from this are all geared toward saving the world from *cheng fu* and its consequences.

Since *cheng fu* is more a societal than an individual issue, standard procedures for healing illness and ensuring good luck are inadequate. This doesn't make them obsolete, of course, but it limits their effectiveness. Individual healing and salvation processes are hampered by the general prevalence of evil. However, in lieu of general conversion, an individual's practice of meditation, and in particular the technique of guarding the one— that is, concern for the coherence and cooperation of all the spiritual and physical elements that together make up a person—can help.

. . .

(48.57) *This slow-witted pupil bows twice before the Celestial Master and says: If a person of great worth hears how a teacher discusses one positive aspect, he will know all four. If a person of lesser worth hears how a teacher discusses one negative aspect, he will know all four.[3] Thus it becomes easy to discuss matters. But I am so foolish and slow-witted that unless an issue has been discussed I continue to be in doubt. So I dare to ask a question: You have explained how majestic heaven hates the reception and transmission [of evil], how the august earth puts forward natural disasters in response to it, how emperors and kings suffer from it, what wrongdoings it evokes among the hundred families, and how it afflicts the twelve thousand plants and beings with punishment.*

He says moreover:[4] *This very foolish pupil is asking questions because heaven wants me to do so. So I would not dare risk leaving something unmentioned but want to hear the meaning of everything.*

What is it? Speak freely.

If emperors and kings as well as the people receive [evil] and pass it on, do all situations contain their own element of such reception and transmission?

Good. The question you have raised on behalf of heaven is sincere, detailed, and circumspect.

Now whenever I meet the Celestial Master it is always understood that I raise questions concerning doubtful matters only because heaven demands it. So how could I dare not to be detailed?

Good. Your intentions are reverent and honest. Let us proceed according to certain situations. Or would you prefer to have me explain it all in full? I would not mind the exertion, but I am afraid a text that is too long might be difficult to put to use. (48.58) If I were to interpret all the world's reception and transmission [of evil], this would be difficult to manage in that ten million characters would still be too few. I will present you with an outline and we will then let everyone who is worthy join the project so that our aim will be reached, as if by contract.

If only the Celestial Master would speak!

You must keep both your ears open, sit still, and listen with a calm heart.

Yes, I will.

Although heaven and earth have given birth to all plants and beings, they also cause injury when virtue is lacking. Thus the world is in disorder as if it were clouded. Families are poor and needy, the old and the weak are hungry and cold, county offices derive no income, the granaries have been emptied. Although such evil stems from the earth inflicting harm on plants, men receive and transmit it. The consequences for one case have now been explained. You must continue to listen carefully.

If one teacher addressing ten students should misrepresent the facts and the ten students in turn each addressed ten students, this would amount to one hundred men speaking falsely. If these hundred men were each to address ten men, this would amount to one thousand men giving wrong accounts. If one thousand men were to each address ten men, there would be ten thousand men speaking falsely. If all these ten thousand men were to raise their voices to the four directions, the world as a whole would speak falsely.

He says moreover:[5] Should a large number of words from various traditions support each other, they would become irrefutable and be considered standard language. This goes back to one single person having missed the truth in what he said. But in turn this made all these men miss the truth, which upset the validity of the correct texts revealed by heaven. This would be the reason why customs would be altered and habits changed. Although the world might see all this as a great ill, they would be unable to bring it to a halt. It would get worse over time because distress would be transmitted from one generation to the next. Clearly, this would not be a mistake committed just by later generations. [However], these later generations would not know that the point from which it came lay in the distance. Instead, they would hold their contemporaries responsible, thereby intensifying the resentment between them. This in turn would not allow the knots in which *qi* had gotten tangled to be untied but would make them daily more resistant.[6] Two cases have been explained now, but you must continue to listen carefully.

Imagine if someone were to put on a great show in the center of town, where roads from all directions cross, in order to trick people. He would proclaim that the earth was flooded and was about to turn into a lake. He might even shed tears while speaking. The people would tell others as they returned home from the market; a thousand households would all learn about it, the aged as well as the infirm, grown-ups as well as children discussing it at the crossroads until the whole world knew. But once the world had been deceived, this deception would increase as if distance made it grow. It stemmed from the words of one man, so responsibility for this deception rests entirely with the receiving and transmitting of empty and false words. What mistake would later generations have committed? The mistake of blaming their contemporaries. Now three situations have been explained. However, you must continue to listen carefully.

There is a large tree in the southern mountains, a tree that is so wide and long that it forms a ceiling over several hundred paces of ground although it has a single trunk. Above the ground, it has innumerable branches, leaves, and fruits, all of which may suffer injury from storms and rain should the root below the ground not cling tightly to the soil. (48.59) If this were the case all the many millions of branches, leaves, and fruits would die from such injury. This is the big evil that is received and transmitted by the ten thousand plants and trees. This evil lies with the root and not with the branches. But if the branches[7] were accused instead, wouldn't they be even more grief-stricken?

But if the branches are without fault, there is no reason why they should suffer death from such disasters.

This is exactly what the punishment of receiving and transmitting [evil] is all about. How can one accuse the latter-born? Four situations have been explained. You must, however, continue to listen carefully.

The southern mountains harbor poisonous *qi* that they don't lock up very well. Thus, in spring, winds from the south bring disease and will even hide the sun and the moon. Large numbers of people become infected and die.[8] At the root is nothing else but the *qi* released by the southern mountains. What reason should there be to let all the world receive and transmit a deadly disease? People of our times will, however, discuss this matter as if there had been some moral transgression and heaven were killing because it found fault with a certain person. How should this not bring about grief? If someone has received and transmitted this disaster without having done any wrong, his spirit will remain resentful [after death]. Thus the living will heap even more accusations on him. Grief-stricken qi will affect heaven above. All this distress is rooted in the mountains' bad qi that is carried by the wind. It is the same with the punishment of receiving and transmitting [evil].

Five situations have been explained, but you must continue to sit straight and listen to the particulars I shall speak about. All that was taught was originally reliable and correct and never corrupt, false, and deceptive. But due to what former kings, teachers, and fathers had taught, men lost a little of this correctness, that is, they lost the correct way of expression as well as the correct way of nourishing their own person. (48.60) Since men learn from imitating each other it became worse from day to day for those born later. This is why over a long period nothing of what they taught each other has been true. They don't have the means to stop the world from being false. Thus natural calamities and disasters occur by the ten thousand, impossible to record. Their causes have been added one to the other over a long time, again and again. Yet foolish men know no better than to find fault with their own leaders and to make accusations against their contemporaries. So how can they avoid becoming even more grief-stricken? Men are wrong, all of them, and can't on their own find out what is right. Even if a single emperor or king had the virtue of ten thousand men, his faculties would be only what they are. So what could he do? How can one find a solution for the conduct of men nowadays? Or supposing that there is food and people wish to get all of it for themselves, so that only the sick cannot eat and end up dying. How can there be any solution? When in intercourse you reach a climax you look forward to having sons and grandsons. You might bring offerings to the deities and beg for happiness but still be unable to have children. How can there be any solution? When men have children they want them to be good and strong, but they might in fact be unworthy of their parents and turn out to be bad. How can there be any solution? All this is proof of the reception and transmission [of evil]. But to turn around and accuse one's contemporaries will only destabilize the government. The men of our times have suffered from corruption and fraud for so long. How should they all of a sudden be capable of reform? This has led to such ongoing grief that heaven is taking pity. Thus you must not be surprised should highest majestic *dao* in concert with primordial qi descend upon us.

Where should we begin?

By guarding the one in your thoughts.[9]

How?

One is the beginning of all figures and the way of life (生 之 道); it gives rise to primordial qi and is the hawser of heaven. Therefore, if you keep thinking of the one, you move from high above to affect changes down below. But the ten thousand beings make the mistake of stressing what equates to the boughs and branches of an activity instead of referring back to its root. A return to the root is even more appropriate so long as these errors remain unresolved.

Thus when the wise men of antiquity were about to take action, they examined the patterns of the sky (*tian wen* 天文) and investigated the structures of the earth. This clearly proves that they went back to the root of things. (48.61) Do you understand?

Yes, I do.

Now out of consideration for your distress I have spelled out the gist of the doctrine of receiving and transmitting [evil].[10] Do you comprehend that all situations in this way involve this reception and transmission?

Yes. Now that you have given me the gist of it, the knot in this foolish pupil's mind has become untied.

Fine. The essential message is the following: In early antiquity, men able to bring peace to their reign through their grasp of *dao* were merely engaged in nourishing their own person and preserving their root. In middle antiquity, when their grasp slackened, they became a little careless in regard to nourishing their own person and lost their root slightly. In late antiquity, plans were not well drafted and men held their bodies in little esteem, arguing that they could get another one. Thus, by erring greatly they brought disorder upon their government. Nevertheless, this is not the mistake committed by the people of late antiquity, but the mistake results from the misery of receiving and transmitting [evil]. All right. Since this has been said repeatedly, I will speak no further. There is nothing to be gained from saying the same thing a hundred times. Now that heaven's words have reached you, there is no need for further additions to this text.

Yes.

You may go; return home to think about the essentials [of this message]. If given to a virtuous lord, these writings should dissolve [explain] the reception and transmission [of evil].

Yes, indeed![11]

NOTES

1. See the commentary to hexagram 2, p. 4, in Baynes's (Wilhelm 1989: 393) slightly biblical translation: "A house that heaps good upon good is sure to have an abundance of

blessings. A house that heaps evil upon evil is sure to have an abundance of ills. Where a servant murders his master, where a son murders his father, the causes do not lie between the morning and evening of one day. It took a long time for things to go so far. It came about because things that should have been stopped were not stopped soon enough."

2. Most of the text depicts *cheng fu* as a trans-family phenomenon (cf. Hendrischke 1991); when family affairs are mentioned they serve only as an example for the transmission of evil from one generation to another (TPJ 103.251). Since what the TPJ has to say on this point is rather isolated it is often misunderstood, and *cheng fu* is frequently seen as representing either family concerns or individual karmic retribution (see, for instance, Maeda 2006). The origin of *cheng fu* is not so much individual guilt as society's general lack of concern for heaven's rules (TPJ 50.70) and *dao*'s intentions (TPJ 58.96), that is, the departure of humankind from the simple and primitive life of early antiquity. The crimes committed must be imagined as the faults mentioned throughout the TPJ: for example, the killing of females, chastity, the digging of wells, and the concern for culture and ornament.

3. This is similar to what Confucius expects from his disciples: see *Lun yu* 7.8.

4. This editorial note introduces a second attempt to discuss the matter of *cheng fu*. The preceding paragraph did not amount to a complete question.

5. At this point, the editorial note interrupts an ongoing argument, which is rare.

6. For the tangling of *qi* caused by the resentment of men who see themselves as maltreated, see section 41, note 45, above. The Celestial Master argues that this resentment will go away once men have become aware of the fact that their sufferings are caused by wrongdoings that occurred in the past.

7. *Wei* 未 (not yet) must be corrected to *mo* 末 (branch); see Yu 2001a: 63.

8. *Bi* 彼 (the other) must be read as *bei* 被 (to suffer); see Yu 2001a: 63.

9. This passage dealing with the guarding of the one has been quoted frequently. It can be found in the *Taiping yulan* (chap. 668), in the *Yunji qiqian* (chap. 49), and also in modified form in the *Chao*. The concept of "guarding the one" (*shou yi* 守一) is the TPJ's most durable and perhaps most prominent contribution to the Daoist tradition. The Celestial Master states explicitly that "guarding the one" is central to his doctrine:

> Should there be disbelief in my text you must show that it is in agreement with the texts on guarding the one from former and present times. When organized according to subject matter these texts provide proof for one another. (TPJ 152.410)

Guarding the one is the most efficient strategy, comparable in this respect to the method of *wu wei* envisaged in the *Laozi*. Great promises are linked to its practice: "If you know how to guard the one, the ten thousand activities are completed" (TPJ 134.369), or, in the words of the later *taiping* text *Secret Advice by the Wise Lord of the Scripture on Great Peace*, "Guard the one without fail and activities are completed of their own accord" (TPJ p. 740).

One of the major problems that the practice of guarding the one can overcome is the inheriting and transmitting of evil as discussed in this section (for this cf. Strickmann 2002: 43). As the *Chao* puts it:

> If you want to dissolve the blame inherited and passed on there is nothing better than guarding the one. If you continue to do this, heaven will have mercy on you. The one is the hawser of heaven and the root of the ten thousand beings. (TPJ p. 60, for section 48)

The other important role played by *shou yi* is related to the search for longevity:

> The essential teachings *(dao)* of former times as well as of today all say that by guarding the one we can exist for a long time without getting old. When someone knows how to guard the one we call this a doctrine *(dao)* that cannot be surpassed. Insofar as someone has a body, he is in constant unison with vital spirits *(jing shen* 精 神*)*. The external figure is what accounts for death, and vital spirits account for life. When [external figure and vital spirits] are constantly together, then there is good luck, but when [vital spirits] go, there is misfortune. Without vital spirits there is death, with them there is life. Togetherness brings forth oneness. Thus you can exist long. Continue to damage the vital spirits and they will depart, no longer assembling in your body. Instead, you will have them traveling about following your thoughts. Therefore, the wise men teach this [method of] guarding of the one when they say that we must guard our person as a whole *(shou yi shen* 守 一 身*)*. . . . Someone who guards the one truly brings it all together in one. He makes the vital spirits of human life completely content, guards them so that they don't disperse, and thus transcends this world, becoming [like] father and mother of people filled with honesty *(liang min fu mu* 良 民 父 母*)*, meeting with the ruler of great peace and becoming beloved by the spirits and other numinous beings. (TPJ p. 716, *Chao,* part 9)

So without *shou yi*, there is no longevity: "If a man does not guard the one, he will not live" (TPJ p. 743, in the *Taiping jing shengjun bizhi,* the *Secret Advice by the Wise Lord*).

The above passage from the *Chao* helps to explain the meaning of "the one" that is to be guarded. It stands here for togetherness and unification, in this case of vital spirits and physical body. In this way, an individual also models himself after the original oneness of the cosmos. Other passages refer to this original state when they speak about the "unification of *qi*":

> The three *qi* combined in one are the spiritual root. One of them is vitality *(jing* 精*)*, the other is spirit, and the last is *qi:* these three, combined in one position *(yi wei* 一 位*)*, are the basic *qi* of heaven, earth, and men. (TPJ p. 728, *Chao,* part 1)

Regarding or treating different entities as one brings them back to their original form, before divisions or, as in the following passage, "structures" *(li* 理*)* were set up:

> One is from the time when primordial *qi* was pure; primordial *qi* had all together no structure, just as wind has no structure. So you can name it all together "one." One congealed into heaven, and because heaven has above and below and the eight directions, it is ten. (TPJ 139.392; cf. TPJ p. 305, *Chao,* part 5)

To this can be added what is said in the section at hand. It does not amount to much. Ontological or cosmological definitions are of little interest to the *taiping* project. Bokenkamp (1993: 46) certainly has a point when he suggests the translation of "maintaining unity" for the term "guarding the one." The Celestial Master is happy to define the one as what is guarded in the practice of guarding the one:

> "One" means that for *dao* to be standard we must begin with guarding the one. Someone who sticks to it without fail will become more enlightened day by day so that even the greatest illusion (*da mi* 大迷) is dissolved. (TPJ 50.64)

The same interest prevails in the *Baopu zi*, where the distinction between *xuanyi* 玄一 (the mysterious one) and *zhenyi* 真一 (the true one) is explained by illustrating the method of how *xuanyi* is preserved (*Baopu zi neipian* 18 *"Di zhen"* 地真; cf. Yoshioka 1967: 496 and Kohn 1989: 140f.).

The practice of guarding the one involved color visualization:

> The practice of guarding the light of the one is the root of longevity. The ten thousand spirits come forth through the gate of brilliant light [as if they were] to receive sacrifices. The moment when you guard the vital light of the one is the same as when fire gets started: you must eagerly guard it without fail. When it starts it is bright red, when it ends it is pure white, and for a long time it is a bluish green. The light shines further than into the most remote distance, and on its return it reigns over all as one, so that there is nothing inside [the body] that is not full of light. The hundred diseases are eliminated. We can call keeping it with unremitting effort a technique to attain ten thousand years of age. The light involved in the method to keep the light of the one has all the brilliance of the rising sun and all the light it has at midday. (TPJ p. 16, *Chao*, part 2)

From the S 4226 table of contents we learn that the original sixth-century TPJ contained more material on the guarding of the one than has been transmitted. The term has been linked to the TPJ ever since Xiang Kai's memorial (*Hou Han shu* 30B.1082), where it is used to describe the Buddha's frame of mind. The fact that it is used in the *Xiang'er* (3.15) in discussion of *Laozi's* "*bao yi*" 抱一 (*Laozi* 10) also shows that the term was an integral element of early Daoist thought. In contrast to the TPJ's Celestial Master, the *Xiang'er* emphasized that obedience to precepts was the best way to "maintain unity," and it saw a need to defend its understanding against "mistaken" opinions (Bokenkamp 1997: 89 and 144f.), which we may interpret as another token of the prominence of the term.

The Celestial Master approached the issue in the same rigidly formalistic manner with which he dealt with many central topics: distinctions are made between the keeping of the one by a great, a medium, and a small man (TPJ 152.410), and also by a great, a medium, and a small worthy (TPJ 152.412). There is also an order from one to five: it is asserted that someone who preserves the one will have heavenly deities at his side; someone who preserves the two will be accompanied by the deities of the earth; someone who preserves the three will be helped by demons from the human world; and someone who preserves the four or five will have only the protection issued by minor beings who convey nothing but unhappiness (TPJ p. 13, *Chao*, part 2).

10. The term *cheng fu* occurs throughout the text, including in sections not in the form of a dialogue between the Celestial Master and Perfected (TPJ 179.534, layer B), but most of the information is no different from what is hinted at in the section at hand. However, the following passage adds certain aspects:

> Instruction on inheriting and transmitting [evil]: Ill-omened *qi* was never dispersed after the division between heaven and earth, or if it ever was, it soon arose again.

> *Why is this so?*

> Now longevity is heaven's greatest treasure. It is attributed to someone with virtue and cannot be achieved by cheating. If you want to know this treasure, [let me tell you]: Should all beings in the six directions and the eight distant regions of heaven and earth be devoid of grief and be completely happy, they would then achieve long life. If but one circumstance remains unresolved, there is at once injury, death, and ruin.

> Some men work hard to do good in everything but the outcome is evil; others vigorously try to do evil but good results. Whether they call themselves worthy has nothing to do with it. If someone works hard to do good but in return fares poorly, this means that he has inherited and is passing on the mistakes made by his ancestors. Rows of calamities from earlier and later times all come together to hurt him. If someone acts badly but receives benefits, this is due to the great merits that his ancestors accumulated with much effort and that now flow toward him. Should his ancestors have achieved merit ten thousand times ten thousand–fold [punctuation by Luo 1996: 35], no misfortune could touch him, even if there were plenty of it. This is so because past events have an impact on later generations, who inherit [the deeds] of five [generations of] ancestors. One small cycle lasts ten generations, and then it starts again. Some people might have done a little good but cannot remain tranquil. They are overwhelmed by the evil passed on by their ancestors and the calamities they have received and are passing on. They die in the middle of their life without children. This is truly grievous (*yuan* 冤).

> As far as receiving and transmitting [evil] is concerned, heaven has three divisions. For emperors and kings it lasts for thirty thousand years, for officials three thousand, and for the people over three hundred years. With all this receiving and transmitting from one to the other, some lie prostrate and others rise up. This can't be separated from decay and prosperity as they occur in ruling over men. (TPJ p. 22, *Chao*, part 2)

The text continues with a discussion of three grades of longevity. This is summarized as:

> If someone unendingly does good, he will surpass [these three degrees of] longevity and we say that he has transcended the world. If he does evil without end, he will not reach the three degrees of longevity but will die too early. If someone dies as a fetus or before reaching adulthood, this is called receiving and transmitting the ancestors' mistakes without any fault of his own. (TPJ p. 23, *Chao*, part 2)

This explains why the fate of human beings does not necessarily follow from their deeds.

This passage consists of separate items. The problem is seen alternately as residing in the general realm of humankind and in the private realm of individual morality. The introduction of ill-omened *qi*, the remark on everyone's happiness, and the claim that the duration of *cheng fu* differs according to one's social stratum points to *cheng fu* as a phenomenon that transcends family tradition. Most of the passage, however, describes the differences in individual fate as being caused by the different performance of previous family members as well as (and, again, this is contradictory) by the moral status of the individual. To combine these points of view is only possible when one assumes as an underlying theory that *cheng fu* is a common phenomenon, affecting every human being, but that its intensity might differ with individual and family differences.

While neither the term *cheng fu* nor the concept it stands for occurs in other transmitted texts, archaeological material points to such a concept. It tells of a burden from which men sought to be delivered. Liu Shaorui (1992: 112–15) has shown that grave-securing writs from the Eastern Han dynasty share not only certain ideas with the TPJ, but also the way that these ideas are phrased. The writs demand that a lead figure be permitted to carry *zhong fu* 重負 in lieu of the descendant, and also that the Great Spirit (*da shen* 大神) may dissolve *zhong fu*, which Liu sees in connection with TPJ 185.561 (layer B), where the Great Spirit helps deliver the adept from *cheng fu*. Liu (1992: 118) also shows that *tu gong* 土功 (construction work) and *xian guan* 縣官 (county offices) are used in grave-securing writs as they are in the TPJ. Whether Liu's identification of *zhong fu*, difficult as this term is, with *cheng fu* is really acceptable is another matter. What is certain is that similarities exist between the materials he compares.

The term *fu ze* 負責, which is rendered by Donald Harper (2004) as "encumbered by debt" (understanding *ze* as *zhai* 債), throws still another light on the phrase. *Fu ze* occurs frequently in a number of illness-dispersing spells (*Xuning bingjian* 序寧病簡) dating from 79 C.E. (cf. Rao Zongyi 1996 and Harper 2004) in the formula 生人不負 責死人不負適, "May living people not be encumbered with debt, may dead people not be penalized" (for instance, on the back of slip 226, Harper 2004: 234). The second part of this formula, that is, the phrase *siren wu shi* 死人毋適, also occurring as *siren bu fu shi*, resembles a phrase that occurs frequently on the grave-securing writs analyzed by Wu Rongzeng (1981: 57), which beg that the dead might "be spared accusations and the living be relieved of all crimes" (*sizhe jie shi, shengren chu zuiguo* 死者 解適生人除罪過). The *Xuning bingjian* formula, with its use of *fu* (encumbered), casts an interesting light on *cheng fu* and might actually explain this expression: what men have been, are presently, and will be encumbered with is the debt they owe heaven, or, when we consider section 61, heaven and earth. In the *Xuning bingjian* material studied by Harper the debt concerns what men owe to spirits, for instance in the fulfillment of sacrificial obligations. For the TPJ this debt would consist of lack of attention to heaven's commandments.

11. The summary says:

This section instructs on the question of how in all affairs [evil] is received and transmitted and how *qi* is tangled up.

An Explanation of
the *Master's Declaration*

The *Master's Declaration* is a prophetic text consisting of thirteen lines of seven characters each that describes the fate of society in general and the chances for individual happiness.[1] The wording suggests that both the short Declaration as well as its exegesis issue from the Celestial Master, who uses the phrase "my declaration." The *Master's Declaration* is almost too vague to attempt a translation, but it must not be left out if we are to present the full spectrum of the original text. It characterizes the transcripts of the Celestial Master's words as exegetical, clarifying, man-made texts as opposed to the revealed, cryptic, even sacred *Declaration*, which was adopted and propagated rather than created by the Master. The following translation of the whole section relies heavily on Max Kaltenmark's work.[2] The translation of the text of the *Declaration* is dependent on the "explanations" that follow.

The topic of the section is the salvation promised to men who convert to the Master's doctrine. Since the language of both the *Declaration* and the *Explanation* is cryptic, as befits prophetic utterances and prognostic exegeses, a synopsis in plain language seems justified.

What the Master says is useful and necessary. It is said at the right point in time, that is, when the phase of fire is strong, as it was seen to be during the later Han period. Order can be established through words only. These must be recited and remembered but not put to use until the time is ripe. Man's happiness consists in living long in this world. Proper government and promotion of the true doctrine enable him to do so. This message is adorned by three images, two of which—the great capital city of Chang'an and the life-strengthening Queen Mother of the West, friend of Emperor Wu—can be seen as related to the Han court. The other is the harmonious sequence of the four seasons, which establishes the time for men's activities and expectations. The *Declaration* is supposed to be entrusted to experts in vitality techniques (*fang shi* 方 士) to make it public; this is the group of people who might be said to have created the Daoist religion.

This section is isolated from previous sections but is linked to the one that follows. Or rather, irrelevant as this short section's contents might be, the author of the following section 51 seems to contrive a link by mentioning that it should follow section 50, which is one of the TPJ's most important sections. The editors have respected this wish. The composition and publication of the *Declaration* are described as if they had preceded the meetings between Master and disciples and the creation of the TPJ. The *Declaration* is quoted in section 212, which in itself is central to *taiping* cosmological beliefs. The passage "Doesn't the *Declaration of the Celestial Master* say '*Bing, wu, ding* and *si* serve as ancestors, as the beginning'?"[3] seems to be the only instance where one passage of the TPJ explicitly refers to another.

The *Declaration* shares a number of features with prognostic literature: a poetic style; an interest in the dissection of characters and in the assortment of heavenly stems and earthly branches; an alternative use of names and concepts; an indirect, enigmatic way of expression; a quotation from the *Book of Changes;* and a certain attention to time and place that is otherwise rare in the TPJ. However, I have not been able to detect any direct parallels in the apocryphal material published by Yasui Kōzan and Nakamura Shōhachi. This seems to hold true for the whole of the TPJ. While it certainly shares aspects of the view of the cosmos and its processes expressed in Han dynasty apocrypha as well as some of their language,[4] it does not have passages in common with them. For the worldview of the TPJ as well as for early religious Daoism in general another set of ideas became crucial. These ideas are hinted at in the *Declaration* when it uses terms like "transcendent" (*xian* 仙), "healing illness," and "expert in vitality techniques." The *Explanation* adds to this the terms *"dao,"* "heaven," "the virtuous ruler," "the inheriting and transmitting of evil," and "the abolition of evil," which are central to the Celestial Master's message of salvation.

The section consists of two more short passages, which do not belong to the *Explanation*. They inform us that the Celestial Master's teacher is heaven and that the combination of the inheritance and transmission of evil makes evil as persistent as it is. Although these passages do not belong here, they also do not seem to belong anywhere else, and if we accept the proposition that the text is based on transcripts of real meetings, then student-instigated changes of topic as documented in this section are plausible.

.   .   .

(50.63) *The Perfected, beating his head on the ground, bows twice before the Master.* Yes?

There is a problem I would like to ask about.

Speak up! What is it?

You have previously given me, foolish and incompetent as I am, a declaration in ninety characters. With due respect I put my mind to it in the dark chamber, refraining from all activities for days on end. But I am by nature dull-witted. I thought about it day and night with unremitting effort, in full concentration, my heart exhausted—in no way at all could I understand what it said. Now if the Celestial Master would only take pity on me, incompetent as I am! I wish you would explain it all to me so that it could be fixed for ten thousand times ten thousand generations and never be forgotten.

This is a good question. We may say that you are someone who is in harmony with heaven.[5] Yes. Listen carefully. I will explain to you the main ideas. (50.64)

(a) "The Master says: The characters I have put down are the ten and are the one.[6] Understand them and you have feet to stand on." "Master" is in correct terms the "master spiritlike man of majestic heaven."[7] "To say" is "words." I took leave[8] from heaven and was sent here in person to explain all details to emperors, kings, and the ten thousand people in order to redeem the million and ten thousand generations from the faults they receive and transmit (*cheng fu zhi zhe* 承負之謫). "Me" (*wu* 吾) is "I" (*wo* 我), "I" is a spiritlike man sent on an urgent mission by heaven. Nowadays heaven spreads the calamities that are received and transmitted (*cheng fu zhi zai* 承負之災) to the four directions. In the beginning, rulers stuck to the root, but in later times they forfeited their reigns as a consequence of these calamities. They had no way to bring them to a standstill. Instead, they robbed and injured others and thus caused even more harm. Now this worries heaven deeply. "Characters" are the characters of the compilation (*leiji* 累積) of celestial writings (*tian shu* 天書), which I am now in the process of explaining. "Ten" means that the writings match heaven in a perfect, sincere, faithful, and identical manner, without the slightest mistake. They don't mislead, not in a single case. As soon as worthy men obtain them they will think deeply about what their ancestors have inherited and transmitted. If they recite them without cease all evil that has been inherited and transmitted, whether big or small, will be completely abolished.[9] "One" means that for *dao* to be standard we must begin with guarding the one. Someone who sticks to it without fail will become more enlightened day by day so that even the greatest illusion[10] is dissolved. "Understand them and you have feet to stand on": "to stand on" (*zhi* 止) means "feet."[11] Feet make beings (*sheng* 生) walk. Once someone walks on this way (*dao* 道) he gains ever more clarity. Never again is he foolishly in the dark. "Ten and one" means "expert" (*shi* 士),[12] "understand them and you have feet to stand on" means "red" (*chi* 赤).[13] This is to say that through these writings *qi* of red flourishes again and reigns (*wang* 王) with great brightness (*da ming* 大明).[14] "To stand on" (*zhi* 止) is the feet of the ten thousand beings. These beings start with germs. When they spread out threads to form a root, "feet" grow. The method (法) of walking on this way[15] is to take primordial *qi* as the root. Then [a man] is in favor with heaven and earth (*de tian di xin* 得天地心). Since this is best, we call it the way of supreme majesty (*shang huang zhi dao* 上皇之道).

(b) "*Bing* [the third celestial stem], *wu* [the fourth terrestrial branch], *ding* [the fourth celestial stem], and *si* [the sixth terrestrial branch] serve as ancestors, as the beginning." *Bing, wu, ding,* and *si* are [like] fire and red. *Bing* and *wu* are pure Yang, *ding* and *si* pure Yin.[16] Yin and Yang are in command of harmonizing everything. It is said that the world would thrive should *qi* of Yin and Yang be together in harmony. "Serve as" (*wei* 為) is to benefit (*wei li* 為利) emperors and kings and free them from disaster and harm. "Ancestor" is "predecessor," which is to resemble the Three Majestic Rulers in virtue.[17] "Beginning" is to return to where the root began. Someone who walks on this way *(dao)* is bound to return to [what things were like under] supreme majesty. (50.65)

(c) "Once you conduct matters through the four [strokes] and 'mouth' the ten thousand beings will be in order." The four [strokes] will become "to say" (言) when they are added to "mouth" (口). Should you manage to daily practice saying the words that I have written, you would take possession of the characters of a scripture that is as correct as is heaven and would be led to understand heaven's full meaning. When, in communion with the intentions of heaven above, the ten thousand beings are each in their place there is no further uproar (*luan* 亂). For this reason it has been said that the ten thousand beings are in order.

(d) "'Son' (*zi* 子) and 'turban' (*jin* 巾), which use the character 'horn' (*jue* 角) to control their right side, amount to the character 'to recite' (*song* 誦)."[18] This means that once you recite these writings without end, all matters will be in unison, and standard. Up on high you will gain heaven's approval; greatly pleased, it will forever be happy. No remnants of anything improper will be left.[19]

(e) "As long as the dragon is asleep don't make use of it.[20] The humble sets the rule."[21] "The dragon is asleep" means that celestial *qi* has returned to a position where nine is at the beginning. The *jiazi* 甲子 year is like the day of the winter solstice[22] and exactly the point from which heaven and earth begin. "Dragon" is the small Yang in the east; it is vital spirit of wood. Thus heaven's way through its origin in wood promotes the phase of fire. As soon as plants and other beings are about to grow they must open the gates and move through. Perfected, at the end of the month, when the moon is full, you must publish these writings in a place that opens up brightness.[23] (50.66) To open is to unlock, to pass through, to get there, that is, to open to the south[24] and to make the *qi* of Yang even more pervading. This ends the evil that has been inherited and transmitted. "To sleep" is to be stored away. Although *dao* has already arrived, it has gone back into hiding. "Don't" is "not to dare to," "not yet." This is when you first see the text and don't yet know how to implement it. "To make use of" is "to rule by it," "to make serve." Nowadays heaven makes use of these writings in order to abolish natural calamities and other harmful events. At *xuanjia* 玄甲 a year brings them forth.[25] At this time, the lord has not yet understood their meaning well enough to enable him to make use of them. For this reason is it said "don't make use." On seeing the celestial text, one does not dare trust it completely but will investigate how to use it. When one puts trust in its use, the arrangements one has made will draw responses as if by echo. This proves the text right. Such a response is derived from the unison with heaven.

"The humble (*kan* 欿) sets rules (*ji* 紀)"[26] means that *zi* 子 [the first branch] is called humble. The stem *jia* is heaven; it is the general guideline (*gang* 綱), it is Yang. The *kan* symbol is the branch *zi*,[27] water, Yin, and sets rules in detail (*ji* 紀). Thus heaven and earth are forever in unison; their rules and guidance begin in *xuanjia*, at the winter solstice and in a *jiazi* year. Since the *kan* symbol can guide and direct the reign of a virtuous lord it is said that the humble sets the rules. What we call the writings of highest majestic heaven have been published for the benefit of the virtuous lord. The true scripture (*zhen jing shu* 真經書) serves to rectify, to cut out what is evil. Its subtle beginnings lie in *xuanjia*. Since all living beings take their origin from *jia* and their root from *zi*, they are derived from *jia* and *zi* at the top.[28]

(f) "What a man may look at is longevity, old age, duration." To be precise, "man" refers to emperors and kings, to the "single man."[29] "Man" is of highest virtue, finds it easy to learn, and knows how to implement the writings revealed by *dao*. Once you rely on propitious signs and agree with [heaven's] patterns, you will have no doubt as to heaven's way. Should you fully understand its intentions you will live long. "Longevity" means that you finish the years heaven has destined for you. "To enjoy old age" means that this doesn't exhaust you. "To endure" means that you continue to exist.

(g) "One lives only between heaven and earth." "To be between" means to be situated. Someone who only lives situated between heaven and earth must learn the true doctrine *(dao)*. Frivolous and superficial texts don't help men to live long. There is always the evil that is inherited and transmitted. For this we must blame doctrines *(dao* 道*)* that lack proper substance. Now heaven will eradicate them.

(h) "Through proper government *(zhi* 治*)* millions of men *(bai wan ren* 百 萬 人*)* are about to become transcendents." "To govern" means to rectify. (50.67) With these writings, heaven rectifies the heart of each worthy man to let him heal his illness, maintain truth, and abolish evil. "Men are about to become transcendents" means that the world has heard about it. The true doctrine *(dao)* has come forth in full so that it might assist the virtuous lord in his reign. The true doctrine is how a man's life is strengthened. Therefore we may say "that they are about to become transcendents."

(i) "Someone apt at healing illness doesn't tell lies."[30] Foolish as men are they don't think for themselves, but in their folly they rely on deceptive forgeries to tell lies. (50.68) How sad! In return, they are severely accused by heaven and create a big load of evil that is transmitted and inherited. For this reason heaven demands that frivolous and superficial texts be discarded. Let each man preserve what is true and essential and safeguard the one [message it conveys]. Let him work at this with energy from morning to night, and he will find it profitable and never again agree to tell lies.[31]

(j) "Joyful indeed is the town of long-lasting security *(chang an* 長 安*)*!"[32] "Joy" means that no joy is greater than the arrival of *qi* of great peace [that has been installed by] supreme majestic heaven. *Hu* 乎 (indeed) is as in the phrase "Indeed *(jietan* 嗟 嘆*)*, his virtue is excellent, without parallel!"[33] "Long" means that while he walks on this way his virtue and goodness will last without fail. "Security" means that there is no longer any risk of destruction. Once someone walks on this way all the accusations by heaven and earth that he has received and is transmitting cease. Long-lasting security reaches far and wide. All worries come to an end. Towns are the places where the men of this world assemble. To implement what these writings say means that a country's population grows and becomes numerous, similar to the men in a city or town.

(k) "To let men live as long as the Kingly Mother of the West":[34] "To let men" means to let emperors and kings have virtue that derives from heaven and to favor men who live by the standard text *(zheng wen* 正 文*)*. "As" means "to follow." Once emperors and kings are able to do most of what my writings say, heaven's way prevails. Act like this and you have great good luck; don't and you will be blamed. "Of the West" (*xi* 西) means that men retain (*xi* 棲) the true doctrine in their breast.[35] "Kingly" means that emperors and kings will act according to heaven's way and thrive in their role as king. They will reign so well that they couldn't do any better. "Mother" is proof of old age and longevity. She is head of all spirits.[36]

(l) "Just as the four seasons return to the beginning." "Just as" is comparative: just as the four seasons bring each other forth, make each other grow, and will never rob or injure each other. Such a reign takes place without a penal code.

(m) "The ninety-character declaration is transmitted to the experts in vitality techniques."[37] "Nine" (*jiu* 九) means "at the end" (*jiu* 究), "to finish." The virtue of someone able to live by these writings completely agrees with the intentions of heaven and earth, Yin and Yang, and the ten thousand beings. "Ten" means a complete, ten-out-of-ten coherence, as in the texts on nonaction.[38] "Written character" means the rows of characters in the texts revealed by heaven. They are comprehensive and put forth all that is needed. "To transmit" a text is to [give men] faith in it. In order to inspire faith in a text's characters and spells (*zi fu* 字 符) you transmit them.[39] "[Experts in] vitality techniques" are quite square (*fang* 方) and upright and quickly convey these teachings *(dao)* to a lord of high moral standing, so that he can abolish the disaster of inheriting and transmitting evil (50.69) and his reign will become square and completely upright. An "expert" is an individual with a determined mind. Any such individual can, when he puts his mind to it, reform a vast number of activities until they agree with these teachings *(dao)*.

What my declaration says will soon become obvious. You have grasped its meaning?

Yes, I have. Excellent! Listening to your words I have become full of joy.

So we may assume that you have understood.[40]

Each time I have a question I know that I distress you. But if I don't ask how can I come to understand?

Yes, it is as you say. When the worthy and the wise are in doubt, they ask. This is why they have their teachers.[41] One should not insist on speaking at random. One might do so once, but must not again elaborate on it.

Yes. This is why I would not dare to insist on speaking. (50.70)

What you say is correct, quite scholarly and modest. Keep it in mind.[42]

Now the Celestial Master has in all respects pointed me in a direction where my doubts will be resolved. So I have already been able to inquire about the things I did not know. I wish to do so again, rude as this might be. May I be allowed to speak?

Please don't hesitate to raise your question.

Yes, I will speak. The worthy and wise have all had teachers, in ancient times as well as today. Now the Celestial Master's teachings (dao) *are as complete as possible. Who was your teacher?*

An excellent question! We may say that you have an eye for subtleties. Yes, when I took up my studies, I also sought the advice of teachers, more than one. Over a long period [my] *dao* matured and [my] virtue ripened. Finally, I came to agree with heaven above. Only then did I understand what heaven wanted to say and it sent great Yang's vital spirit (*jing shen* 精 神) to inform me and make me speak. So I have heaven for my teacher.[43] Although I like to explain things to you, I would not dare to say anything at random if heaven did not want me to speak. For then it would certainly execute me. You know as well that this is truly important, don't you? Heed it!

Yes, I will. All that I have asked you have answered. I am so happy that I can't refrain from speaking. I would like to ask something else!

Go ahead.

Yes, I will. Now you have for the sake of this benighted and shallow pupil outlined the complete theory of receiving and transmitting [evil].[44] I don't understand whether "to receive" and "to transmit" belong together as if they were one or whether they are separate.

Well, "to receive" is first; "to transmit" comes next. "To receive" means that the ancestors originally received heaven's favor. As they went on, they slowly lost it. They did not notice how [their mistakes] increased from day to day. A lot came together. Now the latter-born, as innocent as they might be, meet with these wrongdoings and are forever hit by calamities. For this reason "to receive" is first and "to transmit" comes next. That there is "transmission" means that the cure for rows of disasters cannot come entirely from the reign of one person.[45] One disturbance (*bu ping* 不 平) follows another. We speak of "transmission" because what is first and what comes later are linked to each other. It means that ancestors transmit to descendants. Illness is received and transmitted from one to the other. This means that nobody has yet been capable of putting an end to disasters and other harmful influences.[46] Once they are dissolved, they arise again. In great awe have I obtained these writings from heaven. What they teach *(dao)* can dissolve all this. So they are truly important and invaluable. Do you understand?

Yes, I do. How frightening!

Go now. Don't ask anything else.

Yes.[47]

NOTES

1. The received text has no section 49 or chapter 38. It moves directly from section 48 to section 50 and from chapter 37 to chapter 39. The S 4226 Dunhuang manuscript gives "The method of guarding the one" (*shou yi fa* 守一法) as the title for both. For this reason, Espesset (2002a: 174) has put here as a version of chapter 38 material that has been transmitted as an independent text under the title *Secret Advice by the Wise Lord of the Scripture on Great Peace* (*Taiping jing shengjun bizhi*, TPJ pp. 739–43; cf. Kohn 1993: 194–97). This view is strengthened by Yoshioka's (1967) account of the *Secret Advice*, which sees it as closely connected to the *Chao* and thus to the TPJ itself. *Secret Advice* consists mainly of smoothly composed four-character phrases. Many are rhymed and include other rhetorical devices. The argumentation is elegant and the message clear. The style resembles some layer C passages. Its contents resonate with certain TPJ passages on the "guarding of the one," as Wang Ming (TPJ, "Introduction," pp. 15f.) has pointed out. He suggests that Lüqiu Fangyuan, whom he sees as author of the *Taiping jing chao*, is also responsible for *Secret Advice*. I find it difficult to place this text here, in the middle of part 3, which consists of layer A material. However, the Dunhuang table of contents is to be taken seriously, and we must assume that this section of the sixth-century text dealt with meditation techniques. The *Chao* account of part 3 does not contain any discussion of "guarding the one." It can be argued that this topic was too crucial to have been ignored by the digest and that the original section 49 was already missing when the *Chao* was produced in the late ninth century.

   The *Declaration* is not in the received text. According to the titles recorded in S 4226, in the original text it was in part 1, chapter and section 20. The *Chao* contains no trace of this section, but quotes the *Declaration* in full in part 3 before an almost complete account of the *Explanation*, that is, of section 50. Wang Ming follows the *Chao* when he proposes that section 49 consisted of the *Declaration*. The *Declaration* has also been transmitted in Gan Ji's biography in the *Hunyuan sheng ji* (chap. 7, pp. 17b–18a, by Xie Shouhao, published 1191) and again in the *Lishi zhen xian tidao tongjian* (chap. 20, pp. 1b–2a, by Zhao Daoyi, fl. 1294–1307). It consists of thirteen seven-character phrases, which amount to ninety-one characters. However, it is said to consist of only ninety: see line (m) and also the summary at the end. We can only assume that ninety was considered to be a more meaningful figure than ninety-one.

2. See Kaltenmark 1979: 38–40.

3. See TPJ 212.679.

4. Cf. Espesset 2002a: 435–41.

5. "A person in harmony with heaven" is the definition given of a *tian ren* 天人 (man of heaven), as the passage at hand puts it, in an odd and perhaps corrupt passage of the *Zhuangzi* (64.23.77–79). But some of what the passage says is clear: "Someone who forgets men (*wang ren* 忘人) is a man of heaven. When honored he will not be pleased,

when insulted he will not be angry. He is so only because of being in harmony with heaven." *Zhuangzi* chap. 33 (90.33.3) ranks the *tian ren* before the *shen ren* 神人 and the *zhi ren* 至人. The term occurs only once more in the TPJ: eight ranks, from the celestial (expressed as *"tian"*) and the "earthly" down to the worthy, are called "men of heaven" *(tian ren)* because heaven likes to employ them (p. 223, *Chao*, part 4).

6. This means they are complete, a common meaning of "ten," as explained below, and perhaps "coherent," which is one meaning of "one."

7. The title *shen ren* 神人, by which the Master here refers to himself, is used throughout the *Chao* to indicate the Celestial Master.

8. "To take leave" is written with the same character as "words," *ci* 辭.

9. This almost subitist approach is not within the mainstream of *taiping* thought.

10. As explained in more detail in section 66, great illusion 大迷 results from "frivolous and superficial" material.

11. The character *zhi* 止 is a way of writing *zu* 足 (foot); see *Shuo wen jie zi* p. 173a, and Morohashi (1985) no. 37365 (cf. Yu 2001a: 68).

12. One character put on top of the other; in his account of *shi* 士, Xu Shen (ca. 55–ca. 149) quotes Confucius as having said that a man becomes an expert *(shi)* by pushing *(tui* 推) all ten diverse items to unite them into one *(Shuo wen jie zi* p. 44a; cf. Serruys 1984: 66of.).

13. "Red" does not figure in the *Declaration*'s line (a). In stressing this color, the *Explanation* makes use of line (b). Lines (c) and (d) are also meant to explain each other, as are lines (f), (g), and (h). This might also hold true for the cryptic lines (j) and (k), which both have a concrete entity as their point of departure.

The *Explanation*'s way of dissecting and composing characters is an essential element of Han dynasty and later prognostic arts; cf. below, section 65, and Dubs 1938/1955, vol. 3, p. 540.

14. Fire is the dominating phase and red is the major color of the TPJ in that it is said to be heaven's color (*Chao*, p. 219, part 4, and repeated on p. 647, part 7; the passage is quoted by Li Xian, annotating *Hou Han shu* 30B.1084). Wang Mang (45 B.C.E.–23 C.E.) had declared that the Han had ruled under the auspices of the phase fire (Loewe 1986: 738), and Emperor Guangwu (r. 25–57) made this official in 26 C.E. (Cheng 1985: 33).

The following passage is close to the section at hand. It discusses the date at which the reforms at the outset of the era of great peace should be introduced. The Master says:

> Now is another beginning (*geng shi* 更始) of a great cycle (*da zhou* 大周) of the way of heaven. From above and below pure Yang reigns over heaven and earth. So one must urgently cut off all punishment and penalties. Heaven can be called spirit (*tian zhe cheng shen* 天者稱神), and so can Yang. For this reason heaven sends spirit[-like beings] to reign over men. (TPJ 212.677)

The student questions this proposition:

May I please ask why it is that heaven's *dao* is at present setting a primordial beginning (*yuan chu* 元初) for its great cycle and moreover renewing the numerological system (*geng da shu* 更大數) and putting the standard texts to the test (*kao zheng wen* 考正文)?

The answer is:

The present [the Han period?] is the superior leader of what is grouped [read *wu* 伍 for *wu* 五; see below] with Yang and is the beginning of what is grouped with fire. The utmost of fire in heaven above is the color of the sun and the moon [when they rise]. The red of fire shares its color with heaven; heaven's color is red, and fire is also red. We call fire spirit *(shen)*. When heaven and spirit remain prosperous, they keep things in their original state. For this reason we see the eleventh month as the time when heaven's order is at its starting point (*tian zheng* 天正). Up in heaven it is the same. Therefore, the color of its objects is red: red is the sun when it begins to turn back. (TPJ 212.678)

The student has further questions on this matter:

I would like to know why Yang and fire are in one particular group (*wu* 伍).

The answer:

The *qi* of each phase has its own group, not just fire. Metal and fire are the topmost groups, dominating the Red Emperor. Isn't this why the *Celestial Declaration* (*tian ce wen* 天策文) says "*Bing* 丙, *wu* 午, *ding* 丁, and *si* 巳 are the ancestors, are the beginning"? Beginning is predecessor; it is head. Therefore, the writing says, "are the ancestors, are the beginning." The beginning of all ten thousand activities is their red-colored heart [as can be seen in plants]. The heart on thorough reflection (*dong zhao* 洞照) knows things. Since Yang begins in the middle of Yin, it also reflects thoroughly. For this reason water, which is dark on the outside and bright within, reflects thoroughly. The center holds the vital essence of Yang. So Yang begins in the north, while Yin begins in the south. In the eleventh month it is warm below the ground, whereas in the fifth month it is cold. (TPJ 212.679; for an alternative reading of part of this passage see Petersen 1990b: 28f.).

From this it is clear that whoever governs under the color red is predestined to implement great peace and that the eleventh month is the right time of the year to introduce reforms.

The passage links metal with fire. Another possible link, based on one generating the other, is established between wood and fire (TPJ 99.225).

15. The expression *xing ci dao* 行此道 (he walks on this way) occurs four more times in this section in slightly varied form. It is rare in the rest of the text, and can only be found in section 57 (see below p. 218) and in section 212 (p. 678), in a passage that refers to the Master's declaration, as quoted above.

16. *Bing* and *wu* are equated with fire, according to the *Huainan zi, Bai hu tong*, and other sources; see Eberhard 1970: 62. So, when fire is seen as the dominating phase, they are indeed "at the beginning" and can be called "ancestors." The *Declaration* refers to the leading role of fire only in line (b), and only indirectly, referring to stems and branches

fire is associated with. The *Explanation*, however, dwells on this point. Its analysis follows an established pattern, as presented for instance in the *Huainan ʒi*. In Major's (1993: 88f.) translation of the "Solar Nodes":

> After fifteen more days, [the handle of the Dipper at midnight] points to *si* 巳. This is the Lesser Fullness node. Its sound is like [the pitch pipe] Great Budding. After fifteen more days [the handle of the Dipper at midnight] points to *bing* 丙. This is the Grain in Ear node. Its sound is like [the pitch pipe] Great Regulator. After fifteen more days, [the handle of the Dipper at midnight] points to *wu* 午. Yang *qi* reaches its maximum. Thus, it is said that the forty-sixth day [after the beginning of summer] marks the Summer Solstice [node]. Its sound is like [the pitch pipe] Yellow Bell. After fifteen more days, [the handle of the Dipper at midnight] points to *ding* 丁. This is the Lesser Heat node. Its sound is like [the pitch pipe] Great Regulator. After fifteen more days [the handle of the Dipper at midnight] points to *wei* 未.... This is the Great Heat node. Its (chromatic) note is Great Budding (*Huainan ʒi* 3 *"Tian wen"* 天問, pp. 13a–b).

From this we learn that *bing* and *wu* represent the highest amount of Yang in their respective groups, and that *ding* stands for the first appearance of Yin. It is followed by *wei* as the first branch position (no. 8) with some Yin content. When used to define years, the combinations *bingwu* and *dingwei* indicate dangerous years (Morohashi [1985] no. 35.12). The *Hunyuan sheng ji* (7.17b) quotes the TPJ as reading *wei* instead of *si*. However, the received text with the *Chao* and the *Lishi ʒhen xian tidao tongjian* (20.1b) reads *si*, which does not contradict the general picture in that, like *wei*, *si* also contains a certain spurious amount of Yin. *Si* is also the reading in TPJ 212.679, where the seven characters are quoted.

17. This term is here used to establish chronological order, as in the list of "Three Majestic Rulers, Five Emperors, Three Kings, Five Hegemons" (TPJ 102.236). In this way, the "Three Majestic Rulers" refers to the beginnings of government, when government was one with heaven (TPJ 204.645). But, from a more distant point of view, this period is called middle, not early, antiquity (TPJ 81.206), as if in the earliest period no rulers were needed.

18. Luo (1996: 117) suggests that *ʒi* 子 and *jin* 巾 are elements of *ʒi* 字 (character), which seems to be plausible. Kaltenmark suggests that we might here be confronted with elements of the characters for "(Yellow) Turbans 黃巾" and for "(Zhang) Jue 張角."

In a subitist vein, this passage stresses the recital of texts, as if the situation the text envisages could be reached through reading the appropriate text. In the TPJ this approach is rare but not unique; see above, note 9. Recitals are seen as influential. Reciting the wrong texts endangers life and brings about confusion (TPJ 66.164; 100.229f.). On the other hand, the arrival of great peace is accompanied by the recital of the right scripture (TPJ 66.165). The following statement is almost as strong as what is said in the passage at hand:

> If the whole empire were to recite and read the standard texts, heaven's *qi* would be received and great peace would arrive. (TPJ 78.192)

This resembles the ritual recital of the *Laozi* by adherents of the Celestial Master movement (see the Introduction, above).

19. So the receiving and transmitting of evil would come to an end.

20. This is a quotation from the first *Yi jing* hexagram: "Nine at the beginning means the dragon is hidden: do not act!" Here it means that the celestial book, as great as a dragon, should not yet be shown to the world.

21. The received text's version of *kan* 欽 (humble) must be understood with the *Chao* as *kan* 坎, the diagram.

22. The year of the first stem (*jia* 甲) and the first branch (*zi* 子), on the day of the winter solstice, was seen as the point of origin (see Kaltenmark 1979: 39). In the words of the TPJ:

> *Jiazi* is the starting point for heaven's order (*jiazi tian zheng ye* 甲子天正也). At the winter solstice, the sun begins to go back to its root (*ben* 本). *Yi* 乙 [second stem] *chou* 丑 [second branch] is the starting point for the order of earth, when plants (*wu* 物) sprout (*bu gen* 布根). *Bing* 丙 [third stem] *yin* 寅 [third branch] is the starting point for human order, when men begin to rise early in the morning [*pingdan* 平旦], open the doors, and go to work. These three set the beginning for the start of life for heaven, earth, and men; they are the sprouts and roots (*gen* 根 and *ben* 本) for plants. (TPJ 212.676)

This agrees with what commentators have seen as the meaning of *san zheng* 三正 (the three starting points or three orders), as used in the *Shu jing* ("*Gan shi*" 甘誓, p. 155c).

23. As Luo (1996: 118) says, this must be the southeast.

24. South is the direction fire comes from.

25. As Kaltenmark (1979: 39) has pointed out, the occurrence of *xuanjia* 玄甲 links this passage to another part of the text, where the student raises a question similar to what is discussed in the passage at hand:

> *After we have received the Celestial Master's serious instructions and thorough admonitions, when should we make public these writings, writings that put a stop to malevolence and fraud and promote the dao of heaven and earth?*

> In an *yisi* 乙巳 year [in 16 B.C.E., Jie Guang and Li Xun propagated a *taiping* scripture; in 165 C.E., another *yisi* year, Xiang Kai did the same], they were transmitted to men traveling in government service (*youke* 郵客) and were thus distributed. Later on, they were made public each year at *xuanjia* 玄甲, which is when heaven is first in a *jia* position, in the first week (*xun* 旬), just where primordial *qi* starts from. The writings, from beginning to end, are to be transferred to the country's leaders (*guojia* 國家) so that they will dissolve the evil that from the very beginning of heaven and earth has been received and transmitted.

> *Which characters are to be transferred (bifu 比付)?*

> These teachings in their written form contain masses of characters. Although you yourself know them in depth, you must not let the supreme harmony of majestic heaven and *dao* of first rank leak out. Go about transmitting them to those capable of receiv-

ing (*neng wang fu* 能 往 付) and analyzing them. When it comes to (*bidao* 比 到) *xuan-jia,* should there be someone who is exasperated [*fenfen* 憤 憤—a quality that Confucius (*Lun yu* 7.8) considered essential in a student] searching for my writings, then let him first have material on "guarding the one" and "the frivolous and superficial" [as used in section 72: "avoid the frivolous and superficial"].

We can only conjecture whether there is any historical background to these procedures. In any case, the student sees the contradiction in the Master's words:

> *They have already been transmitted to men traveling in government service and to experts in vitality techniques (youke fang shi* 郵 客 方 士) *so that they can submit them to a ruler of perfect virtue. What does that mean?*

The Master answers that because the implementation of reforms failed, the men who had received the writings must not have been the right men. Thus the process of distribution goes on, and with this also the need to pay attention to *xuanjia* dates (TPJ 165.459f.).

The expression *xuanjia zi,* used a few lines further down, is probably an abbreviation of *xuanjia jiazi.* Luo suggests (1996: 787) that the introduction of *xuanjia* (dark *jia*) refers to the darkness of the north, so that a year's first, most "northern," *jia* date would be called "dark."

26. The terms *ji* 紀 and *gang* 綱, "detailed and general rules" when combined, indicate all administrative activities. See, for example, *Shu jing,* "*Wu zi zhi ge*" 五 子 之 歌, p. 157a. The *Declaration*'s division of government into a lower and a higher stratum agrees with this terminology.

27. Since both are situated in the north, as Luo (1996: 119) points out.

28. This passage belongs to the large number of plant and growth references in the TPJ. Here, the celestial text's first existence is juxtaposed to the very beginnings of life. Time passes between the production of a text and men's awareness of its existence, as it does between the beginnings of a plant's growth and its first physical traces aboveground. However, much of the information given here remains unclear, in particular the interweaving of the *jiazi* nomenclature with the term *xuanjia.*

29. This narrow definition of the word "man" is unusual. It is in accord with the political orientation of this section, which shows much consideration for the ruling dynasty.

30. Wang Ming maintains the reading *dai* 殆 (danger), following the received text and the *Chao,* but states that it means *dai* 紿 (to cheat), as the *Lishi zhen xian tidao tongjian* reads. In the preceding *Chao* version of the *Declaration* (that is, chapter 38), he has corrected the text of the *Chao* accordingly.

31. The line of the *Declaration* that is here under discussion seems to hint at the role of confessions in the healing of illness. Such hints are rare in the TPJ. It is well established, however, that in the second-century Daoist community in Sichuan illness was seen as being caused by moral deficiency and healing involved confessions, which had to be true in order to be effective.

32. Section 50, as well as the *Chao* version, omits *le mo* 樂莫 before *le hu* 樂乎, thus reducing the phrase to five characters. Wang Ming has emended the text on the basis of the *Lishi zhen xian tidao tongjian*.

This reference to Chang'an and to the "Kingly Mother of the West" resembles the use of Chang'an and the west in second-century C.E. grave-securing writs: "The living belong to Chang'an in the west, the dead to Mount Tai in the east" and "The living belong to Chang'an, the dead to Mount Tai" (see Wu Rongzeng 1981: 58). This praise for the capital Chang'an can also be seen as yet another attempt to praise the Han rulers. It was the capital during most of the first Han dynasty, until the northwest came under attack in the first century C.E. It again became the capital in 190 C.E., when the boy emperor Xian (r. 189–220) was forced to leave his capital, Luoyang, for about six years and set up court in the west. Wu Rongzeng argues that it became "the place for the living" during the first centuries of Han rule, and that the role it plays in the second-century C.E. writs is reminiscent of an earlier period. The expression "long-lasting security" occurs throughout the TPJ. The virtuous lord enjoys it (TPJ 132.364), as do all beings (78.192). It is something desired by rulers. *Chang an* can also function as a transitive verb with *shen* (self) as its object (TPJ p. 303, *Chao*, part 5; 167.467). Long-lasting security can be achieved for a state if officials show moral responsibility (*shan;* TPJ 78.191) and the wishes of heaven and earth are respected (TPJ 154.433).

33. "Exclamatory" would be the word for *hu*.

34. The Queen Mother of the West figures prominently in Han dynasty sources; see Cahill 1993: 17–23.

35. In the second century C.E. it was fashionable to propose semantic links between words on the basis of their phonetic similarity, if we are to judge by the methods used by Xu Shen in his *Shuo wen jie zi* (see Rao Zongyi 1972 and Petersen 1990c).

36. Luo 1996: 121 explains that these "spirits" are body spirits.

37. The expression "experts in vitality techniques" *(fang shi)* occurs only here and in the passage quoted above from section 165, which has much in common with the passage at hand. What section 165 seems to say is that experts in vitality techniques received the Master's doctrine, distributed it, and did not bring about great peace or a great peace movement. Therefore, Master and disciples must now try again. As Anne Cheng (2001: 108f.) puts it, *fang shi* were one group of experts who competed for influence at the Han court and in society at large. The *Ru* (Confucianists, here translated as "educated" or "learned") were another such group.

38. The *wu wei wen* 無為文 can refer to the *Laozi*, from a philosophical point of view. However, the *Dongxian zhuan* (see *Yunji qiqian* 110.8b; cf. Bumbacher 2000: 394–99; the text, now lost, is of *Shangqing* or Upper Clarity origin) mentions a *wu wei taiping zhi dao*, so the phrase could just be another word for the material promoted by the TPJ's Celestial Master.

The meaning of *wu wei* in the TPJ is not easy to define. There are passages where it must be understood as "nonintervention," as, for instance, in section 44 (p. 46) and when used together with *chui gong* 垂拱 (to withdraw from business) (TPJ p. 307, *Chao*, part 5; p. 689, *Chao*, part 8). In other contexts, as, for instance, in the expression *yuan qi wu wei* (uncontrived, just like primordial breath) (TPJ 107.282), the TPJ seems to use *wu wei* in the *Xiang'er*'s understanding of *wei* as 偽, "to fabricate" (Bokenkamp 1997: 51f.). This is also the case when *wu wei* is seen as a way to transcend the world, as, for instance, at TPJ 136.381 and 191.588. There is, moreover, a passage in layer C material that refers directly back to *Laozi* 37—*wu wei zhe wu bu wei ye* 無 為 者 無 不 為 也—and goes on to say that this means to return to the beginning or the "root":

> Heaven and earth stem from Yin and Yang. Master the technique of *wu wei* and you can become complete; make the root go away and branches come near you and *dao* will be impaired. (TPJ 168.470)

This is accompanied by the picture of a meditation hall. The passage at hand can thus be understood as referring to texts that are not "fabricated" but devolved from heaven or its messengers.

"Coherence" (*xiang ying* 相應) is the criterion for trustworthiness, as opposed, we might say, to internal contradiction in personal statements (see section 43) as well as in texts (TPJ 78.191).

39. With the *Chao* I read *wen* instead of *wei* 委, so that the text reads *wen zi fu* 文 字 符. The *Chao* mistakenly reads *wen shou fu* 文 守 符.

40. This is the end of the *Explanation*. Three isolated passages follow in this section and the following section 51.

41. Luo 1996: 122 quotes *Bai hu tong* 6 "*Bi yong*" 辟 雍, p. 255, as evidence that the wise men of the past were all known to have had teachers.

42. It is part of the ritual of teaching and learning for the student to question the legitimacy of his contribution to the proceedings. TPJ 44.42 sets forth a similar argument against speaking. In other instances it is seen as an offense for a student not to speak when the Master invites him to do so; see TPJ 54.80.

43. The *Zhuangzi* (70.25.10) says that the wise man who understands all takes heaven for his teacher.

44. This sentence can help to affirm that the order of sections in the received text resembles a real curriculum of instruction, as the preceding sections 47 and 48 do indeed deal with the transmission of evil.

45. There is a tradition of discussing the extent to which a ruler is personally to be blamed for events and can be expected to rectify things; see Tjan 1949/1952, vol. 1, pp. 302f., note 194. The background for this is in the statement of Tang in the *Shu jing* ("*Tang gao*" 湯 誥, p. 162b), in Legge's (1960: 189f.) translation: "When guilt is found anywhere in you who occupy the myriad regions, it must rest on me. When guilt is found in me, the one man, it will not attach to you, who occupy the myriad regions." In contrast to this, the Celestial Master tends to attribute less importance to the ruler. The use of the

word *cheng* 承 is a good example of this, in that *Bai hu tong* 2 *"Hao"* 號, p. 45, identifies what is inherited by *(cheng)* later generations with the emperor's conduct and deeds, while the TPJ sees what is inherited and transmitted as resulting from the conduct of all.

46.   This passage contains a few details that add a little more precision to *cheng fu*. *Cheng* is explained as the aspect of the term oriented toward the past, and *fu* as oriented toward the future. The phenomenon of *cheng fu* is compared to a contagious disease.

47.   The summary says:

This section explains the ninety characters of the *Master's Declaration*.

This short section is placed after the *Declaration*, as the Master demands in this section's last sentence. It touches on the right and wrong of actions and the trustworthiness of actions as well as writings. What it says and how it says it are at odds with the main gist of the discussions between the Celestial Master and disciples. At the start, and without any guidance, the disciple comes up with the right answer. All that is left for the Master to do is elucidate this answer. But, more importantly, what the student says is not in line with the social and political approach that characterizes most of the TPJ. The fact that the Master seems to make a point of promoting this section also throws doubt on it. We must therefore suspect that its origins differ from the sections that precede and follow it.

·   ·   ·

(51.71) Step forward, Perfected. Of all the actions performed under heaven, which are right and which are wrong?

Prove that an action is appropriate and [you may then say that] it has merit. Therefore, whatever heals the illness someone is afflicted with is right.[1] An action you can't prove to be appropriate amounts to conduct without merit: what does not heal an illness is wrong. This applies not only to the ruler.

Excellent. What you have said is quite right. Although you did not say much, this can explain the myriad actions. I have nothing to add to this. Whenever we wish to compare right and wrong, we must always make this the criterion (*fa* 法). When no doubt remains, a tally (*fu* 符) will be trusted.[2]

What do you mean?

All actions are either trustworthy or not.[3] How must we proceed to examine it?

The wise and worthy of old observed how men acted. On this basis, they knew with greater clarity than that of the sun and the moon.

What you have said is so good that it must not be modified. You might wish to know that this is the way in which my writings prove to be trustworthy. Do you understand?

Yes, I do.

Go now. Call this the "true contract" (*zhen quan* 真券)[4] and be careful not to neglect it. Don't put it at the end,[5] but think of it as a section (*shu zhang* 書章) of the *Declaration* (*jue ce* 訣策).[6]

NOTES

1. *Jiechu* 解除 (to heal) is also the word for "exorcism" and the title of *Lun heng* chapter 75. It is what needs to be done to *cheng fu* before a person can be saved (see TPJ 179.534, layer B; cf. Espesset 2002b: 40).

2. So right and wrong cannot be decided through the conduct of an argument but lie beyond, in the results of an action. To prove a statement trustworthy the Master refers to the future, that is, he demands belief, just as a physician who proposes a certain cure does.

3. Yu (2001b: 469) sees this phrase as a question in the form of verb–negation–verb, and he points out that this form is not regularly used in Han dynasty material. Another example can be found at TPJ 66.158.

4. For this expression cf. TPJ p. 712, *Chao*, part 9: Heaven's document or "contract" (*quan wen* 券文) was only made public when men were no longer able to understand heaven's intentions by properly observing natural and social phenomena; cf. also section 63 (p. 140), where *quan shu* 券書 are mentioned together with *He tu* and *Luo shu*, that is, with the charts and texts brought forth by the Yellow River and the Luo. While *quan* occurs in the meaning of "contract" in section 65 (see below), it is not clear whether its usage in the passage at hand and in particular in section 63 allows the conclusion that the Master here deals with a contract between heaven and men similar to that drawn up with deities with regard to the healing of illness, the fate of the deceased, and the use of soil for burials (see Harper 2004). We may, however, assume that the use of the word

quan is meant to remind listeners of these contracts and to thereby stress that the contents of the document in question are binding.

5. The expression *xia fang* 下方 is not clear. I understand *fang* 方 (square) as *fang* 放 (to place), so the Master here advises students in which order they should collate his teachings.

6. The summary says:

This section talks about signs of trust, how to compare writings, and the true contract.

SECTION 52 · How to Work Hard to Do Good

This dense section deals with an individual's accountability for his deeds. This accountability does not end with death but extends to the world beyond. Good deeds guarantee a happy life in the netherworld, and with some luck they can also bring longevity or, when someone's personal disposition is right, an avoidance of death. This main argument is supported by two general observations about the human condition. One is concerned with life's stages and is reminiscent of what is said in section 44 about growing up and raising children. It is argued that full-time religious practice is possible only after one has completed raising a family. The other observation regards humankind's historical development, of which individual life is seen as a replica. After an original state of harmonious interaction with nature, man became a source of damage to his environment and to himself. The good deeds that men perform today are meant to undo such damage. The ruler is in a special position. Good deeds on his part will result in great peace, and the happiness of his afterlife depends on them.

The section is based upon two assumptions, the desirability of living for a long time and the existence of a link between morality and longevity. Doctrines that oppose these assumptions, and in particular the first one, are accused of causing harm and preventing humankind from achieving great peace.

These considerations are placed in the wider context of great peace thought: the chance to abolish inherited evil, the promise to achieve peace and with it longevity and a happy afterlife for many, and, finally, the request to spread this good news widely.

. . .

(52.72) Step forward, Perfected! Living in this world, men are under altogether how many constraints?

What do you mean?

That you state how many constraints men in general suffer from.

They are under many constraints.

But can't you give a name to them?

I can't.

You have no insight, still! In this world, men are under four constraints.

What does that mean?

It means that a child at birth receives life from its father and mother. When it is small, it never imagines that its father and mother will depart. This is the first constraint. When children have grown up, they can't help it:[1] daughters desire a husband and sons a wife. They are unable to control their emotions, and the love they feel does not allow of any separation. This is the second constraint. Their love brings forth children. While man and wife grow older and become less attractive, their children are young and lovely. But they must be brought up. This is the third constraint. When children have grown up and no longer need to be nourished, parents will have become old and unable to do things. This is the fourth constraint. It might still work if men, having been under these four constraints, can find an enlightened teacher and fix their thoughts on safeguarding *dao*. With great talent and the right destiny[2] they might be able to transcend this world or, second best, gain longevity.[3] Or they might enjoy living in their body as long as it lasts and have further cause for joy when their *hun* and *bo* spirit are belowground.[4]

What do you mean?

Down below when they receive someone who has just died, they always ask what he has done and what he achieved while alive. (52.73) Thus the things one does during one's lifetime decide how one is entered in the registers. Men are accountable for their deeds and must for this reason act with great care. Whether someone is safe or in danger depends entirely on himself.[5] Keep it in mind, Perfected. You understand that this is to warn you?

Yes, I do. What the Celestial Master tells me is new to me.

Well, I tell you these things because I see that you continue to have good intentions.

I am afraid you might become idle and weary, so I see the need for clarification, documentation, and instruction.

Yes, indeed.

What do you expect from your present studies, Perfected?[6]

I expect to fulfill my years.

What an excellent aim! We may say that you have grasped what *dao* means. But the common people expect to die of old age while what they really die from is the good and bad of their deeds.[7]

What do you mean? I would like to know.

Well, stick to the study of the good, let your spirit roam about, and be merry and when you die you will become a demon who merrily roams about. It is incontestable that never again will you suffer any distress. Those who bring distress and suffering upon themselves turn into demons who suffer distress after death. A wicked person becomes after death a wicked demon. All these matters are obvious enough for everyone to see, and yet men don't want to do good and make their *hun* spirit happy. This is a most severe fault.

What do you mean?

At birth, men receive the standard *qi* of heaven and earth,[8] and are joined by the four seasons and five phases. This was the situation with the ancestors (*xian ren zhi tong ti* 先人之統體). For a while, they each dwelt as a particular body among the four seasons and five phases of heaven and earth. For their part, they always loved to do good and never had any worries. But life went on. Later generations were different. All along they have plagued the bodies of heaven and earth, the four seasons, and the five phases[9] so that men themselves have become resentful and upon death even their *hun* and *bo* spirit remain in a distressed state. So [we know that] foolish scholars give shallow advice (*bu shen ji* 不深計); since they are unable to prolong [a man's] existence, they make him want to die quickly and to show no regret when he dies. (52.74) The vital spirits [who reside in the human body] are grieved and sad [about this]. They have given these lowly scholars no cause to thus distress and anger them.[10]

So the great worthies and wise men of old, who gave profound counsel and were farsighted, knew what it was like. Therefore, they never ceased studying [how to do good]. A sovereign who enjoys thinking of great peace gains heaven's approval. His merit multiplies. His *hun* spirit roams about happily forever and partakes in heaven's good *qi*.[11]

A ruler not able to bring peace to his reign is not tuned to heaven's will, does not obtain heaven's favor (*yi* 意), and gains no merit with heaven. Even in death his *hun* spirit is still held responsible in the world below and is joined with wicked *qi*. For this reason the lords of supreme wisdom in early antiquity who knew of this worked very hard.[12] Because a foolish man's counsel is shallow he is held to account by heaven as long as he lives and by earth after his death.

How frightening. Although I am foolish and blind, I don't wish to hear of this.

Well, you have come here to learn. If you don't want to hear of such things you just have to work hard to be good!

Yes, I will! For as long as the Celestial Master lives on earth he makes us understand heaven's commands. What we have been taught is deep and substantive. So what can we do to prevent such things?

Excellent. You must quickly spread my teachings so that all men under heaven will follow them. They will for their own person stabilize the vital essence and in their thoughts proceed in communion with great *dao*. Then they will know for themselves where faults and errors come from, and the load of evil that has been received and is transmitted can be abolished. Heaven and earth will rejoice, and the years of life will be multiplied by a return back to [the situation] of early antiquity.[13]

Excellent indeed!

All right. What I have to say has reached a certain conclusion. Study hard and come again another day.

Yes, I will.

Think carefully about the writings you have received, from beginning to end. Not to concentrate on one's studies is, it must be said, a sign of confusion. One has nowhere to go from unless research into things reaches [the realms] where there is neither form nor shape[14] and thinking touches upon what is vital and spiritlike.

Yes, excellent![15]

NOTES

1. I read *bu* 不 (not) for *da* 大 (big) and understand *sheng* 勝 here as it must be understood in the next sentence, that is, as "to control."

2. For some men the length of life is predestined:

Even before their birth, while still in the womb, some men on this earth have their personal and family name on the registers of those who won't die. (TPJ 182.552, layer B)

Such men are, however, exceptional. The Celestial Master's students are not among them; they will be attributed extra years for the service they have rendered to heaven (TPJ 41.34). In general, good deeds were said to influence the length of life, as explained below in this section and in section 182 (layer B). When Ge Hong devised immortality techniques for the educated gentleman who studies the classics he followed more than just his personal interest.

3. One of the Master's attempts to define "longevity" (cf. Kaltenmark 1979: 41f.) is the following:

> When heaven provides men with life, it follows its own rules and models (*ge fa* 格法). Individual life derived from heaven and earth consists of thirty years, just as heaven and earth, sun and moon are interlocked with each other. What is extra is a leap unit. So what goes beyond individual life amounts to being transcendent (*xian ren* 仙人). Of all the years destined by heaven the highest form of longevity measures one hundred and twenty years, earthly longevity measures one hundred years, human longevity eighty, the hegemons' sixty, and the longevity of the neighborhood group of five (*wu* 伍) measures fifty years. Below that, life and death are not of a fixed size, but everyone suffers from the disaster of inherited and transmitted evil (*cheng fu zhi zai ze* 承負之災責). (TPJ p. 464, *Chao*, part 6; cf. also p. 723, *Chao*, part 1)

4. Here, as opposed to section 46, *hun* and *bo* are used in a nondistinct fashion. This is also the way the *Zuo zhuan* (Duke Zhao, twenty-fifth year, p. 2107a), for example, mentions them: they both give liveliness to a person, and both linger around the corpse for a while, possibly in the "shape of an evil apparition," in the words of James Legge (1960: 618, translating Duke Zhao, seventh year, p. 2050b). But at some point their ways must part, if we are to trust the *Huainan zi* dialogue between *hun* and *bo* (chap. 16 *"Shuo shan"* 説山, 1a–b). Brashier (1996: 127–38) calls the dualistic approach to *hun* and *bo* spirit scholastic and argues convincingly that the belief put forth in the section at hand—that at death, both vanish into the ground—was widespread.

To properly evaluate this passage it is useful to look at Confucius's idea of human growth from the age of fifteen until the age of sixty, or at the framework of Confucian-oriented biographical writings, in which interest in life's "higher aims" is often said to become manifest in early youth. Confucius's theoretical appraisal of family life is in contrast to the scant attention his teachings pay to its practical aspects. Instead, Confucius sees a human being's development as intellectual. *Taiping*-oriented human beings differ: the course of their lives is dominated by concern, or we could call it love, for their family.

5. The registers kept in the netherworld or in heaven are of great interest in layer B, which centers on how to become transcendent; their accuracy is mentioned as a threat (TPJ 179.531f.) but also as a promise (TPJ 179.538).

6. This change of topic is abrupt and leaves the previous topic unfinished. The "four constraints" have not yet been fully explored.

7. The relationship between goodness and longevity has many facets. While there is

hardly a passage in the text that would depict longevity as being achieved outside moral restraints, it is not often stated that goodness in itself leads to long life. The connection between the two is less direct. This can be seen from the following passage, which discusses a ruler whose personal goodness is said to attract good officials, who will in turn prolong his life:

> Many officials of early antiquity were transcendent and lived long lives and could thus help their lord to long life. In middle antiquity, many knew how to hold on to *dao* and virtue and could thus help their lord to live without any worries. In late antiquity, there are many fools who don't know the true doctrine *(dao)* and who make their lord quite foolish. (TPJ 155.436)

8. *Zheng qi* 正氣 (standard *qi*) is a word for the natural, unperturbed state of things. It can be rediscovered if lost, and reinstalled together with the *qi* of peace (*ping;* TPJ 209.668). It makes the sun, the moon, and the stars shine brightly, the wind and rain come at the proper time, Yin and Yang cooperate, and the ten thousand beings and plants find their place (TPJ 208.662). Evil deeds, even if they have only partial effect, destroy it (TPJ 134.375; 60.109). The more of such *qi* the better:

> If true *dao* and virtue were ample there would be lots of upright *qi.* In consequence, few men would suffer from illness and many would live long lives. (TPJ 63.139)

Its opposite is "wicked *qi*," which haunts malefactors even in afterlife.

9. The Master reminds us that natural disasters are heaven's reaction to men's trespasses. Since men remained unaware of their own wrongdoings they did not willingly accept the punishment they were afflicted with. Their resentment increased the amount of evil they had created and the misery they had to suffer.

10. "Shallow advice" refers to "mistaken" opinions about moral conduct (TPJ 103.251), the evaluation of textual material (TPJ 132.356), and the attitude toward ominous events (TPJ 204.639). Here the paragraph on "shallow advice" corresponds to the "good counsel" of the following paragraph. Its polemics are directed against nonbelievers, that is, men who don't believe that moral conduct is the basis for health. This is in contrast to those men who give or accept proper advice and who "never cease studying," presumably studying Celestial Master material. When we look for "mistaken" opinions on death and afterlife, passages in the *Liezi* come to mind, which don't depict the netherworld as a place for retribution.

11. *Shan qi* 善氣 and *e qi* 惡氣, "good and wicked *qi*," are a pair, as are standard or upright and evil *qi* (*zheng qi* 正氣 and *xie qi* 邪氣; see TPJ p. 648, *Chao,* part 7). *Shan qi* brings success (*shanshi* 事; see TPJ p. 642, *Chao,* part 7).

12. The *Chao* adds *wei shan* 為善 (to do good), thus making the text tidy.

13. It was assumed that the ancients had a long life span; see *Lun heng* 56 *"Qi shi"* 齊世, p. 803, and *Huangdi neijing suwen* 1 *"Shang gu tian zhen lun"* 上古天真論, p. 2a; cf. Luo 1996: 132f. This belief is also evident in the long reigns attributed to the mythological rulers of the past.

14. Spirit is explained as being "something that changes without ever assuming form and shape and that is never exhausted" (TPJ 156.439). Thus the process of picturing body deities is called the "method of what is without form and shape" (*wu xing xiang zhi fa* 無形象之法) (TPJ 109.293). The expression is rare. It occurs only once in the *Yunji qiqian* (2.4a) in a description of aspects of the original, primordial chaos.

15. The summary says:

> In this section the Celestial Master warns that men who don't work hard during their lifetime will be held responsible after death as *hun* spirits for the reception and transmission [of evil].

This is an adequate summary. The section deals with the continuity of "moral issues" beyond life, although for a definition of "good" *(shan)* we must look elsewhere in the text.

This section loosely connects several topics by proposing that in each of the situations discussed a return to the root will make things right. Giving an example of the role of the root, the Master identifies as a root the original version of a text that must be restored when layers of annotation and corruption have damaged it. He promises that when texts are in proper shape, so, too, will be society at large. Moreover, since brevity and oneness are characteristics of the root, it is best that one stick to a single attempt in the process of divination. "Root" is also the oneness from which the cosmos originates, attested to by a brief review of the changing seasons through the year. We must assume that a return to the oneness and brevity from which things begin is as necessary for man in his confusion as it is for textual materials and cosmic entities.

This argument presents the development of texts in a different light from section 55, for instance, which claims that a complete collection of all written material throughout the ages is necessary for distilling the true doctrine. In this section, texts are seen as corresponding to structures of the universe. They are depicted as if they were in a well-known order and meant to demonstrate the cyclical movement of which everything is part.

The last part deals with teaching and its glory. Thus toward the end of the section, as in sections 50 and 55, the activities and person of the teacher are moved to the fore and it is proclaimed that teaching at its best makes the student fit to save the world.

(53.75) Step forward, Perfected. You have come here to learn. Does it take few items or many to obtain extensive knowledge of what *dao* means?[1]

Well, its prerequisites are many.

Alas! Deep down your knowledge of *dao*'s essential meaning is not yet extensive. *Now heaven is "one." It turns to earth, which is "two." What does this mean? The earth being "two" will turn to man, who is "three."*[2] *Why? I would like to know what this means, that they turn one to the other.*

Well, earth is employed by heaven and man by earth. In a year when heaven rejoices in happiness, it will let the ten thousand plants and beings on earth grow well. Should it be unhappy it will let plants decay, even if earth should wish to nourish them.[3] If earth is good, the people who live on it will love the good. This clearly proves how they employ each other. So, through too many embellishments[4] government turns into disorder and does not obtain heaven's approval. (53.76) Instead, we should return to the root of things.[5] When men speak too much, they don't see this. They should instead return to a basic guideline (*ben yao* 本要) in order to sustain their words and deeds.

Therefore, the original text is completed in a single layer of words. With its transmission comes the creation of chapter and verse commentaries.[6] At the next level is an analysis of difficult passages (*jie nan* 解難). Difficult passages must be explained to prevent men from moving away from truth. The fourth level of words consists of adaptations (*wen ci* 文辭) [of the original text]. At the fifth level, fake texts are produced, and at the sixth level [these fake products] are meant to deceive men. At the seventh level lies the distortion of the original text. At the eighth level, the distance from what has originally been taught is becoming bigger and bigger. At the ninth level, the text is in great disorder; at the tenth, it is completely corrupted. Therefore, a scripture that has reached this tenth stage must be revised, or its further transmission will end in extinction.[7]

Whatever has been destroyed must return to the root. Thus for a new beginning we return to safeguarding the one. This is why the numbers of heaven begin with one and end in ten. This characterizes the nature of heaven's way as it is.[8] So when the wise men of old had a query they undertook a first divination to see whether the situation was auspicious or ominous. In this way they guarded their root and spirits sent by heaven would descend to make the announcement. When one divines a second time, spirits sent by earth will step forward and give information; and at the third time the spiritual beings living among men will do so. Going beyond this and undertaking more divination amounts to deception without any prophetic content. If we divine often we do not hit the truth.[9] When someone's writings and sayings are numerous, they are not held precious.

Excellent, indeed! Now since the Celestial Master constantly takes pity on my short-comings, I would like to beg permission to raise one other point.

Go ahead.

Why do numbers stop at ten?

Excellent. Asking about the pattern that lies behind this matter shows profound knowledge. Well, the numbers of heaven begin with one and end with ten.[10]

Why is this so?

Heaven begins as one. When it moves downward to be with earth there are two. Yin and Yang jointly create life. The ten thousand plants and beings start sprouting in the north, since primordial *qi* arises from *zi*, "son" [the first earthly branch].[11] When primordial *qi* turns toward the northeast, plants spread their roots in *jue*, the "horn" [the first of the twenty-eight lunar mansions],[12] and when it turns toward the east, sprouts shine forth. It turns southeast and branches and leaves grow, becoming thick when it turns south, and almost complete when it moves southwest. (53.77) When primordial *qi* turns west, their produce is ripe, and when it turns toward the north-west, plants die. Since what is dead must again return to its beginning the character *hai* [the twelfth earthly branch][13] consists of two humans who both embrace the one, thus commencing the three majesties [of heaven, earth, and man] (*san huang* 三皇). Therefore, *hai* is "the kernel" (*he* 核), where congealing [freezing] sets in, and that is why water starts freezing in the tenth month. *Ren* [the ninth heavenly stem] is *ren* (pregnant).[14] In this state, a woman is bound to grow bigger each day, so *zi*, "son" [the first branch], is growing. In these three stages,[15] plants and beings turn back to the very beginning after having matured through the harmonious union of Yin and Yang. We call this return to the root *jiazi* [the first stem and branch]. Now when heaven's way gives life to plants and beings they are found everywhere, and they mature by taking in *qi* of heaven and earth, the four seasons, and the five phases. These plants and beings will be somewhat deficient as soon as one single *qi* is not sufficient. Thus, the numbers amount to ten because they take root in heaven and earth and encircle their eight directions. Do you understand any better? (53.78)

Yes! Excellent, indeed! How very kind of you!

Do not say thank you![16]

Why not?

The task of teaching a pupil is as heavy as that of father and mother when they give life to a child. You can't free yourself from your obligation by saying thank you.

What do you mean?

When a couple has not yet brought forth children, they might foolishly spread semen [as if it were] on uncultivated land. Should it suit the soil, then trees and other plants might take root. So [men] produce offspring without knowing how. They spread semen unconsciously. How can they say where? Afterwards plants and trees grow big. [But] man is born from the togetherness of Yin and Yang. So how is his upbringing related to that of plants and trees?[17]

After a man has come to life, he might be careless and, instead of serving a good teacher, he might serve a hideous and foolish one who instructs others in how to do wrong. Learning how to become engaged in evil activities will sometimes lead a man to his death and his family to ruin. He will be accused of crimes and his family will be extinguished, or he will live without knowledge and learning and thus become foolish. Now such a man, ignorant as he is, will not only die in distress and misery, but he will also be accused of his faults in the world below. What his *hun* and *bo* spirits will experience will not allow them to roam about happily, and he himself, when dead, will not manage to become a good demon.[18]

But a man who has learned from a good teacher will change from being foolish and mean to being a good person.[19] Should he not stop at being good he might become worthy. If he should go still further, he might become wise. If this does not stop him, he might acquire some profound knowledge of the true doctrine *(dao)*. Should he safeguard this and go still further, he might transcend death.[20] If being a transcendent he still does not come to a halt, he might become perfected; and if he goes further, he could become like a spirit. If he does not stop there, he will have virtue, as heaven does. If he goes even further his virtue will resemble that of primordial *qi*, which embraces heaven and earth in the eight directions, so that everything lives by receiving its *qi*. Since its virtue continues to cover heaven and earth in the eight directions, vital spirits will come from heaven and earth to drink and eat; no one on earth would not make them offerings. And yet such a person [with the virtue of primordial *qi*] would remain fearful: he might slacken and not be able to make the spirits come. This is the merit we talk of when a very good teacher produces a good student.[21] Is it possible to say thank you for this?

How frightening! Foolish as I am I have broken a sacred rule. I have trespassed in what I have said.

How modest! No more, Perfected! All right, you have understood that a student must not say thank you for having gained knowledge. (53.79)

Yes, I have![22]

NOTES

1. The treatment of "constraints" in section 52 has shown that the student is encouraged to move inductively toward a certain level of abstraction, which allows guidelines to be formulated without going into specifics. So at this stage he should already have learned that "few" must be the answer.

2. This is one way of reading *Laozi* 42.

3. Here the *Chao* reduces the argument beyond recognition: "Now when heaven rejoices in happiness it will let (read *shi ling* 使令 for *shi jin* 使今) the ten thousand beings on earth rejoice in happiness, although earth is the one who nourishes. If it is good, so too will be the people who inhabit it." This eliminates the hint of a possible disagreement between heaven and earth, which makes what the Celestial Master says interesting. Whether the *Chao*'s reading stems from conscious correction or from negligence we cannot tell.

4. The problem of "too many embellishments" is of particular concern in this part of the text. *Duo duan* 多端 are also mentioned in sections 44 and 45 and are contrasted, as here, to "root" and a simplification of government.

5. The *Laozi* deals with the metaphysical place of "root," expressed as *ben* 本 (*Laozi* 26; 39) or *gen* 根 (*Laozi* 6; 16; 26; 59). The image of root and branches played a major role in early Chinese discourse. *Ben* was understood to mean agriculture, as opposed to *mo* (branch), which referred to all other economic activities (see *Shiji* 10.428). The Celestial Master followed suit: For him, "root" (*ben gen* in the passage at hand) is in a general sense "the beginning":

> The noble root at the beginning of heaven and earth is the origin of *qi*. If you wish to achieve great peace, you must keep the root in mind. (TPJ p. 12, *Chao*, part 2)

The unity of the three, which plays a role in this section, can be seen as "root":

> Scholars must practice what these writings say and discover their root *(gen)*. Their root, or their ancestor (*ben zong* 本宗), lies in taking the unity of three as the guiding principle (*san yi wei zhu* 三一為主; as a TPJ quotation ["part 1, no. 1"] in *Daojiao yishu* 2 and *Yunji qiqian* 6, see TPJ p. 9).

As becomes clear from what is said in sections 44 (p. 46) and 50 (p. 64), "root" is a certain state or quality that can be lost through misguided behavior. This loss has disastrous consequences, including the problem of inherited evil. The corruption of textual material is another of its manifestations. In the past, all was well because standard texts were relied on; this proves that:

standard texts and standard sayings are the standard root *(zheng genben)* of heaven, earth, men, and the ten thousand plants and beings. (TPJ 152.416)

This is why rulers are expected to supervise the preservation and collection of texts.

This understanding of "root" prevails throughout the text. In this respect, the root is opposed to the branches: "discard the root and stick to the branches" and you will fail (TPJ 107.284; also 168.470, layer C). This image is occasionally modified by introducing a "center," the trunk:

Stick to the root and you will see it all, stick to the trunk and you will see half of it, stick to the branches and you won't be able to return to the method *(dao)* of self-reflection. (TPJ 107.284; similar passages p. 720, *Chao*, part 1 and 132.361)

Another aspect of the root is its togetherness with the branches. The welfare of the branches depends on the root (TPJ 192.593). The two are related to each other as teacher and disciple (TPJ p. 308, *Chao*, part 5). Thus, concern for the root strengthens the branches (TPJ 186.569).

6. *Zhang ju* 章 句 were a form of annotation popular among Han dynasty scholars. The Celestial Master argues that they were verbose (TPJ 152.420) and superficial (TPJ 106.277f.), but he also attributes to them a high rank compared to other textual material. The term occurs in the *Han shu yi wen zhi* and must have been prominent enough in the early Han period to have been used in a pejorative manner in *Han shu* biographies (see Morohashi [1985] no. 25761.45–48).

7. The corruption of texts is seen as paralleling the increase in inherited evil, so that the history of written material reflects social history:

Standard texts have their root in what heaven and earth feel, they safeguard and structure primordial *qi*. When antiquity's wise writings appeared, they investigated the characters of the original standard [texts]. All that was taught was coherent and the subtle sayings were explained. All this was as demanded by primordial *qi*. Esoteric sayings (*mi ci* 密 辭) came second, and in third place were chapter and verse commentaries. Next came the creation of frivolous and superficial writings. In the fifth place there were divisions of opinion, and these were maintained stubbornly. Then deceptive texts were produced. Chapter and verse commentaries retain a certain respect for their root. What comes after them is unhealthy. It diverts heaven and earth from their course and causes emperors and kings to suffer bitterly without end. This is exactly the reason why [we] don't really obtain order. Luckily you want to respond to heaven's grace and repay heaven's great achievements. Heaven doesn't want men to be involved with products of shallow talent and mannered craftsmanship. It wants men to get together and put these texts in order, and thus avoid confusion. (TPJ 78.190; cf. Hachiya 1983: 51f.)

The passage argues that the world's problems can be mended through maintaining the correctness of texts. It describes how all the texts are to be collected and then proceeds:

To explain [what you have collected and collated] is what we mean by making a chapter and verse commentary. This grasps the intentions of true *dao*. We may say that to collect and explain texts dissolves [or "explains"] heaven's worries and drives great illness away. We may also say that it abolishes earth's sufferings, allows emperors and kings to go on [spiritual] journeys and to find favor with heaven, and helps each of the ten thousand beings to find its place. (TPJ 78.191)

This identifies writing about an issue with understanding it as well as with mending the problem. Certain types of texts are thus seen to represent a certain style of government, as discussed in section 41. The hierarchical order of texts and of political systems is said to be in correlation, and thus the distortion of textual material becomes a symptom of political and social corruption. Just as corruption of a text reaches a certain point at which the text will be lost unless it is rewritten, so too the world can become so depraved that it cannot be redeemed.

8. The expression *shi tian dao ziran zhi xing ye* 是 天 道 自 然 之 性 也 characterizes the preceding statement as a priori, that is, not based on external grounds.

9. Someone who is able to divine correctly is morally superior. A man whose prognoses are always correct can serve emperors and kings; one needs to get nine out of ten right to serve a feudal lord; with eight out of ten right, one can serve men in general. The diviner needs spiritual help. Whether he receives it or not depends on his personal merit:

> To obtain the best warning one must ask spirits to predict events. When predictions are always true, one's method agrees with the spirits of heaven. When nine out of ten are true, it agrees with the earth's spirits, and when eight out of ten are true, it agrees with the spirits of men. Predictions are useless if the result is worse. Someone might get it 100 percent right when he first ventures to consult the spirits but less and less right as time goes on. [This means] he is put on trial in the way *(dao)* of spirits who make him get it wrong. When this happens he [must] rejuvenate himself, straighten out his thinking, and be of vital goodness without any bad intentions. (TPJ 152.413f.)

His predictions will then again prove to be 100 percent right. Divination thus resembles the production of texts; its accuracy signifies a proper attitude. The passage at hand confirms this point when it argues that divination should not be undertaken carelessly and unnecessarily.

The passage doesn't tell us what type of divination the Master is referring to. Considering his frequent references to the *Yijing* we may assume that he means popular Han dynasty techniques that make use of yarrow stalks, numerology, and *Yijing* passages; cf. Loewe 1981: 46–50. It is difficult to find material in the text that could contribute in some detail to Kalinowski's (2003) project on divination in medieval China.

10. This is common knowledge for the Celestial Master: see TPJ 139.391 and 398. In this respect, earth (TPJ 129. 335) and men resemble heaven:

> *I would like to know why the number of heaven is exactly one.*

> One goes back to the time when primordial *qi* was pure; altogether, primordial *qi* had no structure, just as wind has no structure. Therefore, you can name it all together "one."

One congealed into heaven and, because heaven has above and below and the eight directions, it is ten. There are also the five directions, each with its own Yin and Yang, so their figure is ten. Moving downward it comes to rest as earth. Once it rests there, all numerical figures come about through ten. Thus man, who resembles heaven's cipher, is born after ten months. (TPJ 139.392)

The introduction of numerical figures is meant to explain the development of and cooperation between diverse entities. Another structure appears from a threefold occurrence of the five phases: "The figure of heaven is five, that of earth is five, and so is that of man" (TPJ p. 217, *Chao*, part 4).

11. As *Huainan zi* 3 *"Tian wen"* 天問, p. 12b puts it, in Major's (1993: 88) translation, "When the (handle of the) Dipper points to *zi* (at midnight), it is the Winter Solstice (node)."

12. It is situated in the east; see *Huainan zi* 3.31a.

13. Yu (2001a: 76) quotes the *Shuo wen jie zi* (p. 1312a) to explain that *hai* 亥 is a pictograph of a man and a woman in embrace.

14. The character *ren* 任 (in office) is correctly understood by Luo (1996: 136) as *ren* 妊 (pregnant).

15. The "three stages" are, with Luo (1996: 136), those of *hai* 亥, *ren* 壬, and *zi* 子. This outline of the course of the year is unusual in its combination and etymological interpretation of factors from separate tables. Also, the argumentative purpose of the passage is thin. It does not seem to reach beyond numerological speculation, as opposed to section 60, for instance, where the Master gives a mainstream version of the occurrence of growth through the seasons, linked to the demand for benevolent government.

16. This is repeated in section 209 (p. 668), where the Master argues that he instructs the disciple because heaven bids him do so and not in order to do the disciple a favor.

17. This is making the best of a passage of which Luo and Long don't seem to produce coherent translations and which did not make it into the *Chao*. Since this passage would perhaps fall under "sexual techniques," censorship might have resulted in the received text being as difficult as it is. What the passage seems to be saying is that it is easy to be born but much more demanding to become a proper person since latter involves education.

18. That is, he will not be of benefit to his descendants.

19. A "good person" is here someone who believes in *dao*, as above, in section 41. Religious ranks are conceived as steps in an ongoing process of learning:

A foolish man becomes worthy through learning. When a worthy man learns without interruption he becomes wise. A wise man who continues to learn becomes a man of *dao*, who will through study turn into a transcendent. A transcendent can learn to become perfected, and through continuous learning a perfected becomes spiritlike. (TPJ p. 725, *Chao*, part 1)

20. Throughout layer A the avoidance of death, important as it is (see below, section

66, p. 335, for instance), is not the only aim of the *taiping* adept. Here it is depicted as nothing but one step in a spiritual career that extends all the way to saving the world. The *taiping* believer is expected to "nourish the vital principle," which is necessarily a personal and private activity with a society-oriented consciousness.

21. This passage is not in the *Chao* but is quoted in the *Daoxue zhuan* and the *Taiping yulan*, both of which give the TPJ as their source. Neither gives a hint of the general direction of the passage, that is, the argument about saying "thank you." They both quote the stages of learning as proof of the benefits to be gained from relying on a teacher. The *Taiping yulan* (659.2945a) adds a few sentences that are almost too smooth to be from the TPJ:

> Not to get a good teacher is to go astray. Teachers transmit their knowledge to each other until it is more solid than metal and rock. What has not been transmitted by a teacher we call a random fabrication, which will lead to evil. To depart from such a teacher is to depart from the true doctrine *(dao)*. In this consists the art of self-destruction. [Teaching the] doctrine *(dao)* are ancestral teachers of two ranks, *zong shi* 宗師 and *zu shi* 組師害.

The gist of this TPJ passage is unusual. The path outlined for the disciple reaches far beyond the human realm. The person who reaches primordial *qi* and what is as it is becomes a cosmic force. All this refers to stages of meditation, which explains the expressive, exalted use of language.

22. The summary says:

> This section explains the difference between root and branches and the figures for the end and the beginning; it is the essential text on meritorious conduct between father and son and teacher and student.

How to Enjoy Giving Life
Wins Favor with Heaven

The text in this section is damaged. It seems to consist of the transcripts of two separate dialogues, both of which are corrupt beyond any hope of emendation. The first
dialogue concerns moral action. The issue is raised in a broad context that includes
one's personal life as well as political policy, and it is dealt with in a practical manner,
integrating rather than excluding a wide range of approaches. Although it is best to
resemble heaven, bring things to life, and let the country's administration take care
of itself, not everyone is free to act that way. The Master here shows some understanding of the difficult decisions a public servant might have to make. Once in government a person must strive to do without the penal code, we are told, since punishments cause grief and thus perturb heaven. If they must be applied, however, it is
good to limit the number of people put to death. A person who goes so far as to eradicate a family or a group of neighbors can no longer be called good. Such criticism
of strict rule was common. The saying "The dead cannot be brought back to life, nor
the amputated parts of the body rejoined" has been transmitted in various places.[1]

   This section throws some light on the justification used by members of the Taiping and other popular Han dynasty movements for attacking and killing the
officials they could get hold of, as was described above in the introduction. Severe
officials are, in the Celestial Master's opinion, evil, since they destroy life instead of
protecting it as well as they can. This makes them morally inferior and deprives them,
we might conclude, of the authority and respect that they would otherwise be entitled to due to their position.

The transmitted text of the second session does not seem to refer to any particular topic of discussion. Instead, the student's words take up more space than usual. He describes his own inferior position but otherwise does not say much. Most of the passage consists of those admonitions that generally introduce and appear at the conclusion of discussions. The text mentions the Celestial Master's personal excellence, the student's eagerness, and the way in which the Master's message is to be distributed. Perhaps this is all that the second half of this section originally consisted of. This content agrees with the account of the section in the summary, "polite conduct between teacher and disciple."

· · ·

(54.80) Step forward, Perfected. In the deeds of men and the reign of kings—what is best?

It is best to have sympathy with all and harm no one, as heaven does.

Your words, we must say, agree with *dao*'s intentions.[2] However, although no government is more outstanding than the one that resembles heaven, there must also be one next in line.

What do you mean? I have with great care been able to say one thing. I will not speak twice. Would that the Celestial Master would explain it all!

Well, the best way for a man to act and for a king to reign is to always desire to give life. Always be as eager in this as someone who draws water from a well when thirsty and you will do the right thing. In the next turn, nothing is better than to enjoy bringing life to perfection.[3] Always be as anxious to do this as you are worried about your own person and you will do right. Benevolence and generosity are the next best. It is right to feel as much distress for others when you see them poor and exhausted as you would about your own hunger and cold.[4] The next best is to promulgate laws efficiently. Without taking any interest or joy in causing anybody harm, you must let laws spread fear.[5] Next, nothing is better if someone has trespassed than administrative acts, which don't involve anyone in a criminal investigation. This is the right thing to do. Next is the wish not to do serious harm to the person involved in the crime.[6] Next, the right thing to do when nothing can be done about someone's execution is to try to prevent family and neighborhood groups from getting involved.[7] Next, when a crime involves a family and neighborhood group we must focus on those who committed the crime and take care not to completely wipe out a specific set of people. Man exists in the spiritlike dispensation of heaven and earth. To annihilate means to cut off this dispensation, which might wound and injure the substance (*ti* 體) of heaven and earth. This is severe damage. Heaven [might] respond by striking dead a whole generation.[8] This is not an easy matter for forefathers,[9] family ancestors, and parents, who must plan for later generations and protect sons and grandsons against the peril of inheriting and transmitting evil. That is why wise men always reign with great peace in mind. They might set up a penal code but will not make use of it.[10] In this way, they plan for later generations. Have you understood what these subtle sayings mean?[11]

Yes, I have!

(54.81) Step forward, Perfected![12]

Yes, here I am.

Perfected, are you not up to speaking your mind?[13] Or are you too modest? Just one word?

My dispensation is attached to earth; my destiny lies with the Kunlun. Now the destiny of the Celestial Master lies with heaven, with the Purple Palace of the [celestial] North Pole.[14] Now earth must be void and empty if it is to receive heaven's mercy. As a pupil, I must comport myself in a semblance of the earth's void heart. Only after I have respectfully received your instruction will I reach dao's essential words . . .[15]

(54.82) *Some live earlier, others later, some know more, others less, their position is honored or lowly, they rank high or low. Now what I could say would not match your words. What a young man might say is not how an old man views dao; it is not of first-rate clarity. The Celestial Master has already paid attention to me, foolish and inadequate as I am, and made me begin to see things. To know good and bad is difficult[16]—how could I get there as if at one stroke? For the sake of majestic heaven and august earth, please don't abandon me halfway.*

Well, you have spoken in the name of heaven. I won't give you up. But I thought[17] that out of fear you might never say a word. This is why I have asked you this question.

I would not dare be so fearful. When I hear the Celestial Master speak, I am just too happy and too afraid.

How is that?

I am happy to have met the Master. I am afraid because I fear that I am too slow and dull to learn everything before the Master goes away. I am as eager to ask a question as thirsty people are for the water of a well.[18]

Why is that so?

I want to obtain your teachings (dao) *and deliver them to disciples who will give them to a virtuous lord so that he can make use of them. Should[19] Yin and Yang each be in their place, all the world's diseases that are inherited and passed on would be completely healed.*

You have put this well. Carefully investigate my writings and the doctrine *(dao)* will be complete. If you go through them from beginning to end, they will become clearer than the sun and the moon as they interact while rotating around themselves. If you daily think about how to live by these teachings, all diseases will of themselves be completely healed and all will be resolved. Then everything can really be called happy.

Yes, indeed.[20]

NOTES

1. See *Kong Congzi* 4 *"Xing lun"* 形論, p. 27; Ariel (1989: 170) refers to the remnants of Fu Sheng's 伏勝 (third to second century B.C.E.) *Shang shu da zhuan* 4.112 and to *Shuo yuan* 7 *"Zheng li"* 政理, p. 60 for similar observations.

2. *Dao yi* 道意 (*dao's* intentions) is rarely used. In contrast to the *Xiang'er* (for *Laozi* 9, 13, 20, and 21), the Celestial Master and the TPJ in general don't personalize *dao*. This function is marked out for heaven; cf. Asano 1982: 14–16.

3. The *Chao* interprets *cheng* 成 (to bring life to perfection) in the sense of *Lun yu* 12.16: *junzi cheng ren zhi mei* 君子成人之美 ("The gentleman helps others to realize what is good in them," in D. C. Lau's [1979] words). Luo (1996: 138) adheres to this when he interprets the passage as "to make others perfect" in a moral sense. I follow Long's (2000: 169) broader understanding of the word as "to help things to ripen."

4. The *Chao* is here further than usual from the received text of the TPJ. The *Chao* seems to misinterpret the last sentence: "Next, nothing is better than benevolence (the text mistakenly reads *ren* [man] for *ren* [humaneness]) and generosity. It is right when you see them poor and exhausted to feel their distress (*wei qi chouxin* 為, (corrected from 謂) 其愁心) as if you were worried about hunger and cold (*zi* 自 "your own" is missing)." The large number of variants points to a high degree of textual corruption.

5. Not to prosecute can be seen as a virtue. Hulsewe (1955: 137) mentions Yuan An 袁安, who, as governor between 73 and 83 C.E., chose not to follow up a case of substantial corruption in order not to be forced to exclude a number of his subordinates from office (*Hou Han shu* 45.1518).

6. As Hulsewe (1955: 129) points out, hard labor was the primary alternative to the death penalty.

7. Hulsewe (1955: 114–18) shows that the execution of a culprit's relatives, including grandparents and grandchildren, was common during the Han, although it met with some resistance (see *Han shu* 23.1104f.). When the Wei (220–65) came to power, it was seen as necessary to exclude grandparents, grandchildren, and married daughters from such

collective punishment (*Jin shu* 30.925f.), in line with the demands put forth in the passage at hand. The report on legal matters of the *Sui shu* does not mention collective responsibility. It does, however, note that Emperor Yang argued in 607 for the employment of descendants of criminal offenders in public service; cf. Balazs 1954: 90f.

8.   This consequence of damaging the sequence of generations is the same as that which results from chastity; see section 42.

9.   The expression *xiansheng* 先生 covers a wider group of men than *zu* 組 (ancestors); see TPJ 73.178 and 141.401. This wider group is also thematized when the Celestial Master discusses the origin of "inherited evil" *(cheng fu)*.

10.   This characterizes good government. Emperor Wen of the Han was thus praised; see *Han shu* 4.135 and cf. Hulsewe 1955: 334 and note 155 on pp. 375f.

11.   This passage ties general ideas about good government to specific *taiping* notions about the need to protect life.

12.   What follows consists of fragments without any line of argumentation. Some passages are badly damaged. As far as their contents can be made out, they are similar to the beginning or the end of many layer A dialogues.

13.   The transmitted text must be spurious; otherwise, this remark makes no sense.

14.   The TPJ's understanding of these matters agrees to some extent with common patterns. Mount Kunlun is seen as reigning over earth as the central pole star (*zhongji* 中極) does over the sky (TPJ 137.384). It is the place where lists are kept with the names of the long-lived (TPJ 179.532, layer B) and, according to the *Zhuangzi* (46.18.20), is the resting place of the Yellow Emperor. It is said to be close to heaven:

> Registers of spiritlike men and transcendents are kept at the [celestial] North Pole (*beiji* 北極), adjacent to the Kunlun, on whose grounds the Perfected reside, according to their rank. They are in charge of the men registered. They list family name and personal name in good order. The one known to be on top is put on top, someone in the middle is put there, and a person who is at the bottom is put at the bottom. (TPJ 190.583, layer B)

Transcendents who have not yet achieved access to heaven reside on the "Kunlun of the [celestial] North Pole" *(beiji kunlun)*, amidst clouds and winds (TPJ p. 698, *Chao*, part 8). The Celestial Master has achieved this access and thus resides in the palace of the celestial North Pole, the abode of spiritlike men who resemble the supreme celestial emperor (see below, section 56). They bend *qi* (*wei qi* 委氣), and have a voice for instruction but no corporeal form (TPJ p. 222, *Chao*, part 4). All this creates a bond between Master and disciples. Their worlds are different, but they belong together as Mount Kunlun belongs to the sky to which it reaches. This use of the mountain and the constellation that is supposed to adjoin it signifies a certain unity of the *textus receptus* in that it recurs in layer A as well as in layer B. Moreover, while all the elements mentioned belong to a standard Daoist scenario (see, for instance, Schipper 1996: 105–7), I have not found any exact parallels to the TPJ's way of arranging them.

15.   The topics dealt with in this corrupt passage are the proper way of teaching and the relationship between teacher and student. The following is a tentative translation of the isolated elements that have been transmitted:

> *model for emperors* and be able to obtain . . . [seven characters missing] . . . without the proper etiquette between teacher and student. This, however, is called by name to exchange . . . [six characters missing] . . . his talents. This we call chaotic learning without order . . . [eight characters missing] . . . instructions cause the doctrine *(dao)* to become indistinct, sometimes right and sometimes wrong. Such sayings must not be transmitted to become the model for emperors and kings.
>
> *That is why I don't dare to speak.*
>
> Don't say that (*bu ye* 不 也; see Yu 2001b: 467)! How modest! I would like to discuss with you how to do good. There is indeed no harm in talking . . . [four characters missing] . . . how?

The TPJ's colloquial prose style makes it even more difficult to emend this passage. The tenor of its message is probably similar to that of the following, better preserved, sentences.

16.   Through guarding the one we know good and bad (TPJ 152.412). The expression occurs frequently, including in layer B (TPJ 194.598; 179.528). Heaven takes an interest in this knowledge:

> Heaven makes men know good and bad, do good, and be trustworthy (*you xin* 有 信). It does not want them to have a bad name (*e wen* 惡 聞). (TPJ 179.535, layer B)

17.   As Yu Liming (1997: 50) points out, the character *xie* 些 is miswritten for *zi* 訾, which in the TPJ is used for "to worry"; see TPJ 48.61.

18.   This is the second time this expression is used in this section. The fact that it occurs here could have persuaded the editors to collate the section as they did. It is used at only one other place in the TPJ (61.112).

19.   Yu (2001a: 79) corrects *jin* 今 (now) to *ling* 令 (to let). Throughout the received text one of the two characters is frequently taken for the other.

20.   The summary says:

> This section explains the evaluation of government policy and how to respond to heaven's will; it talks about the use of polite language between teacher and student.

The short section does indeed deal with two topics.

The task of putting written material in order not only resembles redeeming the world, it also promotes such redemption. The following section instructs a ruler in how to go about assembling texts. The first step, only vaguely defined, is the division of all writings from all ages into different categories. There are meant to be writings on *dao* and heaven; writings on "wisdom," which probably means moral questions; writings on "worthy action," that is, on political issues; and manuscripts without any official status, "which the people have put forth."

Memorable passages from these four sets of writings are to be excerpted and made into books. Together they amount to the "Scripture That Pervades All," the scripture of scriptures, which is impossible to improve.

We may call all of this material man-made. The disciple mentions another set of texts whose origin lies in the world of spirits and in heaven. The Master argues that these texts lack perfection: they contradict each other, and none of them gives the complete picture. So we may assume that the *taiping* material, which the disciples read in the course of their training, was not seen as going directly back to a supernatural source. Man-made, it was authorized by heaven but did not originate from it.

The last passages of the section approach the issue from another angle. It is here presumed that the text entitled "Great All-Pervading Reign of Heaven" is already available. It has been created by the Celestial Master and is perfect; it is beyond any further improvement.

This reference to the Celestial Master's own work has perhaps slipped into the section because the term "all-pervading" occurs in its title as well as in the title of the scripture that is supposed to be collated under the auspices of a *taiping* ruler. The section, however, does not focus on any particular scripture. It focuses on the process of compiling textual materials, which in itself is seen as part of the reform process and thus as a great peace-promoting activity. Given the way this scripture has been collected and edited, we cannot expect any authorial voice or coherent argument. Also, commentaries don't seem to play a role in it. We must expect this scripture to have been a *leishu*, that is, an encyclopedia or anthology. *Leishu* were, in the words of Teng and Biggerstaff, "compiled for the purpose of providing the emperor and ministers of state with conveniently arranged summaries of all that was known at the time."[1]

The contradiction between the availability of a perfect scripture and the ongoing need to produce one encapsulates the practicalities of the reform process. To produce the true scripture is to do as it says. It is therefore a social and a continuous activity. It cannot be replaced; it can only be guided by the text the Master himself has put forth.

·　　·　　·

(55.83) *From day to day more foolish, dull and blind as I am, I bow twice before you. Could I please ask something?*

Go ahead! You are improving yourself,[2] and you study with unremitting effort. Your questions are on behalf of heaven. It is my task to listen to what you have to say. I would not dare to spare myself. Speak right away.

Yes, I will. Nowadays little that has been written on dao *can be considered a celestial scripture. [We must] collect and revise[3] the words of wise men from early, middle, and late antiquity for a scripture of wisdom. We must do likewise for the words of men of great virtue for a scripture of virtue, and we must compile the words of the worthy and enlightened from early, middle, and late antiquity for a scripture of worth. Now when I think of what you have said, I can't fully comprehend the intention of these collations. Could you please enlighten us on what should be done first and what next, so that a virtuous lord may obtain [this material] for his personal instruction and then engage the worthy men around him to extract from it opinions that are valuable?[4]*

Well, your question is essential, just as it should be.[5] Excellent, indeed! Yes,[6] I shall explain it all; you may record it in the way it suits you, but be careful not to forget my words. I speak for heaven and earth, and lay out rules that the lord of supreme virtue must follow in order to abolish the peril that has resulted from the reception and transmission of evil since the division between heaven and earth. (55.84) One must not dare speak at random, as this would surely be resented by majestic heaven and august earth and would disappoint the most worthy, enlightened, and virtuous (*dao de* 道 德) lord, and we would have to view it as a great crime. Do you understand?

Yes, I do.

Well, this is what is meant by collecting and revising what has been written on *dao* from early, middle, and late antiquity:[7] it is only to let all worthy men jointly recite and glance at all of *dao*'s texts, the old ones and those of a more recent date. If a scroll contains one valuable expression (*shan zi* 善 字) or instruction (*shan jue* 善 訣), they should at once take note of this piece of writing and make an excerpt. One scroll might contain one valuable expression, ten scrolls ten, and so forth for one hundred, one thousand, ten thousand, and one hundred thousand scrolls, which might contain one hundred thousand valuable expressions. If there were ten valuable expressions or instructions per scroll there might be one million, and if one scroll contained one hundred this would make ten million. [What is valuable] should be recorded in writing and put together in one place.

The worthies should take a look at all essays (*wenzhang* 文 章), old and new, and compile their complete list, organized according to subject, each under the heading of their school (*ge zong qi jia* 各 從 其 家), cutting out duplicates. They should edit them in the order of certain key words (*yao wen zi* 要 文 字).[8] This done, we gain thorough knowledge of the essential meaning of heaven and earth, humankind, and the ten thousand beings in previous times as well as nowadays. From these texts the celestial scriptures (*tian jing* 天 經) are derived. Do you understand?

Yes, excellent.

So you have understood! When you collect and revise the valuable expressions (*shan zi* 善 字) and instructions (*jue shi* 訣 事) from scriptures by wise men from early, middle, and late antiquity, you might find one in one scroll, ten in ten scrolls, and so forth up to one hundred thousand expressions in one hundred thousand scrolls. Should there be ten to a scroll, we would have a million; if a hundred, we would have ten million. Men considered worthy and enlightened should list these writings, assemble them in one appropriate place, and compile them all by subject. If the worthy and enlightened were to examine this material, put it in proper order, and cut out duplicates it would make up a scripture of wisdom.[9] Do you understand?

Yes, I do.

Good. When one collects and revises expressions by the worthy and enlightened from early, middle, and late antiquity there might be one truly valuable one in one scroll, ten in ten scrolls, one hundred in one hundred scrolls, and so forth up to one hundred thousand. Should there be ten to a scroll that would be one million; should there be one hundred that would be ten million. Once they are complete, they must be brought into sequence by subject, so that one follows the other. (55.85) The worthy and enlightened should undertake an examination, cut out duplicates, and then edit and display the material. This would constitute a scripture on worthy [action]. Do you understand?

Yes, I do.

So you have understood. If you wish to collect and revise essays, scriptures, and writings of *dao*, including the writings of worthy men as well as the valuable expressions and instructions[10] that the people have put forth, you must record all that is valuable and assemble it in one secluded place. Having done this, give them to the worthy, enlightened, and truly virtuous to organize according to subject matter so that they prove and clarify each other.[11] One must cut out duplicates and arrange the expressions in sequence. These are called writings and texts on heaven and earth and words about the condition of men.

When all this has been finished, these valuable instructions omit nothing, not even something the size of a thin strand of hair. They are *dao*'s own teachings, entitled "All-Pervading Scripture on Heaven and Earth and on Yin and Yang."[12] Tens of thousands of generations will not be able to improve them.

Excellent indeed!

All right. I would say you have mastered it.

I am foolish, I am not good enough. Now I would like to ask one more question.

Go ahead.

The division between heaven and earth took place long ago. The Yellow River and the Luo have issued texts and maps. Occasionally spirit writings (shen wen shu 神文書) *have appeared. Some sacred phoenixes on their tour of inspection came to spit out texts.[13] Texts were collected in many ways, not just from one source. There have also been many made by wise and worthy men. In the end, each has its own merit. What questions do you raise in regard to this material, how do you peruse and view it? [Despite the existence of this material], you suddenly instruct the worthy and enlightened of late antiquity to collect and revise old and new texts and men's sayings!*

Yes, I have perused and viewed this material. I would not dare annoy the worthy and virtuous men of late antiquity without proper cause. I am now banished to the realms below heaven (55.86) and must explain (*jie* 解) to a lord of outstanding morality that the reception and transmission of evil are to blame for the strings of calamities and poisonous influences (*liu ʐai wei du* 流 災 委 毒) [that have been around] since the division between heaven and earth. Old and new celestial texts, wise writings, and worthy sayings are complete enough, but when put together[14] the trouble is that each excels in one topic. If you rely on the model [set up by] one school [only], you will not be able to abolish all the disasters that happen in heaven and on earth, and they will continue to be received and transmitted without end. Later generations suffer from calamity and illness that increase every day.[15] For this reason heaven feels for the virtuous lord and his ongoing reception and transmission [of evil]. It knows[16] that because of these calamities later generations are unable to survive on their own.[17] The mistake lies really with the worthy and wise men of former generations. They all excelled in one thing, but there was also a lot they misunderstood or neglected. Since heaven knew that something was missing, it occasionally issued the Yellow River and Luo texts and maps and other spirit writings. These again differed from each other in what they said. The great worthy and wise of different generations each dealt with one specific matter. They again differed from each other in what they said. On some issues, they were not good. Each had their weak and their strong points. Thus it is clear that all of them were unable to fully understand what "all-pervading" *(dongji)* means. Thus between heaven and earth calamities never ceased to occur. They were never brought to a halt, not in former times or in later times, but sometimes they were increasing and sometimes they were not.

Therefore, heaven above thought about it, and now there are written texts that from beginning to end are complete and perfect. Were another wise man to be born there is nothing further he would be able to write, to add, to formulate in sentences and to benefit heaven, earth, and virtuous lords. If heaven gave birth to another wise man, his words might excel in one particular field, but, even so, the growth of natural disasters would never come to an end, just as was the case for the wise and worthy of previous ages. For this reason heaven has sent me to strictly command you to give texts to a virtuous lord so that he can show them to all the worthy and enlightened men around him. They must collect and revise these writings together with all the world's texts and the instructions and expressions men have given voice to, which from beginning to end support each other. They must cut out duplicates, put forth a digest of instructions, and record it as a scripture. When this has been done the true texts, standard terms, and valuable expressions of heaven and earth can all be made public. Deceptive forgeries[18] will be completely eradicated, the great illness of heaven and earth will vanish, calamities will be completely abolished, and the people and the ten thousand beings will each be able to live where they belong and will no longer suffer from hardship.

For this reason heaven has instructed me in how to collect and revise material. The writings I have produced put together proofs, not words. Once they are examined and enacted in heaven and on earth, calamities (*zai* 災), disasters (*bian* 變), anomalies (*guai* 怪), illnesses (*ji* 疾), epidemics (*bing* 病), and jealous, cunning, and despotic officials as well as ill-fated and deceptive forgeries are all bound to go away, just as clouds are dispersed on an overcast day.[19] (55.87) Compare this to what I have said and what I have written—they are exactly the same.[20] Now I have received these texts with great respect from heaven and have passed on what they say. Why would heaven without cause put an end to calamities if it sees that men do not vigorously enact these texts? It is natural that men will be in disorder if their written texts are in disorder. Under these circumstances there is no chance that calamities will go away. Do you understand?

Yes, I do.

Fine, so you know.

I would like to ask a question.

Go ahead.

Now, since the division between heaven and earth, heaven has brought forth spiritlike, wise, and worthy men so that throughout the ages they would be in charge of the sayings of heaven and earth. They designed models for kings to follow in order to end natural disasters and make the world secure. Emperors and kings of today make use of them. Texts were written [for them] so that they won't ignore heaven's intentions and the rules [set by] Yin and Yang. These texts all have titles. Now what does one call the writings on dao *and its virtue that the Celestial Master has produced?*

This is a good question. Well, the title is "Great All-Pervading Reign of Heaven."[21]

Why is its correct title "Great All-Pervading Reign of Heaven"?

Well, "great" is "big." The government of someone who puts this into practice is of highest unsurpassable excellence. *Dong* means that *dao*, virtue, and the [knowledge] of good and bad of such a man reach out to heaven and earth, that Yin and Yang cooperate with him, and that in all six directions everything will be responsive to him.

Since all are concerned with doing good, nothing is not in its right place. On behalf of *dao* men are to collect and revise the heavenly, earthly, human, and spirit writings that have come out since the division of heaven and earth and select from them valuable points to make the "Scripture That Pervades All." Once emperors and kings rely on it and let the worthy men around them work at applying it, within the four oceans and the four borders[22] all natural disasters will vanish as if they had been swept away. The reign will become penetrating, pure, and brilliant and the ruler's personal stature will resemble that of the spirits and numinous beings *(shen* and *ling)* of heaven and earth. For this reason [the scripture] is entitled "Great All-Pervading Reign of Heaven." Do you understand?

Yes, I do! How alarming!

Well, now you know.[23]

NOTES

1. See Teng and Biggerstaff 1971: 83. They mention the *Huang lan* 皇覽 as the earliest encyclopedia to have been collated under imperial auspices, in about 220 C.E. Cao Cao (155–220), then in charge of much of the empire, initiated it for his personal instruction. This section of the TPJ could well be the earliest description of how such a compilation was organized.

2. I read *ri* 日 (daily more) for *yue* 曰 (to say). What follows is too self-confident to be part of the disciple's speech. More importantly, *yue* is very rarely used to introduce master or disciple as speaker. Where its occurrence must not be interpreted as erroneous—that is, TPJ 105.261, throughout section 108, and TPJ 153.426—the text seems to consist of a condensed version of the original transcripts; this holds true in particular for section 108, which has several features in common with the *Chao* and where *yue* is used frequently.

3. "To collect and to revise" (*ju jiao* 拘校) is an activity *taiping* adherents are expected to master, as documented in the list of nineteen essential commandments (TPJ 173.510; cf. Espesset 2002c: 83f.).

4. We must assume that the "valuable opinions" (*shan yi* 善意) are those that further great peace:

> Some among the millions of scrolls of writings can increase men's longevity, improve their life, give them security. These are true texts (*zhen wen* 真文), the rest are not. In the rooms filled with writings are some that can help in understanding heaven's intentions and bringing peaceful order to government. These are true texts, the rest are not. (TPJ 158.446)

In more abstract terms, the definition of what is "true" or "valuable"—here the two terms are close—is more difficult. It is, however, not in conflict with what has been said above:

> When men talk, they each say something. You must extract what is valuable *(shan)* from the texts *(wen)* and the sentences (*yan* 言) that nobody objects to. You must put

together explanations that everyone sees as best so that they clarify and prove each other. They will agree with the heart of men and thus also with the heart of heaven and earth.

Since the disciple claims that he doesn't understand, the Master continues:

A man's actions are examined by the heart. We may call everything that agrees with the heart of the worthy and the wise "valuable" *(shan)*. It is bound to agree with the heart of heaven. Should there be doubts when you examine something in your heart, have it examined by the worthy and the wise down to the small men. What they say "no" to is inauspicious *(xiong* 凶 *)* and heaven is also bound to see it as such. That is the proof. Therefore, if you collect these words *(shuo* 説 *)* to make them into a scripture, [keep in mind that] what agrees with a man's heart is right *(shi* 是 *)* and what doesn't is wrong *(fei* 非 *)*. (TPJ 132.354)

5. A major topic is how to handle writings. Sections 47, 55, 61, 73, 75, 77, 79, 132, 165, 167, and 169 in the received part of the TPJ deal with it. The S 4226 table of contents lists more: for instance, sections 8 and 39.

6. The Master's language shows that he finds the question exciting. "Excellent, indeed" and "yes" are in general the response of a student, but in this case it is hard to say what the student would be responding to.

7. The Master mentions texts going back to *dao,* to wise men, to worthy men, and to the people. This last point is his own addition to the scriptures of wisdom, of virtue, and of worth that the disciple had asked about. The classification of writings given here is one of many possible classifications and is concerned not so much with texts as such (for this, see section 53), but rather with material that is to be newly collated. The hierarchical order of texts and materials is flexible. Compare, for instance, the following amazingly egalitarian approach:

Sometimes the spirit texts of heaven *(tian shen wen* 天神文*)* might omit something, but the wise texts have grasped it. At other times, wise texts omit something that the texts of the worthy have understood, or these texts neglect something that the people's *(bai xing)* texts deal with. Or the people's texts omit what the Yi and Di barbarians have grasped. Sometimes the texts produced internally *(nei)* miss it, while those produced outside *(wai)* have it, or the other way around. (TPJ 132.352)

Another classification is by age:

What men of early antiquity have omitted, men in middle antiquity may have included. What the men of middle antiquity have omitted, men of late antiquity may include. (TPJ 132.352)

Intellectual status can also be used for classification:

Occasionally superior men have been slightly neglectful and inferior men have achieved something, or a superior man has grasped a point that has been omitted by inferior men. Or both superior and inferior men might have ignored something that a man of middle rank might have understood, or the other way around. (TPJ 132.352)

Women and serfs are included in this task. They are expected to contribute to the production of texts.

8. This is how anthologies of a limited and thus realistic scope such as the *Daojiao yishu* were, in fact, organized. The figures mentioned by the Celestial Master add a fantastic touch to his own project.

9. "Scripture of wisdom" (*sheng jing* 聖經) is the term later used for the classical scriptures promoted by Confucianism; see *Hanyu da cidian* vol. 8, p. 674, which quotes Wang Tong's (583–616) *Zhong shuo* (chap. *"Tian di"* 天地, p. 9a).

10. This last group of texts seems to refer to material not produced within the academic environment, from which the above-mentioned texts from "early, middle, and late antiquity" probably came.

11. Yu (2001a: 81) corrects *wei* 微 (subtle) to *zheng* 徵 (to prove).

12. This is the *Dongji tian di yin yang zhi jing* 洞極天地陰陽之經. *Dongji* (all-pervading) is the opposite of rupture and blockage, which are seen as life-threatening perversions of the natural course of things. It is pointed out at the end of this section that *dongji* is the word for the almost utopian concept of total communication that is expected to link all the participants of a *taiping* society. The term is used throughout layer A with the meaning of "reaching everyone" and "covering everything" (TPJ 139.397; 104.258) and occurs in praise of the Celestial Master (TPJ 209.668; 207.629), in praise of methods of government (TPJ 65.152; 103.253), and in praise of *qi* (TPJ p. 651, *Chao*, part 7). Everything will be well governed with the arrival of *dongji qi* (TPJ 136.378). The term serves as an abbreviation for expressions like *dong liu ji* (pervade the six most outward points) (TPJ 104.258; 151.408; p. 222, *Chao*, part 4; 105.273f.).

A scripture entitled *Dongji jing* or *Dongji zhi jing* is depicted as being instrumental in the arrival of a state of great peace:

> I would like to ask why, all of a sudden, heaven and earth let the men of this world collect [popular] sayings and the texts of spiritlike and wise men of past and present times to make the "Scripture That Pervades All."

The Master answers that heaven and earth intend thereby to cure all ills; see TPJ 132.349f.

The following passage adds more details:

> Nowadays, when another great cycle of heaven and earth is about to begin, natural disasters and other evil influences must all come to an end. Nobody must again (commit the crime of) hoarding goods. Therefore, teach men how to collect and revise old and new texts and put together what is valuable. Thus will they get the "Scripture That Pervades All" and determine forever, unchangeably, what is "good." Even sages and worthies won't again attain what it says. It is what heaven and earth and Yin and Yang put forth. Thus, it instructs and reprimands a ruler and his worthies in their search for great peace. (TPJ p. 686, *Chao*, part 8)

The scripture is thus part and parcel of the *taiping* reform project. Without the instructions it contains men can't achieve great peace. This agrees with the TPJ's general appraisal of texts (cf. Kaltenmark 1979: 24–29; Hachiya 1983):

> Give this to a lord of outstanding virtue. He will let the people know what heaven wants. They will then spontaneously be secure and have all they need, without any doubt or error. He will correct everything, thoroughly investigate the root of heaven and earth, eradicate the harm done to a country by heaven's resentment and earth's accusations, and set up the "Scripture That Pervades All." (TPJ p. 467, *Chao*, part 6)

Editors of the "Scripture That Pervades All" are said to be the "worthy and enlightened." They are seen to make use of a wide range of materials, including memorials collected all over the country (TPJ 129.333). There are also the "spirit writings":

> What the Celestial Master puts forth today agrees completely with material like the spirit writings and valuable texts from the Yellow River and the Luo issued in former times as well as today and also with instructions that have been uttered by worthy and enlightened men. Once this has been made into the "Scripture That Pervades All," the calamities that have come about since the origin of heaven and earth can all be abolished. (TPJ 129.331f.)

How this scripture is related to the writings put forth by the Celestial Master is left as unclear on other occasions as it is in this section. However, it is safe to say that the scripture is—or, with regard to the section at hand, after its completion it will be—authorized by the Master, and in this sense it is "his." The following passage reflects the ambiguities of section 55, but in more compact form:

> *I would like to ask about the Celestial Master's writings that collate [ju jiao] texts by worthy and wise men from earlier and later times, going back to the origin of heaven and earth, including spirit writings from the Yellow River and the Luo and also what the people have to say, including serfs and barbarians . . .*

> . . . The best, first-ranking scripture from which all errors have been removed is the "Scripture That Pervades All." It is called "Heaven's All-Pervading Reign" (*tian dongji zheng shi* 天洞極政事). Consequent upon it, all the ills of heaven and earth will be driven away. (TPJ 132.348)

The use of the term *dongji* signifies the relevance of the scripture concerned, regardless of whether it is the text initiated by the Celestial Master, or the text promulgated by officials of the virtuous *taiping* ruler, or whether the two texts are identical. This scripture comprises all that is needed to implement *taiping*-related reforms and is expected to reach everyone and everything. Furthermore, in another sense of *dong* (to reach), the term also signifies the range of the missionary project, which does not permit any exclusions.

13. This is mentioned, for instance, in *Lun yu* 9.9.

14. *Ju* 居 is put to unusual use. There is a parallel passage:

> If we consider the textual material that reaches from old to modern times it is quite complete. But the trouble is that put together (*chou qi ji ju* 愁 其 集 居), nothing is pure. Put side by side (*ji ce* 集 厠), [words] contradict (*luan* 亂) each other so that the worthy

and enlightened have questions, misgivings, and doubts and don't know which [words] to follow and which to trust. (TPJ 78.188)

Both *ji ju* and *ji ce* refer to the edition of textual material. *Ji ce* is also used in this sense at TPJ 71.174, layer unclear.

15.   *Yue* (to speak) must be read *ri* (day); see Long 2000: 180 and Yu 2001a: 82.

16.   Yu (2001a: 82) corrects *he* 和 (harmony) to *zhi* 知 (to know).

17.   This explains the timing and the novelty of *taiping* missionary activities. They are taking place now; they did not happen in the distant past.

18.   In line with this section, which identifies the fate of a society with that of its texts, *xie wei* 邪偽 can also be translated as "evil and deceptive conduct." This same point is also expressed below, at TPJ 57.92, and throughout the sections here translated, where *xie wei* serves as a broad term of social and cultural criticism.

19.   This passage is a rhetorical expression of exultation. The "true text" is being composed in separate, ritualized stages. Once the whole ritual has been performed and the text has been created, its existence puts an end to all calamities. This message is set forth in a verbose, enthusiastic manner, unlike the more prosaic way in which other subjects are treated. This choice of words signifies the central function of texts in the world of great peace (cf. Hendrischke 1992).

20.   There are frequent lacunas before the phrase *wan bu shi yi* 萬不失一—see TPJ 57.92; 60.111; 67.169; 78.190; 208.664—perhaps as a means of abbreviation. It was clear what was meant anyway. For the passage at hand the two missing characters could be *shi zhe* 是者 (see TPJ 78.191), *yi ci* 以此 (TPJ 83.210), or *ci zhe* 此者 (TPJ 86.320), all of which occur before *wan bu shi yi*.

21.   This is the *Da dongji tian zhi zhengshi* 大洞極天之政事; see also TPJ 132.348.

22.   Here two expressions are combined. The four oceans (*Shu jing*, chap. "*Da Yu mou*" 大禹謨, p. 134b–c) and the four borders (*Mengzi* 1B6) both serve to define the world of men. Many of the TPJ's word clusters are created in a similar fashion.

23.   The summary says:

This section explains how to collate writings and men's sayings from early, middle, and late antiquity.

This section documents how all social groups cooperate in a society at peace.[1] Their togetherness is the ruler's responsibility, and his success depends on their support. He creates the environment in which each task can be performed and thus attracts the right men to perform those tasks. The interconnection between these groups and between their tasks resembles the relationship between Yin and Yang, where each element is of similar or perhaps even equal importance. We are told that this ideal society functions so well because each group exerts its own influence on the common *qi*. Hierarchies are taken for granted, but cooperation and integration are stressed in a way that portrays social harmony or "balance" (*ping* 平) as slightly different from the harmony envisaged by Mengzi, for instance, or the harmony in the *Wenzi*, which puts men into twenty-five different ranks and argues that the top five are related to the five at the bottom, just as men are related to oxen and horses.[2]

The second part of this section is only loosely linked to what precedes it. The discussion of *qi* brings the two parts together. A man can learn to control *qi* through diet and meditation in order to become heaven's servant and the direct subordinate of heaven's vital spirits. He will then be in a position as "heaven's servant" to mediate between heaven and men and to act as a potential savior. The *Zhuangzi* has something to say on this through the voice of Confucius:[3] when Yan Hui is about to take up an official position, Confucius advises him to practice "fasting of the heart," which would put him in full control of *qi* and thus improve his safety and chance of success.

On the one hand, this section stresses the coherence of the reform project and the inclusion of all activities. On the other hand, and in slight contradiction, it mentions the critical importance of spiritual expertise and the special role reserved for the individual who excels in the control of *qi*.

·　　·　　·

(56.88) *What does it mean that heaven has set up nine groups of men in regard to the effects of Yin and Yang?*[4]

Man is the leader [responsible for] managing the ten thousand beings. There are spiritlike men among them who are without bodily form and who bend *qi*.[5] Their task is to look after primordial *qi*. Men of great spirit are in charge of heaven, the perfected are responsible for order on earth, transcendents must regulate the four seasons, and men of great *dao* the five phases. The wise must look after Yin and Yang, and the worthy have the task of putting texts and writings in order and receiving everything that is put in words. The common people are in charge of looking after plants, trees, and the five crops of grains. Serfs are responsible for overseeing goods and commodities.[6]

Why is this so?

Everything is managed according to its kind. The spiritlike man who is without bodily form bends *qi* and resembles primordial *qi*,[7] so he looks after it. The man of great spirit has a body; great spirits[8] resemble heaven, so such a man keeps matters that concern heaven in order. The perfected concentrates his energy and deserves trust, similar to earth, so he is responsible for it.[9] The transcendent ensures that the four seasons [are respected] since he is transformed in the same way as they are.[10] The man of great *dao* presides over prognosticating good and bad luck.[11] He resembles the five phases and is for this reason responsible for their movement. The wise man presides over harmonizing *qi*. Since he resembles [the balance between] Yin and Yang, he controls all that relates to them. The worthy revises writings and speaks well. He resembles [the regular pattern of] texts and is therefore in charge of the realm of texts and writings.[12] The common people are disorderly, troubled, and without insight, just like the ten thousand plants and beings, so that is what they are put in charge of. Serfs handle goods since they resemble goods and commodities. (56.89) The rich have them, the poor don't. Since serfs can keep track of what goes and what comes, they oversee goods and commodities. In defining responsibilities, majestic heaven does not violate any feelings. It allows each man without fail to be concerned with what is of his own kind. If this were not the case, great damage might occur. So this is the way in which we must organize the people who live under heaven. The wise men of old knew this well. Therefore, they did not miss heaven's intentions but gained favor with it. You had better comprehend this!

Excellent, indeed.

I have said this to warn you not to forget.

Yes, I won't.

Work hard!

Now I am perplexed[13] *and don't know the answer. Are you saying that these nine groups of men with their different activities are of a certain advantage to the king's reign?*

No.[14] A government that meets heaven's intentions will harmonize these nine *qi* and create agreement among the nine groups of men. It will thus be able to achieve great peace of highest majesty (*shang huang taiping* 上皇太平). Should these nine activities conflict rather than be in accord with each other, great peace will not be achieved. These activities generate each other in turn.[15] But men are not well informed about it. The wise and worthy of former times did not explain it in full. That is why it has long remained undetected.[16] But if one single activity is not in order, peace can not prevail.

Why is this so?

For the *qi* of highest majesty to arrive on a grand scale,[17] these nine groups of men must all come to help the king govern. As soon as one single *qi* [as represented by one of these nine groups of men] does not cooperate, something will not be right. For this reason one will not be able to harmonize Yin and Yang and reign in peace.

How about their "coming [to help]"?

The spiritlike man without bodily form will come to make the announcement to the king, so that his heart becomes more enlightened from day to day. (56.90) The man of great spirit will occasionally appear to teach about the purpose of government. The perfected, the transcendent, and the man of great *dao* will all act as teachers to assist this process of education. The wise and the worthy will come to the fore. From their midst detached scholars will come to serve as officials. The common people and serfs will behave well and do nothing wicked and evil. This proves that heaven and earth are very pleased.

What is the meaning of "As soon as one single qi *does not cooperate, this will not happen"?*[18]

Should primordial *qi* not cooperate, the spiritlike man without bodily form will not

arrive, and if heaven's *qi* does not do so, the man of great spirit will not come. Problems with earth's *qi* will prevent the perfected from coming. Disharmony of the four
seasons will prevent the arrival of the transcendent. Should the five phases lack harmony, the man of great *dao* will not step forward. If Yin and Yang are not in cooperation, wise men will not appear. Should what the texts say not be true, officials of
great worth will not come. Should they not be able to harvest the ten thousand crops,
the common people will be in disorder, there will be few goods and commodities,
and serfs will run away. Men will ignore their responsibility in all their activities.
This is precisely the damage [that results from a disharmony of *qi*]. Should you wish
to deliver heaven from disorderly *qi* you have to work hard and unremittingly at
creating balance (平). Heed my words!

Yes, I will.

Once [all] *qi* has been obtained, the nine groups of men will safeguard *dao*. The inheriting and transmitting of the calamities [that were caused by] ten thousand generations of former kings will come to an end. But should these men forget their place,
the damage derived from this inheritance will increase daily. Should these nine, from
the man without bodily form down to the serf, each adjust to one *qi*, the nine *qi* will
blend in the way of Yin and Yang.

But for heaven to bring about this harmonious blending of *qi* men must first feed
on *qi*.[19] For this reason a superior scholar who is about to enter *dao* will first give up
eating solid food and instead feed on *qi*.[20] This means that he is about to mix with primordial *qi*. So nourishment must be set up inside the grass hut[21] to let him celebrate
a fast. He must look at nothing wicked or evil but daily refine his body. When nothing attracts his desire, he will be able to step out into the space without crevices [as if
he were not solid][22] and will offer his assistance to transcendents, perfected, and primordial *qi* to keep heaven in order. This makes him something of a spiritlike scholar[23]
and a servant of heaven.[24] Don't restrain yourself and don't give up. You will truly
be able to do it. You will be called a celestial scholar *(tian shi)*[25] and will be selected to
the group of good men. Heaven will be greatly pleased and will in turn benefit men.

What does this mean?

Someone who has thus achieved *dao* and moves away from this world might be of
no use in the eyes of men but will harmonize *qi* of Yin and Yang. When emperors
and kings of old offered a sacrifice, spirits from heaven would come down to feast.
This is what is meant. (56.91)

But would heaven's vital spirits in person come down to feast?[26]

Very good, what you have said. Well, if a man should rise to become heaven's servant, heaven's vital spirits become his superiors. Lord and servant affect each other. The servant's task lies in supervising [human] conduct. Whenever the servant says that men are good and have gained merit, the lord descends with him and is pleased and happy down below.[27] Thus will the evil that men have inherited and that they transmit be abolished. Should the servant not be pleased, he will say that men trespass against heaven. Neither lord nor servant would want to descend and get close enough to men to share their food. For this reason, there would be an increase in the number of crimes. Since men would themselves commit more trespasses, how would they be able to put an end to the chain of calamities that reaches back to former kings? You should really comprehend this!

How frightening! I am in great fear, as confused as if I had lost my breath (qi). *If I had not asked you, I would not have had a chance to hear this mentioned.*

All right. Work hard! Our talk is finished. You'd better go.

Yes, I will.[28]

NOTES

1. The title of the section reads "nine heavens." It is corrected to "nine men" *(ren)*.

2. See *Wenzi* 7 *"Weiming"* 微明, p. 337.

3. See *Zhuangzi* (*"Ren jian shi"* 人間世) 9.4.24–35.

4. The text is corrupt beyond hope of emendation. This translation follows Yu 2001a: 84, but the result is not satisfactory in that Yin and Yang are hardly thematized in this section. Also, *er* 而 does not usually link characters that function as nouns. Moreover, the section begins abruptly, without an exchange of greetings and questions. We must assume that the first part has not been well transmitted.

5. "Bending *qi*" (*wei qi* 委氣) is a breathing technique, mentioned together with *lian* 鍊 (smelting), *bi* 閉 (stopping), and *bu* 布 (extending) *qi* (*Yunji qiqian* 60.19a–b) in a text entitled *Zhongshan yugui fuqi jing* 中山玉櫃服氣經, which was supposedly written by a certain Bi Yan 碧嚴 "Blue Peak," annotated by *Huang yuan jun* 黃元君 (Lord of Yellow Origin), and frequently quotes the *Huangting jing;* it does not figure elsewhere in the *Yunji qiqian* or in other material consulted by Ōfuchi and Ishii (1988). Long and Luo prefer to render the term as "accumulating *qi*." Although *wei* can mean "to store," this is an activity that the TPJ authors meet with disdain; *wei* (to bend) is taken from *wei shen*, the "bent body" that is a sign of respect; "to bend *qi*" resembles in structure the "smelting" and "extending" of the *Yunji qiqian*.

In the TPJ "to bend *qi*" is an important activity. It is mentioned in a passage on meditation in connection with the first of nine grades of being Daoist. It belongs to layer A, but the topic is personal salvation. It says that adepts who master the first three techniques will be able to transcend the world (*du shi* 度世):

> The most high-ranking first grade is to consider yourself ("your body" *shen* 身) in the way of primordial *qi* without falsity (*yuan qi wu wei* 元氣無為). Utterly uncontrived you will only think of yourself as being white all through, as if you bent *qi* and were without shape. If you make this your permanent model you will get to the point where you will achieve and know everything. (TPJ 107.282)

The TPJ also uses the term in a different, slightly puzzling manner, as Max Kaltenmark (1979: 31) has pointed out, as if the "bent *qi*" were an entity similar to primordial *qi*. In a passage that does not contain distinctive stylistic elements but that probably belongs to layer B, it is said that the spiritlike man who studies the way *(dao)* of life "shares the wishes of bent *qi* (*yu wei qi tong yuan* 與委氣同願)" and "would not dare forget the intentions of bent *qi* (*bu gan shi wei qi zhi yi* 不敢失委氣之意)," in the same way as the pious child will always think of his parents (TPJ 185.563, layer B [?]). The term occurs altogether four times in this passage. Another layer B passage (*Chao*, p. 710, part 9; cf. Espesset 2002b: 11) links the term closely to the layer B figure "Great Spirit."

6. The nine groups mentioned here resemble a set of eight—or, in fact, nine—groups introduced in a *Chao* passage (pp. 221–22) from part 4, which can be identified with section 96 of the S 4226 table of contents, entitled "Instruction on how to explain heaven's nine groups of men (*jiu ren* 九人)." (Yoshioka [1970: 31] sees the character after *tian* (heaven) as not identifiable. See Zhang Gong 1992: 3; it seems to consist of radical 213, "tortoise," under radical 41, "roof.")

> Now what do the spiritlike man, the perfected, the transcendent, the man of *dao*, the wise man, the worthy, the people, and the serfs resemble? (TPJ p. 221)

The spiritlike man resembles heaven's omniscience while the perfected resembles earth's sincerity—it will never deceive heaven. The transcendent resembles the four season's changeability; the man of *dao* resembles the five phases and can thus prognosticate good and bad luck and stay in control of security and danger. The wise man resembles Yin and Yang and is thus in harmonious cooperation with the ten thousand beings, and the worthy reaches into the distance, similar to mountains and rivers, and thus serves emperors and kings. The people resemble the ten thousand plants (*wan wu* 萬物); they grow everywhere, high and low. Serfs and slaves resemble low-growing plants (*cao mu* 草木). This list is depicted as being the outcome of a twofold division of society, that is, into male and female or lord and servant in line with the forces of Yin and Yang. The passage also discusses the issue of social or at least Daoist mobility:

> Serfs who obey their master and learn how to be good (*xue shan* 學善) can become worthy. If they don't, they become good men (*shan ren* 善人) and honest subjects (*liang min* 良民); if honest subjects and good men study without let-up, they become worthy men. (TPJ p. 222)

This is the wording of a TPJ quotation in the *Zhengyi fawen taishang wai lu yi*. The *Chao* text gives the full list, but with less detail:

> When serfs are worthy, they can become good men *(shan ren)*. When a good man likes studying, he becomes a worthy. If a worthy man studies without giving up, he becomes wise. A wise man who continues to study knows the gate of heaven's *dao*. Should he continue to enter *dao* and complete the task of avoiding death he becomes a transcendent. A transcendent who does not give up becomes perfected. A perfected who perseveres becomes spirit, and a spirit who does not give up shares the body of majestic heaven. For this reason the spiritlike man of the highest order lives in the [celestial] North Pole in the same constellation as the supreme emperor of heaven and is called "spirit of the celestial heart" *(tian xin shen 天心神)*. Should such a spirit not give up, he will transcend heaven, undertake the bending of *qi*, and instruct by sound while being without shape. He will belong to the region above heaven. (TPJ p. 222, *Chao*, part 4)

The last, most illustrious, being, who transcends heaven and bends *qi*, is not in the list of eight introduced in part 4 of the *Chao*, but his addition creates the more meaningful figure of nine and thus brings section 96 very close to the section at hand. So we may assume that in the Celestial Master's opinion the origin of human rank depends on the Yin and Yang dichotomy, while the move from one rank to the next relies on "learning." This suggestion is repeated in the *Chao* version of part 1 (p. 725), where it is explained that through learning a foolish person will become worthy, a worthy one will become wise, a wise one will gain *dao*, followed by becoming a transcendent, a perfected, and a spirit. There are seven groups all together. This process of learning is not specified, but we must assume that it consists of learning what the Celestial Master teaches. One major subject in this curriculum is "to learn to search for the way *(dao)* of life" *(xue qiu sheng dao 學求生道)* (TPJ 185.563, layer B[?], cf. Kaltenmark 1979: 31), a study undertaken in particular by the spiritlike man without bodily form. So learning is promoted as the basis for social mobility. The passage at hand attests to the *taiping* doctrine's "totalitarian" or holistic approach. It integrates social and spiritual ranks into one single system that renders religious instruction mobile and flexible. This system played a role in attracting followers; see sections 58 and 61. The following passage throws a different light on the issue:

> The Perfected said: *My life does indeed depend on predestined fate* (lu ming 緣命)! *It is my good fortune that I have been able to meet with you.*
>
> The spiritlike man [in this section, as in the *Chao*, *shen ren* is used for the Celestial Master; the section contains the expression "Now that I have heard the spiritlike man, the Celestial Master *(shen ren tian shi 神人天師)*, speak, my heart is greatly delighted ... ," p. 287] answered:
>
> > Yes, the six ways of human life each have their fate. The first is that of a spiritlike man, the second is a perfected, the third a transcendent, the fourth a man of *dao*, the fifth is wise, the sixth worthy. They all support heaven's rule. The spiritlike man is in charge of heaven, the perfected of earth, and the transcendent of wind and rain. The man of *dao* is educated in matters of good and bad luck, the wise man rules over the

hundred surnames, and the worthy assists the wise in keeping the registers of the ten thousand subjects in order and in extending support in all six directions to where there is insufficiency. For this reason each human life has its fate. If it is someone's fate to be in a high position he can't be lowly, and if he is fated to be humble he can't rise. Do you want to know how I can prove this? Although a fish avails itself of water, it would not fly in the water's *qi;* a dragon also avails itself of water, and from the water's *qi* it rises into a green cloud and becomes heaven's envoy! The honored and the lowly both have their fate; it is foolish to talk about it at random. (TPJ 108.288f)

The dialogue then moves toward a compromise. Heaven's fate also includes the ability to learn *dao,* and thus progress is possible.

7. According to the *"Lüli zhi"* 律 歷 志 of the *Han shu* (21A.964), "primordial *qi"* (*yuan qi* 元 氣) is the root of the universe. The term is frequently used in a similar sense in the TPJ. *Yuan qi* is situated in the neighborhood of *ziran* (TPJ p. 17, *Chao,* part 2): "Primordial *qi* has three names: great Yang, great Yin, and their harmony" (TPJ p. 19, *Chao,* part 2). It is among the highest-ranking cosmogonic and thus cosmological principles:

Primordial *qi* is Yang and is in charge of giving life. What is as it is causes change; it is Yin and in charge of nourishing all beings (*fan wu* 凡 物). Heaven's Yang is in charge of life; the Yin of earth is in charge of nourishing. (TPJ p. 220, *Chao,* part 4)

For this reason, neglect of "the method of heaven and earth, of primordial *qi,* and of what is as it is" causes disaster (TPJ 65.151).

The Celestial Master's understanding of *yuan qi* differs from other Daoist usage of the term. In the third-century *Commands and Admonitions of the Families of the Great Dao (Da dao jia lingjie),* primordial *qi* is only one of three pneumas that go back to *dao* as creative force, which reduces the cosmogonic function of the term, and Bokenkamp (1997: 159f.) concludes that here *yuan qi* is the element that makes cosmic *dao* accessible to humans.

The maintenance of this *qi* requires returning backward and holding on to the root (TPJ, pp. 12–15, *Chao,* part 2; cf. Kaltenmark 1979: 23). The need for return applies to society as a whole just as it does for the individual. For this reason, for the Celestial Master, primordial *qi* is the source of individual life (see TPJ 44.43) as well as a method of government:

There are altogether ten methods that provide support for the government of emperors and kings: government by primordial *qi,* by what is as it is, by *dao,* by virtue, by benevolence, by propriety, by ritual, by texts *(wen),* by a legal code *(fa),* and by war. (TPJ 103.254; and see above, section 41)

8. *Da shen* (Great Spirit) is here used as an abbreviation for *da shen ren* 大 神 人, as in the above paragraph. The TPJ speaks of him as a ruler who governs in the knowledge of all written material on all three *dao:*

In his meditation he understands what the world *(tianxia)* wants and [what causes] movement and rest in all transformation. (TPJ 132.360)

We must assume that a *da shen ren*—the term is rare—is a human being resembling a "great spirit," as introduced in the *Zhou li* (*"Chun guan, si shi"* 春官肆事, p. 769c) and in the *Zuo zhuan* (Duke Xiang, ninth year, p. 1943a), where spirits or, perhaps better, deities are "great" and powerful in the same sense in which a country can be great.

In TPJ layer B material, a Great Spirit takes the place of the layer A Celestial Master. His position is high:

> The honorable personage of the spiritlike man of supreme majesty who is personally known as Duke Who Bends *Qi* and also by the name of Great Spirit is always situated to the left of the Celestial Lord (*tian jun* 天君). He is in charge of putting in order the writings that are in the Hall of Light. (TPJ p. 710, *Chao*, part 9, layer B)

9. When one considers the whole of the TPJ, this order of ranks allows the Great Spirit, who in layer B acts as mentor to the well-deserving disciple, to be positioned above the Perfected, the rank held by the Celestial Master's disciples.

10. "Transformation" (*bianhua* 變化) is a *Zhuangzi* (34.13.30; 72.25.64) and a *Yi jing* term (hexagram 1, p. 1). It points to the way beings exist in this world.

11. Prognostication is one of the TPJ's major topics. Judging by their titles, sections 1, 35, 36, 37, 67, 68, 88, 105, 121, and 215 deal with the topic.

12. This is the worthy's task throughout the TPJ. Since so much depends on texts, his work is crucial. He is an assistant to the wise man, *sheng ren*. Neither of them is an expert in specific life-prolonging arts. They can be seen as one group, as the "wise and worthy of old" (*guzhe sheng xian*) (TPJ 66.157–67). This group can also contain a third component, as in phrases like "the worthy, wise, and highly educated of old" (*guzhe xian sheng da ru* 古者賢聖大儒) (TPJ 66.159; see also 162). They are literate and in a position of responsibility. Their cooperation is essential for the success of *taiping* reforms, but they can't be expected to initiate these reforms on their own.

13. "Perplexed" (*xinjie* 心結): When the heart is "tangled up," no understanding (*cong ming* 聰明) is possible; see TPJ 132.357 (also 208.662). The Celestial Master is capable of untying it; see section 48, p. 146, above. The character *jie* is also used to intensify the meaning of *yuan* 冤 (grief); for *yuanjie* (grief-stricken), see sections 41 and 48.

14. I follow Yu's (2001a: 85) punctuation, reading *bu ye* 不也 as the answer to the question *he yi yu wang zhi hu* 何益於王治乎.

15. The *Chao* reduces the TPJ's pleonastic expression *ci jiu shi nai geng die xiang sheng cheng* 此九事迺更迭相生成 by cutting out *nai geng*.

16. The philosophers have been more concerned with explaining the need for a division of labor and the ensuing social hierarchy (*Mengzi* 3A4) than with explaining the need for cooperation between the different strata, as if the second point were more self-evident than the first. However, the need for "stomach and limbs" to cooperate was well understood: see *Mozi* 46 *"Geng zhu"* 耕柱 (79.46.10) or *Guanzi* 48 *"Zhi guo"* 治國, p. 262.

17. "To arrive on a grand scale" (*tai zhi* 太至): the adverbial use of *tai* and the brevity of the expression are unusual.

18. The argument is bidirectional: *qi* must be in order for the nine groups of men to help the lord, and these men must help the lord for *qi* to be in order. Order is obviously achieved in certain successive layers of activity. The mode of expression signifies the necessity of the linkage, the interdependence of factors. It all makes perfect sense, despite such formal intricacies.

19. Breathing techniques are the skill all men must have if they want to do their job. This is referred to in the *Mengzi* (2A2) and analyzed in the *Guanzi* (*"Nei ye"* 內業), as well as mentioned in a host of Daoist material. Breathing techniques are related to the role played by the method of guarding the one in achieving great peace.

20. The division of men into superior, average, and inferior *(shang, zhong, xia)* pertains to three different aims in life. Between them, the three groups represent the whole variety of how things can be done, as is the case with most TPJ divisions into three. The Celestial Master needs to define the different approaches to the study of his teachings so that individual failure can be explained. The following pattern is laid out:

> The superior person studies *dao* in order to assist emperors and kings. He must love life and gain merit and will then live long. An average person studies *dao* because he wishes his family to transcend the world. An inferior person studies *dao* simply to cast off his own body. (TPJ p. 724, *Chao,* part 1)

The next passage can help explain why this is so:

> The superior person is a worthy of high rank (or "superior persons and worthies of high rank" [*shang shi gao xian* 上士高賢]) who stands in complete awe of all activities, may they be big or small. The average person is half in awe, the inferior person not at all. The reason why the superior person is in awe is what is demanded of him, not what he would demand of others. His heart is open; his mind (*yi* 意) is immersed in nothingness and embraces tolerance. He knows that primordial *qi* is at the root of what is as it is (*zhi yuan qi ziran zhi gen* 知元氣自然之根). (TPJ p. 724, *Chao,* part 1)

For this reason, all beings and all natural phenomena inspire him with awe. The average person has no insight into the arts (*shu* 術) involved in primordial breath and what is as it is and therefore has little respect for astronomical phenomena. The inferior person is not even amazed at the size of the earth's mountains and rivers. All he knows is how to till the soil, sow, and keep his house in order (TPJ p. 724, *Chao,* part 10).

These passages depict the superior person as a leading personality who has a wide soteriological impact. This is also upheld in the rather unusual section 191, which represents the whole of chapter 113 and has traces of a Celestial Master-type dialogue. It explains how the three types differ in their attitude toward music and what they achieve by it. Through nonaction the superior person enables others to turn into transcendents; the average person makes society harmonious; the inferior person sees to it that there is food (TPJ 191.588).

21. A grass hut is a simple place for a simple meal. See *Han Feizi* 21.768.12.

22. See *Laozi* 43.

23. The term *shen shi* 神士 (spiritlike scholar) is used only here in the TPJ and does not occur in the dictionaries.

24. Spirits are heaven's servants (*tian zhi li* 天之吏); see TPJ p. 221, *Chao*, part 4. They are also its envoys (*shi* 使) (see TPJ p. 218, *Chao*, part 4), or both its servants and envoys (TPJ p. 15, *Chao*, part 2). The two characters can easily be confused. In the passage at hand the phrase "lord and servant" on the next page makes it likely that "servant" is the correct character.

25. The term *tian shi* 天士 occurs once more in the TPJ (TPJ 179.541), probably mistaken for *tian shang* 上, but it is used in Han dynasty historical writings (see *Hanyu da cidian*, vol. 2, p. 1405) in the meaning of "someone who knows the way of heaven," as Yan Shigu explains.

26. The presence of spirits *(shen)* was auspicious, as the following *Zhong yong* account indicates:

> The Master said: "The way demons and spirits show their virtue is marvelous. When we look at them we don't see them, when we listen to them we can't hear them. They are at the core of things and must not be forgotten. They make everyone in the world observe fasts and purification rituals and put on a ceremonial gown to attend to their sacrifice. The spirits seem to float just above the heads of the sacrificers, all around them. It is said in the *Book of Odes* that 'The approaches of spirits are unfathomable. How could one be unmoved by this?' This is what is meant when we say that what can barely be detected becomes evident, and what is sincere cannot be kept concealed." (See *Li Ji*, "*Zhong yong,* " p. 1628a: cf. Legge 1960, vol. 2, pp. 397f.; Sommer 1995: 37f.)

This renders more pertinent what is said in section 46 about the need to contain the presence of demons *(gui)*.

27. The Celestial Master is such a servant. He is here said to fulfill the tasks of an informant, as do the body spirits.

28. The summary says:

> This section examines how the nine groups of men bring peace to the king's reign by fulfilling their ambition without resentment. Thus heaven is happy to abolish [the evil] that has been inherited and transmitted by former kings.

How to Examine What Is
True and What Is False *Dao*

This section gives a short preview of the entire missionary process, a long-lasting course that is begun in the presence of the Master and his disciples through the distribution of texts. From this beginning, a process of corrections follows, first of texts and then of men's understanding. Schools assembled around standard texts will eventually improve men's behavior and thus reduce the load of inherited evil. Since this load is big, no sudden relief can be expected. Still, progress is observable and proves the validity of the Master's texts.

There is an apparent contradiction between the long process through which reforms evolve and the opportunity to observe some proof of the program's validity more or less at the outset. This problem is not solved in principle, but rather put aside by the personal testimony of the Master, as proclaimed in this section—"I am here in person to verify"—or by reference to heaven's testimony. Disciples and followers are provided with some proof, but they are also expected to believe.

The section also attempts to provide an explanation of the origin of false texts and thus evil action. False words are occasioned by an increasing number of mistakes, just as an increasing quantity of something cold reduces the heat of a substance. The process of deterioration is depicted here as being as gradual as the reform process. It has different stages, moving from the accidental mistake to intentional deceit, and finally to a state of general distrust.

The section is very short and has an unusual number of lacunae. However, it is introduced and completed in the usual manner and has a clear message. What it says contradicts the more fundamentalist approach of other sections[1]—where it is argued that with one *qi* in disorder the world is in disorder—but the Celestial Master makes similar remarks elsewhere, for example, in the subsequent section, section 58. The central point is that the state of great peace can be achieved. It seems to be of lesser interest to the believers whether it will happen in a subitist or in a more gradualist manner.

· · ·

(57.92) This business will indeed be finished before too long. Step forward, Perfected. Pay attention to these instructions.

Yes, I will!

After you have come to live by these teachings *(dao)* in person, the long-lasting causes for the inheritance and transmission [of evil] will gradually recede into the distance. But there is so much peril; *qi* is tangled, and calamities, grievances, and poisonous influences are truly many. They cannot come to an end at a moment's notice. Once men have learned to put all their energy into following these teachings, the peril of inheriting and transmitting evil will lessen day by day, it will be reduced month by month, and it will vanish year by year.

How would one know this?

Very good, your objection! One may say that you understand what *dao* is all about. Well, listen carefully. All texts and writings under heaven will become standard after men have learned to live by these teachings *(dao)*. Thus men will also [follow] the standard [norms]. There won't be any deceptive forgeries[2] after everyone has been initiated to the true doctrine *(dao)*; they will all cease to exist. Men will be ever more attentive, of their own account, from generation to generation. They will imitate and teach each other, so that all will know *dao* and turn inward, keep their own person in view, and show concern for their own self. Their progeny will therefore be pious (*xiao* 孝), live a long time, and put effort into growing old. The color of their face will not be the same as it was during the times without the true doctrine. Later generations will know more and more of [*dao*'s] supreme meaning and form a school. Their learning will continue to surpass that of their predecessors. From day to day they will become more generous and friendly toward each other. They will cherish and value men in possession of *dao* (*you dao ren* 有道人). Weapons and armaments, jealousy, and treachery will be of no further avail. So the peril of inheriting and transmitting [evil] will lessen. This is the art of what is as it is. That it always succeeds[3] proves the validity of my text. One must not carelessly set aside good words. I am here in person to verify that [these sayings] are as an echo to heaven and earth. How could they be mistaken? It is so that in the course of time texts and writings have come out in which men—not just one—have collected [accounts of] circumstances that are difficult to understand.[4] This is the reason why my teachings *(dao)* are sincere. You have come for some time to study and ask questions,[5] so you must be glad to know that there is proof for what I say. It works with opposites, as with cold and heat: when there is too much heat there is too little cold, and when there is too much cold there is too little heat.[6] Now, since the division between heaven and earth, teachers who formerly instructed others often hid away the true doctrine *(dao)* and instead taught [others] frivolous and superficial [material]. Through carelessness faults slowly became bigger. They grew and expanded even more upon reaching later generations. This is the reason why men were finally transmitting to each other false teachings, separated by a great distance[7] from heaven's way.[8] At first, the creation of texts became an occasion for deceiving others. Just happening once, it went unnoticed. Later on it was used for profit. (57.93) This meant that men in a leading position were no longer trustworthy, and subordinates ceased to pledge allegiance. Disorder arose because each harbored doubts about the other. Later generations inherited [these evils] and passed them on, so that the perils their forefathers had encountered were multiplied. That is why they increased even more.[9] Since heaven grieves about this, I advise you to pay attention.[10] It is in your own interest to study vigorously. Then you will abolish illness in the name of heaven and remove danger for the sake of emperors and kings. Up in heaven your great merit will be known.

I would not dare to accept this.[11]

NOTES

1. For instance, section 56.
2. See above, TPJ 55.86.
3. See TPJ 55.87 for characters missing before the phrase *wan bu shi yi* 萬不失一. I insert *ci zhe* 此者, following TPJ 127.320. Yu (2001a: 87) inserts *xing zhi* 行之.
4. Heaven wants men to know about such issues (*nan zhi qing* 難知情), but does not, or rather cannot, tell them directly:

   Truly, heaven has grabbed your heart and made you speak. At one moment you were completely in the dark, not knowing what to do, and in the next it made you aware and your insight is as clear as sun and moon. You don't believe me? Heaven would like to make things public but it can't speak to men and has difficulty letting them know (*nan zhi qing* 難知情). My writings convey heaven's instructions, in clear colors. (TPJ 166.462)

The fact that heaven does not speak with a human voice is the reason for the origin of texts.

5. The two missing characters are read as *lai xue* 來學. The phrase "you have been coming for some time to study" (TPJ 60.108) or ". . . to study *dao*" (TPJ 41.29) is common. So is the phrase *xue wen* (to study and raise questions), e.g., TPJ 53.78. Yu (2001a: 87) adds *lai nan* 來難.

6. Yin and Yang must be in balance.

7. With Yang (1994: 316), I read *li* 離 (distance) for *sui* 雖 (although).

8. Heaven, or rather the reliable order of the heavenly bodies, is "truth." Texts are an approximation. In their realm error and thus deceit become possible.

9. The character *yue* (to say) must be corrected to *ri* (daily more); see Yu (2001a: 87). The passage is difficult. If I read it correctly, this is a harsh critique of the core of classical erudition. The Celestial Master argues that the scriptures that Han dynasty scholars studied were meant to deceive people. We must, however, remind ourselves that the Master does not, as did Zhuangzi (see 36.13.68–74 and 39.14.75–79), attack books as such.

10. The two missing characters are read as *da jie* 大戒 (general advice); cf. TPJ 152.420, *yu zi yi da jie* 語子一大戒, and the frequent use of *da jie* in section 156 (pp. 438–40).

11. The summary says:

This section gives instruction on how to verify *dao* through comparison and how to know true and false.

On the Four Ways of Conduct
and on [the Relationship between]
Root and Branches

This section begins with a discussion of human conduct with respect to the rules laid out by the prognostic sciences. The argument is abstract and formalistic. We are not told what the rules in question are, but the discussion leaves no doubt that they do not involve any moral or political considerations. At stake are advantage, auspiciousness, good fortune, and their opposites, to various degrees and in surprising combinations. The approach is that of an expert in the diagnosis of options for future development. He is involved in prognostics as a scholarly subject. Thus for him the fortunate and the unfortunate rank first, since their case is clear, and what exists in the gray area between the two extremes is problematic.

This radical approach is modified in the second part of the section, in which the origins of inauspicious conduct are analyzed through the use of the root and branches analogy. Each move away from the root or, in other words, the slightest negligent behavior is said to incur risk. Such movement gains its own momentum, just as a river grows larger by flowing downward. Thus deterioration appears to be a natural outcome of historical development and beyond individual influence. But a "return to the root" is always an option for the individual, particularly at that moment when the movement away from the root—or from Yang—has peaked. The disciple is bound to recognize this point as the moment he lives in, with all the devastation and the promise this entails.

The last paragraph returns to the issue of change. The disciple is assured that the education he has received has not been in vain. The career trajectory that has led him to become a Perfected will not be reversed now, while he is close to the peak.

Though the section covers a variety of topics, there is a certain common thread, which is the systematic approach to human conduct. The Master calls this system the way of the great ultimate. It is not accidental that the Celestial Master here mentions the great ultimate, an entity that in the *Book of Changes* is said to have initiated the division of all that is into the spheres of Yin and of Yang. Between these spheres there is thought to be a continuous interchange, in which human conduct is included.

·   ·   ·

(58.93) Step forward, Perfected!

Yes.

How many modes of conduct does man have?

Hundreds and thousands.

No. What you have said is the same as common people would say. Man has four modes of conduct. One of them is puzzling.[1]

How would you call them?

Well, when conduct is not good, it is bad.[2] Conduct that is neither good nor bad maintains a certain unstable balance. If it is good at one time and bad at another, it is messy and inconstant. If it cannot be relied upon to be either good or bad, then fortune and misfortune will have no [well-defined] place.

Excellent.

How many ways of conduct are there in regard to fortune and misfortune?

Thousands and millions.

You speak as common people might do. There are four different ways of conduct for fortune and misfortune, one of them puzzling.

How would you call them?

Well, when we are not fortunate in all we do we suffer from misfortune. Should we be neither fortunate nor the opposite, our fate is in some unstable balance. If we are sometimes in luck and sometimes unlucky, both mixed together, this is messy and inconstant, and fortune and misfortune cannot be prognosticated.[3]

Excellent.

All right. [Now] to the nature (*xing* 性) of heaven and earth: How many [combinations of] good and bad are there in a year, a month, and a day?[4]

Too many to list them.

What you say is confused and unclear, as if you were drunk. Year, month, and day develop in four different ways in the realms of heaven and earth. As soon as one is in a messy state, disasters and anomalies occur.

What do you mean?

Well, listen closely! (58.94) Now should a year in heaven and on earth not be prosperous, it is bound to be bad. When it is neither prosperous nor bad it maintains a certain balance. Should it be good for some time and then bad at another time, it is a year when heaven is changeable and puzzling.[5] Now if it's a day, it is bound to be bad if it is not good. If it is neither good nor bad it will be a day—or a month—of some unstable balance. Conduct that is good for some time and bad at some other time will be puzzling and bring forth anomalies, irregular events, and disasters. I can only give you a general idea and show how it all begins.[6] This is the way things happen in this world.

What do you mean?

Well, unless they are good, the world's ten thousand beings, as well as its people, are all steeped in evil. To be neither good nor bad is balanced conduct. To be good at times and bad at other times is deceptive conduct; it can't achieve anything. Balanced conduct must not be encouraged. Only men who are really good or really bad make a name for themselves.[7]

Why are there exactly four modes of conduct?[8]

This is a good question. We may say that you understand *dao*'s intention. Well, to be really good resembles the pure conduct of great Yang, while to be really evil is like the malignant behavior of great Yin. There is both good and evil in their intercourse (*zhonghe* 中合). Should [human] conduct lack constancy, heaven and earth, the intercourse between [Yin and Yang], the lord, his subordinates, the people, and the ten thousand plants and beings miss the right way (*daolu* 道路). This is why men must follow standard [norms]. You will be quite good if you stick to Yang, and quite bad if you stick to Yin. Act according to their intercourse and you will arrive[9] at a balance. Should fortune and misfortune not be constant, one's conduct follows neither model nor measure.[10] For this reason the wise and worthy of old thoroughly observed heaven and earth; the year, month, and day; the people; and the ten thousand plants and beings. They looked at increase and decrease, at excess and balance, and at progress and decline. Hence they knew for themselves which conduct would succeed and which would fail, just as your appearance becomes distinct when you look at yourself in a bright mirror.[11]

Excellent, indeed! Now what does one have to do?

Well, in your conduct hold onto the root, and take heaven as your model. This is the beginning. Once you take earth as your model, outlaws become rampant. To take the space between the two as your model is next best. To be without constancy ranks last.[12]

Why have men nowadays become so inconstant in their conduct?

Well, the ancestors erred a little through neglect, next came small-scale misbehavior, then some on a large scale, and finally they erred a lot. The way's *(daolu)* root *(genben)* became fussy and confused, and one could no longer rely on its intentions. That is why men's conduct became inconstant. They made changes to what they had said earlier, and the years of their life did not pass uniformly. So, clearly, *dao* had been corrupted to the extreme[13] and there was a need to return to the root. But when the wise men of old saw this, they knew that what had been dispersed was bound to turn back once it had reached the outer end. Therefore, they remained in power and kept their celestial mandate. So when the great worthy and wise observe matters they see clearly that good fortune comes from nothing but constancy. (58.95) Would you like to hear some further proof?

If the Celestial Master would only be so kind as to let us know about it!

All right. The course of the year is prosperous in its root and bad when it finishes, since Yin and Yang have then reached their end.[14] Latter-born men are evil and petty when [the course of] generations has reached an end. The ten thousand beings are prosperous at their root and without yield toward their death: they have reached their end. Latter-born men utter many empty lies without real content, since the quality of speaking has reached its lowest point. When texts and writings are composed in large numbers and all they say is untrue, [the skill of] writing has come to an end. All of this means that you move toward the branches once you lose your root, and are left with [only] blossoms when you let the fruit go. So to cause heaven and earth to bring forth the ten thousand plants and beings we must stress the core of things and not their ramifications. Certainly, the fault lies in drifting away from the root toward the branches.[15] We are deceived once we give up what is true, just as we become poor when we lose our means. So let us remain constant![16]

Thus, men became evil in their daily habits without being aware of it, just by increasingly ignoring the model set up by heaven. Latter-born generations continued to take things easy. They turned to deceit and fraud. They continually practiced how to become spiritlike.[17] Although no longer able to restrain themselves, they falsely claimed to have full understanding, so they inherited and transmitted more and more [evil]. They made heaven and earth spread their punishment and warnings to the four directions. Nobody can stop this. Even humane and worthy lords and kings would not be able to end mistakes that were committed by one generation after the other, more than ten thousand times in a row. An error might be small to begin with, just like a grain of millet, but to miss heaven's way by the tiniest margin amounts to an error of one thousand miles. When millet is collected, it grows to thousands and millions of measures that fill storage houses of many levels. And rain, falling incessantly, drop by drop, becomes one hundred streams that make up the mass of water of the four oceans. You must not let go of the root. So use true *dao* as your measure and you will arrive back at the root once you turn away from the branches' tips. Fruit grows by discarding the blossoms. Truth reappears as soon as you turn away from fraud. Once the tip of a branch has been reached one must return to the root; when a journey is at its end one must go home: this is heaven's way. Now to disregard standard *dao* in its uprightness is not just a small indisposition; it is a mistake that will be inherited and carried on after a man's life is over. The latter-born suffer from further confusion and error, so that standard *dao* becomes increasingly obscure and men go even further astray. Once heaven's *qi* is perverted, how can government achieve peace? How can men who have been poisoned or wounded live long? Since the ten thousand plants and beings suffer from numerous injuries and die early, I entreat you again and again to transmit my writings. Let men see for themselves: disregard *dao*'s intentions and you will fall ill and suffer personal grief. How, then, can heaven and earth, emperors and kings, the people and the ten thousand beings be safe? If you wish to please heaven's feelings you must not be idle or negligent.

Yes, indeed. I would like to ask one other question. Will the fortune and misfortune you have talked about arrive only when it is their turn?

Fine! Your question shows insight into *dao*'s intentions. (58.96) What has reached a peak must return to the bottom, what has been stretched out as far as possible must again be drawn in. Once the utmost of Yang has been achieved, there will be a return to Yin. What has reached the bottom must return to the peak. So when Yin is at its extreme point, it revolves back into Yang. This extreme point lies in the branches. From there, one must return to the root. Now since the division between heaven and earth, men slowly but gradually have come to disregard *dao*'s intentions.

The longer this has been inherited and transmitted the more it has brought corruption and fraud to their peak.

How does one know this?

By the fact that so many among the ten thousand beings and all the people turn bad in their later years when at first they were good, and that few achieve anything.[18]

What do you mean by "first" and "later"?[19]

At first is the true thing, and what comes later is hollow. The wise men of old knew about this since they always watched the activities of the ten thousand people. Thus they never went astray.

Excellent! I would like to ask one more question.

Go ahead.

Now if you are saying that there is a lowest and a highest state for beings, and if we consider the spiritlike man who bends qi[20] to be at the top of the nine groups of men and the serf at the bottom, then through study someone at the bottom will reach the top. But will someone who is at the top also be obliged to move downwards?

Fine; so this is your question. Now you are still, as always, foolish and confused, with no understanding for the workings *(dao)* of the great ultimate.[21]

Now the body and the strength of this spiritlike man who bends *qi* are the same as that of primordial *qi*. In unison with the four seasons and five phases, he brings forth life. All spirits who serve men are derived from celestial *qi* that has received them from primordial *qi*. Spirits move about riding on *qi*. Thus a man in possession of *qi* has spirits, too, and while in possession of spirits he also has *qi*. Should spirits go away, *qi* will face an interruption, and should *qi* be lost, spirits will go away. That is why one dies without spirits as one dies without *qi*.[22] How should a spiritlike man who bends *qi* ever find entry into the belly of a man?[23]

Yes, indeed.

Also, the five phases grow from primordial *qi*, while spirit has the same body and the same activities as primordial *qi*. The five phases move inside [a man] to form his five bodily organs. Should the most exalted of these nine groups of men move downward and return to someone's body?

Excellent! Although I have studied for quite a while, this is the first time I have heard this.

Well, you must concentrate on your studies. Otherwise, you won't benefit from them.

Yes. When I hear the Celestial Master speak, it is as if heaven's way was moving on its circle.

All right. Let us assume that you have understood. Go, but don't hesitate to ask when there is a question. (58.97)

Yes, certainly.[24]

NOTES

1. *Huo* 或 must be understood as 惑 (puzzling); cf. the sentence preceding note 5 of this section.

2. In this context, "good" and "bad" can hardly be seen as moral values. In a similar vein, section 106 talks about the "good and bad" in man's nature (*xing* 性) as if this meant "prosperous and disadvantageous":

> So when the nature *(xing)* [someone has received from] heaven and earth is good, it not only becomes manifest in himself; it also spreads to his descendants, as becomes clear from their actions. If his nature is bad, this also does not rest with him only but reaches to his descendants and in a perverse way becomes manifest in their actions. Therefore good and bad must become manifest. But to be good is like the brightness that spreads with sunrise; to be wicked is like the darkness after sunset. This is what the nature [someone has received from] heaven and earth, Yin and Yang, and what is as it is, is like. Heaven brings forth the ten thousand beings, each follows its path (*xing* 行) and becomes distinct, and nothing remains hidden. Thus the good man moves upward, and his fate lies with heaven, just like the living belongs to heaven. The wicked man moves downward, and his fate lies with earth; just like a dead person the wicked therefore moves downward, to the Yellow Springs. This is what it means. (TPJ 106.279)

3. This section discusses action from what we might call a "scientific" point of view rather than from a moral point of view. The viewpoint is that of a prognosticator who needs to establish well-defined criteria to predict the future. The Master's approach here can be compared to that of a physician who sees his skills made irrelevant by a patient who recovers although predicted to die and by another patient who dies despite the existence of a promising cure.

4. In the following, the formation of "good" and "bad" is linked to the occurrence of Yin and Yang. This relationship is taken up in another passage that deals with "good" and "bad" in a nondistinct manner, as if what is "good" would include rich harvests and lucky days as well as moral conduct:

> The nature [that has been received from] heaven and earth is half Yang and half Yin. Insofar as it is Yang, it is good and obtains rewards and remunerations. Insofar as it is Yin, it is bad. The bad man is being punished and his actions are corrupt. When rewards are many, punishments are few. When there is a lot of knavery, rewards are few and the gate to corruption is open. . . . The nature [that has been received from] heaven and earth is half good and half bad, so the ruler elevates the good to shut out what is corrupt. Promote the good and you will have good results. Elevate bad people and your results will be bad. (TPJ p. 702, *Chao,* part 9)

5. This is said from the prognosticator's point of view.

6. This phrase is repeated frequently, with minor variations, throughout layer A (TPJ 103.244 and 245; 104.260; 137.384; 152.421; 156.440; 177.518; 191.588; 207.654; p. 648, *Chao*, part 7). Its meaning is expressed as "I can't tell you all and give you only the main points" (TPJ 158.446) or "I can't change it. I can only give you the main points and let you see how it all begins" (TPJ 103.251). This phrase must be seen as a stylistic characteristic of layer A.

7. This argument is based on common sense and is strikingly devoid of moral considerations. Concern with fame is rare in layer A, but it is expressed several times in layer B (TPJ 179.532 and 540; 197.609).

8. Another division into auspicious and inauspicious modes of conduct is attempted in section 178 (pp. 520–22), which distinguishes four auspicious and four inauspicious ways of ruling a country. The four auspicious modes are the employment of, from top to bottom, a person who accumulates merit and achieves permanent stability (*chang an* 常 安), someone who makes a good administrator, someone who sheds light on his teacher's doctrine, and someone who believes in this doctrine. The inauspicious modes are the employment of a man who doesn't benefit his sovereign, of someone who undertakes criminal activities, of someone who discards the doctrine he has learned, and of a disbeliever, whom heaven and earth detest.

9. *Zhe* 適 (this) is understood as *shi* 適 (to go to); see Yu (2001a: 88). Yu (1997: 53) points to several similar cases in the TPJ and also to early translations of Buddhist texts.

10. "Model and measure" (*fa du* 法 度) is a term for rules of personal conduct used without specification, as if what was meant was clear. The warning not to ignore "model and measure" goes back to the *Book* of Documents (*Da Yu mou;* see Legge 1960, vol. 3, p. 55). In this sense they are also supposed to guide the personal conduct of the *taiping* adherent: "When you personally stick to model and measure, you will not lose constancy (*chang* 常)" (TPJ p. 214, *Chao*, part 4). The Celestial Master integrates the term into his own argument and proposes that the people's contribution to cosmic and social order can be seen to consist of attending to "model and measure":

> When great *dao* was corrupted the fault lay with the people of lower antiquity who taught each other to ignore model and measure *(shi fa du)*. (TPJ 208.663)

The consequence of such neglect is the end of life:

> When heaven's way is in disorder and uproar (*luan hui* 亂 毀), the danger of extinction arises through the loss of model and measure. (TPJ p. 701, *Chao*, part 9)

11. *Dongming* 洞 明 is the brightness that meditation results in. It follows after envisaging red, white, and green (TPJ p. 16, *Chao*, part 2). It is the way in which heaven reflects a man's heart (TPJ 65.154). The concept occurs in the *Yunji qiqian* (88.9b; referring to a *Xian ji zhijue* 仙 籍 旨 訣, which is not mentioned elsewhere) in a similar context: when a person looks after his vital energy properly his inner organs will be *dongming*.

12. *Wei* 未 is corrected to *mo* 末; see Yang 1994: 317.

13. *Wei* is corrected to *mo*, as above.

14. The section takes a turn at this point from stressing "constancy" to stressing the "root." However, as the root is lost by a lack of constancy, the two parts are linked, as pointed out below.

15. For the image of root and branches, see section 53.

16. The Celestial Master's use of the word "constant" must be seen against the background of its prominent position in the first line of the *Laozi*. The TPJ occasionally uses the term "inconstant" in a purely descriptive way, for instance, in the sense that all beings change their shape with the change of seasons (TPJ p. 221, *Chao*, part 4), or when water and wind are called inconstant because they can fill a circle as well as a square (p. 738, in a quotation in the *Daoyao lingqi shengui pin jing*, an anthology of passages from pre–Sui dynasty texts). However, "inconstancy" is mainly used to point to problems, including the joy and anger of the population (TPJ 108.287), good and bad fortune (TPJ 152.414), and flood and drought (TPJ 190.584). Inconstancy needs to be avoided in all these cases, so the passage at hand is by no means isolated.

17. In the TPJ, the expression "to turn into a spirit" or "to become spiritlike" (*cheng shen* 成 神) is used as if it were a technical term. It describes one step toward avoiding death and transcending this life into otherworldly realms. It is used in this sense in layer B (TPJ 182.551; 184.561; 197.609; 198.612) and in the following layer A' passage:

> The key to understanding the method of implementing *dao* and avoiding death lies in making yourself spiritlike. Thus will you transcend the world (*du shi* 度 世), as pledged by heaven. (TPJ 173.511)

In the passage at hand, "to turn into a spirit" is seen as a manifestation of a successful religious career, as in layer B. In contrast to this usage, in section 54 (p. 78), "to turn into a spirit" is used to describe one step toward becoming the universe's savior.

18. This is another statement that runs counter to general opinion.

19. With Yu (2001a: 90), the two missing characters are read as *hou he* 後 何.

20. On the "spiritlike man who bends *qi*" (*wei qi*), see above, section 56. Spirit that ranks with life-giving *qi* can't move into a man's belly. One's Daoist rank is, as we would expect, defined by physical as well as by spiritual substance.

21. The *Xi ci* in the *Book of Changes* says, "In change there is the great ultimate, which generates the two modes [of Yin and of Yang]" (*Yi jing*, "*Xi ci*" A, p. 43.11). In this section the Celestial Master uses the "great ultimate" with the same meaning. For him this concept guides the movement of beings and actions between the spheres of Yin and of Yang. The only other TPJ reference to the concept is far removed from the *Book of Changes*:

> So what do we mean by acting according to the great, medium, and small ultimate? Someone who acts according to the great ultimate is in charge of the realm that is with-

out outside; someone who acts according to the medium ultimate is in charge of the central realm; and when someone acts according to the small ultimate, everything keeps within its own division. (TPJ 139.396)

This reinterpretation of the great ultimate is closer to Ge Hong's understanding than to the *Book of Changes*. For Ge Hong the great ultimate was the heavenly abode where the transcendents sojourned (*Baopu zi waipian* 34, *"Wu shi"* 吳失 p. 160).

22.　As an aside, and as if what he says is well known and clear, the Master here points to the role played by the body spirits. They must not go away; if they do, illness occurs. Tanaka Fumio (1984) has shown that the TPJ shares the concern for body spirits with the *Huangting jing* and the *Baopu zi*. Since their departure was seen as causing illness, these spirits had to be asked, in ritual form, to come back. For this, the believer fasted and then envisaged them in great detail (TPJ 109.292). The writing of confessions was meant to appease heaven and in particular the body spirits, who were its servants (see Masaaki 2002).

23.　The answer does not seem to fit the question. The Master replies that the spiritlike man is spirit of such high quality that he cannot be transformed into a low-ranking body spirit. The disciple's question, however, is concerned with the hierarchy of human rank. The answer seems to take for granted that the worlds of men and of spirits are parallel, as outlined in much detail in layer B.

24.　The summary says:

This section examines the essence of heaven's four modes of conduct, root and branches, and the great ultimate with the aim of returning back to standard [norms] (I read *zheng* 正 for *zheng* 政).

This section stresses the importance of communication and openness to the flow of information. While this is a topic of mainstream political thinking—as expressed, for instance, in the *Mengzi*[1]—it also agrees with the *taiping* ideal of sharing and co-operation. The Celestial Master places this subject in a cosmic context, in the tradition of cosmological and prognostic reasoning. All deviations from the regular course of nature must be seen as willed by heaven. If men refuse to interpret these deviations as warnings or decide not to act upon them, their fate is sealed. The Master makes this point repeatedly in strong terms, as if, despite the prestige that disaster analysis enjoyed during much of the Han dynasty, he still had to convince his audience. He seems not to have been mistaken, as the disciple questions the main point of his argument, which requires the Master to repeat it: once the tokens heaven has sent to signal its reproach have been ignored, heaven will cease to send them. Men might then feel secure while being truly on the brink of ruin. The large amount of detail in this section is perhaps more than a simple rhetorical device. The details also function as a list of points an official must be expected to check in order to be aware of all cosmic warnings. The division into "small" and "big" reproaches is formalized, as if to simplify the proper implementation of prognostic calculation.

However, despite the description of natural disasters in this section, the focus is on the relationship between the ruler and his advisors. If the official is the main human source of warnings, corresponding in this respect to heaven, then the period immediately preceding a breakdown might appear unperturbed, at least for the ruler, whose official advisors have learned to flatter him persistently. The reduction in the number of omens that were reported during the reigns of Emperor Shun (r. 125–44) and, in particular, Emperor Xian (r. 189–220) could actually be a case in point.[2] Such a reduction of omens on a regional scale may well be the background and the reason for what is here said about heaven cutting off disasters when humankind is doomed. But there is also a direct link between the breakdown of communication on the cosmic and human levels. A treacherous contentment will in both cases block the flow of information: heaven will not send signs, thus stupefying ruler and officials; the official will not speak up; and if he did speak up, his mission might be hampered by heaven, which has ceased to communicate, and by the ruler who has ceased to listen.

The thesis set forth in this section conflicts to some extent with the idea that an increase in human guilt leads to an increase in natural disasters, as described in sections 47 and 48, as well as in the section at hand.

.   .   .

(59.98) The Perfected beats his head on the ground. He says:

I am a foolish pupil, blind and dull. I truly don't know anything about dao. *Thanks to heaven I have now had a glimpse of safety and danger, fortune and misfortune.[3] So I dare to ask all I can about* dao's *commandments. Are there any expressions of reproach[4] in the way the spirits of heaven and earth [move about] in this world? If the Celestial Master would only instruct us and direct us to what* dao *means.*

You have asked about something that is mysterious[5] and far-reaching.

I have observed that men reproach each other. Thus my question is whether heaven does likewise.

Good! With this question you have grasped the true center of heaven's way. Heaven's vital beings[6] will come forth, and spirits of heaven and earth will rejoice. The main points of this I will now explain to you so that[7] for ten thousand times ten thousand generations they will not be forgotten.

Yes!

Well, heaven utters a small reproach by changing color, and a big one by splitting open. Should this not be heeded it does not occur again. When the three luminaries reprimand men in regard to small matters, stars change color. In the case of a big rebuke, the luminaries stray from their course and lose brightness. Should this not be obeyed it will cease. Earth shakes to give a slight warning, but mountains collapse and the soil splits open for a big reproach. If men were not to pay attention such phenomena would no longer be seen.

For a small reproach by the five phases, calamities occur. In the case of a big reproach, the eastern phase kills men through worms,[8] the southern phase kills them through poison[ous winds],[9] the western phase through tiger and wolf,[10] and the northern phase through water animals.[11] In the case of the central phase, petty officials and ordinary subjects use poison and turn to robbery and murder. (59.99) All this will come to an end should men ignore it. Should the four seasons utter a slight rebuke, cold and heat will not be in balance. When it is an earnest reproach, they change places so that the seasons no longer occur in proper order. Should men not pay heed such warnings cease.

Vital qi[12] of the six directions wreaks havoc for a small reproach, again and again. Vital qi breeds plagues of flying and creeping insects. It assembles masses of clouds and wind that don't cause rain to fall, and thus the husks remain empty, without grain. When the reproach is big, periods of flood and drought are irregular and bandits cause damage to things (wan wu 萬物) and to the people. Should men not pay heed to such warnings they will end. When birds and four-legged animals slightly reproach men, they send natural calamities. Once the reproach is severe, they devour men and send locusts forth in large numbers. This will come to an end should the reproach not be heeded. Demons, spirits, and other vital beings[13] that utter a slight rebuke haunt petty officials and the people with small numbers of bandits and diseases. In the case of a severe rebuke, they rip men apart and wipe out whole families. Should this not be heeded such warnings will come to an end. In the case of a subtle warning of the six directions, rain and wind turn disorderly and violent. They injure men in conjunction with evil and poisonous vapors. If it is a great warning they stretch sideways to tear the structure of the earth apart, let tiles and rocks fly about, let soil pile up against majestic heaven, wreck houses, and move mountains. If this is not heeded it will come to an end. (59.100)

When the sounds of heaven and earth utter a slight warning, thunder and lightning become mildly frightening. Should they utter a severe warning men will defile and pervert each other on numerous occasions and make thunder clap loudly, again and again. This will come to an end should men not pay attention. Petty officials and ordinary subjects who utter a slight warning frequently change allegiance. In the case of a severe warning, they turn to robbery and violence. These warnings will end should nobody pay attention.

A severe warning by the six directions and the eight ends of heaven and earth means that they wish the writings brought forth by the Yellow River and the Luo to be in standard order and bear witness of heaven. Auspicious texts appear in the world to set lords and kings right so that everything under heaven is in correspondence. Should these warnings not be heeded they will no longer take place. Since scriptures on heaven's way should always be put to use we must act as they instruct us. For this reason, as soon as the wise and worthy of old noticed an event they did nothing but discuss and deliberate[14] its meaning. They did not dare remain idle and negligent and thereby lose the breadth of a hair in their understanding of the subtle message this event had put forth. Since they did not ignore what majestic heaven had on its mind, they were able to maintain their person and secure their abode[15] free from worries and peril. Disaster did not strike. Plans and calculations met heaven's intentions.

Excellent, indeed. I have understood. Only now do I clearly see the model you have outlined. I would like to hear the meaning of "therefore [warnings] would come to an end." It must be brought to light.[16]

Your attitude is excellent! Well, heaven's way assists and eases education. It helps men to be completely sincere[17] as well as attentive and observant.[18] It helps and eases understanding and instruction. It teaches a sovereign it wants to be mighty (*hou* 厚).[19] Otherwise, it won't teach him. This is similar to men who explain events to those they are intimate with (*qin hou* 親厚) and don't like to give explanations to others they are not intimate with. Should someone not pay attention when taught, heaven will be annoyed that it has spoken at the wrong time and will therefore discard and dismiss such a person and never again attempt to teach and guide him. At this point, natural calamities, disasters, and other anomalies will come to a standstill. When [heaven] no longer guides and instructs men, even the worthy and the wise become deaf; they are in the dark and know nothing. All their insight is blocked. Should the spirits of heaven and earth no longer wish to reproach men, natural calamities and other irregular events would happen more and more frequently. There is no remedy against it, and men will become weaker from day to day until they lose their position in the world.[20] (59.101)

This is why the wise and worthy of old withdrew day and night from business in order to think deeply. They never dared ignore what heaven felt, so they were able to serve majestic heaven as father and majestic earth as mother, the sun as older brother and the moon as younger brother. They kept the firmament (*tian wen* 天文) in correct shape and the five phases stable. By following the four seasons they observed their coming and going. Through self-reflection,[21] they corrected their conduct. By understanding [things] thoroughly they knew about gain and loss.[22] Their essential *dao*[23] was simply [the way in which] heaven and earth maintained themselves. They took heaven's support, expressed in Yellow River maps and Luo writings, as their mandate. (59.102) For this reason all their actions were in correspondence, as if they were spirits. Only by these means did they thoroughly fulfill heaven's wishes. Their words were a precise fit, as if compasses and carpenter's square had been applied. So spirits and other numinous beings were busy on their behalf. Should men be obstinate and refuse to heed such reproach heaven will go backward and the earth astray. In uproar, the five phases and four seasons will go the wrong way and lose their order. Then activities will go wrong and big disasters will occur. This is what is meant by "[warnings] will come to an end." Is this any clearer?

Yes, it is.

So it is in unison with the nature of heaven and earth that subordinates reprimand their superiors and that superiors reproach their subordinates. Each has strong points as well as shortcomings. Only when both support each other will each of the heavenly way's ten thousand activities (*fan wan* 凡 萬) be in its right place. So, when compared to earth, majestic heaven, spiritlike and wise as it may be, has certain weak points.[24] The reason is that, although the ten thousand beings receive life from heaven, they gain food for their body from earth. The three luminaries in one respect fall short of fire: although spiritlike and bright, they cannot shine in a dark chamber as fire can. A great wise man has shortcomings when compared to a worthy, and men have shortcomings when compared to the ten thousand beings. Once the system of mutual reproach reaches all the way down to the very smallest item, we won't lose *dao* or ignore heaven's intentions. For this reason heaven has brought forth all activities in such a way that they sometimes undergo reform.[25] To reproach the ruler of men is always a token of perfect virtue that deserves full attention.[26] This is what we mean by mutual criticism of heaven, earth, and the ten thousand beings.

Yes, indeed. I wish men would put into effect the explanations that the Master of Majestic Heaven (huang tian shi 皇 天 師) *has put forward!*

Fine. Make sure to heed what I say and to think about it. If a loyal and faithful official were to reprimand his superior and the lord did not listen but instead tried to harm him, the official would turn frightened and tongue-tied, as if he were dumb. Nothing would get through [to the lord], as if he were behind doors closed in all six directions. The worthy and learned[27] would hide in fear. The loyal and the faithful would shut themselves in and the true doctrine *(dao)* would nowhere be seen. Then, even if the lord were wise and worthy, he would have no way to hear about things. He would thus turn deaf and blind. He would have no means to observe unusual and strange occurrences. Increasingly, they would be shrouded in darkness, the lord deaf and the official dumb. If this misfortune were not checked, the official would be in the dark and the lord blind. Depravity and evil would spread widely. Should the official be dumb and the lord deaf the world would not reach them. Good and evil would not be distinguished. Heaven-sent calamities would become universal, fighting would break out at the six ends of the world, disasters would occur one after the other, everywhere.[28] How can one not pay attention to this!

Yes, indeed.

For this reason the wise and worthy of old paid close attention to natural calamities, disasters, and other irregular events. They set things right in person, as if with a marking line, so that nothing went wrong. They were truly in agreement with the great teachings of the major texts. (59.103) Completely loyal in all their undertakings, they suffered from no further disasters. You have been warned repeatedly; pay attention to my words.

Yes, I will.

Well, heaven is not high and bright because of the merit and virtue of one single vital spirit (*jing* 精). The government of emperors and kings does not meet heaven's approval just because of one single worthy official. Now my words are a general outline to point out where to begin. It is not possible to write or speak about every detail. You will have to figure out for yourself what it all means.

Yes, I will.

All right, you may go. How should words [ever] reach to the end? Ask no more questions.

Yes, I understand.[29]

NOTES

1. See *Mengzi* 2B2.
2. See Bielenstein 1984: 104.
3. "Fortune and misfortune" (*ji xiong* 吉凶) is a frequent topic in the TPJ; the two characters occur in the titles of sections 45 and 191. "Safety and danger" (*an wei* 安危) occurs in the title of section 275. Much of section 58 deals with this topic.
4. "To reproach" (*jian* 諫) is a layer B term. Someone who is good *(shan)* makes use of reproofs (TPJ 185.564), and men who do the right thing speak up and reproach each other (TPJ 169.530), as opposed to those who don't do so (TPJ 182.550). It is said that when three reproofs are not heeded no further criticism will be heard (TPJ 188.577). In a *Chao* passage, it is said that reproof must reach the lowliest of the distant regions in

the four directions so that its inhabitants won't despair (TPJ 468). Layer B passages depict reproach as a way to safeguard personal accomplishment, while in the passage at hand communal well-being is at stake.

5. Luo (1996: 174) is right when he identifies the expression *miaoyao* 妙要 (mysterious) with the *yaomiao* of *Laozi* 27, which also occurs in TPJ 111.554 (layer B) and p. 214, *Chao*, part 4.

6. According to *Huainan zi* 8 *"Ben jing"* 本經, p. 11b, *tian jing* 天精, "heaven's vital beings," means "natural phenomena," that is, the sun, moon, stars, constellations, thunder, lightning, wind, and rain. The *Huainan zi* sees heaven's *jing* as the equivalent of earth's "balance" (*ping* 平) and men's "endowment" (*qing* 情), that is, man's thinking, understanding, and feeling. In the *Laozi zhongjing* (老子中經) (see *Yunji qiqian* 19.2b and 3a) the white and yellow *qi* of "celestial essence" refers to a specific type of *jing* (sperma). The "lord of celestial essence" (*tian jing jun*, or *tian jing da jun* 天精大君) is a body deity (*Yunji qiqian* 52.1a–b, based on the *Za yao tu jue fa* 雜要圖訣法; see also 55.8b, in the commentary to a section [*Cun shen shen fa* 存身神法] that deals with body deities).

The shades of the term *jing* as used in the TPJ vary. The term means fine, essential *qi*, as in the *Huainan zi*, and it also means *jing shen*, that is, spiritual beings of high rank who reside in the human body but who also act as heaven's servants and envoys. In discussing the TPJ's use of the term, Harada (1984) stresses the first aspect and arrives at the convincing conclusion that in both respects *jing* is an important element of a human being's longevity. As Bokenkamp (1993: 47) shows, this is based on the character's pointing to semen and to menstrual fluid. As agents of procreation, these liquids can be seen as manifesting the human life force. See also note 12, below.

Tian jing occurs only here in the TPJ, and it probably means the same as the full expression *tian jing shen* 天精神 of section 56—they do men the honor of partaking in properly administered sacrifices. So the passage at hand talks about *jing* and *shen* spirits from heaven, and *qi* 祇 spirits from earth.

7. *Jin* is corrected to *ling*; see Yu 2001a: 91.

8. According to *Lun heng* 49 *"Shang chong"* 商蟲, p. 719, the growth of all insects has something to do with weather conditions and thus with the relationship between Yin and Yang, for which the government of the day must be held responsible.

The five phases are here identified by direction from *dong xing* 東行 to *zhong* 中 *xing*. This is unusual. Also, for the rest of this passage I have not managed to find an exact parallel that would comprise all the same correlations between the five phases and the damage they may cause.

9. Wang Chong sees the "hot air of the sun" as poisonous and the south as the place where poison originates (see *Lun heng* 66 *"Yan du"* 言毒, pp. 949f.).

10. Wang Chong sees a need to refute the idea that tigers are particularly prone to devouring men in regions that are poorly administered by corrupt officials (see *Lun heng* 48 *"Zao hu"* 遭虎, p. 707).

11. *Chun qiu fan lu* 60 *"Wu xing shun ni"* 五行順逆, pp. 377–80, explains the linkage between water, winter, and the turtle.

12. "Vital *qi*" (*jing qi* 精氣) is an expression for spiritual beings, used in parallel and often together with "spirits" *(shen)*; see TPJ 153.425 and 211.673, *gui shen jing qi* 鬼神精氣; p. 698, *Chao*, part 8, *shen ming jing qi* 神明精氣; p. 706, *Chao*, part 9, *jing qi gui shen*. The expression is also used often in layer B: see TPJ 185.563; 186.567, *shen jing qi;* 187.572. Illness occurs if vital *qi* and spirits are cut off, if their impact does not reach men (TPJ 153.425; cf. 107.284). However, the expression *jing qi* is also used as "life-giving *qi*," for which the *Hanyu da cidian* (vol. 9, p. 222) refers to *Lun heng* 65 *"Ding gui"* 訂鬼, p. 946. *Jing qi* is said to bring about knowing, just as bones give strength. This resembles the point made in TPJ p. 723, *Chao*, part 1: "When *dao* brings forth men, they are originally all vital *qi*."

Luo's interpretation (1996: 176) stresses the six directions and takes its clues from the *Huangdi neijing suwen* 67 *"Wu yun xing da lun"* 五運行大論, pp. 15a–25b, which mentions wind, cold, heat, mildness, dryness, and fire.

13. Wang Ming corrects *jing* to *jingwu* 精物 following the reading of the *Chao*, but in this section the single character *jing* is used in the meaning of *jingwu*, as, for instance, in *tian jing* 天精 in the last paragraph.

14. "Discuss and deliberate" is expressed by the compound *wei lun si* 惟論思; see Yu 2001a: 92.

15. The *Chao* reads more plausibly, "to secure the people's [in the received text *min* is corrupted to *ju* 居] nurturing of all ten thousand plants and beings."

16. I correct *dang* 黨 (group), which is rarely used in the TPJ, to *dang* 當 (must). Yu Liming (1997: 51) argues that *dang* 黨 is here used to mean "to learn," which, according to the *Fang yan*, is Chu usage. However, Yu admits that the character is rarely used in this sense.

17. The general understanding of "sincerity" (*cheng* 誠) as a virtue through which we implement what we have understood, or through which spiritual achievement becomes physically manifest, is the background for the Celestial Master's use of the term, for this is the virtue in men that moves heaven (TPJ 63.134; 83.210; 131.342; p. 719, *Chao*, part 1). To be "sincere" is to be "true" (*shi* 實) (TPJ 153.425), and the opposite of "deceitful" (*qi* 欺) (TPJ p. 221, *Chao*, part 4; 131.344; 152.414). Section 153 gives detailed information on the term. Heaven's concern with the lack of complete sincerity among men has caused it to send the Perfected to learn from the Celestial Master. Through complete sincerity, a man corresponds to heaven and earth (153.425). His impact on heaven derives from the fact that his actions are oriented toward it:

As for "complete sincerity," when we call a man completely sincere we mean that he either looks up to heaven when he acts and achieves things by imitating heaven's way, or that he looks down to earth and reforms things by reflecting its virtue. . . . So the sun reigns as king through fire. It is a [source of] correctness for heaven and brings everything to light. Therefore, when a man is completely sincere he sets right all that is troubling, from within his heart. The heart's spirit in its complete wisdom informs the sun, which then informs heaven. In this way, complete sincerity of the five inner organs moves spirits and other numinous beings (*shen ling* 神靈). . . . When a man in complete sincerity is concerned about something, he approaches troubles from within his heart. Documenting [the state of] the heart, the stomach won't take any nourishment [I read *er* 而 as *neng* 能 with Long 2000: 879]. What is at issue is the heart, the will. When there is something heart and will can't forget, the liver presents itself as most humane *(ren)*. And since it rules the eyes, they shed tears. This is what is meant by the completely sincere way in which vital energy thinks (*jing si* 精思). . . . So all human action in search of *dao* and virtue starts from complete sincerity. Heaven and earth respond to it, spirits and other numinous beings come to announce it. Without complete sincerity, men won't have an impact on heaven and earth, and they won't influence spirits and other numinous beings. Thus since the inheriting and transmitting [of evil] commenced, the men of later antiquity have been truly without faith (*xin* 信), they have lacked complete sincerity, and they have not had impact on heaven and earth, but instead have deceived them. So spirits and other numinous beings do harm without end. (TPJ 153.426–27).

Tsuchiya Masaaki (2002: 45–51) adds an important perspective to this, as he sees "sincerity" as telling the truth when confessing offenses. This can help to explain why a sincere person does not suffer from illness. A believer's self-critical, penitent attitude makes the spirits who watch over him return to their places in his body and thus restore his health. This also provides another possible explanation of why heaven responds to a man's sincerity. It is moved by the confession of sins, just as a judge might show leniency toward the culprit who admits his guilt.

18. This is how men must behave toward the four seasons (TPJ 140.400), toward heaven's way (204.630), and toward the good (TPJ 103.250). It is only here that the two characters *jin shun* 謹順 occur without an accompanying object.

19. This passage goes back to the *Shijing* song (no. 166) "*Tian bao*" 天保 (heaven protects you). The meaning of *bao* is here expressed by *you* 祐 (to help), but the term *tian bao* occurs a little further down, on p. 101 of this section. The song addresses the lord (as translated by Karlgren 1950: 109):

Heaven protects and secures you, doing it very solidly; it causes you to be richly endowed (*hou* 厚); what felicity is not heaped [on you]?

20. This passage mentions in close proximity the two contradictory functions of "unusual occurrences." They communicate heaven's will and are thus a sign of its benevolence. They are also the means by which humankind will eventually be exterminated.

21. "Self-reflection" (*zi zhao* 自照) is a way to heal illness:

When your innermost heart entertains evil intentions, uproar develops in distant regions and your spirits (*shen qi* 神氣) spread about faster than thunder and lightning. You must then urgently make spirits and other enlightened beings (*shen ming* 神明) return so that self-reflection takes place. Thus illness is healed and men are well governed. (TPJ pp. 722f., *Chao*, part 1)

22. The text is perhaps corrupt, but there is no obvious emendation. Neither the phrase *zhi tian* 知天 nor the phrase *tian de shi* 天得失 occurs elsewhere in the TPJ. The reading of the *Chao* differs, which might point to problems with the textual transmission: "Through self-reflection they made their conduct upright and knew of themselves about gain and loss (*zi zhi de shi* 自知得失)." The quotation ends at this point. The *Chao* quotes section 59 more fully than other sections and places it prominently at the end of part three. We must assume that the passage was already difficult when the *Chao* was written. I have changed *tian* 天 to *zhi* 知 in an attempt to achieve some parallelism with the preceding sentence. The text, then, would read *yi shen zhi zhi de shi ye* 以深知知得失 也. It is quite plausible that some corruption occurred around the reduplicated *zhi*.

23. See above, 47.55 *(zhen yao dao zhi wen)*, and section 154, passim, where "essential *dao*" (*yao dao* 要道) is used similarly to *dao* in its ontological sense ("Now heaven creates beings through essential, true *dao* . . ." [TPJ 154.430]), and also in the sense of "doctrine" ("educate and reform the small-minded through essential *dao* and virtue" [TPJ 154.432], or "Now essential *dao* and excellent *(shan)* virtue come forth to educate the small-minded" [TPJ 154.430]).

24. The main concern of this section is that an official must be frank with his superior, so even when stressing that reproach must be mutual, the emphasis is on its upward direction. Through the juxtaposition of heaven and earth, even heaven is included in this scheme, which then naturally also includes the ruler.

25. *Biange* 變革 is a *Li ji* (34 "*Da zhuan*" 大傳, p. 1506c) term for "reform."

26. This is Mengzi's (2B2) point of view.

27. *Xian ru* 賢儒 (worthy and learned) is a regular TPJ word for officials of rank (TPJ 62.128, 65.155, 66.162), as it is in, for instance, *Lun heng* 40 "*Zhuang liu*," pp. 619–22. It is clear that the officials who were expected to implement *taiping* reforms were the officials of the day.

28. These last sentences, starting with "the lord deaf and the official dumb," are of unusual rhetorical vigor. This is achieved by the persistent juxtaposing of ruler and servant, by a sequence of brief four-character sentences, and by the use of rhymes; see Yu (2001a: 93f.).

29. The summary says:

This section provides correct instruction on heaven's reproaches.

How Books Illustrate [Rule by]
Punishment and [by] Virtue

Rulers who establish their authority by applying the penal code prevent the arrival of great peace. The Celestial Master states this repeatedly, arguing that the misery of those who perish in prisons and those whose lives are cut short causes heaven to be vengeful and inclines it to send calamities. Another, more formalistic, train of thought follows in this section. Here, the course of the year is said to represent what severe government and what a reign by virtue can achieve. As if it were self-evident, the text identifies Yang with virtue on the one hand, and Yin with punishment on the other. The ruler is expected to ensure that his government corresponds with the span of the year from midwinter to midsummer, that is, to the period of growing Yang and growing virtue. Since this section takes up a topic that has always been central to Chinese political philosophy, presuppositions abound. That the people as well as the ruler both desire a stable and permanent government is taken for granted, and so is the sovereign's dependence on the social elite. The ruler here is compared to the natural force that makes the seasons follow one another. This comparison throws a new light on the ruler's relationship to the other groups in the political arena.

The section is unusually long and contains two separate dialogues on the same topic. The dialogues are arranged differently but convey roughly the same message. The changing influence of "virtue" and "punishment" from day to day and from month to month was a well-known aspect of ancient cosmology,[1] but there do not seem to be any other examples of the way in which this section applies it.

The text argues that the relationship between punishment and virtue is the essential lesson to be drawn from the course of nature. Virtue is shown as growing with the growth of plants from one month to the next until it has matured and gives way to punishment, whose growth coincides with the decay of vegetation in autumn and winter.

This is followed by a passage on the antagonism that violent rule creates and the popularity that results from virtuous conduct. The argument is not fundamentalist but allows for degrees. The more punishment a ruler applies, the more insurrections he will face, while the extent of his benevolence directly affects the obedience he can expect from his subjects. A violent ruler will lack men who support him and will therefore lose his position. On the other hand, moral conduct and benevolent practices enable a man to assemble followers, to become a king, and to reign successfully.

At this point the first dialogue ends and is followed by the second, which raises the same points in a different order. The disciple argues that a strong and severe government should be able to coerce people into submission. This forces the Master into an argument that hints at historical reality, though without giving names and details. The Master argues that severe government drives men into hiding rather than into submission. This is followed by another, slightly more concise, account of the annual cycle of "virtue" and "punishment." The Master takes a more radical stance here than in the first dialogue, and he argues that each act of violence and of virtue has widespread repercussions.

This section can be seen as a reaction to certain political tendencies that became manifest during the reign of Emperor Huan.[2] One was the attempt by Cui Shi 崔寔 and others to make punishment more severe.[3] Another, described by Rafe de Crespigny, was an increasing tendency among those selected for office not to accept it, out of contempt for the emperor and his surroundings and because of the great risk involved in raising any objections against the emperor's way of ruling. Wei Huan's 魏桓 response to his neighbors, who wanted him to take the position at court that he had been offered, says it all:

> "If I were seeking salary and advancement I would thereby get what I want. Yet there are thousands of women in the imperial chambers, and how shall their number be reduced? There are tens of thousands of horses in the imperial stables, and how shall their number be diminished? The attendants at the imperial court are powerful and oppressive, and how can they be removed?" All replied, "This cannot be done." Then Huan sighed and said, "You ask that I should go away alive and come back dead [for I should inevitably be killed

when criticizing these abuses]. How can you require this of me?" So he went into hiding and would not go.[4]

.   .   .

(60.104) Perfected Chun bows respectfully [and says]:

Now in asking this question I am bound to commit a serious offense. When I ponder the master's writings I know they are all true and contain nothing that needs modification. But this pupil is foolish and dull. It vexes me not to know where you found the model that you have shown us. I know that you are the illustrious teacher, the spiritlike man sent by majestic heaven, but still I am perplexed by the sheer number of your words. If you would only[5] have mercy and point to the essential proof for the lessons we are to draw from heaven's Yin and Yang and for the predictions cast by the spirits of heaven and earth.[6] I am annoyed and confused because I cannot figure it out. Of course, what I say goes against your prohibitions, but I am unable to control the desire to speak out. Although you will criticize me, I wish that you would give us a clear illustration of the token and the model provided by heaven[7] so that it can be transmitted for ten thousand times ten thousand generations, brilliant beyond all doubt and bright as the sun at noon, never to be changed and never to go away.

Well, you are determined not to trust my words, aren't you? As if you, for your part, had not yet properly learned to understand heaven's intentions! As if you were a fool! You are hardly better than the common people if you think that my words can be opposed! Whoever opposes them will be in disarray. Whoever acts against them will suffer defeat. Everything I tell you is supported by the patterns of heaven.[8] Everything I say agrees with the great lesson we can draw from Yin and Yang. You have come to ask questions on behalf of heaven; I transmit orders on its behalf. I would not dare to say anything improper, meaningless, and false or to use artful language. You have lived through quite a number of years, months, and days and experienced quite a lot. Yet you still don't see how the ten thousand beings in their confusion[9] (60.105) all tend to stay where there is virtue and to avoid *qi* that arises from punishment. This is the clear token set up by pure, majestic heaven. It thereby sends a severe warning to rulers of how government achieves gain and loss.

Yes, indeed. Now this is as if I had understood, although I have not yet understood. I would like to ask for more instruction.

Well, [the relationship between] punishment and virtue is a clear token of the spiritlike reign of heaven and earth and Yin and Yang. It sets the rule for the ten thousand beings and for the people. Thus in the eleventh month great virtue is positioned as nine in first place,[10] below the ground. At this time virtue is within the chamber,[11] so *qi* is inside and the ten thousand plants and beings return to it. Punishment is at the same time positioned as six in top position,[12] in the four distant regions of open fields. So outside there is no *qi*, everything is bare. Since the outside is devoid of the ten thousand plants and beings, [spirit] cohorts return to virtue.[13] They follow it to the region below the Yellow Springs.[14]

In the twelfth month, virtue is positioned as nine in second place. [The handle of the Dipper at midnight points to] *chou* [, the second earthly branch]. [Plants] are within the soil of the earth and not yet coming forth. At this time, virtue resides in the Hall of Light.[15] The ten thousand plants and beings follow it and begin to rise but don't yet dare show themselves. Up above, punishment reigns.

In the first month, [the handle of the Dipper points to] *yin* [, the third of the twelve branches]. Virtue is positioned as nine in third place. Each of the ten thousand plants and beings follows perfect virtue and delights in peeping out at heaven and earth.[16] Thus they all grow. At this time, virtue resides at court.

In the second month, virtue is positioned as nine in fourth place. [The handle of the Dipper points to] *mao* [, the fourth branch]. [Plants] are already leaving the ground. They have not yet quite reached the open (*tian*, "sky") but are just above the border [between heaven and earth]. Virtue is at the gate. Thus the ten thousand plants enjoy peeping through it.

In the third month, virtue, now in perfect form, is positioned as nine in fifth place. [The handle of the Dipper points to] *chen* [, the fifth earthly branch]. Stretching upward to the middle of the sky *(tian)*,[17] perfect virtue is at this time outside on the roads and in the alleys. Thus the ten thousand plants all step forth to live outside.

In the fourth month, [the handle of the Dipper points to] *si* [, the sixth branch]. Virtue is positioned as nine at the top of the hexagram. It stretches all the way to the six distances and eight borders.[18] It has grown to perfect size in the eight directions. When *qi* is good and is Yang, everything responds and brings forth life. (60.106) In confusion, things leave the inner chamber and go to the open fields. Punishment is at the root of the ten thousand plants, situated in the inner chamber, at this time. Thus in the void down below there are no plants, while they grow in abundance aboveground. They all want to follow virtue and be governed by it. This is a great token for [the need] to reign by virtue.

Now that I have been privileged to hear about the function of virtue, I would like to hear about that of punishment.

Well, in the fifth month, punishment is positioned as six in first place. [The handle of the Dipper at midnight points to] *wu* [, the seventh earthly branch]. Punishment is belowground. It is bare down there, without *qi*. The realms belowground are empty. At this time, punishment resides in the chamber. Plants are not inside, but all out in the open.

In the sixth month, punishment is positioned as six in second place. [The handle of the Dipper points to] *wei* [, the eighth branch]. Punishment is situated within the soil and has not yet become manifest. While it resides in the hall, its *qi* is inside and virtue's *qi* is outside. All beings and plants in their confusion enjoy presenting themselves and flocking to perfect virtue.

In the seventh month, punishment is positioned as six in third place. [The handle of the Dipper points to] *shen* [, the ninth branch]. Punishment resides at court at this time. The ten thousand plants and beings don't yet dare go inside but are determined to enjoy their stay outside.

In the eighth month, punishment is positioned as six in fourth place. [The handle of the Dipper points to] *you* [, the tenth branch]. At this time punishment, although moving upward, has not yet reached the horizon. Virtue is at the gate at this time, so the ten thousand plants and beings take pleasure in peeping through it. They would like to follow virtue and come back in.

In the ninth month, punishment is positioned as six in fifth place. [The handle of the Dipper points to] *xu* [, the eleventh branch]. Punishment, stretching to the middle of the sky *(tian)*, is at this time on the roads and in the alleys. The ten thousand plants are on the verge of dying. They follow virtue and move into places of storage, so there is continuous growth on the inside while the outside becomes empty and void.

In the tenth month, punishment is positioned as six on top of the hexagram. [The handle of the Dipper points to] *hai* [, the twelfth branch]. At this time, punishment reaches the six distant regions, eight borders, and four stretches of open field. The ten thousand plants in their confusion escape to storage places. They go with virtue until they reach the Hall of Light. Four-legged creatures cuddle up inside. Outlying regions are empty. There are no cohorts in sight. Someone who likes to apply punishments will see [others] move away.[19] Or don't you think so?

Should you attempt to control your cohorts in a frame of mind that endorses punishment their number will lessen from one day to the next. Thus in the fifth month, when one set of punishments is endorsed, one group will stage an insurrection. In the sixth month, when two sets of punishments are endorsed, two groups will rise up and so forth, until in the tenth month six groups will rebel.[20] Thus the outside will be deprived of all plants and beings. Everything takes refuge inside. This clearly proves it. So if you govern by punishing others they will show awe and respect on the outside, but inside there will be rebellion. Therefore, your cohorts will lessen from day to day.

One group will show deference for one portion of virtue harbored [by a ruler], [as is the case] in the eleventh month; (60.107) two groups will submit for two portions of virtue, [as shown] in the twelfth month; three groups will submit for three portions of virtue, [as] in the first month; and groups from the four directions will respond to four portions of virtue, [as] in the second month. Five groups of worthies will become his followers if [the ruler] harbors five portions of perfect Yang-type virtue, [as] in the third month. The ten thousand plants and beings will make an appearance if he harbors all six portions of virtue,[21] [as is the case] in the fourth month. They will all, in their confusion, return from within to the outside. This is heaven's clear token.

Virtue and punishment are on a par in the second and the eighth months; thus plants are halfway damaged by the cold in the second month, just as in the eighth month. In the second month virtue wishes to send its cohorts out through the gate. At the same time, punishment expects to move its cohorts inside through the gate. They are all situated at the border [between heaven and earth]. Thus in the second and the eighth months punishment and virtue happen to meet each other in the ten thousand plants and beings. Life and death are on a par; half the amount of possible damage takes place. If you want to know the constant model that heaven and earth have set up and have a clear token of how Yin and Yang work, this is it.[22]

Now since men detest and fear a ruler who makes punishment ever more oppressive, they do not give him their labor power. Instead, the ruler has fewer and fewer men to employ. But more and more [men] would yield if he were to let virtue expand and grow from day to day, to apply neither punishment nor penalties, and not to create fear among the ten thousand beings. They would all return to him and support his reign. This is heaven's clear token. It is so striking that no doubt is possible.

Nowadays subjects cannot be governed unless they are in awe and fear. What about this? (60.108)

Well, the wise men and exemplary gentlemen (*junzi* 君子) of old inspired awe in others through *dao* and its virtue, not by physical strength or punishment and penalties. Men who don't enjoy virtuous conduct will instead attempt to support their rule through punishment and penalties, fear and terror. Yet all they achieve is others moving away [from them]. All punishment does is make people give up, become destitute, depart, and desert; it is not what is required for the ten thousand plants and beings to grow. It clearly increases their confusion. Now this makes people disregard authority[23] and turn to deceptive methods. It is a great mistake.

Now you have been coming to study for quite some time. You have asked a number of questions and have collected a great many writings, but you still can't believe my words. You still don't understand?

Chun beats his head on the ground and bows respectfully before the Master. [He says]:

I am greatly to blame. I have turned my back on the words of an enlightened teacher and spiritlike man. Deeply mortified, I perspire from shame. I am indeed foolish: I have accomplished little and feel utterly worthless. Although I have studied many a day, I am still benighted and unable to fully comprehend the enlightened teacher's words. I dare not ask any further questions. I have been greatly immodest. I have annoyed you so much for such a long time.

No, don't say that.[24] It is because you don't pay attention to your studies. Be on guard. Heaven sets up images as a model for men and as a lesson for emperors and kings on how to conduct themselves without fail while they rule. If you wish to know, this is the precise meaning of this model. Should government not have recourse to it, heaven will remain restless and angry. If this is not resolved, disaster and calamity are bound to follow. Be warned! For heaven to provide prosperity, choose virtue as the image that guides you. Someone who is about to lose chooses punishment. This is what I want to say.

What I say shows regard for heaven and earth and Yin and Yang and conforms to their rules and regulations. It complies with the order of heaven and earth. I enlighten you by explaining the records and by means of moral instruction, for the sake of heaven. I don't err by the tip of an arrow. Follow my words and you will continue to prosper. Oppose them and you will perish.

Heaven's model is wonderful, just like a spirit!

This is the reason why the spiritlike, the perfected, and the great wise men of old were well equipped to set up model and measure. They all observed heaven's vital patterns when they defined rules and regulations on behalf of emperors and kings. Knowing deep inside what Yin and Yang meant, they were able to rule in obedience to heaven and earth. (60.109) Being of one mind with spirits and other enlightened beings and observing their actions, they ruled without the slightest fault. Nowadays certain foolish petty officials and ordinary people believe that the example set by heaven can be ignored or opposed. So they don't rely on model and law, which quite upsets their lord's reign. All this is most blameworthy.

Now that you have received writings, why don't you investigate their concern and intention? Think about it again and again while you are inside the dark chamber. Once you keep in mind heaven's movements, you can transmit its teachings, that is, advise men who are foolish and help emperors and kings set up model and measure. Someone about to employ punishment and penalties must deeply ponder their effect. He will see all his followers[25] leaving him. Isolated, without cohorts, he will be on his own, just as in winter punishment resides in the four regions of open fields devoid of men, while the ten thousand plants and beings move in protest to places of storage to avoid punishment as best as they can. In summer, when punishment is inside, the ten thousand plants and beings return outside to virtue and the underground chambers become empty. Punishment resides isolated on its own, since everyone has followed virtue to the open fields. As long as virtue is outside, the ten thousand plants and beings will turn back to the outside. When it resides within the dark hollow, they all return inside.

Now[26] [I understand that whoever rules by] punishment is extreme in his severity and takes pleasure in his ability to subdue the people and the ten thousand plants and beings. But why is he unable to keep his cohorts under control? Isn't this unusual?

It shows that punishment must not be applied in a lighthearted and careless manner. Injure one single item of upright qi and heaven's qi will be in uproar. Damage one qi that moves in the right way and all of earth's qi will go the wrong way. Offend one educated gentleman and they will all vanish; harm one worthy person and they will all go into hiding.[27] All activities are under some influence. For this reason the wise men, wise kings, and emperors of the past saw it as their priority to look thoroughly at such writings that convey heaven's warnings. Full of fear they did not dare to act at random. They were afraid of failing to grasp heaven's intention and thus of risking their own safety. A man whose virtue derives from highest majestic heaven thoroughly understands the tokens of *dao* and its virtue; he will never be severe and rigid, nor frighten and terrify others. So cohorts will come to stay with him. Thus you must safeguard *dao* to keep yourself intact and safeguard virtue so that you don't venture any loss.

Since you have received my writings you must recite and read them. (60.110) Should you have any doubts, investigate each chapter again and again, from morning to night, until you will perceive what it warns against and how it proves it. You will then be close to grasping heaven's feelings and intentions. To act against them is to oppose heaven, just as the ["male," first] *qian* 乾 and the ["female," second] *kun* 坤 hexagrams of the *Yi jing* must not turn into their opposites, the six *jia* 甲

dates must not change their order, the eternal model of the five phases must not be neglected, and the brightness of the sun and the moon must not be covered up.[28] That the lord is placed up on high and the official down below must not be overturned. From this it is clear that the reign of heaven and earth and Yin and Yang favors virtuous conduct. There are some foolish men who are fond of punishing [others], and they must continue to look at these writings until their misconceptions are resolved. The task is to instruct people to become good and educated, to safeguard *dao* and virtue, and to attempt to avoid the use of punishment and penalties. What my writings say agrees with[29] the model and measure of upright heaven. To go by *dao* and virtue is easy, to employ punishment and penalties difficult. Continuous growth stems from loving concern and loss stems from severity. Go quickly to transmit my writings, on behalf of heaven. Be confident! What they say deals with all the confusion that prevails in the world.

Yes, indeed. I will sincerely think about the mistakes that have been made. I will ponder [your text] from beginning to end. I would not dare omit a single item.

Fine, just be careful and attentive. If you can't figure out in detail what my writings mean, just look at the general picture of heaven and earth and Yin and Yang. From spring to autumn, when virtue remains outside, the ten thousand plants and beings go back outside. Insects that had been hibernating come from their caves, and people step out of their houses. From autumn to spring, when virtue is inside, the ten thousand plants and beings return inside. Hibernating [insects] and stored [produce] go inside, and people enter their houses. This is the token of virtue's reign.

From spring to autumn punishment rules inside, so the ten thousand plants and beings step outside. Inside it is empty. [Punishment] resides there isolated and on its own. From autumn to spring, as long as punishment reigns outside, there are neither plants nor *qi*. It is void, without any cohorts, all of which are inside, having joined virtue. This proves clearly that one cannot rule through punishment.

Thus the virtuous man agrees with heaven and joins forces with it. Going outside when Yang moves outside, he steps inside when Yang does. [To apply] punishment [means to] join forces and agree with the earth, and in this way [someone] moves outside when Yin moves outside while coming in when Yin does. Since the virtuous man joins forces with life's *qi*, he steps outside and returns inside as life's *qi* does. [But] by [applying] punishment [a man] joins *qi* of death and comes forth and retires together with it. The virtuous man moves upward joining heaven, while by applying punishment one moves downward, in line with earth. (60.111) Virtue is always together with things that are full; punishment is in the empty space where there is nothing. Virtue is always where growth is, so when things grow outside it steps out, and when they move inside, it moves indoors. This is why it comes in during winter and moves outside in summer. Punishment keeps company with *qi* of decay and death. Thus it moves outdoors in winter and comes in during summer. Since *qi* of death is bare, its surroundings are bare. Therefore virtue shares *qi* with emperors and kings. When kings rule through external relatives they bring Yin forward, and when they rule through the royal family punishment is kept inside.[30] Punishment is of the same rank as small-minded men. Thus the place where it resides is devoid of cohorts.

Someone to whom beings return will accumulate the virtue of an emperor or a king. Since everything returns to him, he is given the name "emperor" or "king." Punishment never shares a place with beings, and someone without cohorts won't be called a gentleman (*junzi* 君子). For this reason the wise men of old independently and thoroughly thought about and watched the ways of heaven and earth and Yin and Yang to make them a teacher and a model.[31] You can't go wrong when you know this great reliable proof.[32] Thus, don't dare oppose it. This is exactly the token that has been set up by heaven and earth. It must not be slighted! It must not be ignored! It is the model of what is as it is (*ziran fa* 自然法) and does not stem from human beings but from the constant movement of heaven and earth. This is all I have to tell you for now. You must continue to ponder its meaning and be careful in what you do.

Yes, I will. I would not dare turn away from it.

All right. Now I have transmitted to you all the truly exemplary sayings. My worries are over. On behalf of heaven I have attempted to set an end to wrongdoings in order to promote perfect virtue and strengthen the king's government. Don't give this up. Otherwise, you might run into trouble.

Yes, indeed.[33]

NOTES

1. John Major (1987) argues that the two terms *xing* 刑 and *de* 德 are used with two distinct meanings. One meaning is similar to *Han Feizi*'s "two handles," that is, punishment and reward (or "punishment and favor" in Watson's [1964: 30] translation). The other is, in Major's translation, "recision and accretion," referring to the annual cycle of Yin and Yang growth and decline. However, the function of *xing* and *de* for distinguishing days and larger units of the calendar is more complex than the simple correspondence with the flux between Yin and Yang. Marc Kalinowski (1995) has explained

the yearly and daily sequence of *xing* and *de* situations in great detail on the basis of the
Mawangdui manuscript *Xing de* and what Kalinowski calls its cord-hook diagram. He
concludes that the purpose of the *Xing de* was prognostic. Donald Harper (1999:
849–51) has pointed out that the multiplicity of *xing de*'s astro-calendrical function must
be kept in mind in reading the *Huainan zi*'s "Treatise on the Patterns of Heaven" (*tian
wen* 天文), on which Major bases his understanding.

For the section at hand calendrical and hemerological speculation is of little relevance.
The cycle of *xing* and *de* stands for Yin/Yang-based seasonal change, but it is clear that
the cosmological meaning of the terms cannot be separated from their political context.
Here they mean "reign by punishment" and "reign by virtue." The passage at the beginning of p. 108 does not allow any other explanation. What the benign ruler is asked
to achieve is a continuing reign by virtue, impossible as this might be from a cosmological point of view. The argument goes that the ideal way of acting is not an imitation of nature as such, but rather an imitation of certain specific patterns or methods
that can be observed in nature.

2. See de Crespigny 1980; cf. also Watanabe's (2001) account of the debate toward the
end of the second and the beginning of the third century C.E. between those who promoted "lenient rule" and those who promoted "severe government."

3. See Balazs 1964: 208–11; de Crespigny 1980: 44–51.

4. *Hou Han shu* 53.1741, in de Crespigny's translation (1980: 54), slightly modified.

5. I read the two missing characters as *jin wei*, as, for instance, used in TPJ 44.42: *jin
wei tian shi wei qi chenlie* 今唯天師為其陳列 (If only the Celestial Master were to explain in detail . . .).

6. The Celestial Master places *shen* 神 and *qi* 祇 spirits, that is, the spirits of heaven
and earth, in a lowly position just above humankind and the ten thousand beings (TPJ
127.323). However, they do as heaven does (TPJ p. 212, *Chao*, part 4) and thus hold certain moral power over men: when they accuse a man, he has no place to escape (TPJ
78.189; see also TPJ 132.354). Their coming and going among men is a positive sign
(TPJ 129.336).

7. *Mingzheng fa:* The cluster of *mingzheng* 明證 (token), as also used below in this section (pp. 244, 246 and 250) and *fa* 法 (model) does not occur anywhere else in the text.
Fa seems to act as a gloss for *mingzheng*.

8. *Tian wen* 天文 is used throughout the TPJ for astronomical phenomena and for texts
issuing from heaven. Occasionally *wen* seems to mean a combination of the two, just as
"dao" is an ordering principle and the doctrine that explains it.

9. *Raorao* 擾擾 (in confusion) is a term a quietist thinker would use to describe the
world of daily life and worries when looking at it from a distance (*Zhuangzi* 35.13.44).
The best example is in the *Liezi* (3 *"Zhou Mu Wang"* 周穆王, p. 110; cf. Graham 1991:
71), where a man whose memory has just been restored complains about all his likes and
dislikes returning to him "in confusion." Throughout section 60 the word is used for

"the world as it is," as opposed to what is explicitly "good" and brings forth life (p. 106, beginning). Thus punishment is said to increase "confusion" (p. 108, beginning), and in this sense the Master's writings deal with "confusion" (p. 110, middle). The word is characteristic of this section. It occurs here more often than in the rest of the transmitted text.

10. This integrates the topic at hand with *Yijing* symbolism. Each amount of punishment and virtue has its distinctive place in the order of the sixty-four hexagrams. A "nine" line is an uninterrupted, Yang-type line. "In the first place" means that it is positioned at the bottom, where the counting starts.

11. This is one of the seven imaginary places where *xing* and *de* can be found, according to the *Huainan zi* (3.11a–12b; see Major 1987: 284f.). In the TPJ, there are only six distinct places: chamber, hall, court, gate, roads and alleys, and distant fields. Nevertheless, the similarities are such that the TPJ passage must come from material similar to the *Huainan zi*:

TPJ		HUAINAN ZI		
xing	*de*	*xing*	*de*	
				month
roads and alleys	"inside"			ninth
distant fields	"inside"			tenth
fields	chamber	fields	chamber	eleventh
"outside"	hall	roads	hall	twelfth
court	alleys	court		first
gate		gate		second and eighth
	roads and alleys			third
inner chamber	distant fields			fourth
chamber				fifth
hall				sixth
court	"outside"			seventh

In the TPJ the "outside" consists of distant places at the end of the world, and the inside is as far below the ground as the Yellow Springs.

12. A "six" line is an interrupted Yin-type line. From the top position lines are imagined as leaving the hexagram.

13. The expression *shizhong* 士眾 (cohorts) is characteristic of this passage. It occurs in only two other places in the text. In section 64 (p. 143) it is said that to scare *shizhong* through severity and the use of punishment is poor leadership. In layer B (TPJ 179.534), the word is used for the spirits of heaven and of earth as they are addressed by the Celestial Lord. The arguments raised throughout section 60 seem to point to the creation of regional power bases through attracting large groups of followers, which was a feature of the outgoing Han dynasty. In some instances, we must imagine these supporters to be spirits; in others they are the civil and military followers of a lord, regardless

of the size of his reign. The example of Liu An comes to mind. In the outgoing Han dynasty the large number of clients whom certain patrons managed to assemble became a political force.

14. Here the Yellow Springs are not so much the abode of the dead but a place deep down in the ground where, according to the *Mengzi* (3B.10), earthworms drink.

15. The hall, which at this stage is the abode of virtue, is here and further below, on p. 245, given the honorific name Hall of Light, which was a center of Han dynasty ritual concerns. When it is the turn of punishment to abide there it is called "hall" (see p. 245).

16. The prognostic meaning of *xing* and *de* is touched on at this point. Plants and all beings must make sure whether *xing* or *de* reigns before they make a move. It was considered particularly important for the military strategist to be able to distinguish a *xing* situation from a *de* situation: see Kalinowski 1995: 84.

17. This is the position punishment occupies in the ninth month; see below, p. 106. *Lun heng* 31 "*Tan tian*" 談天, p. 478 explains that according to Zou Yan the "middle of heaven" (*tian zhong* 天中) is the constellation Pole. This agrees with the TPJ. The celestial North Pole is said to be heaven's center (TPJ p. 20, *Chao*, part 2).

18. "Six distances and eight borders" (六遠八境) is an unusual expression. TPJ 104.258 says that someone who wishes to completely tidy up (*zheng* 正) the six distances and eight regions (*liu yuan ba fang* 六遠八方) must first turn to what is in his own person (*nei* 內).

19. *Zong* 從 (to follow) must be corrected to *xi* 徙 (to move); see Yu (2001a: 97). The *Chao* reads *tu* 徒 (on foot).

20. This is a new account of instances that the course of the year and political policy have in common. It is not in the *Huainan zi* passage on *xing* and *de*. It here strengthens the Celestial Master's basic proposition of a correspondence between the two realms.

21. They are, according to *Zhou li*, for instance, "*Di guan, Da si tu*" 地官大司徒, p. 707b: knowledge, humaneness, wisdom, righteousness, loyalty, and harmony.

22. This dramatic moment is described in the following manner in the *Huainan zi:*

> When the power of Yin is like that of Yang, punishment and virtue are both at the gate. In the eighth and the second months, *qi* of Yin and Yang are in balance and the portions of day and night are equal. For this reason we say that punishment and virtue are both at the gate (*Huainan zi* 3.12a; see Major 1993: 87).

23. The expression *nei fu* 內附 is used in this sense in *Lun heng* 58 "*Hui guo*" 恢國, p. 825.

24. This is expressed by *bu ye* 不也. Yu (2001b: 467) explains that this use of the phrase, which he terms "colloquial," occurs in Han dynasty material only in the TPJ.

25. *Zong* 從 is corrected to *xi* 徙; see Yu (2001a: 98).

26. *Tian* 天 is here erroneous and must be corrected to *fu* 夫. "Heaven's punishment" is of a different order.

27. Here human beings are seen to react to others' behavior as natural forces react to

each other. So norms for human conduct resemble natural laws, and infringements are seen to have drastic consequences.

28. The standards that the Master points to stem from astronomical as well as prognostic and calendrical reasoning. Since he sees a need to refer to them in support of his faith in heaven we may assume that they were more widely respected than heaven's divine role. The expression *liu jia* represents here and throughout the TPJ the whole system of heavenly stems and earthly branches (cf. *Hanyu da cidian,* vol. 2, p. 28).

29. The two missing characters are read as *yan ying* 言 應: *yan* is used here as it is used a little further down in *wu shu yan* 吾 書 言 and throughout the TPJ, and *ying* is used here as it is used in TPJ 134.370, *gu wu shu ying tian jiao* 故 吾 書 應 天 教.

30. This translation is tentative. It attempts to do justice to the context, but it goes against the common understanding of *wai* 外 as male and *nei* 內 as female, as observed by Luo 1996: 197, where he translates, "When the legitimate emperor rules he abolishes the power of empresses and eunuchs (this is "Yin"); under female rule a system of punishments is introduced." The difficulty with this version is the translation of *chu* 出 as "to abolish." In the rest of this section, *chu* is "to bring forth." Yu (2001a: 101) tries to solve this problem by transposing the positions of *chu* and *ru* 入.

31. "Teacher" and "model" (*shi fa* 師 法) are prominent terms in the *Xunzi* (24.8.107–8 and 87.23.6), where it is said that morality has no chance unless someone has both.

32. The two missing characters are read as *xinxiao* 信 效, as in TPJ 152.414: *zi yu zhong zhi qi da xinxiao* 子 欲 重 知 其 大 信 效.

33. The summary says:

This section is based on the model of heaven. It clarifies how governments in former times and nowadays, in earlier and later periods, came to win and to lose.

· On Digging Up Soil
and Publishing Books

Although this section is long and long-winded, it is well composed and not repetitive. The disciple's questions and objections make the argument plausible and convincing. The section takes as its starting point the close resemblance between soil and mother. The section stresses the close relationship between people and their natural surroundings. Heaven and earth are depicted as mother and father, the former nagging, the latter punishing. Earth nurses its children through its natural springs; it suffers pain from injuries to its skin and body. Men can be to earth what intestinal worms, fleas, and tooth bugs are to men. The parallels drawn between the human realm and that of heaven and earth are carried so far that the Celestial Master adds the reminder that heaven and earth are nature *(tian)*, and therefore different from men.

In this section the Master also issues drastic restrictions. Wells and canals, as well as newly constructed houses and grave mounds, must be limited in size and number. These commandments are new, a point that is stressed twice.[1] The final part of the section deals with the missionary project, the disciples' role in it, and its historical time frame. The world must presently be reformed because great peace is about to arrive and heaven's position is strong. For the first time in history heaven is able to employ assistants of its own choice, among them the Perfected, and thus make its intentions public.

Although the Master's message cannot be found in other material in these exact terms, it is embedded in a long tradition of environmental concern.[2] The *Huainan ʒi,* for instance, has much to say on the abuse of natural resources. Mining, construction work, building, and hunting endanger the authority and power of a sovereign.[3] Or, to give another example, the *180 Precepts* of the later Daoist tradition contain a number of commandments that have an environmental impact: "You should not improperly dig the earth or spoil mountains and rivers"; "You should not block up ponds and wells"; "You should not throw foul things into wells."[4]

The TPJ makes a major contribution to this tradition, mainly because of the Celestial Master's great interest in and philosophical approach to the people's daily life. As he sees it, human survival is based upon a compromise between man's interests and those of heaven and earth. Man may take from earth the water he can't do without and build some shelter for his protection, but if he goes further than this, earth's distress and heaven's anger will put all human existence at risk. In addition, the clearing of hillsides by burning grass, bushes, and trees is not permitted, although these methods may be attempted on level ground.[5]

The internal coherence of this section is combined with several formal ruptures. The section consists of three parts; these are, as I see it, the notes of three different dialogues. The first explains and defends a set of prohibitions: it is the nature of earth that certain offenses will make it barren. This part is interrupted by the editorial note "He also says." The second part, which starts with "Step forward, Perfected"[6] and deals with the digging of wells, is closely related to the first part, merely adding another prohibition. The last part, separated from the second by a sequence of admonitions and the sending away of the disciple, views the preceding prohibitions in a historical light: their implementation is more important now than ever before because of heaven's increasingly direct involvement in the affairs of men.

· · ·

(61.112) *I am foolish and worth nothing, but I still can't help wishing to ask a question. Although it is a great fault to offend the Celestial Master's prohibitions, I can't subdue my wish to speak, as if I were a small-minded man unable to control his desires. My body's five organs are tormented and anxious. Please allow me to raise one big question. If you would only deal with me as if I were a small child that must be forgiven its craving and greed!*

Speak up! How modest you are!

Yes, I will speak. Now the Celestial Master always shares the vital thoughts of majestic heaven and venerable earth. Your heart is in profound agreement with their intentions, as

if compasses and carpenter's square had been used. Not the breadth of a hair is amiss. I
know that heaven and earth are always worried and tormented,[7] *which mortifies even me,*
foolish and inadequate as I am. Thus I dare to step forward and ask all sorts of questions.
I would like to know what the major prohibitions are that are eternally upheld by spirits
and other numinous beings of heaven and earth.

Good, you are becoming more refined! What you are now asking pertains directly
to the feelings and the intention of heaven and earth. Let someone understand them,
enlighten the worthies about it, and [this knowledge] will not be lost for another ten
thousand generations. I have always wanted to discuss this matter, but there had been
no occasion.[8] Now that you have asked, I am quite happy. I am about to explain it
to you in all its different parts. I would not dare keep anything hidden. If I did, I am
afraid that heaven's and earth's spirits and other numinous beings would deeply
detest me and might in consequence strike me with disaster. You must sit still and
pay attention. What heaven and earth find most detestable is a wicked person who
is disobedient and lacks filial piety. (61.113)

What do you mean? I wish I knew!

A good question. Now the three *qi* of heaven, earth, and the space between them
belong close together, as if they were one family. Moreover, they are jointly in control of life and nourish the ten thousand beings. Heaven dominates the creation of
life and is called father. Earth is in charge of nurture and is called mother. Man is
responsible for putting things in order and is called son. The father presides over
the process of education in stages and sections. Guided by him the mother undertakes the task of nourishing. Receiving life from the father and nourishment from
the mother, the son exists. Being the son, he must with due respect serve his father
and love his mother.

Why is this so?

Well, a father educates in stages and sections. Thus heaven relies on the four seasons
to let all that lives grow until it is mature. End and beginning have their own specific
time. An evil man who acts against this order is like a son who disobeys his father,
or *qi* of heaven that forgets what it was asked to do. He doesn't find favor with heaven.
Since heaven detests him so much, it creates calamities to make the son ill. This is the
same as in a family where the father rules over his son in anger. Disturbing things
happen: father and son disagree and, filled with hatred, a son disobeys the precepts
issued by a severe father. So Yin rises over Yang and inferiors betray their superiors.
Rebellious sons step forth in large numbers, officials neglect their tasks, demons pros-

per and make men ill, treacherous fellows live by the side of the road, and the dark gives cover to unruly elements. The mistake lies in opposing heaven and earth.

Perfected, you must never disobey! The method of what is as it is resembles a shadow in its response to a body, or a cart when it follows a horse. They cannot be shaken off.[9] Heed this!

Yes, I will. (61.114) *Now that I have learned with great respect what you had to say about heaven's teachings and admonitions, I would like to hear how men transgress earth's prohibitions.*

Fine, pay attention.

Yes, I will!

Heaven is father, earth is mother.

Father and mother are both human. So where is the difference?

Heaven is also nature (*tian* 天), and so is earth. Father and mother are distinct by being Yin and being Yang, being male and being female. But what they love and hate is the same. Heaven nourishes man's life; earth nourishes man's body. Men must be very foolish, blind, and benighted not to know how to pay respect to father and mother. Such men make heaven and earth forever regret that they have produced humankind. Both are desperate beyond any hope of relief.

Why is this so?

What you say is fine.[10] You thoroughly understand what heaven and earth want. The period of great disaster is about to end. So men must be happy and good.

What do you mean? Please explain!

Well, nowadays the people of this world all behave like bandits. They cause father and mother grief.

How?

The four seasons' celestial *qi* was put in place by heaven. To oppose it is to rob your father.

What do you mean?

Now human beings consider earth to be their mother from whom they obtain clothes and food. But instead of showing love and care, they raid it.

What do you mean?

Well, listen! Men are really useless. They bore into the soil and undertake big construction projects without concern for the proper order of things (*dao li* 道理).

When they go deep, they reach down to the Yellow Springs, and even when they don't go that far, they still go a number of *zhang*.[11] The mother is in distress and enraged, but the children don't show respect or piety. Although she is forever bitter, angry, apprehensive, and anxious,[12] she has no way to communicate this in words. In the course of time, the wise men of old had not yet got around to instructing on these matters, so the people acted carelessly.[13] They argued that earth did not feel bad about it. But earth could not restrain its bad feelings and involved heaven above, without men's knowledge. She resented that the children were not to be controlled and complained about men to their father. She did this so many times, again and again.[14] Thus the father's anger never came to a halt. Natural calamities, disasters, and other anomalies occurred by the ten thousand. The mother became more unhappy (61.115) and too indignant to put any effort into feeding the people and the ten thousand plants and beings. Once father and mother have both become desolate, the ten thousand beings will perish, as well as the people. The fault lies in their neglect of proper order *(dao li)*.

The conduct of latter-born generations is worsening from day to day. Unable to understand the intention of heaven and earth, they turn their hatred against both and accuse them of not cooperating.[15] They also attack emperors and kings, saying that they are unable to pacify the rebels within their realm. People trespass against heaven and earth without being aware of it. Instead, they accuse their superiors of wrongdoing. For this reason heaven and earth no longer care for man. They view his end as irrelevant. Although a man might scream and moan when he is ill and close to death, as if he were well aware of his crime, heaven and earth as father and mother won't rescue him. His crime is too great. This is what happens to someone who shirks responsibility for his faults. In later generations, this behavior has gone even further. People have learned from each other until this behavior has become the rule and it is now impossible to restrain them. Calamities increase day by day because they have no means of restricting each other. Human beings truly cause grief to heaven and earth, their father and mother. When a child harms father and mother it is as if a robber were inflicting wounds. It is not a small crime. For this reason heaven and earth severely reprove the unfilial and disobedient, without pardon. Even though a man's life is short and there are countless ways of dying, he has no reason to be resentful. You understand, don't you?

Yes, I do! (61.116)

Now that heaven has sent you to ask these questions I know that I may speak. But you must not take it easy. You must pay heed!

Yes, I will.

Now if someone injures father and mother and opposes their commands, should he continue to be supported, in your opinion? This is the reason why heaven does not feel much pity.

Now the Celestial Master has been kind to this foolish pupil. You have explained it all to me. But how do we know that heaven and earth are still filled with anger and indignation and blame men for numerous instances of digging up soil?

Good. Heaven has sent you to pose such tormenting questions. So you naturally ask this on behalf of heaven and earth.

Yes.

I deeply fear heaven. I would not dare keep anything hidden, afraid as I am of calamities that might hit me. So I will now let you have a clear idea. Keep it eternally written in your breast, so that you will never forget!

Now if one family undertakes construction through which soil is dug up, many families will suffer for it. Some will perish. Or bandits will invade the government precincts. Elsewhere weapons will be raised and fights will occur. Snakes, hornets, tigers, wolves, and other evil animals will injure men. When much soil is dug up, big disasters will occur; when little soil is dug up, the disasters will be small. This means that earth in its anger asks spirits and other numinous beings to cause such calamities. This clearly proves how heaven and earth make men ill. Do you understand?

Yes, I do! But nowadays some people remain lucky and in good health despite digging up soil. Why is this so?

Good, your question! There are always impediments, but a man who has obtained good soil does not suffer right away. Instead, disasters occur in the four directions, so that over a period of time they will reach him as well. A man who has obtained bad soil that can't tolerate what men do to it will suffer harm right away. Later on, it will spread to distant regions.

Why?

This is the same as with a good-natured man. Should he suffer a grievance he might be able to tolerate it for the moment, but he will not forget, and he will injure [others] on a later occasion. A wicked person, on the other hand, would not be able to bear it but get his revenge right away.

Excellent, indeed! Now the earth's body is huge. Man is quite tiny by comparison. Thus what he achieves is little and not worth mentioning. How can he be capable of molesting earth?

A good question. Heaven has sent you to sort out all that is unclear.

How do you know?

Because you take words so seriously. In your heart you are attentive and anxious about what you want to say. (61.117) You urgently wish to speak.[16] The spirits and other vital beings of heaven and earth that reside in your belly hasten your words without your being fully aware of it. In everything men want to do, heaven urges them on.

Yes, I would not dare keep anything secret.

So listen attentively!

Yes, I will.

Now you have said that men are too small for their movements to be capable of injuring earth. The body of an adult may be one *zhang* tall and ten spans big.[17] Little insects live in his teeth.[18] Although they are so small that they hardly deserve mentioning, they afflict a man's teeth with great pain. When they are thus at work a man will cry and moan. Teeth will one after the other fall out until they are all gone. But the size of a man in relation to heaven and earth is the same as this insect's size [in relation to] the man it harms. Moreover, teeth are more solid than metal, stone, or bone, while the insect consists of flesh. So how can it injure anybody? The pain man inflicts on earth is the same. Do you know what I mean?

All right.

You will soon understand better.

Yes, indeed. (61.118)

But some men are more than one *zhang* tall and more than ten spans big. The insect that causes ulcers is no bigger than one *cun*.[19] Its body is small, so small that it does not deserve mentioning. Should it live in someone's skin and chisel away day and night, he will fall ill and die. Now man's respective size in relation to earth is similar to this insect's [size in relation to him].

How can these small insects, even in large numbers, attack and kill a human being?

Perfected, why do you have to be so foolish and so blind? Almost as much so as the common people!

I am no good!

But if you are no good, what do you call the common people?

I am at fault, I have been foolish. If the Celestial Master would only raise the issues I don't fully understand and be kind enough to explain to me what it all means.

Yes, let us not hide anything. I know that heaven and earth suffer much pain, so I will speak to you again.[20] All right. I will tell you something else. Examine it and you will know better.

Yes, I will do so.

Now it is not so that a grown man and a strong fellow should not be able to keep insects that cause scabies under control. They are so small that one can hardly see them. But about one cup of them can eat up a man. They make him ill so that he cannot sleep, lying tormented on his bed. Now these scabies causing fleas and other insects are tiny, but when many of them get together they eat up a man. Intestinal worms kill a man.[21] Scabies causing insects give rise to itching, which gives a man so much discomfort that he cannot sit anywhere in peace and will develop sores. Now man's size in relation to earth is the same [as the size of these insects in comparison to man's size]. Do you understand?

Yes, I do!

All right. Now you might perhaps think that what I say is not enough to show the pattern *(fa)*. What I am telling you is that man, small as he is, causes grief and distress to earth's body. (61.119) He should clearly understand that he is committing a severe crime. This is obvious. Now with one hundred households to a village there would be one hundred wells; with one thousand households to a district there would be one thousand wells, ten thousand in one county, one hundred thousand in one commandery, and one million[22] in a province. A large well has [a diameter of] one *zhang*, a medium-sized one has [a diameter of] several feet, and a small one [a diameter of] three feet.

Now to the world as a whole: how often will men dig up soil to reach the Yellow Springs? One house might perhaps have several wells. Let us just take small wells into account: ten of them will amount to thirty feet, one hundred to three hundred feet, one thousand to three thousand feet, and ten thousand will amount to thirty thousand feet. How many such wells are there all over the world? All are dug into earth to obtain water, which is earth's blood in its veins. Now if someone dug up your body to get to your veins, you would be in pain, don't you think? Now how many miles do one million wells cover? You can calculate this for yourself. How many million wells does the world have? Thus it is proven that men cause heaven and earth grief. What adds to the mother's pain is that it is her own children who make her ill. Earth's *qi* leaks out. Although such an illness would be seen as quite severe in a man, human beings show neither concern nor compassion. Instead, in what they say they forever voice resentment against heaven and earth as if both were not cooperative. Isn't this perverse!

So far I have only mentioned wells. But nowadays we have large houses and big grave mounds.[23] Moreover, we dig up mountains and hills to get metal and stone. We burn tiles and push columns into the ground. We dig out drains and ditches at random. Some of them have been obstructed and brought to a standstill. How many hold water that can't keep moving as it should? For some the spring must be activated, while for others it must be kept flowing.[24]

He also says:[25] How many springs have been blocked and then excavated? Springs must be kept flowing. Water must be spread to be of use. All drains in use between heaven and earth will bring downward what is high up. Now this is sometimes not as it should be.[26]

To carelessly dig up earth's body creates sores. Sometimes obstruction occurs: what should be in motion is not. The king's reign is inept (*bu he* 不 和) and earth suffers greatly. No one is willing to address its discomfort, illness, and misery.[27] Day after day earth's vital spirits complain to heaven that [what should be moving] can't do so. Thus heaven and earth are both unhappy. This is why it is difficult for the pure *qi* of great harmony to arrive. You must understand this, Perfected!

Yes, I do. (61.120) Now men live between heaven and earth. Don't they need a roof above their head and a well to drink from? What about that?

This is a good question. Now heaven does not begrudge men their homes. But when they dig too deep they create sores. Some fetch earth's bones, others its blood.

What do you mean?

Springs are earth's blood, stones are its bones, soil is its flesh. To unearth a spring is to obtain blood. To quarry stone is to break bones. If you dig deep into good soil and throw tiles, stones, and hard wood inside for enforcement, earth feels pain inside. What makes it worse is that it is not just one person doing this.

So what should we do?

Earth is mother of the ten thousand beings. It takes delight in loving and nourishing them. It doesn't mind their weight, as if it were a human being pregnant with child. Someone who safeguards *dao* will not dig up his mother at random, and she won't make him ill. But if a man digs her up as he chooses in his search for a livelihood, she will make him ill. He must not dig at random and he must not dig deep, but must live aboveground, content with finding some protection. Then earth will not make him ill but will greatly love him and make him happy.

I would like to ask how big the protection can be that men might be permitted to have.

Altogether, when removing soil and digging into earth, it should not be more than three feet.[28]

Why is it the rule to stop within three feet?

The first foot is illuminated by Yang; its *qi* is that of heaven. Plants grow by means of the second foot; its *qi* belongs to the harmonious intercourse between Yin and Yang. The third foot belongs to the earth itself; its *qi* is Yin. When you go deeper than this, you injure earth's body, which would be disastrous.

How about the ancients, who lived in caves?[29]

They also violated earth's body, that's all. They often made their caves along mountain valleys, that is, in earth. They also pushed wooden weirs and piles into the ground. They gave earth only little pain since there were few of these and men relied mainly on water that flowed by. Thus illness was rare. Later generations did not know the proper limit. They frequently violated earth, and thus they often did not live long.

Why was that?

There was more illness. (61.121)

Nowadays so many men live next to flowing water and don't dig wells. Why do they often suffer from illness and not live long?

The anger of heaven and earth extends to all members of a neighborhood group of shared responsibility. They inherit and transmit evil from one to the other, in the same way as the faults committed within one family extend to older and younger brothers.

Now some men don't move earth. When they settle they choose an auspicious time to move into old lodgings. They are as prone to meet with disaster as they were before. Why is this so?

Their actions were disadvantageous and antagonized certain spirits.

Which spirits?

Not just one. It is impossible to tell in advance who it would be.[30] Do you understand?

Yes, I do. (61.122)

So men live on this earth without taking the trouble to teach each other how to be good. Thus mistakes are made that bring forth more mistakes. This is grievous.

Now some men live far away from flowing waters. Their life depends on obtaining water to drink from a well. What should they do?

Good, what you have said. But where there are old wells people must be encouraged to continue to drink together from where they have always drunk.[31] They must be careful not to initiate frequent changes. With each change they will have to fill up the old well and block earth's *qi* so that it does not come forth. If you drink from earth's body it will become weak and unable to nourish plants. When you fill up an old well you must take out what is in it to enforce it.

What do you mean?

I mean the tiles, stones, and timber that are put into the well, where they didn't belong in the first place. But there they are. Similarly, a man would become ill if there was something foreign in his body.

How frightening! I would never have known this had you not looked at the question in such detail!

Step forward, Perfected![32]

Yes [, here I am].

Why do you always ask questions in such detail?[33]

Through these details I will see things as you do. It is being said that human life depends on heaven and earth. When they remain happy the order of things achieves great peace. Longevity is the consequence.[34] This is the reason why, living between heaven and earth, I am always in fear[35] of making them both angry. That is why I work hard. Should heaven and earth not be in harmony I will not be able to finish the years that have been allotted to me.

You have said the right thing.

I am forever fearful because I see so much poisonous qi *accumulate in heaven and on earth. Violence and murder continue. Emperors and kings suffer bitterly, their government not at peace. I always want to support them in their troubles.*

Why are you prepared to help them?

I have heard that merit earned among men will be acknowledged by heaven. So I am always happy to fulfill heaven's wishes.

You have the right intention!

Since the Celestial Master is showing heaven's prohibitions to this foolish pupil, I would like to be permitted to ask another question. Now some people build houses on ground that is below rivers and the sea. They will possibly obtain water without piles and weirs before they remove three feet of soil.[36] What about this?

This is a good question. They are also causing some injury. They must not go that deep. They are where the earth's skin is thin. (61.123) They have moved too close to its veins. Take, for example, a man with thick skin. It is difficult to get at his blood, but when blood does come forth he is wounded. It might be easy to obtain blood from a thin-skinned person, but when it comes forth he, too, is wounded. In both cases, there is injury. This proves the importance of blood for heaven and earth. It is clearly a crime to make blood come forth, regardless of whether the person who is wounded is thick-skinned or thin-skinned, but man resembles heaven and earth in his dislike of being wounded. Should you wound someone, he will detest you. Should earth alone wish to receive wounds? But heaven and earth are man's true root, they are father and mother of Yin and Yang. Why must a child injure its father and mother? Do take this to heart. Foolish men might perhaps from carelessness take things easy, not being aware of the great crime they are involved in.

Now a child must get food and drink from its mother. So why are humans so much to blame when they dig a well to drink?

What you say goes clearly against heaven's intentions. Now man turns to where his mother puts forth a spring in order to drink. Human beings are therefore nursed where a human spring bursts forth. The place where a child is nursed resembles the spring of water that earth provides men to drink. So why must we dig up its skin and drink its blood without reason? Your question does not make any sense. (61.124)

I am at fault! I have offended against your prohibitions!

Don't be too modest! If your questions did not go as far as they do we would not be able to learn *dao*'s complete lesson. I have nothing against what you say. Majestic heaven must be quite anxious to have sent you to ask question after question.[37] This is the reason why your questions continue to go this way and that way.

If the Celestial Master would only forgive me and pardon my faults. I am a foolish pupil who can't refrain from talking.

It's all right. Why are you so modest? You have already labored in the interest of heaven and earth by coming from afar to ask questions.[38] Make sure not to keep my writings secret.

Yes, I will.

Should men in general fail to look at them they will not of themselves realize the severity of their crime. Instead, they will simply continue to offend heaven and earth.

Why don't they understand?[39] *Why is government completely evil and without peace?*[40]

They don't realize that when generations of men trespass against heaven and earth this is inherited and passed on from one to the next. Since the latter-born are met with such calamities, they don't complete their natural life span.[41] Life and death don't come at the set time. Work hard! Don't dismiss these writings, or heaven and earth will oppose and detest men even more.

Yes!

Should you be found guilty of this offense a disaster will occur.

Yes!

Give the writings to a virtuous lord, who should show them to everyone! Men are children of heaven and earth and hold the rank of elders among the ten thousand beings. These are my instructions for you.

What should we do?

Each of you must deeply think about this. From now on, if you wish to enjoy wealth and longevity and remain free from illness, you must ponder what these writings say. Inscribe them into your heart. You must make this a personal project. Don't keep them secret. Share them with others and make them known. Now spirits of heaven and earth follow the path of these writings and keep an eye on the person [who is handling them].

What are you saying?

Are you aware of this?

Now how does one know that these spirits keep a watch over a man's conduct?

You don't trust my words! Just try to hide these writings and you will fall ill. Should you dare to prevent their distribution you will be out of luck.[42] This clearly proves that the spirits of heaven and earth keep men under observation. Pay heed!

Yes, I will.

You may go. Take courage.

  Human life lies with heaven and earth. If you want to be safe, you must first make heaven and earth safe. Only then will you be able to enjoy long-lasting stability.[43] But if instead you annoy heaven and earth, violate and injure father and mother, how can you be safe and in luck? Since what happened earlier and what happens later come together, natural disasters occur without interruption. I am not mistaken. I am always seeing earth's spirits go up [to heaven] to demand justice. There is no end to this. That is why I truly know of earth's distress.[44] (61.125) When I now see how you persist in raising questions, I know that you have been sent by heaven to do it. The reason is that heaven wishes to bring these matters to light and to let men know for themselves. The hundred families know how to accuse heaven but they don't understand the need to accuse themselves.

Now why would heaven all of a sudden send me to ask questions?

The reason you were sent is that *qi* of great peace of heaven's highest majesty is about to arrive, so government must be in great peace. I am afraid that foolish people endlessly violate prohibitions set up by heaven and earth and thus bring disorder to upright *qi* and cause disaster and harm. This being the case, *qi* of great peace will not arrive at the proper time. That is why you were sent to ask questions. [Heaven] does not want the people to go on with their violations, for if they don't, then heaven and earth won't cause illness but will instead love man and let the five grains and ten thousand plants grow well to provide him with food. Should man ignore this, heaven and earth will become angry, withdraw their love, and refuse to feed him. So if heaven and earth make the year disastrous nothing will grow well, and if they make it prosper, harvests will be good. This is what it means. Do you understand?

Excellent! In the past great peace was general. Why weren't the people forbidden to move soil?

A good question. In the beginning, heaven and earth were not in the position in which they are today.

How can this be explained?

Nowadays heaven makes all the appointments. It selects the man who bends *qi*, the spiritlike man, the perfected, the transcendent, the man of *dao*, the wise man, and the worthy.[45] They must all step forward to support the virtuous ruler's government. This was not the case in the past. Heaven's subjects[46] have never been chosen for office since the division between Yin and Yang. So this is really something great.

How very alarming!

So it all amounts to the first lesson *(dao)*, [which says] that we must teach the world's people models of moral behavior. When men are good, their government will be stable, and the king who reigns over them will roam about without worries.[47]

Excellent! What a great joy!

That is why I instruct you to quickly publish this book. Take care not to keep anything hidden! Show it to everyone! Once the hundred families see the prohibitions, they will practice restraint. Otherwise, misfortune will befall later generations with no further chance of redemption. Prayers don't help when it is a case of crimes against heaven and earth.[48] Do you understand this?

Yes, I do.

You may go. Should you have questions about these writings, come and ask.

Yes, I will.[49]

NOTES

1. See below, 61.114 and 125.
2. Cf. Callicott and Ames (1989).
3. See *Huainan zi* 8 *"Ben jing"* 本經.
4. See *Laojun shuo yibai bashi jie,* precepts 47, 101, and 100 (cf. Hendrischke and Penny 1996).
5. See sections 209 and 210.
6. On p. 122.
7. I read the two missing characters as *huan ye* 患也. *You huan* 優患 occurs frequently; see, for instance, TPJ 207.652: *tian chang yi shi wei you huan* 天常以是為優患. The *Chao* reads *you yu* 優預, which does not make sense and seems to indicate that the text was corrupt at the time the *Chao* was produced. Yu 2001a: 101 reads *yu ye* 預也.
8. See *Lun yu* (15.8) on the need to address the right audience when speaking.
9. *Yu* 與 (with) is corrected to *yu* 輿 (cart); see Yu (2001a: 102). Retaliation for evil deeds is as certain as that a shadow will follow a figure.
10. The original text is perhaps incomplete. The student did not say anything. On the other hand, the Master's remark is puzzling even to the student, as the next question shows.
11. The height of a tall man is one *zhang* 丈; see below, 61.117.
12. "Apprehensive and anxious" (*kun yi* 悃悒) are two characters characteristic of this section. They occur here, on p. 114, speaking about earth, and again on p. 117 with respect to the disciple, as in TPJ 60.104, and also on p. 112, when the disciple describes his feelings. Another occurrence is in TPJ 127.318, at a mention of heaven's anxiety. In the TPJ, *kun* occurs only in combination with *yi* and does not, as Yu (1997: 50) points out, mean "sincere" (see *Hanyu da cidian* vol. 7, p. 544) but stands for *kun* 困.
13. Toward the end, this section gives another explanation for the novelty of the prohibition: the proximity of the new era of great peace creates the need to stick to prohibitions more closely than men did in the past. Both passages agree about the novelty of the prohibition. The Master claims that heaven did not make the prohibition known before the student's questions forced the Master to discuss the matter. This assumption is not historically correct. The *Shi ji* (88. 2570) reports that Meng Tian 蒙恬, the First Emperor's general and architect of the Great Wall, at first declared himself innocent when condemned to commit suicide by the First Emperor's son and successor: "By which crime did I offend heaven? I die innocent." However, he soon recollected, "I am guilty and deserve to die. When constructing the link between Liaodong and Lintiao, a wall of more

than ten thousand miles, I could not avoid cutting the veins of the earth. This is my crime." Sima Qian argues that Meng was wrong. His real crime had been cruelty against men, and that is why he deserved death. Wang Chong, who quotes the passage (*Lun heng* 21 *"Huo xu"* 禍虛, pp. 275f.), can see some sense in Meng Tian's words, as if it were indeed wrong to hurt the earth, but he doesn't see heaven in the role of a punishing sovereign. Wang Chong's conclusion provides the intellectual background against which the Celestial Master directs his arguments. It is the following, in Forke's (1962, vol. 1, p. 172) translation:

> Yet one succeeds, the other fails; one gets on, the other falls off, one is penniless, the other well-to-do, one thriving, the other ruined. All this is the result of chance and luck, and the upshot of fate and time. (*Lun heng*, p. 281)

14. This image of heaven and earth as a married couple has a replica in the *Chun qiu fan lu* (38 *"Wu xing dui"* 五行對, p. 316), where it is said that earth does not call her achievements her own. So we say that "heaven rains" (*tian yu* 天雨) and "heaven raises wind" (*tian feng* 天風), despite the fact that rain and wind are earth's doing. The account of heaven and earth in this section is more anthropomorphic than is usual in the TPJ. Earth talks heaven into punishing men for disrespecting her, heaven resembles an angry father who doesn't get on with this son, and men hold heaven responsible for their misery, in the same way as they accuse a bad ruler.

15. Disobedience of heaven and accusations against heaven are juxtaposed with disobedience and accusations in regard to political leaders. Both of these types of accusation are seen as particularly severe forms of disobedience and are thus said to intensify the consequences of trespasses.

16. This section contains an unusual number of reminders that both the Celestial Master and his disciples speak for heaven. This can be explained by the relative novelty of the matter under discussion.

17. This is a tall and a big man, when we consider that, as the *Han shu* says (21A *"Lüli zhi,"* p. 966), one *zhang* is always ten "feet" (*chi* 尺) long. Yanzi 晏子, for instance, who was known as having been small, was supposed to have been less than six *chi* tall (see *Yanzi chun qiu* 5.25, p. 146). The legendary Emperor Yao was supposed to have been ten feet tall (*Kong Congzi* 7 *"Ju wei"* 居闈, p. 40). Ten spans was given as the size of a big tree (*Hanyu da cidian* vol. 1, p. 827), but there is also the *Shi shuo xin yu* (14 *"Rong zhi"* 容止, p. 161) passage, which mentions a person who is seven *chi* tall and ten spans big.

18. *Qu* 齲 insects were known to cause toothache (see Morohashi [1985] no. 48716). However, I have not found parallels for this and the following passages in any medical material.

19. In the Han dynasty, ten *cun* 寸 were one *chi*, usually translated as "foot," and said to have been about nine inches (see Swann 1950: 362). Needless to say, this is not plausible for section 61. An insect of almost an inch is not "tiny," and a man ten feet tall, that is, one *"zhang,"* is a giant.

20. *Kou kou* 口 口 is corrected to the sign for two missing characters, which are read as *fan fu* 反復, as suggested by Yu (2001a: 105).

21. To be more precise, these are the three worms, *san chong* 三蟲, that exist in a man's belly. The text deals with them at some length in another context, where the assaults of intestinal parasites are paralleled to men's unruliness and the occurrence of natural disasters (TPJ 136.378–80).

22. *Yi* 億 stands for one million here, following the figure of *shi wan* 十萬, which does not occur elsewhere in the text. The general sequence (see TPJ 67.169 and passim) is *qian, wan, yi*, which makes *yi* into "one hundred thousand." Morohashi (1985; no. 1178), quoting a *Shi jing* (no. 249; cf. Karlgren 1950: 204f.) passage, argues that one hundred thousand *(shi wan)* is the character's oldest meaning, that hundred million *(wan wan)* came later, and that "one million" *(bai wan)* and "ten million" *(qian wan)* occur occasionally.

23. The TPJ is by no means alone in this social critique. Poo (1990) has collected accounts of burials, most of them highly critical. The following passage is from a memorial in which Liu Xiang tries to prevent the emperor from building his own mausoleum. It is quoted here in full since it resembles *taiping* concerns:

> When Chang mausoleum (*chang ling* 昌陵) was built, height was added to small mounds, and earth was piled up into a mountain. People's graves were destroyed, to the extent of tens of thousands, to make room for the building of mortuary structures. The schedule was pressing, and the cost amounted to more than one million. The dead underground were in grief and the living up above in distress (*chou* 愁). Resentful (*yuan* 怨) feelings upset Yin and Yang, which caused famines. Hundreds of thousands of men perished or were made homeless. (*Han shu* 36.1956; translation, slightly modified, by Poo 1990: 49)

It was commonly believed that digging up soil created a problem. Grave-securing writs from the second century C.E. often include a passage of apology to the earth's spirits for the disturbance caused by entombing the dead; see Wu Rongzeng 1981.

24. "A good canal is scoured by its own water" is how it is phrased in the *Zhou li* ("*Dong guan kao gong*" 冬官考工, p. 933a). Zhang Rong, a contemporary of Wang Mang, argued in detail how too much irrigation slowed the flow of water and thus increased the build-up of sediment (Needham 1971: 229).

25. This is an editorial note that does not signify a change of topic. For a similar use of *you yan* 又言, see TPJ 48.57f. Yu (2001a: 106) attempts to correct *yan* (to speak) to *wang* 妄 (at random), which occurs several times in this passage. This still leaves the problem of *you; ren wang* 人妄 might be more appropriate, but there is really no need to change the text.

26. From the limited material assembled by Hsu (1980: 255–75) on irrigation projects, the Han dynasty experts placed at least as much stress on building new canals as they did on the repair of existing facilities, if not more. This seems to be what the Celestial Master intends to criticize here.

27. The three-character compound *bing ji tong* 病疾痛, which occurs only here, is typical of the TPJ's word formation. The translation tries to do justice to the expression's rhetorical value.

28. Judging by the other measures given in this passage—the size of a man, supposedly ten feet, and the size of a tiny insect, which is said to be one *cun* (inch)—we must assume that the three feet mentioned here amount to less than the 70 cm that tables of Han dynasty measures (Twitchett and Loewe 1986: xxxviii) would suggest.

29. *Li ji* 9 "*Li yun*" 禮運, p. 1416a, says that the ancient kings had no houses, but lived in caves during the winter and in nests in summer.

30. This answer makes man more the spirits' plaything than is customary in the TPJ, or would be appropriate for a merit-oriented depiction of the spiritual world.

31. *Gu xiang* 故相 is corrected to *gu xiang* 故鄉, as in Luo's (1996: 218) translation. It is said in the *Yi jing* (hexagram 48, p. 29) that when you move into a new abode you must not change the wells.

32. This serves as an introduction to a new dialogue and could introduce a new section. As it stands, section 61 is unusually long.

33. This question, which seems to take up the student's last remark, could be one reason why the following dialogue was put here.

34. This is the central *taiping* message: men must make heaven happy, which will then create great peace; great peace enables men to live long.

35. "In fear," and "fearful" in the next paragraph, are both expressed by *hai* 駭, with the radical "horse." The same character is used on p. 125 in "how alarming": *ke hai zai, ke hai zai* 可駭哉. The same meaning is expressed on other occasions by *hai*, with the radical "heart," as, for instance, on p. 122: "how frightening." Yu Liming (1997: 50; the quotations are not quite accurate) points out that this use of *hai* (with the "heart" radical) is nonstandard and that both forms of the character are used in section 61. This difference can perhaps be explained by a difference in note takers for the first (before the phrase "Step forward!") and second dialogues. No similar explanation is possible for section 78, however, which also has both forms of the character (pp. 189 and 191). The variations are proof of the leniency of the text's sixth-century editors.

36. With Yu (2001a: 108) I read *wei* 未 for *fa* 法.

37. With Yu (2001a: 108) the two missing characters are read as *fan fu* 反復; cf. TPJ 132:350.

38. As Confucius's disciples did; see *Lun yu* 1.1.

39. I read *zhi* 知 (to know) for *he* 和 (harmony).

40. The wording is *zhi he yi e bu ping ye* 治何一惡不平也, which is perhaps corrupt. Punctuation and attribution to speakers are my own. Yu 2001a: 109 sticks to Wang Ming's text and punctuation.

41. I read *de* 得 (to be able to) for *fu* 復 (again).

42. The Celestial Master often points to future developments to prove his point. He ar-

gues, for instance, that his text must be studied and *taiping* reforms must be undertaken because once this has happened people will see the improvement (TPJ 50.66; 57.92; 65.152).

43. For "long-lasting stability" (*chang an* 長安), see above, section 50.

44. With Yu (2001a: 109), I read the two missing characters as *yuan jin* 冤今.

45. For these ranks, see above, section 56.

46. The term "heaven's subjects" (*tian min* 天民) is here used as in the *Mengzi* (7A19), where it is said that heaven's subjects practice only what is of value to the whole world (Lau 1970: 185), as opposed to "the ruler's men" *(jun ren)*, who are at a ruler's command, and to "community's officials," who serve the interests of a particular community. Mengzi proposes that only "great men" with overriding moral power are in rank above heaven's subjects. *Tian min* does not seem to be a Daoist term, except for the difficult *Zhuangzi* passage (63.23.43), according to which heaven's subjects are those men whom others must let go (Graham 1981: 103). Its use in this TPJ passage aligns it closely with the "good people," or, in later language use, the "seed people," that is, the believers in *dao*. Cf. section 66, below, and the following passage in the *Preface to the Double Character Talismans of the Scripture on Great Peace (Taiping jing fuwen xu):*

> When a *renchen* 壬辰 (year) comes around we will see the wise lord (*sheng jun* 聖君) descend and will experience the perfect order of great peace. Noble transcendents will manage affairs, and the subjects of heaven will be rewarded. (TPJ p. 745)

47. See below, section 65, for a similar argument; good people bring about a good ruler, an ideal ruler.

48. See below, section 66, for details on the limits within which prayers might improve the culprit's lot.

49. The summary says:

This section explains the grievances of heaven and earth.

SECTION 62 · *Dao* is Priceless and
Overcomes Yi and
Di Barbarians

The Celestial Master's doctrine leads to the political pacification of humankind and is thus immeasurably valuable. It is certainly worth more than beautiful women and heaps of gold. This is the answer to one of the more banal of the disciple's questions.[1]

This pacification is to be achieved in a traditional manner: A ruler is presented with the Master's writings, studies them, and does what they say, then worthy men come to offer their support and make all the people content. As a result, natural disasters cease and the ruler's position is secured.

Most of this section is written in a lively and unusually coherent style. A short and rather puzzling dialogue deals with a new aspect of the topic "the Master's doctrine" toward the end. Its message is somewhat surprising, as it demands secrecy, as opposed to the Celestial Master's almost constant encouragement to propagate his teachings. It makes sense to include this message in section 62, in that the demand not to spread it indiscriminately enhances the value of what the Master says. Section 62 as a whole includes a number of statements that can be seen as hinting at concrete events: the fight between factions, the private assembling of learned men, the awareness of imminent cyclical change and, perhaps in conclusion, the need to be selective in choosing the audience for propagating the *taiping* program. The Master demands that disciples share his message only with men of influence and not with inconsequential "small men," who cannot be trusted with the implementation of great peace. All of these demands enhance the scripture's value for those who receive it. There is an aura of secrecy and elitism that does not often accompany layer A dialogues.

The section's message adheres closely to the Master's central teachings. To succeed, the argument goes, the timing of the reform process must strictly conform to the turning of a cosmic cycle. Only reforms implemented at the right time can succeed.

.   .   .

(62.126) *Celestial Master, you are about to go away. No time has been set for your return. I would like to be permitted to ask another few questions.*[2]

Go ahead! Speak up quickly. There are still a few days before my departure. What do you wish to ask?

I would like to ask something about the writings on dao (dao shu)[3] *that you have previously given to me. I want to put forward something that is immodest and should not be said. But if I don't ask now, I will never find out.*

Go ahead! Don't be shy!

If the illustrious teacher would only instruct this foolish pupil!

Yes, I will.

Now then, what is the worth of the writings that I have received from you over the course of time?

Oh, your foolishness is indeed enormous. You are saying that my teachings *(dao)* have a price?

Yes, I am.

All I have explained to you in order to enlighten you and give you a profound knowledge of the way of heaven—how much does it weigh? What is it worth? If I were to bestow on you instead one thousand pounds of gold to give to a country, would this better enable you to make heaven and earth happy, harmonize Yin and Yang, let calamities cease, let rulers, emperors, and kings live for a long time and their government achieve supreme peace? If you were presented with ten thousand pairs of jade discs to give to a country to store them as a treasure, this would be the world's most precious thing. But would this better enable you to let *qi* of great harmony reveal itself in the six directions, let portents of prosperity come forth, and let Yi and Di barbarians retreat ten thousand miles so that they would not cause any harm? The teachings I have given you are complete. (62.127) They enable emperors and kings truly to make heaven and earth happy, all the world's officials perfectly content, all living beings joyous, and Yi and Di barbarians return to allegiance. Portents of prosperity will appear everywhere, and natural disasters will cease. Ruling houses will prolong their reigns; the people will live long lives, taking great care to do good, in line with my writings. Just grasp their main idea and everything will fit, just as if you were applying compasses and carpenter's square. Without exception, you will achieve as much as can be achieved.[4] I speak on behalf of heaven, I don't lead you astray. If you were to support a virtuous emperor or king with the patterns that heaven promulgates, you would do away with all his worries. Day after day he could freely roam about. This is "how much it is worth." Have you grasped it, foolish as you are?

Yes, I have.

I will talk to you about another matter. Of all that is good and delightful, the men of this world like nothing better than the right (*hao* 好) woman. When a man finds her, they bring forth children together and are both of one heart. Nothing can match a woman who is truly good and lovely. If you gave ten thousand women to a country, everyone would be delighted and happy. Looking at these women men would forget their age. But would this really help to make heaven and earth safe, the ten thousand countries content, the eight distant regions submissive, and the world a place of great peace? My teachings can make heaven up above secure in its infinity; they can bring order to earth down below in its endlessness. Everyone from the eight directions will wish to pledge allegiance. All that is in confusion will be reformed by virtue and find its proper place. "How much is it worth?" You must thoroughly figure out for yourself what this means. (62.128)

If you would like to return heaven's many merits and obtain its favor you must urgently make my writings known. Heaven will not be pleased if you wish to support it by masses of man-made precious objects, and you will not gain much favor with it. If you wish to gain favor, you must think day and night about what my writings say. As soon as you understand what they say, you will also obtain heaven's favor. "How much would that be worth?"

You would not promote as much good government if you gave a country one thousand pieces of gold as you might with one piece of sound advice. Giving a country ten thousand pairs of jade disks won't match the promotion of two worthy men. Good advice, men of worth, and exquisite teachings make it possible for emperors and kings to reign even when they sleep soundly at night and to achieve great peace while still enjoying themselves. They can put an end to disasters and other irregular events and make the world safe. This is achieved by men of worth, sound advice, and exquisite teachings. "How much are they worth?"

So in antiquity the wise and the worthy, emperors and kings were never short of material wealth but always suffered from a shortage of scholars. What distressed them was that men of worth would not come to them and the people in general would not flock to them, but would instead wish to be allied to others, so that the numbers [of their own supporters] were dwindling. In this way someone who has fallen from majestic heaven's grace must forever suffer severely. But by all means find joy in precious man-made objects if you wish to do so; you won't be able to gain favor with heaven and earth and secure the realm between the four oceans, though. Let [emperors and kings] assemble enough precious objects of gold and jade to cover an area of one thousand miles in breadth and width and reach up to heaven—this will not make worthy and wise men, transcendents and scholars come and support their reign.

Study my writings carefully and worthy men will come of their own accord to support and assist the rule of emperors and kings. One morning they will all of a sudden come together to help making plans, just as one morning, when merchants get together, ten thousand goods are piled up high and all provisions are in store: one can go out and look for them. Act in accord with my writings. Heaven and earth will become brighter; the sun, the moon, and the stars will have a halo[5] and shine in the eight directions into the vast distant regions so that the four barbarian peoples will take note of it and will all wish to come and submit themselves. The worthy and the learned will come forth from their hiding places. Their warfare will come to a complete stop. Without the use of official insignia,[6] the world will be all right. Men will no longer try to hurt each other, but will together strive to be good and make emperors and kings happy.[7] My writings can bring this about. "How much are they worth?" You understand, don't you? (62.129)

So the wise men of old did nothing else but to think deeply of *dao* and pay attention to the balancing of *qi*.[8] They did not rely on scholars of their own,[9] but instead attached themselves to a man of virtue. Such a man would know the intentions of heaven and earth and would therefore honor *dao* and think highly of virtue. Because foolish men made much of precious man-made objects, heavenly writings were not revealed and the worthy and wise didn't receive them. This is what it means. Heed this; what I say does not mislead you. Pay attention to my teachings. Men whose aim it is to hold onto precious objects like jade discs and golden coins will sit up in the dark to protect them, unable to sleep. But these are only precious objects. How about the treasures of heaven, secret maps and writings, which make the six ends and eight outlying regions of heaven and earth safe? They have become known to the world, so you must be even more attentive.

Yes, I will.

Spirit messengers sent by heaven always sit next to my writings to guard them. Again, be warned!

Yes, I will.

Spirit messengers sent by the three luminaries are always at hand in all their brilliance to look after my writings.

Yes, indeed!

My writings say what heaven intends and what earth wants. You must again thoroughly and clearly memorize them.

Yes, I will!

Since you are able to understand what I say, I will again explain to you a matter that is hard to detect.

Yes!

What leaves the mouth and enters the ear must not be transmitted to everyone. Should an emperor or king obtain [this message], the world would submit to him. Spirits and other numinous beings would support his government. People would of themselves become good. They would behave in a balanced manner (*jun* 均) without being daily ordered to do so.[10]

Yes! All six of us are foolish and dumb. We can't help it. What we say is bound to go against the prohibitions. Now[11] if the Master would only outline dao *and virtue on behalf of majestic heaven and thus give emperors and kings a precious tool that will last for ten thousand times ten thousand generations.* (62.130) *You must make known to us all inside matters[12] without restraint. Truly, once we have humbly received certain awe-inspiring doctrines and secret admonitions, we will not dare let anything leak out.*

Yes. Now for your sake I have inquired with majestic heaven: it must all be told and I would indeed not dare hide anything. If it were not permitted to make things known I would indeed not dare do so on my own account.

The rotations of heaven and earth both have their sequence. What is made known at the right point of a rotation can be achieved forever.[13] Thus countries will remain happy and be in no danger of ruin. That is why you must not attach yourself to a small man, but only to an emperor or a king. Emperors and kings who appear at the right point in this historical sequence stay forever attuned to heaven and earth. They are able to achieve this, but a small-minded man is not. So I request that you[14] attach yourself to such a person.[15]

NOTES

1. Wolfgang Bauer translated most of this section into German in 1971 as part of his *China and the Search for Happiness*, which was translated into English in 1976; cf. Bauer 1976: 121–24.

2. The Master no longer resides on earth but in heaven, in the celestial North Pole, as has been established in section 54. The disciples will eventually follow in the Master's footsteps, as stated in section 63. As the Master puts it:

> I have already departed from the world and cannot reappear among the people as I might choose. Therefore, I have handed the book to you, Perfected. You are also leaving the world behind, however, and will thus be unable to teach the people. So I ask you to search for honest people with full understanding, hand it to them, and let them quickly deposit it with a virtuous ruler. What an offense it would be not to go and hand it over but to remain inactive and keep it. (TPJ 103.255)

For the present, however, the disciple is in charge of initiating the missionary movement, as explained below, in section 65.

3. The Celestial Master's own writings are *dao shu;* see TPJ 66.161: *wu dao shu* 吾道. They rank first in certain textual hierarchies:

> The first group is writings on spiritlike *dao (shen dao shu)*, the second is texts that examine affairs, the third is reports that oppose frivolous and superficial material. They all teach what is appropriate (*da shun* 大順). (TPJ p. 718, *Chao*, part 1, and quoted with textual variants in *Yunji qiqian* 6 as "TPJ, part 1"; see TPJ p. 9)

Another word for the Celestial Master's writings is *san dao shu* 三道書; see below, section 65.

4. I read the two missing characters as *wu shang* 無上; see TPJ 55.87: *zui you da wu shang* 最優大無上.

5. This is an auspicious portent; see, for instance, Li Ji's 李奇 (from Nanyang, as Yan Shigu tells us in his introduction; see *Han shu*, p. 4) commentary on *Han shu* 58.2632, as quoted by Yan Shigu: "In a world of great peace the sun has a halo, which means it is a double sun."

6. Not to use official insignia is an expression of *wu wei* 無為:

> When emperors and kings act accordingly the world will prosper. Laying down the official insignia and practicing nonaction, they transcend the world and live long lives. (TPJ pp. 688f., *Chao*, part 8)
>
> Someone who lays down the official insignia and practices nonaction drives away all ill luck. (TPJ p. 307, *Chao*, part 5)

7. Although such fights were a constant feature of political life, it can be argued that

the controversies between the "clean party," made up of career officials, and their upstart enemies during the reign of Emperor Ling (r. 168–89) were among the most prominent of these fights.

8. *Qi ping* refers to the balancing of natural forces. *Qi* is here *tian qi* (heaven's *qi*); see TPJ 132.362 and 208.666.

9. I follow Long (2000: 262) in correcting *tu* 土 (soil) to *shi* 士 (scholar) (see also Yu 2001a: 113) and *he* 和 (harmony) to *si* 私 (private). Yu (2001a: 113) suggests reading *zhi* 知 (to know) for *he*. The passage is an attack on the formation of schools and perhaps also on the attempts by powerful individuals to assemble not only their own armies, but also pools of advisors. *Guanzi* 45 "*Ren fa*" 任法, p. 256 uses the expression *si shi* in this meaning. The conclusion the Master's disciples are expected to draw is clear. They are not meant to take the initiative in the political realm but are to remain in the background in a supportive, advisory function.

10. As Luo (1996: 225) points out, this passage resembles *Laozi* 32 read in the way of the *Xiang'er* commentary (p. 12), which in Bokenkamp's translation (1997: 133) reads:

> Text: The populace would naturally make themselves equals (*jun* 均) without having been ordered to do so.

> Commentary: When the king reveres the *Dao*, his officers and subjects will desire to emulate him. They will not fear laws and regulations, but the spirits of heaven. They will not dare commit wrongs but will desire only to perfect their bodies. They will make themselves equals without having been commanded to do so.

Jun is used in the TPJ in the sense of adjusting differences of social rank:

> When heaven and earth bring about equality (*shi hua de jun* 施化得均), the honored and the lowly, great and small men are all alike and don't fight with each other, so that the ruler becomes [like] father and mother. (TPJ 213.683)

Sharing things has something to do with this:

> When someone receives life (*ming* 命) from heaven and is then in his behavior (*gong xing qi* 共行氣) not harmonious and fair (*tiao jun* 調均) in what he gives away to others (*yu ze* 與澤), the world will not be at peace. He behaves like an official who, although employed *(ming)* by emperors and kings, turns away from his superiors and, smiling on those below him, spreads favors without consideration for harmony and fairness; officials will then, as a group, forget about loyalty and faithfulness and instead betray their superior. (TPJ 151.406)

Merit and achievement must be the basis for distributing favors. The demand for fairness extends to heaven's conduct of business, as described in passages from or close to layer B. It is striking that even in regard to heaven, fairness is occasionally expressed as a demand and not as an observation of what is actually happening. As the Celestial Lord put it:

> The memorials that are submitted [must all be treated] in a balanced and fair manner (*ping jun* 平均), without resentment and dispute. (TPJ 180.544, layer B)

Moreover, heaven's personnel must be remunerated according to their performance, that is, with "fairness" (TPJ 188.579, layer not clear). Heaven's dealings with humankind follow a similar logic:

> Now that heaven sends the spirits it has appointed [to distribute gifts] in harmony (*tiao he* 調和) and fairness *(ping jun)*, let everyone get what he wants and not take away what anybody is entitled to (*an* 安). (TPJ 200.616, layer B)

We may conclude that *jun* points to general impartiality and moderation in the execution of control and represents one aspect of the state of *ping* (peace, balance). In the following passage, then, *jun* is used as if it were a gloss of *ping:*

> "Peace" *(ping)* means that a reign is completely balanced *(taiping jun)* so that all activities are kept in order (*li* 理), without further jealousy and selfishness. (TPJ 65.148)

11. For *ju* 俱 (all) I read *qie* 且. *Jin qie* 今且 is used frequently throughout the text to introduce a sentence.

12. "Inside matters" (*nei shi* 內事) is used in the sense of "vitality recipes" (*fang shu* 方術) in a *Wei lue* quotation in Bei Songzhi's commentary to *San guo zhi* 19.365, a quotation that explains the early career of a certain Han Pin 寒貧, who moved from the study of the *Book of Odes* and *Book of Documents* to a love for *nei shi* and, when he turned sixteen years of age, began to read the *Laozi* and other *nei shu* 內書. This remark shows a certain contempt for *nei shi*, and in the *Inner Chapters* of the *Baopu zi* (chap. 15, "*Za ying*" 雜應, p. 68), it is in similarly critical fashion pointed out that there are better remedies. "Inside matters" have a certain touch of the esoteric: they belong to one teacher and his school, as well as to this school's friends. The TPJ contains a passage in which inside matters are put on a par with *dao;* this is reminiscent of the *Laozi*'s (48) proposition that while learning (which is inferior) grows, the doctrine *(dao)* becomes less. As the TPJ puts it:

> The learning of external [matters] (*wai xue* 外學) involves a lot, while learning inside [matters] (*nei xue* 內學) involves little. When external matters (*wai shi* 外事) grow from day to day, inside matters (*nei shi* 內事) become less and less. (TPJ p. 720, *Chao*, part 1)

13. The Master sees the world as moving in cycles (*da zhou* 大周; see TPJ 212.678), as Petersen (1990b: 27) has pointed out. This cyclical movement has two facets. At the end of one cycle, the danger of extinction coexists with the chance for beginning a new and better regime (TPJ 212.686). As the Master puts it:

> The great cycle that began with the way of heaven is at present complete. The future depends on human beings and on Yang. Yang loves life and hates death. . . . Now at the start of another great cycle of heaven's way, pure Yang reigns over heaven and earth from top to bottom, so we must quickly get rid of punishment and crimes. (TPJ 212.676f.)

When the disciples want to know why this is happening now, the Master explains that it is caused by the phase of fire becoming dominant (TPJ 212.678; see Petersen 1990b: 28).

Kamitsuka (1999: 316–25) discusses the relationship between the concept of *cheng fu* (see section 48) and a cyclical explanation for the occurrence and ending of disasters. She points out that both explanations coexisted in Han dynasty disaster analysis. The Celestial Master clearly takes more interest in the moral aspect of natural calamities than in the numerological configurations that were produced around them.

14.   I change *junzi* 君子 (gentleman) to *zi* 子 (you). The occurrence of "small-minded man" in the preceding sentence has triggered this error. The small-minded man is here the opposite of "emperors and kings."

15.   This is an unusual ending in that the departure of the students does not involve any further admonitions, but the content of this passage does not differ from the rest. It argues that the writings revealed by heaven are destined for the "virtuous lord," who will implement their prohibitions among the populace at large. They are not meant to be distributed directly among the people. The summary says:

> This section is on peace, *dao*, and virtue; it attributes high and low rank; it explains the feelings of foolish men.

Officials, Sons, and Disciples of
Outstanding Goodness Find Ways
for Their Lord, Father, and
Master to Become Transcendent

In promoting *taiping* morality the Celestial Master does not oppose commonly accepted moral norms but rather argues that conformity with them is not enough. Goodness does not result merely from sticking to norms. Instead, it requires taking initiative, active involvement, and self-denial in the service of others. Considering the great value the Celestial Master places upon life and its protection, it is not surprising that a good person is described as someone who makes others happy and prolongs their lives. However, the TPJ is not a text about philosophical principles for their own sake, but rather a manual on how to lead a *dao*-oriented life. So the question of what it means to be good is not raised for man in general but in separate accounts for a subject, a son, and a disciple, in line with the social philosophy of the "five relationships" (*wu lun* 五倫).[1] The last of these relationships, which is not dictated by birth or social necessity and is commonly equated with the relationship between friends, is here the bond between master and disciple. In all three roles, a good man takes the other's mortality into consideration. To postpone and soften death is considered good by the Celestial Master. The argument involves a certain degree of fundamentalism, as it excludes all nonbelievers from the realm of moral excellence.

The Master demands that *taiping* adepts feel responsible for the length of their parents' lives, thus creating an unusual link between filial piety and the search for longevity. The *Baopu zi* posits a different link between the two. Here Ge Hong integrates established ideas based on the ancestral cult with his own personal interest in longevity and argues that the personal search for longevity is in itself an act of filial piety. As he sees it, the Daoist adept is someone who keeps the body that nature and his parents have given him completely intact. He even improves it through the use of Daoist techniques. Such practices demonstrate his piety by enabling his ancestors to partake in the glory of his achievements. His ancestors are also said to take special delight in the exotic food their Daoist descendant prefers and in which they may partake through ancestral offerings.[2] In contrast to this preoccupation with one's own longevity, the *taiping* ideas have a more traditional concern—one might even say a more social concern.

The second part of the section is separated from the first by a marked caesura. Straying from the topic at hand, the Celestial Master explains the problems his missionary movement has been confronted with in the past and, in particular, the lack of a receptive audience. He then sends his disciples away, thus finishing the session. However, he gives in when confronted with another question and proceeds with a discussion of the availability of immortality tools. He stresses the resemblance between heaven's system of rewards and that of the state. Men with merit will live long. Those without will not, just as a county office provides resources only to those men who deserve them. This adds another dimension to what has been said in the first part of this section. It now becomes clear that only good deeds, as the Master defines them, enable a man to partake in heaven's benefits and thus really enjoy his life.

The last part of the section affirms that nowadays only a few men are worthy of longevity. The deterioration of the doctrine and of the texts that present it is at fault. The situation outlined for the latter age, which is distant from *dao,* has all the negative characteristics that were outlined in earlier sections. Texts promote the application of punishment, rulers can't attract honest and worthy staff, and authentic material and good officials are scarce. At the end of the section the Master returns to the need to publicize and support the new longevity-oriented behavior patterns that he described at the beginning of the section.

·   ·   ·

(63.131) Step forward, Perfected. Why are some men, officials and ordinary subjects alike, so excellent in their goodness? You must think hard to come up with a reasonable explanation, difficult as this is.

Yes, I will, but I am afraid I might say something wrong.

Why, so modest!

Yes, we may rightfully say that nowadays we must call a country's officials[3] and ordinary subjects truly good should they always remain attentive and faithful,[4] never daring to break the king's laws, from birth to death never committing a serious mistake, and throughout their lives never being found guilty of a criminal offense.

Oh! The sort of thing you have said looks all right but is in fact wrong. You have described what we must call a person of average goodness, but not "the best." Well, describe to me also what the conduct of the most filial son should be. Think hard so that you will tell me all.

What I have just said did not meet with your approval. I would not dare speak again.

How modest! Just say what you know. Should it not suffice I will help you get there.

Yes! Now in all he does the most filial son will forever safeguard dao. *He won't dare cause father and mother any worries and will always nourish them well, by remaining day and night at their side. From the time he is born, for as long as he has been aware of himself, he has never committed a mistake serious enough to be called a crime. Such a person we may call most filial.*

Oh! The description you have given looks all right but is again wrong. (63.132) We may call the person you have described as of average goodness. He doesn't match the highest level of filial piety.

I am not good enough! I am to blame.

It doesn't matter. But when we consider that you might be in a position to instruct students, your conduct sets a pattern and you must watch all you say. Now if you don't speak any better than you do, the common people in their foolishness, blindness, and ignorance will be really difficult to teach. This foolishness will increase without end until they might consider a man of excellent goodness and piety, should they find one, odd. Since you can't do it, I will explain it to you.

Yes!

All right. But, difficult as it may be, you must also describe to me the best disciple.

Now I have already offended you twice. I would not dare speak again.

All right. Just concentrate on what you say! To be someone's disciple and refuse to speak[5] is indeed a severe offense. But to be inadequate has been common for as long as the world has been in existence. Speak up!

Yes, I will. Now as a disciple one must always, day and night, be obedient and attentive. A disciple must follow the master's instructions and admonitions without forgetting the smallest part of what is said. He must not dare to speak at random or bring disorder into the master's writings. In going away and coming back, he must never dare worry the master. After a disciple has been instructed, he must not dare be aggressive, negligent, offensive, or wicked.[6] *He should strive to be good, in a happy mood, day after day, have no evil intentions, and never counteract his master's wishes. We would call such a man the best disciple.*

Oh! There is some similarity, but it is not the best disciple whom you have described. It just about fits the average one.

Really, I am no good. Since you have severely reprimanded me, I have forced myself to speak three times. Three times I have not met with the illustrious teacher's approval. The mistakes I have made are severe. I am afraid I have once again committed a crime that cannot be pardoned.

Everyone has certain shortcomings. Your intentions are not bad, so there is no crime. Nowadays the men who live in this world are all foolish and completely in the dark. Not a single one of them knows what is right. Even you keep talking about issues as you do. So what can one expect from ordinary folk and foolish men? They will never understand. They trust their own foolish opinion, that's why.

Luckily, the Celestial Master has been overwhelmingly kind and has explained things to me. Please go again through the points that I don't understand. Show mercy and be my enlightened teacher.

All right, I will explain it all, for your sake. You must be careful to take notes.

Yes, I will!

Yes.[7] Well, this is the conduct of officials and ordinary subjects who excel in goodness: Always, day and night, they feel concern for their sovereign. They want him to be secure, and in their heart they feel what pains him. (63.133) They are always pleased to watch how the ruler lays down his official insignia and government occurs on its own. [When this happens] subjects and officials follow suit and become filial and generous. The men in government are happy for the king to sit in meditation and [let his spirit] roam afar. Such a reign finds favor with heaven high above and agrees with the wishes of earth down below. In the center, the ten thousand people are contented, so that none stricken with grief would neglect their duty. Creeping insects and other beings change form as is proper for their kind. Therefore nobody dies from epidemics, and all the ten thousand beings are in their right place. With heaven and earth in harmony, the three qi[8] delight in each other. Thus the ruler's long life is further prolonged. Moreover, the hundred families keep searching for special recipes and rare ways of treatment[9] for their emperors and kings.

[They make public] writings that they had locked up and hidden away until all is out in the open. The world responds. Full of surprise, everyone says, "How splendid. It has never been like this!" No one, old or young, will ever again know how to do evil. They submit their special and rare recipes to emperors and kings, who are thus able to live [even] longer. Everyone is concerned about the lord growing old. But since his reign finds favor with heaven, heaven and earth might send spirits to bring medicine and announce to their son to take it: such a person's health won't deteriorate until the end of his life. This is what an "official" or an "ordinary subject of excellent goodness" can achieve. You understand, don't you?

Yes, I do! (63.134)

So we may say that this is clear to you.

This is how the majestic emperor's best officials and best subjects conducted themselves in early antiquity. How were they able to find out about it and to achieve such rectitude?

Through these teachings *(dao)*. My teachings are indeed like the first-ranking texts of early antiquity. Ponder their meaning deeply and you will understand heaven's wishes. With due respect have I received [these teachings] from the heart of heaven to pass them on to a virtuous lord so that he might cut off calamities and put an end to all harmful influences. I fear heaven's severity. How would I dare not put forth all there is? But it is still angry.[10] So I let you have these writings. Give them[11] quickly to a lord of supreme virtue and his reign will resemble heaven. How should it differ from heaven?

Excellent, indeed! Now I have learned from what you say that qi *of peace* (ping), *which goes back to heaven's great peace, has truly arrived.[12] The text that has brought this about has been made public. This is splendid. What would be left to worry about?*

Now why should people who have not become disciples be happy when they see what is good and worry about the evil that they perceive?[13]

For the following reason: Upon the arrival of good qi, *evil* qi *goes into hiding, which makes us forever safe and free from illness and injury. But when evil* qi *arrives, good* qi *goes into hiding so that we fear calamities and don't dare move. This is what the world is like. So we are happy when we see what is good.[14]*

What you have said is right!

The Celestial Master is kind! You have already explained to me the model of an official and an ordinary subject of supreme goodness. Would you please also talk to me about the conduct[15] of the most filial son?

What a good question! Well, a son of excellent filial piety always keeps in mind that his parents are getting older and will pass away. If he lives on his own, he thinks of them whenever he has leisure. He is always most eager[16] to find methods that keep death at bay. If possible, he lives with his parents. His life consists of nothing but contempt for material wealth on the one hand and reverence for *dao* on the other. He entertains his parents by singing melancholic songs to the lute, making them relax and helping them enter *dao*. He enjoys staying with them until the end, while making them forget that they are old. He is always in search of special recipes in all the remote places. His sincerity has such an impact on heaven that he succeeds even after he has exhausted his strength. He has no more clothes, food, or property than what he needs. He does not lay aside rare treasures for future generations, but he protects his father and mother from any grievances that they might suffer.[17] Should one of them die, the [son's] *hun* spirit is unhappy and suffers distress. He maintains himself but does not search for happiness. That is to say, he tries hard to look after his own person[18] only for the sake of those below the ground. He must not, thinking of one of his parents, cause harm to himself. (63.135) Now this is what we call the conduct of most filial sons of highest majesty[19] in early antiquity. When such goodness becomes known to the four directions, everyone far and wide will, before long, rejoice and think of doing likewise, intent on copying [such conduct]. This gives emperors and kings friendly and filial officials.

Now a filial son is concerned about father and mother. In the same way, a good official worries about his ruler. But what you have just described amounts only to average conduct, in that someone keeps his own person intact. How could this benefit ruler, father, and teacher? And yet you call this person a man of excellent morality! He deserves only the name of someone who looks after his own profit. If even you deem this to be "good," how about the common people? Someone appearing to be attentive and faithful, who does not offend against the king's laws and has no criminal record, will immediately and passionately declare himself to be a person who doesn't turn his back on heaven and never fails lord, father, and teacher. If your conduct were just good enough to safeguard your own person, you would be a great fool to invoke heaven and earth to insist that you have achieved merit. We could never consider you to be a person of outstanding goodness.

Now this is what I have explained to you in detail. I want you to give it in written form to a lord who is of supreme virtue. With this in hand, he will very earnestly advise the worthy men in his service. All of a sudden, they will understand and know for themselves the difference between right and wrong. Wouldn't this indeed benefit lord, father, and teacher?

Men have become more foolish since earliest and middle antiquity. They have become wealthier each day through corrupt practices although they have proclaimed that they have performed meritorious deeds on behalf of heaven, earth, lord, father, and teacher. Such men are obstinate and unreasonable. You see this, don't you?

Yes, I do! (63.136)

So we may assume that you have understood. Nowadays, good conduct is really difficult. Take care. You must try hard to understand what my text says. Then you will put an end to the great illness that has gripped heaven and earth. This will allow emperors and kings to let their spirits roam about, untroubled and at their leisure. So the whole world, including plants and trees, will rejoice. Otherwise, you will never be able to match what is expected of a person of excellent goodness, but only deserve the name of a person who looks after himself.

But why should anyone dismiss heaven and earth?

People take delight in looking after their own person. This holds true even more for the small-minded *(xiao ren)*. Are you aware of this?

Yes, I am!

So we may say that you know. Take care!

Yes, I will! Now you have been very kind to this foolish, lowly, unreasonable pupil! I would also like to hear something about the conduct of a disciple of outstanding goodness.

Well, after he has learned about *dao* and its virtue, such a student will bear the master's generosity in mind. When he has grown up and local leaders and worthy men seek his company, he will not forget the neighborhood group he belongs to. Perhaps he might obtain an official position and will then show his gratitude to father and mother. Or he might enter deep into *dao* and understand the art of nourishing his own person. Men receive life from their father and mother, become accomplished in *dao* and virtue with the help of a teacher, and obtain glory and honor from a lord. Each man in his own realm of life must keep in mind that once lord, father, and teacher have grown old there will be no chance to repay them. Always think of them and it will be all right. If you find special recipes and rare texts, you thank the teacher for what he has done for you. But simply to remember them will soothe the pain in your heart. If special [ways of treatment] and rare [texts] cannot be found, it is all right to simply think of [your teacher]. However, if you have a worthy[20] for your teacher, obtain a commission for him, speak on his behalf, and perhaps you can help him become a country's trusted advisor. Being in such a top position, he would benefit the reign of emperors and kings for a long time. All this is what a disciple of supreme morality in earliest antiquity would have done. When his influence extends to latter-born generations and to an enlightened ruler, together with a ruler's worthy officials, we call him a man of excellent morality.[21]

Now we might say that a disciple as attentive and faithful as you, Perfected, is easy to teach, but such a one who did not understand his master's intentions would only be what we would call an obedient disciple, who labors toward perfecting his own person. How would this benefit his superiors? How could he call himself a good disciple? Since even you talk like this, it is no wonder that certain common fools continue to claim that they have done something for their teacher. But to be an official, a disciple, or a son and not to follow the instructions of lord, father, and teacher amounts to the crime of great contrariness.[22] It cannot be called anything else. (63.137) The good son, good official, and good disciple that you describe doesn't commit a criminal offense, but that's all. How foolish! How can you call this "being good"?

This is [exactly] why common men are so foolish, as has been obvious for quite some time. We really know that it is true when we go by what you have just said: they have lost the right way, they are getting involved in corrupt practices, and they have long been in confusion and doubt. That is why heaven, which alone knows all this, is angry and displeased. So calamities are increasing and are inherited and passed on from one generation to the next. All that men who behave as you have described achieve is to safeguard their own person and not commit an offense. Their great folly is even greater when they claim to have performed meritorious deeds on behalf of heaven, earth, and other human beings. You must heed this! What you say does not yet fully agree with heaven's intentions. But when I ask you to speak, this is not aimed at you. I wish to see the right and wrong of the common people and what they would consider a great crime. By encouraging you to speak, I have seen that what they deem to be crooked and what they deem straight is not so.[23] You really understand, don't you?

Yes, I do.

All right, it's clear to you. (63.138) I had originally thought I would talk to you only until I had made you understand. I could see that you were eager and getting better each day. Therefore, I have had serious talks with you. I have taught you what heaven and earth want, explained to you why emperors and kings suffer bitterly, why the hundred families are grief-stricken, and how the ten thousand beings and plants have lost their proper order. There is nothing else to take care of now that I have explained to you the model [set by heaven] and talked about its meaning. You must simply make the effort to remember it.

Yes, I will.

I had certain students I could not talk to, so with them I did not study to the end. That is why my teachings *(dao)* have not yet been made public. You understand, don't you?[24]

Yes, I do.

You may go; you have learned it all![25]

Well, the Celestial Master has been so kind as to permit us to speak directly,[26] without reserve. The more worthy the lord, the more loyal is his official; the more illustrious the teacher, the less reserved is the disciple in what he says.

That's right. You are aware of the gist of it. Speak up.

Now if we assume that in heaven and on earth there really are methods to become a tran-scendent and avoid death and that there are recipes against old age, how can we find them?

Yes, this is a good question. Well, they can be obtained. Up in heaven there are as many drugs for becoming transcendent and avoiding death as there is grain in a large granary. There are as many garments for transcendents as there are bales of cloth in a large government compound.[27] Abodes for transcendents are as numerous as the rooms in a county office.[28] Stay forever with great *dao* and you will be permitted to enter heaven. Someone of great *dao* may find room in the relay stations reserved for spirits and other numinous beings, just as a man with moral achievements (*dao de* 道 德) is permitted to stay in the county's rest house.[29] Up in heaven one does not begrudge human beings the garments of transcendents or recipes against death but does not give them away too easily. Heaven will not give any recipes against death or the garments of a transcendent to any man who has not gained merit with heaven and earth. It will not give them to any man who has not managed to cure their big ills, who does not let Yin and Yang *qi* move freely and is of benefit to the three lu-minaries, the four seasons, the five phases and spirits, and other numinous beings of heaven and earth. Heaven will offer[30] such special and rare things only to a man of merit. Should you wish to see some strong proof of this, just take a look at the grain in the large granaries or at the bales of cloth [stored] in government precincts. There are so many pecks in a large granary, but a man without merit and moral achieve-ment won't be able to get a single pint. Should someone trespass he will enter prison, be charged directly, and await sentencing for this crime. This proves it.

Nowadays men are truly evil. They don't fulfill heaven's intentions. This is why heaven does not let them have all its powerful medicinal substances. (63.139) Instead, day after day it sends demons, spirits, and other vital beings to investigate and flog men who misbehave.[31] That is why there is no end to illness and death occurs in many forms. For the same reason, county offices quell disorder by filling prisons with criminals, many of whom die a violent death. This is what it means. A man who performs meritorious deeds on behalf of emperors and kings has many palaces; he can always avail himself of official grain and bales of cloth for his clothes and food.

Heaven[32] demands that emperors and kings always attempt to govern in unison with good men (*shan ren* 善人). Why would it begrudge its love? It's the ruler's task to [join forces] with all worthy and learned men and bring peace to the world (*ping zhi* 平治).[33] But a lord without worthy officials, a father without filial sons, or a teacher without obedient and capable students is more grieved than can be put into words. This is why the Three Majestic Rulers of early antiquity laid down their official insignia and remained free from business and without worries. [Therefore,] their officials were attentive and honest. They cared for their lord, soothed his eternal sorrow, and ventured to help him bring peace to the world. They also searched heaven on his behalf for methods to become transcendent and offered them to the lord so that he might live a long time. Some men earned great merit. The most meritorious became transcendents and went away to administer the affairs of heaven. Thus heaven provided them with clothes and food. There is clear proof for this; I don't tell lies.

Since middle antiquity, men have often intercepted the true teachings *(dao)* out of jealousy. Moreover, they have deceived each other with mistaken doctrines *(dao)* and made fools of other people. In consequence, worthy men are rare, so that both lord and officials suffer bitterly, don't manage to bring peace to the world, and often don't live long. This is not only caused by the mistakes men have made in late antiquity. It reaches back. You know that it involves certain great faults, don't you?

Yes, I do.

Now there are so many rare recipes and so many garments for transcendents in heaven that they cannot be counted by hundreds of thousands, yet a man without great merit won't get any. In the same way, there are the county office's rooms, money, grain, and cloth in the realms of men. If someone always holds onto great *dao,* his family will never be obscure, but a person without merit and virtue can't get one peck of grain, one single coin, or one inch of cloth. This proves it.

Since there have been fewer and fewer true teachings *(dao)* since early and middle antiquity, the true method for living long and becoming transcendent can no longer be found. So someone who just happens[34] to live a long time truly becomes this world's most long-lived man.

Why is this so?

If true teachings and true virtue were ample there would be lots of upright *qi*. In consequence, few men would suffer from illness and many would live long lives. [But] when wicked and fraudulent writings abound there is much wrong and evil *qi*. (63.140) For this reason men often fall ill and don't live long lives. This [follows] the model of heaven as it is *(tian ziran zhi fa).*[35] Therefore in antiquity many lords lived a long time because the officials [who served] the Three Majestic Rulers often adhered to the true doctrine *(dao).* The Five Emperors did not live quite as long because their officials only followed the true doctrine sometimes. Officials [in service] of the Three Kings knew still less about it, and so the kings did not fare as well as the Five Emperors. It was unfortunate for the Five Hegemons[36] that their officials presented them with cleverly[37] faked writings, which did not contain a single true sentence. Thus many of them died young, which is a clear proof. The few of them who lived long lives were indeed the world's longest living. You must cherish this knowledge!

I do!

So when wise and worthy men wish to predict the future they look at what is auspicious and what is ill-omened in the portents that they have received. Then they know for themselves where security and risk are, where advantage and where danger. Whoever receives prophetic texts of excellent quality rules in the best possible way. Anyone who received texts of medium quality would resemble an average man. But to get some of inferior quality points to a lowly man.

What do you mean?

In regard to receiving texts, the Three Majestic Rulers had the best texts, the Five Emperors average ones, and those of the Three Kings were below average. Whoever gets the texts [which were in use under] the Five Hegemons has the most inferior ones.

How do you recognize these texts?

A good question! Texts that teach how government happens on its own without [the use of] punishment are best. Those that set forth advice and commandments that are respected and that instill some fear are of medium value. Texts that teach how to govern through moderate punishment come next. All texts that teach a lot about deceptive skills and how to make lies look true, how to forget about precedents (*fa* 法), how to handle memorials in a frivolous and superficial manner, and how to rule through a violent use of the penal code are quite wicked. Not to adhere to the true teachings results in the way [things were run by] the Hegemons. The wise and worthy of antiquity were able to observe heaven's instructions, so they knew for themselves the difference between magnificent and inferior.

Should [heaven] want to instruct, whom would it send to assist a king?[38]

For this purpose heaven might perhaps bring forth worthy officials to support a [king's] reign, in the same way as a family that is moving upward is bound to have worthy sons; Yellow River and Luo might for this purpose issue auspicious texts and maps to bring about a contract.[39] This is how it is. Do you understand?

Yes, I do!

So we may assume that you have gained more insight. When a family is on the verge of perishing, its young men are violent and bad. When a ruler is about to fall, heaven doesn't send worthy and honest men in his support. When a family[40] is about to die out, sons and grandsons refuse to stick to the true and upright *dao* and virtue. Instead, they take an interest in what is artful, deceptive, frivolous, and superficial and set up evil and vile models. (63.141) This makes a family unlucky and rebellious. It would prosper, if [its members] were to search for true teachings and true virtue, rare texts, and special recipes and thus save themselves. For a ruler to prosper, heaven must give him true texts, true teachings, and true virtue. Good men would reign in unison with him, Yellow River and Luo would from time to time send their advice, natural calamities and other harmful events would decrease while auspicious portents would increase, and [heaven] would respond more and more favorably. This proves it.

Excellent, indeed!

You may go now. You must work hard. You must perform meritorious deeds on behalf of heaven; you must help the virtuous lord to gain insight.

What do you mean by that?

You wish to gain a lot of merit in your service of heaven. But you are at present in the position of having left the world behind.[41] You can't gain credit through your conduct of government affairs. How will you do deeds for heaven?

So what should I do?

You must convey writings to a virtuous lord. Being heaven's son, he must be guided by its wishes. If he were to rule accordingly, he would repay heaven for its great deeds and make the world safe and his own person prosperous. Then you would also become happy and secure a long life for yourself.

Fine. Yes, I will do so.

You may go now. We have finished discussing the three types of behavior. Point them out to worthy officials and also to the common people, and later generations will do well. This is what you must do.

I hardly dare to accept this task.

But to do nothing else but look after your own profit and then to say that you are doing good deeds is to dismiss heaven, lord, father, and teacher.

We could say that the type of behavior you have talked about extends from conduct slightly above average to great foolishness that involves more evil feelings and wicked acts than can be named. Distribute these writings and each person [who lives now], in the age of late antiquity, can truly conceive which actions are of benefit to heaven, lord, father, and teacher. Certainly not the type of behavior that is of profit only to oneself![42] Heaven knows what man's heart is like![43] This is why so many people fall ill.

Fine. I can now see what heaven's intentions are. Your words have been enlightening.

We may say that you learn easily. Nowadays, a number of very foolish men trust their own foolish hearts and not what they are told by others. This is their mistake. It destroys heaven's way and makes emperors and kings suffer bitterly. It all begins with certain ignorant scholars who are envious of true *dao* and excellent virtue and say that these two are not good enough. Instead, they trust in ways of thinking that neglect benevolence. Since heaven suffers bitterly, it has sent me to publish these texts so that a virtuous ruler can achieve his aim, (63.142) [that is,] safeguard his own person and bring peace to his reign. It is precisely for this reason that the highest majestic lords of early antiquity obtained favor with heaven and shared its opulence. Do you know what I mean?

Yes, I do.

All right. Now that you have understood you may go. Think about it.

Yes, I will. I would like to ask one more question.

Go ahead.

Why are the texts in which you outline what we must learn from this model altogether as many as there are?

This is a good question. We may say that you understand what *dao* wants. Well, the world's love for good and for evil is expressed in various degrees and through different intentions. *Dao,* although identical in general, contains many small differences.

By dividing the whole into 11,520 characters,[44] [we manage] to have heaven's way presented in small sections[45] and the kings' way in minute detail. But if we were to speak *(dao)* about the whole of heaven and earth, up above and down below, reaching in the eight directions and to the six extremities, from an outside and an inside perspective, we would have to say that these writings were insufficient. Can you understand this?

Yes I can.

All right, you know. Give these writings to a lord who follows *dao* and its virtue to make them public. Let the common people think for themselves about gain and loss. Thereby you will dissolve the anxiety of heaven and earth, safeguard emperors and kings, and make their reigns peaceful. You are aware of this?

Yes, I am.

You may go. Never forget to stay in control of yourself!

No, I won't.[46]

NOTES

1.   See above, section 44.

2.   See *Baopu zi neipian* 3 *"Dui su"* 對 俗, p. 11.

3.   The text reads *guo jun chen* 國 君 臣. The inclusion of *jun* does not agree with the context and must be seen as the result of negligence. *Jun chen* frequently occurs as a pair.

4.   According to the *Lun yu* (1.6) a young man should be *jin* 謹 and *xin* 信 (attentive and faithful) or, in D. C. Lau's (1979: 60) rendering, "sparing in speech but trustworthy in what he says." They occur together in the TPJ only in this section. They are labels for the mainstream moral values that the disciple believes in.

5.   I read *xin* 信 (trust) as *yan* 言 (speech).

6.   Here wrong conduct consists of *fan fei li xie* 犯 非 歷 邪. The four characters also occur in a passage on reckless, irresponsible, uncivilized men, who are said to see some merit in such conduct (TPJ 196.603, layer B).

7.   The speaker of *nuo* 諾 (yes) is difficult to determine. The dictionaries tell us that it is a sign of agreement mainly used by someone superior in rank (as Zheng Xuan [127–200] comments in *Li ji, "Qu li"* 典 禮, *shang*, p. 1240a). Throughout layer A this is the Celestial Master, and in layer B (see TPJ 198.612) it is the Celestial Lord. There are instances, however, when only the disciple can be the speaker (see, for instance, TPJ 47.54). When we must assume it is the Celestial Master who is saying *nuo*, as in the phrase at hand, it functions as an introductory particle, often followed by the command to sit still and listen carefully (TPJ 55.83; 59.102; 61.114 and 118).

8.   This can be Yin, Yang, and their intercourse (see section 61), heaven, earth, and men

(TPJ 79.196), or heaven, earth, and the space between them (TPJ 103.248). The communion of the three points to general cosmic harmony; cf. Espesset 2002a.

9. The existence of life-prolonging and death-avoiding treatments and medications was a generally accepted fact of Han dynasty life; see, for instance, Akahori 1989.

10. Here the Master tells us again that his movement has lasted for a while, that it has not always been successful, and that it has been conducted in different ways.

11. This is expressed by the three-character expression *wang fu gui* 往付歸.

12. "*Qi* of peace" (*ping qi*) can be used as another term for great peace (see above, section 42), but the term can also point to a certain potentiality. It often indicates an opportunity to achieve peace, an opportunity that men must utilize in order to finally achieve actual peace. Since *ping qi* stems from heaven, it has splendid characteristics. It is "highest" (TPJ 140.400), "honest" (*liang;* TPJ 46.52), "honest and good" (*liang shan;* TPJ 211.672), and "all-prevailing" (*dong;* TPJ p. 649, *Chao,* part 7). Besides the *qi* of peace sent by heaven there is earth's "*qi* of peace," and the cooperation of both produces a situation of "great peace."

13. Which words are spoken by which speaker is not clear in this passage. The question raised is of some depth, taking up the issue discussed by Mengzi and Xunzi of how we can explain that men know good from bad unless we assume that they are born good. The answer given here is practical, or perhaps utilitarian: morality changes the world for the better, these changes are noticeable, and, for this reason, men like what is good. These changes resemble the course of nature, as pointed out in section 60. We like goodness in the same way that we like spring and summer.

14. Good and bad are mutually exclusive, as are management by virtue and by punishment.

15. I read *xing* 行 (conduct) for *shu* 術 (technique).

16. This passage is probably corrupt. Tentatively, I read *ji xia* 疾下 as *jiji* 疾疾. Yu (2001a: 117) understands *xia* as "with the passage of time."

17. For the expression *chou ku fu mu* 愁苦父母 (to cause parents grief), see TPJ 173.512.

18. *Laozi* 72 contrasts *zi ai* 自愛 (to look after one's own person) with *zi gui* 自貴 (to think highly of oneself). A Daoist does the first but never the second.

19. The expression "highest majesty" is here attached to "early antiquity" with little regard for the context.

20. A "worthy" is a person who is qualified for public service. The phrasing of the passage suggests that not all teachers were qualified. This agrees with what we know of practices of *fang shi* (experts in vitality techniques), and in particular of figures like Gan Ji, who was linked to the origins of a scripture on great peace. Recommendation, in a formal—linked to regional quotas—as well as in a less formal sense, was the way to official appointment (cf. Hsu 1988: 184f.).

Zi yang 自養, "nourishing one's own self," is another term for the nourishing of the vital principle *(yang xing)*, which is the art that the disciples expect to learn from the Celestial Master (see above section 47).

21. This passage touches on the fact that one individual can be both outstanding disciple and outstanding subject.

22. The term *da ni* 大逆 does not refer to a specific crime but is used to categorize crimes. Its meaning is close to that of *bu dao* 不道. The murder of father and mother, as well as acts against the reigning house and its property, fall into this category (see Hulsewe 1955: 156–68). The punishment is severe:

> In case of *da ni wu dao,* great refractoriness and impiety, [the culprit] is cut in two at the waist; the father, mother, wife and children, brothers and sisters [of the culprit] are all, without distinction between old and young, publicly executed. (Hulsewe 1955: 158; see *Han shu* 81.3355 and 49.2302)

23. Here the Master gives voice to a characteristic element of layer A dialogue: the disciple expresses what the people at large think (see sections 41 and 64; TPJ 103.241). By refuting the disciple the Master corrects what we might call public opinion.

24. The scenario depicted in the TPJ is not the Master's first attempt to start a missionary movement. The problem was—and we may perhaps gather it still is—the disciples' commitment.

25. The following dialogue is closely linked to the first. It points to the rewards that await someone whose conduct is "excellent," as the Master understands the term.

26. With Yu (2001a: 120), I read *zhi* 直 (direct) for *zhen* 真 (true).

27. The situation in heaven is a replica of life on earth. Medicine and garments are plentiful for the spirits residing in heaven, but even in heaven distribution is linked to merit, in this case in the fulfillment of celestial duties; see TPJ 188.579, layer unclear. The TPJ authors agree with hagiographic accounts of the way a transcendent lives. His appearance was said to undergo changes (TPJ p. 221, *Chao,* part 4), and he was seen as riding through the clouds on a dragon (TPJ 108.289; p. 403, *Chao,* part 4; 187.571, layer B). The text provides such different answers to the questions why and how to become transcendent that these answers can help distinguish textual layers. In the Celestial Master sections of the text (layer A) it is taken for granted that men want to live long, just as they want to eat, drink, and love. The desire for longevity is used to set men on the right track, as a short *Chao* passage puts it: "Since they are greedy for life, they won't dare do wrong" (TPJ p. 223, part 4, probably layer A). In section 50, men will become transcendent, that is, avoid death, when the reign of great peace has begun, and in the first half of the section at hand men prove to be good by providing others with the means to live long. As opposed to this, layer B material proposes that the search for longevity is man's main interest and promises help. Layer B explains the function of the celestial "bureau for long life" *(zhang shou zhi cao* 長壽之曹 TPJ 179.531, layer B) and provides insight into the functioning of the celestial bureaucracy (TPJ 188.579, layer not clear; 199.614, layer B).

28. Access to such rooms, and in particular to county postal relay stations (*xian guan you ting* 縣官郵亭), was strictly regulated, not only here on earth but also, as we are told, in heaven and in the netherworld. In heaven such places are destined for *shen xian ren* 神仙人, spiritlike transcendents; those on earth are for the worthy; and those belowground are where good spirits and good demons are expected to stay (TPJ p. 698, *Chao*, part 8). There were similar rules for official rest houses (*zhuan she* 傳舍). See TPJ 199.614, layer B; cf. Espesset 2002b: 13.

29. The system of official recommendation made it obligatory for officials to regularly recommend "the virtuous and the wise" (see Ch'ü 1972: 205) who were entitled to enjoy certain privileges.

30. I read *ci* 賜 (to give) for *ci* 此 (this).

31. Lian Shaoming (2002) refers to this passage in a discussion of the different spirits and the roles they play in the Qin dynasty Yunmeng bamboo slips. He shows that there are parallels to a list of spirits set forth in TPJ section 107. In the passage at hand (referred to by an incorrect chapter number), he reads *wu gu* 無故 for *wu zhuang* 無狀, so we would have to translate it as "and flog even innocent men." My reading relies on the mention of special wickedness in the previous and following passages.

32. With Yu (2001a: 120), I read *tian* 天 (heaven) for *ren* 人 (men).

33. *Rou* 柔 (weak, or perhaps conciliatory) is understood as *ru* 儒 (learned). The *Laozi* praises the *dao*-like quality of *rou:* "What is of all things most yielding can overwhelm that which is of all things most hard" (*Laozi* 43), or "Truly, the hard and mighty are cast down; the soft and weak set on high (*Laozi* 76, translations by Waley 1934). However, *xian* 賢 *rou* is a confusing combination of characters, and *rou* can stand for *ru* (educated), based on the two characters' joint meaning of "weak" and their phonetic resemblance; see *Shuo wen jie zi*, p. 681b. Throughout the TPJ, when *rou* is added to *xian* (TPJ p. 304, *Chao*, part 5; 160.451; 66.160), the two characters point to a person who has administrative skills, as does the character *xian* on its own and as does the combination *xian ru* (TPJ 59.102; 62.128; 65.155; 66.162; 100.230; 129.335 and passim throughout layer A).

34. With Yu (2001a: 121), I correct *guo* 過 (mistake) to *yu* 遇 (to happen).

35. While TPJ ideas about the preservation of life have many roots—Harada (1984: 72–76) points to the *Laozi*, the *Yi jing*, and Han dynasty cosmological speculation set forth in the *Huainan zi*, for instance—the text is also in itself an authority on the subject. It is self-evident for the Celestial Master and his adepts that a man's thoughts and actions influence the quality of his *qi*, which then decides the length of his life; they do not need to discuss it. It is one of the Master's basic doctrines and stated clearly and authoritatively throughout the text, as demonstrated by Harada (1984).

36. Throughout the TPJ the rule of the *ba*, the "Hegemons," is criticized, as it is in the *Huainan zi* (chap. 13 *"Fan lun,"* p. 20b) and much of the earlier tradition. However, in the second century C.E. the powerful and efficient political methods of certain Warring States Hegemons were reconsidered and newly appraised. Cui Shi (fl. 145–67) came

to the conclusion that at certain times the reign of a hegemon would be preferable to that of the true, virtuous king (Hsiao 1979: 535).

37. With Yu (2001a: 121), I correct *gong* 功 (merit) to *qiao* 巧 (clever).

38. *Wang* 往 (to go) is read as *wang* 王 (king).

39. For the expression *quan shu* 券書, see above, section 51.

40. In this section *renjia* 人家 and *jiaren* 家人 both seem to mean "family." Yu 2001a: 122 understands *jiaren* as "one of the family."

41. See above, section 62.

42. With Yu (2001a: 122), I read *zeng* 增 (increase) as *zeng* 曾 in the meaning of *nai* 乃. In this passage, the Celestial Master makes it clear that to seek *li* 利 , here in the sense of profit, for oneself is wrong. His warning against selfishness includes a critique of concentrating on the search for personal longevity to the detriment of one's social obligations. It is left open how such a critique is to be reconciled with the demand for nourishing one's own vitality, a demand that is stressed in section 47 and throughout the text, as, for example, in this section (on p. 136), when an excellent student is said to understand the art of nourishing his own person.

43. The two missing characters are read as *ruo ci* 若此 (like this).

44. This is the figure the astrologer Zhang Heng (ca. 100 C.E.) gives for the number of stars: *Ling xian*, p. 4a.

45. With Yu (2001a: 123), I read the final particle *er* 耳 as *ju* 具 (to write out).

46. The summary says:

> This section analyzes [the relationship] between lord and official, father and son, master and disciple. It makes known their good and bad conduct and portents of success and failure.

· How to Subdue Others
by Means of *Dao* and
Not by Means of Severity

This section contrasts the effects of moral example with those of physical violence
and clever stratagems. Violent conduct is seen as wrong for a number of reasons:
the spirits detest it, it resembles the way criminals act, and it causes cosmic disorder
by interrupting the flow of information between heaven and men. However, this is
only one aspect of the issue. What must also be considered is heaven's own use of
violence when it punishes men by thunder and lightning. A second contrast thus
emerges, a contrast between violent action and the use of force intended to control
such action and protect its victims.

The arguments put forth in this section are not new. The Celestial Master repeats
concerns that belong to the main tradition of political thought. Wang Fu expressed
them in the following terms:

> So heaven installed a ruler not because it was partial to him as a person and to
> let him employ the people as his servants, but so that he should punish violent
> action, eradicate harmful influences, and be of benefit to the masses.[1]

This point, however, is emphasized in a unique way in the TPJ. The Master uses
strong words to accuse the oppressor and the clever manipulator who treats others
as if they were animals. To intimidate others so that they don't dare speak up against
a perpetrator of violence is to treat them as badly as bandits might do.

This section elaborates upon previous comparisons in the TPJ between rule by virtuous example and the application of punishment. The use of violence gains a new dimension because the discussion of violent action is not, as is customary, limited to the apparatus of the state and its administration, and the Master speaks up in defense of what we could term strong government. Although this seems to contradict arguments made elsewhere in the TPJ, it can be explained by a difference in perspective. The ideal ruler is expected to use violent means only in retaliation, and to protect the people from certain powerful tormentors. Such an expectation suits the situation of the second century C.E., when a weak political center and deficient state apparatus were surrounded by strong and independent-minded local magnates.

.　　.　　.

(64.142) Step forward, Perfected! Should men in general use severity and deceit to overcome[2] others? Or is this wrong? Think carefully about what you say.

Well, why would men go about overcoming others by severity and deceit? So that they might become orderly and upright.

Oh! Deep inside, your knowledge is just like that of everyone else. We must not yet call you "Perfected of highest rank." The words you have just uttered resemble what everyone would say. You don't understand what heaven wants: what a Perfected of highest rank says is identical with what heaven wants. (64.143) Now demons and spirits detest a man who overcomes others by severity and deceit, and they are not the only ones to detest him. Yin and Yang spirits do the same. And, again, Yin and Yang spirits are not the only ones who do. Since the division between heaven and earth this is what the world has suffered and how it was put to order. When someone subdues others by force, he does not reign over them properly, so the people he suppresses become resentful. But demons and spirits help them, and so do heaven and earth. Since heaven and earth come to help, men must also rein in those who suppress others, and help to subdue those who subdue others.[3]

Therefore, when men of outstanding wisdom who served the ancient Three Majestic Rulers triumphed, they ruled through perfect *dao* and virtue. They never oppressed others with severity and deceit. Should you use such means and also punishments you are nothing but a thief, a robber, and a bandit. That is how such men oppress others. How could a lord who uses such methods distinguish himself? Would he look any different? And yet, this is what you said! Wasn't this foolish? Do you understand that this is what has caused uproar in heaven and on earth ever since middle antiquity? In early antiquity, a lord of *dao* and virtue never used severity and deceit to rule the people. In middle antiquity, laws were promulgated but nobody dared make use of them. In late antiquity, some severity, deceit, and penalties were implemented to govern the people. This led to some minor disorder. Certain men of great foolishness promoted the Hegemons' method of government. They created fear among their clients (shizhong 土眾) through strict regulations and harsh penalties, so that petty officials and the population at large rose in numerous rebellions.

Therefore, rule by *dao* and everything will be pure and bright; govern by virtue and both advance and retreat will be in measure. Thus, [men's] advance and retreat have been difficult to control in late antiquity, since deceit has become rampant. Since heaven rules through *dao*, its shape is pure and the three luminaries are bright. Since earth rules by virtue, it bears [its load] patiently. (64.144) Since man rules through the harmonious [intercourse between Yin and Yang], he advances and retreats in frequent alternation and what he says is versatile and without constancy. Heaven's order is first, earth's order is in the middle, and man's order is at the bottom.[4] What is at the very bottom will move upward.

How does one know that one is at the bottom?

It means that advance and retreat lack constancy and that exit and entry are explained differently.[5] [Man's order] is the lowest of the three *qi* [of heaven, earth, and man]. What has reached its lowest point must move upward. Once we reach *dao*, we will obtain great peace, [which is] just like heaven. Once we reach virtue, there is an average level of peace, similar to earth. On reaching harmony, a small amount of disorder comes forth, as is the case with man. Disorder increases once severity, deceit, and punishments are in place, as it would under the rule of the Hegemons when punishments played a big role. What you have just said in your answer about the use of severity and deceit throws into confusion what heaven means to tell us.

Now you have said that one must not use severity and penalties. Why does [heaven] employ the terror of thunder and lightning to keep men in check?[6]

That is a good question. You have understood what I want to say. The reason why thunder and lightning keep men in check is that rulers who in their exalted position act with evil intent make light of antagonizing others. Man is the most honored and important being. Heaven reins in anyone who has human beings eat the same food as the six domestic animals, and helps men who are oppressed and have to eat such food. It detests [anyone who acts like this]. So [it holds true for] every man, great and small alike, that anyone who makes light of antagonizing others comes under [heaven's] control, which pities and helps the oppressed.

So when a lord overcomes others he must do so only by means of *dao* and its virtue. He must not overpower and grieve them in a cruel and offensive manner. Severity and deceit must be employed only to restrain unruly men. One cannot bring men to submission by *dao* and virtue if they want to act without *dao*. Such men must be subdued in the way mentioned, just as the Duke of Thunder[7] keeps unruly men in check. But this must not be a constant practice since it offends heaven's intentions. If someone wants to obtain favor with heaven and earth, he must proceed through *dao* and its virtue.

That is why the wise and worthy of old esteemed the use of *dao* and virtue, and won men over through benevolence and love, and it was not deemed right to oppress others through severity, punishments, and terror. Should someone continue[8] to overawe, intimidate, and subdue others by such crooked means, the highest majestic *qi* of great peace won't come to support his reign. Since this is so the men over whom he rules will not agree with him.[9] Grief stricken, they won't dare to speak up from fear, just as men whose clothes have been stolen by a robber might not dare to speak up, even though they know the culprit quite well. Instead, they might use fine words and call the robber "general" and "supreme ruler." Or men might be too weak to appeal on their own account (64.145) and won't dare speak up. We must call all of this "rupture" and "lack of pervasion."[10] It prevents the celestial *qi* of Yin and Yang from being in agreement.

Heaven is in command of a man who rules over others and sets him the basic task of keeping the strong under control and supporting the lowly and the weak. But certain petty officials are cruel. They intimidate and frighten others with severity, or scare and terrify them with intrigues and deceit. When *qi* of peace is about to arrive and a virtuous lord reigns, it must be feared that upright *qi* might become perverted by these [wrongdoings]. This is why I inform you. Pass it on to a lord of supreme virtue. Let him inform his worthy advisors and the people at large. If petty officials and the whole population were to think for themselves about how to maintain order, this would benefit those in power. One must be careful to avoid disorder. You understand, don't you?

Yes, I do!

All right, now that you have understood you may go. You must always watch your words. Don't talk nonsense. Heaven keeps track of men.[11]

No, I won't!

Nobody is perfect. The best thing to do is to ask.

Yes, indeed![12]

NOTES

1. See *Qian fu lun* 15 *"Ban lu"* 班 祿, p. 161–63; cf. Hsiao 1979: 538. Using quotations from the *Xunzi* and the *Huainan zi*, Peng Duo's annotation supports the idea that this was a common perception.

2. The term used for "to overcome" is *sheng fu* 勝 服, which does not seem to occur in the dictionaries. However, Schuessler (1987: 171 and 539) gives evidence of the meaning "to overcome" in regard to external as well as internal enemies for both characters.

3. This is nothing more than a new formulation of time-honored political principles, contrasting "punitive action" with "aggressive war," as does, for instance, Mengzi (1B8 and 2B8), when he evaluates the rebellions started by King Tang and King Wu or Qi's attempt to overcome Yan (cf. Hsiao 1979: 271).

4. According to *san zheng* 三 正 (three-orders) speculation, heaven's year begins with *zi*, the first earthly branch; the year of the earth with *chou*, the second branch; and man's year with *yin*, the third branch (*Han shu* 21A *"Lü li zhi,"* p. 962). This difference was supposedly reflected in calendrical arrangements, as the Zhou dynasty's year was said to have started in the eleventh month, the Shang dynasty year in the twelfth month, and the Xia year in the first month. In 104 B.C.E., calendrical reforms aligned the Han dynasty calendar with what was supposed to have been the Xia dynasty arrangement (see Kalinowski 1991: 538). The Celestial Master refers to these well-known ideas to give a certain precision to his own account of historical change.

5. The expression *jin tui* 進 退 (advance and retreat) occurs four times in this short section. It is the word for the changes between the four seasons (TPJ 59.101) and for movement and change in general (TPJ 109.294; 58.94). Knowledge of this movement is essential; the Master puts it thus:

> You want to understand [the meaning of] "complete pervasion"—[but] do you know how spirits and other numinous beings advance and retreat? (TPJ 107.281)

When the disciples don't know the answer, they are told about the nine ways of contemplation, in proper order, through which to approach *dao*. We must assume that such contemplation is directed toward the coming and going of spirits and their effects (cf. also TPJ 203.626, layer B, and p. 722, *Chao*, part 1).

In this passage, the Celestial Master stresses that advance and retreat must be kept constant, particularly where Yin and Yang are concerned (this is also expressed in TPJ p. 213, *Chao*, part 4). Given the conclusion drawn here from the lack of constancy, it must also be considered that in the *Yi jing*, advance and retreat are the movements that a change from broken to unbroken lines and vice versa represents (*Yi jing*, *"Xi ci"* A, p. 39.2). Orderly exit and entry (*chu ru* 出 入) of lines signify smooth change (*Yi jing*, *"Xi ci"* B, p. 48.7), which leaves no room for differing explanations, or for what the Celestial Master would call disorder and deceit.

The determinative force of cyclic movement plays a strong role in this particular section of the TPJ, as pointed out toward the end: the *qi* of great peace will definitely arrive, for cyclical reasons. Master, disciples, and the proper doctrine can only help the government of the day to make the best use of it.

6. The expression *qu ren* (to keep men in check) must be understood in the sense of *qu tianxia* in *Laozi* 48. The *Lun heng* chapter "On Thunder and Lightning" attests to the belief in the punishing effect of thunder.

7. The Duke of Thunder (*lei gong* 雷公) was a well-known deity. The *Huainan zi* (chap. 2 "*Chu zhen*" 俶真, p. 12a) says that the perfected "employs wind and rain and makes the Duke of Thunder his official." The TPJ explains that a person who is one with *dao* communicates with spirits and rises up to the clouds to ride on a dragon and share the abode of the Duke of Thunder (TPJ p. 306, *Chao*, part 5). *Lun heng* 23 "*Lei xu*" 雷虚, p. 303 describes how artists depicted the Duke of Thunder, with a drum in his left hand and a hammer in his right hand. Hayashi (1989: 162–66) introduces several wall paintings showing him on a wagon drawn by his helpers or by dragons and surrounded by many smaller figures with metal tools. He often appears together with the Lord of the Winds, *Feng bo* 風伯.

8. With Yu (2001a: 125), *an* 安 is corrected to *chang* 常. *An* (pacification) is rarely, if ever, used in a negative sense.

9. *Zhi* 知 (to know) is corrected to *he* 和 (to agree); see Yu 2001a: 125.

10. This passage states that the TPJ's demand for "pervasion" is driven by moral considerations, and in particular by the idea of a cohesive, comprehensive society in which happiness is general. The doctrine and its effects (*dao* and *de;* TPJ 66.160; 155.436), as well as the Master's book (TPJ 61.124), must certainly "pervade," that is, they must be distributed.

11. The phrase *tian fei ren* 天非人 is also used in TPJ 152.417 with the same meaning.

12. The summary says:

> This section analyzes and distinguishes [ways] of subduing [others], and why demons and spirits of heaven, earth and men are mischievous and why they support government.

Threefold Cooperation
and Interaction

This section, repetitive and lengthy as it is, deals with topics that are relevant to social relations and political hierarchies. The claim that the world as we know it functions only because everything is made up of three components leads the disciple to
conclude that the arrival of "the *qi* of great peace" *(taiping qi)* results from the cooperation of three. The existence of three safeguards the continuity of each single
one, or, considered from the opposite perspective, if one were missing, all three
would no longer exist. This line of argumentation points to the concept of equality. Although the demand for "threefold cooperation" is derived from the structure
of the family, its main application is in the realm of politics, where rupture and isolation are said to cause severe harm.

The Master stresses the need for cooperation in this section. A rather similar TPJ
section praises cooperation between two, which is said to bring forth a third, based
upon the observation that things are created by two hands, not just by one. Heaven
and earth, the four seasons, the five phases, man and woman, master and disciple,
ruler and official— each consist of "both hands":

"Both hands" means to work evenly together, neither moving to the fore
nor falling behind. In this way, something can be achieved. Nothing will be
achieved unless both hands work together. All activities resemble [the use of]
these two hands. Everything must find the right person. When [we] work
together with one identical aim *(tong xin)*, as both hands do, *qi* of happiness,

stability, and great peace will be established. If we don't, we won't be able to bring forth *qi* of majestic great peace in many millions of years. *Qi* of great peace always wants to come forth, just as heaven always wishes to depend on "both hands." When they never cooperate harmoniously, they lock *qi* of great peace up so that it can't get through. This brings forth unrest and disgust. The fault lies in the lack of cooperation between both hands.[1]

After he has established the need for cooperation, the Master explains how to bring it about. In doing so, he raises two issues: the submission of memorials, through which communication between the three tiers is maintained, and the allocation of tasks. He elaborates on the latter, arguing that a subordinate must always be given tasks within his capability. Otherwise, his frustration and disappointment might cause a major disturbance. Also—and this is outlined in great detail—the subordinate's performance must be continuously assessed, in a formalized manner.

It is a commonly pronounced thesis of Chinese political thought that ruler, officials, and the people depend on each other. The Celestial Master accepts this thesis, but lays stress on the people. The lower strata's moral attitudes have, as he puts it, an impact on the morality of their ruler; when they behave well, the ruler will react to their behavior, just as the natural environment does. This proposition supports the argument that the Master's audience consisted of people who were outside the official political system, or at its lowest end. Another point is more common but is of some interest, considering the place the Master attributes to heaven. He claims that the well-being of the people shows that heaven is contented.

The Master concludes that "threefold cooperation" is, for the present, the way heaven's will can be fulfilled. This was not always the case, as the disciple points out. The problem of rupture and lack of mutual understanding did not arise in antiquity because everyone adhered to *dao* and the unity that is achieved through meditation, thus making superfluous arrangements such as the division of beings into entities of three.

·   ·   ·

(65.146) *With due respect Chun salutes the Master twice: May I please ask something?* What is it that you would like to know?

In the morning I come to study; at night I return home. I always stay where it is quiet to think about what it really means. I wouldn't dare to be idle. Now your writings always

mention that qi of highest majestic great peace is about to arrive. What do you mean by
"high," "majestic," "great," "peace," and "qi"?[2]

Now you throw everything into question! All of a sudden you wish to inquire about the meaning of certain subtle words!

The reason is this: I want to learn from you everything about these writings, and they often say "highest majestic qi is about to arrive." I cannot understand what this means. If I don't ask after your secrets—you are heaven's enlightened teacher—I am afraid I won't have another chance of finding out. So how should I dare not ask all I can?

What you have said is right and will remain so for ten thousand generations. When heaven's perfect *dao*, great virtue, and full benevolence arrive, the majestic numinous[3] will want men to act quickly. That is why heaven's *qi* has touched your heart so that you raise questions from morning to night. The model set by heaven is so distinct[4] that I am quite perplexed.

Yes. Sit quietly and I will explain to you the meaning of these characters so that it will be transmitted until the end of time. Well, the character *shang* 上 (high) consists of the stroke for "one."[5] In the center, there is another "one" in the vertical direction. Moving upward there is contained yet another "one." Altogether the character for "high" has three single strokes for "one." It is called "high" because the character reaches upward without being cut short and does not move back downward. (65.147) There is nothing above this character. The opposite of "high" is *xia* 下 (low), which consists of the stroke for "one," with another stroke for "one" in the center, in the vertical direction. Moving downward there is contained another "one." We call this character "low" because it moves downward without any chance to turn upward. The intention is always to move downward, on and on to the deepest point, until there is nothing further down below, like mud, for example, which tends to sink into the ground and become soil. Soil is thus at the very bottom, with nothing beneath it. The character for "high" always moves upward and can't turn back downward, like clean water, for example, which tends to move upward and turn into sky ("heaven"), which is highest of all and thus sets the model. Each word has its own character and its own definition. This holds true for all we undertake, and this is how models promulgated by wise men always reflect heaven's intentions.

To stick to the character "one" (予 一) and aim upward is "to divine" (*bu* 卜). "To divine" means to raise a question. If you divine without interruption, all the while wishing to move upward, you are on the road to a peak of good fortune. That is why the character "high" has the character *bu* (to divine) right above the stroke for "one," while "low" has this character beneath the stroke for "one." "To divine" is "to question." If you are always intent on raising questions, you move downward until you cannot go any further down. So if you move too far in aiming downward you will not manage to turn upward again. Thus, "high" [is the character for something that] never has anything above it, and when we say that someone's reign is moving in an upward direction, we mean that it matches heaven's will and has nothing above it.

Excellent! The illustrious teacher has been kind enough to explain to me the character "high." I would also like to hear about the character "majestic" (huang 皇).

The character "majestic" consists of the elements "one" (*yi* 一), "sun" (*ri* 日), and "king" (*wang* 王).[6] The "one" [that is] above "sun" is the sky (*tian*, "heaven"). Heaven has the figure of one. Obtaining the sun, [something majestic] shines forth in great brightness and is king. Hence, when written down, "one," "sun," and "king" make up the character "majestic." "One" stands for heaven. All three of them— heaven, sun, and king—rule. So three rulers jointly make up the character we call "majestic." To be majestic means that someone's spirit has gained brilliance. That is why we call him "majestic."[7] To be majestic means to be first in the world, with nothing above.[8] (65.148)

Excellent! You have been so kind as to explain the character "majestic." I would like to hear about the characters "great," "peace," and "qi."

"Great" is "big." It means to achieve big things, as heaven does, which is big in all respects. Nothing is bigger than heaven. "Peace" means that a reign is completely balanced (*tai ping jun* 太平均) so that all activities are kept in order, without further jealousy and selfishness. "Peace" resembles the way in which earth remains below us. It is in charge of keeping balance (*ping* 平). This happens in the same way in which a man who sows good seeds reaps well, while someone who sows evil reaps evil. A man who really exerts himself will have a good harvest,[9] while the harvest of someone who invests only a little energy will be poor.

"*Qi*" means heaven's *qi* enjoys creating life beneath heaven, and earth's *qi* likes to nourish what is above earth. It is the model for *qi* to be active below heaven and above earth. When Yin and Yang get together, they create harmony. When we include the harmonious intercourse between these two there are three *qi* that nourish all beings and objects. No more damage will occur once these three *qi* love and pervade each other. "Great" is "big," "peace" is "upright," "*qi*" nurtures by making harmony pervasive. Rule through these three and great peace, harmony, and great uprightness will prevail. Then might we say that *qi* of great peace has arrived.

Excellent! This is saying nothing less than that qi *of heaven, earth, and their harmo-*

nious intercourse must interact with each other and rule in unison. Am I right? And that in all activities three must get together?

Excellent! What you have said agrees with the model set by heaven. If emperors and kings were to copy it they would reign as if they were spirits *(shen).* Well, I will tell you all, and you must, as it suits you, write it all down.

Yes, I will.

When *qi* of the primordial, of what is as it is, and of great harmony [between Yin and Yang] interact with each other, combine their energy, and are of the same mind they are for a while indistinct and not yet in any shape.[10] When these three *qi* congeal into form, they bring forth heaven and earth.

When heaven, earth, and the harmony between them get together, combine their strength, and are of the same mind, they create all objects and beings *(fan wu),* which then interact with the three luminaries, combine their efforts, and, all thinking alike, illuminate heaven and earth.

When the hardness and softness in all objects that is derived from the five phases interacts with the harmony between them (65.149), they will, combining their efforts and intentions, bring forth the ten thousand plants and beings.[11] When *qi* of the four seasons, Yin and Yang, and the harmonious intercourse that exists between heaven and earth interact, combine their efforts, and are of the same mind, they give rise to the wealth *(wuli* 物利) of heaven and earth.[12]

When the first, second, and third months of each season interact, combine their efforts, and are of the same mind, each presents one aspect [of the year]. When the earth's heights, deep valleys, and plains pervade one another, combine their efforts, and are of one mind, they nurture the produce of heaven and earth. When male and female reptiles and insects in mutual agreement[13] work together and are of the same mind, they continue their species.

When man and woman get together, combine their efforts, and are of the same mind, they bring forth children. When three individuals join forces and are of one mind, they create a family. When lord, official, and the people get together, combine their efforts, and are in agreement, they build a country. They all receive life from primordial *qi,* what is as it is, and heaven and earth. Whenever three parties interact, *dao* can come about.[14] When three beings in agreement stay with each other forever, combining their efforts and being of the same mind, they fulfill one joint task, achieving one common objective.

It would be disastrous if one [of the three] were amiss.[15] Yang on its own, without Yin, could not bring forth life, and all order (*zhi* 治) would break down. The problem would be the same if there were Yin but not Yang. The species could not be continued if there were Yin and Yang but no intercourse (*he* 和) between them. A breakdown of order would certainly occur. So if there were heaven but not earth, beings and plants would have nothing to grow from. If there were earth but not heaven, they would have no way to obtain life. If there were heaven and earth one next to the other without having intercourse, beings and plants would not hold onto each other and rear themselves. Thus a male cannot give life on his own, and a female cannot nurture on her own. If male and female cannot bring forth children, how will they set up a family and be called father and mother? (65.150) So it is heaven's model that there must always be three who get together to create something.

This is why, in their profound knowledge of the conditions of heaven (*tian qing* 天情), the wise men of the past reigned in close resemblance to heaven['s order]. Thus the lord was father, like heaven, the official was mother, like earth, and the people were children, as if they were the harmonious intercourse [between father and mother]. Heaven commands all beings in their confusion to interact as groups of three, combine their energy, and be of the same mind. Then they can achieve one common objective, build one family, and form one body. Heaven makes them depend on each other. None of the three must be amiss. Should one of them be grief-stricken and not play its role, all three risk destruction. Thus only when the lord depends on officials, officials depend on the people, the people depend on officials, and officials depend on the lord can they achieve their common objective.

Should one not suffice, all three would remain incomplete. Thus, we would not call a lord without people and officials "lord." Officials and people without a lord would not really be officials and people. Disorder would occur if they were to remain without a lord. They would not be able to put [their affairs] in order and become good officials and good subjects. The three depend on each other to take up their position. Only in relation to each other can they become [what they are]. So lord, officials, and people must match the model set by heaven. The three must interact, combine their efforts, and be of one mind. Together they will become like one family, in the same way as husband, wife, and children are one family only because they rely on each other. This is heaven's essential *dao*. In this way, a man's head, feet, and stomach form one body. None of them can be done away with. Should one be gone, [what was left] would not suffice and would not make a man. This is the cipher of what is as it is in heaven and on earth.

It is for this reason that the wise men of old took heaven as their model and that a man must find a good wife to conduct his affairs with her. Only then will there be good children. Man resembles a lord, the wife an official, and the children the people. The way in which heaven commands that a country be ruled [for the ruler] is to befriend wise and intelligent officials. Through her goodness, a wife makes children agreeable. A good official ensures the people live in harmony. Only a good wife gives birth to good children. None but a good official brings about good people. If people and officials both love to do good they are able to allow their superiors to rest securely forever.[16] If you want proof of this, [let us consider] heaven as lord and earth as official. Heaven's rain falls everywhere. When it rains on good soil it brings forth a good harvest; when it rains on bad soil, harvests are bad. This is what is meant. But father and mother must hold onto general rules and guidelines, [just as] lord and official do. The main thing is that for clothes and food they depend on their children. Men without children lack posterity. When a lord has few people, clothes and food will not suffice, which will make him suffer bitterly in his heart.[17] (65.151) Thus the way *(dao)* of ruling a country is to make people the basis. Without people, lord and officials can't conduct affairs and establish order.

For this reason, when the great worthy and wise of old were in government, they saw the people as their most pressing concern, from morning to night. They thought of the people as in a family a father and mother fret about not having children. Without children, how would they be called father and mother? How would someone be called lord if there were no people? So it is heaven's example *(fa)* that makes lord, official, and people stay together forever, under one command, sharing the same good and bad fortune and fulfilling one task. There will be general misfortune if one activity should go wrong *(shi zheng* 失 正*)*. The rules and guidelines of proper government have often been forgotten since middle antiquity. This has created the problem of inheriting [evil] and passing [it] on. So later generations have suffered a great number of widespread disasters, all because lord, officials, and people have forgotten their aim. They didn't know how to think thoroughly, care for and cooperate with each other *(xiang tong* 相 通*)*, combine their efforts, and be of one mind. Instead, they have made each other suffer bitterly.

Now should the lord remain isolated *(yi ren)* or even in deep hiding, the grievances of the four outlying regions[18] would be cut off and not become known, and his reign won't find favor with heaven. Masses of natural calamities, disasters, anomalies, and irregular events would come about, impossible to stop, and the ruler would not be able to understand what heaven and earth wish to say. This must be greatly condemned. Since the three don't combine their energy, the flow of intelligence is interrupted. Evil *qi* is tangled up and not put in order. Majestic heaven above greatly detests this, earth below greatly condemns it, and it is a big worry for emperors and kings. With numerous disasters and no solution in sight, there is great harm for the people and much illness for all beings. Since all this has come together over a long time it has not been caused by mistakes made only today in the period of late antiquity. Do you understand?

I understand that this has been going on for a while. But I really don't know what has caused it. So I ask: where do these grievances truly come from?

Well, as soon as *qi* of heaven's great peace arrives, government must find favor with heaven, and then these evils will all disappear on their own. This is why heaven has sent me to explain it all. It wants me to save [men] from these errors and bring forth the standard texts. So it has caused you to come and ask, as you do, where the trouble comes from. We don't try to resemble the model set by heaven and earth, primordial *qi*, and what is as it is, and to cooperate with each other [in groups of] three, combine our efforts, and be of one mind—that is why such [trouble] has come about. If three were to interact with each other, combine their efforts, and be of one mind they would achieve peace, great contentment, and a state without natural calamities.

I would like to know how one should conduct one's affairs.

One must stick to the model set up by heaven, as I have said earlier.[19] Heaven sets the example of combining efforts and being of the same mind in all matters. Thus it takes the three luminaries as the pattern (*wen* 文). By working together, they shine forever without interruption. (65.152) Since the appearance of celestial contracts,[20] men have conducted their affairs through writings, just as heaven [does through] the three luminaries. So from time to time heaven bids the Yellow River and the Luo to bring forth writings. Texts made by men must repeat the orders [thus bestowed by heaven]. Goodness grows and wickedness shrinks as long as men enjoy copying the model and measure of heaven's all-pervading *(dongji)* spiritlike regiment.[21]

With regard to "writings," all texts that provide information are "threefold writings."[22] A lord must properly guide his subordinates, give clear orders, issue commandments, and teach each subject to remain in his place and submit memorials that mention all the good and all the wicked that he has heard about. One can send memorials with someone who travels on foot or on a merchant's cart or even deliver them oneself, clearly stating one's own family name and style name (*zi* 字).[23] Conducting affairs in this way brings to light all the world's good and wicked acts. The lord causes heaven's *qi* to reach downward, the official lets *qi* of earth move upward, and the people let *qi* of harmonious intercourse [between heaven and earth] spread upward. You must transmit writings. Give them to a virtuous lord. Let him examine and comprehend what I say. This will bring peace and contentment. Disasters and other irregular events will cease. Not a single point is missed. My writings attempt to take heaven as their model; they are not just a senseless elaboration that I have made up. [If this were the case] heaven would slay me. You know well what a severe offense that would be, or don't you?

I do.

Anyone who wants to see how reliable my writings are need only practice what they say as soon as he has received them and heaven and earth will respond as if by echo. That is how reliable my text is. With such great and clear proof there can't be any doubt: the way *(dao)* to govern a country is to find favor with heaven and be sure of oneself. Practice proves this right. An echolike response in heaven is a clear token that heaven talks to men.

But I can see that you like helping a virtuous lord and wish to repay heaven for all it has done for you. That is why I have told you a few things. I know how wrong it would be not to tell you all.[24] Now once a lord has these writings he will reign through their clear instructions and good directives. We may say that from now on each petty official and ordinary subject must fill his place and try hard to submit memorials that report every good and wicked deed, to enlighten the reign of emperors and kings, and to spread heaven's *qi*. It is not permissible to intercept [memorials]. Anyone who does so must on this account spend three years in prison. Anyone who submits memorials that are completely reliable and contain no falsehood will, I say, be invited to take office.

What will be his office?

Each man will be asked where his strength lies and will be employed for a task he can accomplish.

Why must he be given work that agrees with his talents?

It is heaven's will to employ each man on the basis of his ability. Where this is not the case, we must say that it gives a man cause for resentment so that *qi* is tangled up and natural calamities occur. Since this is so a man can't fulfill his task. From birth until death he won't achieve anything. (65.153)

Now what the people like best is to obtain good harvests and precious objects. Now suppose an enlightened lord were to let it be known that a man could have gold, silver, and other treasures stored in the empire's county offices with a clap of his hands: "You will not be accused of a crime; it is all for you." Such a man will be very happy to obtain these things. [But] if his strength were not up to it, he will not be able to succeed, even if the objects were tied to his hand, and he would exhaust his energy. Now a lord [is like] father and mother to others. If he assigns men an official task that is not geared to what they are good at, he virtually murders them. Not only will they be unable to fulfill their commitments in an orderly manner; they will with futile effort bring uproar to the office and make the population at large suffer bitterly. With the office in uproar, ordinary subjects and officials alike will call to heaven in their distress to voice their resentment and will move heaven to send even more disasters and other anomalies. That is why in their desire to find favor with heaven the wise and worthy of old were doubly careful in filling offices.[25] They always met men's wishes (*ren xin* 人心) and thus were able to fulfill heaven's wishes (*tian xin* 天心).[26]

How does one fulfill heaven's wishes?

What you do must agree with the people. The sign of your success is that petty officials become better men from day to day, and also more faithful and loyal. You must then promote them at the right time, which helps the country['s ruler] to be someone who obtains heaven's favor. But some individuals are inclined to take office one morning because they wish to earn fame. Their conduct does not signify success; they neither fulfill heaven's will nor agree [with the people]. But emperors and kings who attempt to base their rule on heaven's will must fulfill all of it. Not to do so would be wrong. If their reign does not respond well [to heaven][27] and agree [with the people], they must retire and think about what went wrong. This is enough to make heaven content and everyone in the world loyal and faithful and let them exert their skills and their strengths. Even in dark, hidden, and faraway places men will hear about it and will no longer hide their skills. They will submit memorials eagerly: human life is of greatest importance; not a minute must be lost. As long as men bemoan grievances, *[qi]* is tangled up into ever more anomalies and disasters.[28] Rush forth instantly to address this! Problems that are less pressing must wait until autumn and winter.

Why wait until autumn and winter?

Well, in autumn everything is ready, and in winter it is all stored, as decided by heaven's *qi*. Plants have ripened by the eighth month of mid-autumn, so yields can be divided up. Thus according to the model set by heaven and earth one must start in the eighth month to divide things up and inspect them in detail.[29] In the ninth month, heaven's *qi* has come to an end. By this month, plants are prepared to die. So in the ninth month our inspections are concluded[30] and we understand good and bad points. Ten is the last figure. When plants reach the tenth month they return to the beginning. For heaven, the eighth month is [like the last,] the tenth month. So this is the time when plants are ready. For earth, the ninth month comes last, for by then everything has turned old. For men, the period of *hai* [the twelfth earthly branch] is the last month, for by then everything has died. (65.154) Once these three months are over, plants come to life again. Thus *qian* [the first diagram] is situated in the northwest. Plants start from their seeds in *hai* [the twelfth earthly branch].[31] According to the model set by heaven, we divide things up in the eighth month, arrive at conclusions in the ninth, and have these verified in the tenth month. So the three dispensations of heaven, earth, and man arrive at their end in unison. Verification takes place in the *hai* [period], so in the tenth month results are verified and transmitted to subordinates. Since this is so, everything in heaven, on earth, and among men is finished and returns to where it came from in these three months, that is, from the eighth month to the tenth month. Should there be no verification of any sort, [this means that] the aim has not been reached, and since heaven and earth will not be pleased and content, the natural calamities they send will go on and cause damage for years to come. For this reason one inspects in detail in the eighth month, arrives at conclusions in the ninth month and verifies it all and makes it public in the tenth month.[32]

If we make petty officials and ordinary subjects think critically of all they did wrong they won't dare do it again. In the years to come they will show more respect and everything will turn out well. If [results] are not passed down and mistakes are not reflected on, ordinary subjects and low-ranking officials will stubbornly ignore directions. Their hearts will not change unless they see for themselves the mistakes that they have made. Heaven's *dao* is stubborn in its hatred for [people who] don't change.

That is why [results] must be passed down. I can prove this to you. [Let us assume that the results] passed down for this year have all been put forth in writing by [the lord] himself, and that petty officials and ordinary subjects were instructed to do the same on their own behalf. What shows the amount of good and bad [results] is called "celestial contract" (*tian quan* 天券). The next year, the results are again passed down and put on a list to show how much good and bad there was. Exactly the same thing is done the following year. What subordinates submit and superiors report must, although distant from each other, be in agreement.[33] This is what we call "Heaven shows its approval by matching the tallies."

Once petty officials and ordinary subjects change their minds and become good[34] they find favor with heaven, and a man in superior position must become even better. Once they change a great deal there is bound to be a lot of good. [But] should they stubbornly stay as they are and refuse to change, their superior would remain stubborn. Should [small officials] not stop being wicked, their superior will be even more so. When petty officials and ordinary subjects make heaven quite angry by trying to deceive it, the man in a superior position is bound to become even more evil.[35]

Thus heaven is like a mirror that clearly reflects the heart. It does not fail in the slightest to bring to light how petty officials and ordinary subjects conduct their affairs. Heaven and earth resemble a shadow that follows a man and that he can't get rid of. Fortunately, you are a person with good intentions, which you pursue with much energy and care. Although you come to ask about these matters as if this were nothing and of no benefit, heaven in its deep silence takes note of what your mouth has to say.

How do we know this?

By the words [you use]. When a man talks about a matter in words that are auspicious and good, others reply with goodness. They respond with goodness like an echo. When someone's words are ominous, wicked, and inauspicious, others reply with wickedness. (65.155) They respond with wickedness, as if they were an echo. Events in general are in response (*ying he* 應和), [since] they are all sent by heaven. Do you understand this?

Yes, I do.

Now heaven is high above us, and it is distant, high-ranking, and stern. How could it possibly talk personally in each case to a man who is down below? Thus its method is to respond through what is as it is *(ziran)*.[36] Is this clear to you?

Yes, it is, my question has been answered. I want you to tell me one more thing.

Go ahead.

Middle antiquity's majestic rulers had no texts. There was no "Cooperation of the Three." How were they able to pacify the realm?

What a good question! Following heaven's movement, men were straightforward and plain at this time. They all held on to *dao* and had only faith in the one. Speaking in many ways they understood each other. Everyone intended to be perfectly sincere and faithful and thought of fulfilling heaven's will. Nobody was there to deceive others. That is why lord, official, and ordinary subject—all three of them— combined their efforts, were of the same mind, and interacted so that they could conduct their affairs. Disorder will arise if a family is made up of men who are not of the same mind. Nowadays, [in an age when] evil is inherited and transmitted, there are many texts and writings. With ever more texts, men deceive each other.

Moreover, [this material] is frivolous and superficial. The worthy and learned become perplexed and no longer meet heaven's wishes. Once heaven brings forth texts, one must no longer spread words without verifying the truth of what they say. With the "Cooperation of the Three" heaven's *qi* is in balance *(ping)*. Heaven's models are many: one hundred thousand or ten thousand and never the same. Each way of government is different; each method is special. Nowadays, when *qi* of great peace is about to arrive, one must examine whether texts are in their original form and written with standard characters so that they conform to heaven's intention. You are not able to analyze the many, many different ways of conducting affairs that have come about since heaven and earth have set things up. Whatever in one's activities agrees with heaven is right, and what doesn't is wrong. This is a very clear proof of the fact that there is a contract with heaven. Do you understand?

Yes, I do.

Go now, don't ask any more questions. Now it is not that I couldn't tell you all that has happened since heaven and earth set things up[37] and interpret for you[38] all the world's writings, but there is a problem with writing down too much text. If it can't be put to use it is of no benefit for the king's reign. So we must only say what is essential: lack of order in a government stems from too many texts,[39] and this is where the great illness of heaven and earth comes from. In ancient times, all of the worthy and the wise hated and detested [this situation]. When *dao* was practiced by a virtuous lord he did not dare produce texts but made everyone hold on to substance, search for the root, and guard the beginnings, so that the way of heaven was orderly and the country rested secure. Although you like to ask questions, don't cause any more text to be written. (65.156) Go and think about it.

Yes, I will.[40]

NOTES

1. TPJ 177.518f.
2. The meaning of *shang huang taiping qi* does not differ from that of *taiping qi*, which abounds in the text. The belief in its imminent arrival is the central point of the Master's missionary program. The question at hand is also raised elsewhere:

> The writings often say that heaven's highest majestic *qi (shang huang qi)* is about to descend. Now I don't know what "highest majestic *qi*" means. (TPJ 102.234)

In response, the Master gives a longish list of the constituents of the Three Majesties of heaven (the sun, moon, and constellations), of earth (the five peaks, the plains, and the valleys) and of humankind (sovereign, official, and the people). Only toward the end of the section and when reminded by questions does he return to the topic and explain that the ancients were well informed about the chances for the arrival of "highest majestic *qi*":

> The ancients undertook the following divination in regard to their government: they analyzed the solidity of their virtue *(de)*, investigated what their *qi* responded to, and thus knew exactly, as clearly as the sun and the moon, their reign's gains and losses, weak and strong points.
>
> *Very good, but how can one avoid losses?*
>
> Yes, you are already familiar with celestial scriptures, so you must bring to an end the calamities that the ten thousand beings inherit and transmit.
>
> *But how can this be done? If the Celestial Master would only advise the worthies on how to achieve highest majestic* qi! (TPJ 102.238)

The arrival of such *qi* signifies the success of the reform program. Should a society still lack perfection, the arriving *qi* would be less satisfactory, promoting, for instance, three-fourths of peace rather than the whole lot (TPJ 102.238).

Huang is used throughout the text in connection with personages, powers, and actions that originate from heaven and thus possess the highest possible authority. The word is therefore occasionally linked with *taiping*, which is mainly referred to as *taiping qi*, "*qi* of *taiping*," but occasionally as *tian shang huang taiping qi* (TPJ 50.68) or as *shang huang taiping qi*, as in the passage at hand. It follows that *huang* (majestic) does not appear in connection with *yuan qi* 元氣 (the primordial *qi*), which is not seen as originating from heaven, but rather as representing an independent ontological entity.

3. The "majestic numinous" (*huang ling* 皇靈) is another word for heaven. The disciple raises questions on its behalf (TPJ 127.312; 129.332), as he does on behalf of *tian*; cf. also TPJ 163.456. The *Hanyu da cidian* (vol. 8, p. 266) quotes Cao Zhi 曹植 (192–232) to document that the two characters mean "emperor of heaven."

4. The expression "distinct" (*chacha* 察察) is used in *Laozi* 20 for the mind of the people in contrast to the mind of "I," and in *Laozi* 58 for a government that encourages people to use stratagems. The positive meaning it conveys in this passage can be found in *Xunzi* 8.4.3, for instance, where it means "careful investigation" in Knoblock's (1988: 186) rendering. Throughout the TPJ, it means "clear" in the sense that the Master makes things clear (TPJ 99.225; 110.295), or that the sun, moon, and stars shine brightly (TPJ p. 648, *Chao*, part 7). It is of interest that here the *Laozi*'s understanding of *chacha* seems to be of no impact.

5. The Celestial Master attempts to analyze language as a scholar would. As the *Chun qiu fan lu* says:

> Names and appellations obtain their correctness from heaven and earth, which give them their meaning. . . . What is spoken loudly in imitation of heaven and earth is an appellation, and what is cried by way of commanding is a name. Names and appellations, though they all sound different, have one common root. They are all uttered to convey what heaven wants. Heaven does not speak; it lets men put forth what it wants. It does

not act; it lets men do what it intends. (Chap. 35 *"Shen cha ming hao"* 深察名號, p. 285; cf. Bodde's translation in Fung 1952/53, vol. 2, pp. 85f.)

6. The explanation of *wang* (king) and *jun* (ruler) in *Chun qiu fan lu* (35.289) is less analytical, but it shares with the Celestial Master's approach an interest in pronunciation and, in particular, rhyme. See, for instance, the five aspects (*ke* 科) of the character *wang* 王, which are said to be *huang* 皇 (majestic), *fang* 方 (square), *kuang* 匡 (square and full), *huang* 黃 (yellow), and *wang* 往 (to go toward). The fact that "to go toward" was a common explanation of *wang*, from the *Gu liang zhuan* to apocryphal scriptures (see Tjan 1949/52, vol. 1, p. 300, note 187, and *Bai hu tong* 2 *"Hao"* 號, p. 45), shows that the Celestial Master's approach to concepts is rather mainstream.

7. The character *huang* 煌 (brilliant) is pronounced like *huang* (majestic). *Huang huang*, in Tjan Tjoe Som's translation (1949/1952, vol. 1, pp. 296f., note 178) "resplendent," occurs frequently to explain "majestic," as for instance *Bai hu tong* 2 *"Hao,"* p. 45: "He was called majestic, shedding forth a brilliance that none could escape" (cf. Tjan 1949/1952, vol. 1, p. 230).

8. The *Bai hu tong*'s way of explaining "majestic" is more straightforward:

    What is the meaning of *huang?* It is also an appellation. It means *jun* 君 (lord), *mei* 美 (beautiful), and *da* 大 (great). (*Bai hu tong* 2 *"Hao"* 號, p. 44)

9. This translation follows Luo (1996: 260). The character *zi* 子 is here used in a nominalizing function; *wuzi* 物子 means "harvest."

10. This cosmogonic sequence is complex. Also, the proposition that there were three before the beginning of creation is remarkable against a background of dualistic Yin/Yang–, male/female–based cosmogonic images. For the power the TPJ assigns to a threefold approach, see Espesset 2002a, part 3. The passage at hand argues carefully. It pays more attention to what we might call reality than to empty formalism. The three luminaries—another trinity—are introduced as if they were a second entity beyond or above all other things and beings that were created by heaven, earth, and their intercourse. Also, in a nonformalistic manner, the origin of the family is laid out in plain terms as a man and woman getting together and bringing forth children. Only then does the argument move back to the "cooperation of the three," that is, to the three who make up the family.

11. "Hard and soft" are juxtaposed in *Laozi* 78. Here they mean "quality." It was generally believed that "quality" was an effect of five phases activity.

12. All of these factors influence harvest results. In this passage, the term *zhonghe* is the word for the active, involved presence of cosmological entities, as opposed to their being just as they are. I have not found the term *wuli* anywhere else, not even in the TPJ.

13. The expression *sheng he* 生和 (not mentioned in the dictionaries) is poorly translated by "in agreement." It recurs later on in this passage: "When three are in agreement . . . " It points to the physical, concrete outcome that is derived from an agreement between beings or objects.

14. This is perhaps as abstract as the TPJ gets. Three triggers the process of becoming, which is termed *"dao."* This position deserves some attention within the narrow spectrum of Chinese ontological speculation. Elsewhere in the text *dao* is one of the entities involved in the cosmogonic process, as are primordial *qi*, what is as it is, the intercourse between Yin and Yang, and heaven and earth; see also p. 85 above.

15. *Shi* 事 (activity) is corrected to *shi* 使 (to cause), as in the phrase "Should one not suffice all three would remain incomplete" on p. 150. The mistake is caused by the occurrence of *yi shi* 一 事 in the previous sentence.

16. For "to rest secure forever" (*chang an* 長 安), see above, section 50.

17. Section 60 repeats the proposition that scarcity of people makes a country poor. The opposite claim, which is put forth in the *Han Feizi* (chap. 49 *"Wu du"* 五 蠹 , p. 856.2: "In the past . . . people were few and goods many. So men never quarreled"), for instance, does not seem to occur in the Celestial Master's arguments.

18. The four outlying regions are mentioned throughout the text, for instance, as an abbreviation of "the countries of the four outlying regions" (TPJ 134.368). They are situated in all eight directions (TPJ p. 729, *Chao*, part 1).

19. "Heaven's model" here refers to cooperating in threes.

20. The term "celestial document" or "celestial contract" (*tian quan* 天 券) occurs only in this section, altogether three times (see pp. 317 and 319), and in part 9 of the *Chao* (p. 712), where it seems to figure as another word for "writings" and where the Master talks about the relationship between heaven and men as if they had a contract consisting of a list of a man's deeds agreed on by both parties. *Zhen quan* (the true contract) is used in this sense in section 51. The section at hand deals with the proper supervision of subordinates. The introduction of a celestial contract enhances the role of heaven as a source of authority for political leaders. The contract referred to here resembles a form of agreement that was common between sovereign and official (see *Xunzi* 44.12.7 and 13), as discussed by Lewis (1999: 30 and note 49, p. 374). Such documents were produced annually to oblige the subordinate to achieve certain mutually agreed upon performance goals. Contracts were also used in the ritual of "rending of the tally" (*fen quan* 分 券) that was meant to bind a disciple to his master (Benn 2000: 318, 330).

21. See above, section 55.

22. "Threefold writings" (*san dao xing shu* 三 道 行 書) are said to be texts of the highest quality because they help to detect malpractice. In their comprehensiveness and investigative clarity they are said to resemble the three luminaries:

> Only a man who resembles heaven can, by understanding its will, grow old and live a long life. Someone who resembles earth and understands its intentions does not live quite so long. To resemble men means to enjoy hardly any longevity but to die as the ten thousand beings all do, not at the [proper] time and without the [right] cipher. What resembles heaven is the threefold texts (*san dao tong wen* 三 道 通 文). Heaven has three patterns (*wen* 文), whose clarity is that of the three sources of light, namely the sun, the moon,

and the stars. The sun scrutinizes Yang [that is, what is in the light], the moon Yin [lying in the shade], and the stars what lies in between. That is why threefold writings undertake to provide explanations. Writings that reach the authorities must give only the name of the author; there is no need to ask who submits them. Writings that resemble earth are twofold, and those that resemble man go only in one way, which is blocked, moreover. What resemble the ten thousand animals are words arranged on the spur of the moment; they are not set in writing. (TPJ 79.198; see Long 2000: 311)

Hachiya (1983) points to the origin of *xing shu* when he explains them as "texts circulating [among the people]" (see TPJ 68.171). They come from the grassroots. They were collected by petty officials and the people (TPJ 132.360) and consist of reports submitted by local officials, townspeople, and travelers on all the unusual occurrences they have observed in towns and marketplaces, on the roads, and in the countryside (TPJ 167.467; cf. also 127.328). The "three ways" of the text's title might actually refer to these three groups of men if "threefold writings" were not also the means by which wrongdoings are reported (*ji guo* 記過) in heaven and by spirits (TPJ 211.673). It was clearly faults and trespasses that were reported (TPJ 152.420), as Max Kaltenmark (1979: 26) has observed: he sees the *"san dao"* as referring to heaven, earth, and men. This understanding links the procedures described here to the *san guan shou shu* 三官手書 with which adherents of Celestial Master Daoism addressed the netherworld's justice department to be spared intrusions from mischievous demons (Cedzich 1987: 54). These memorials dealt with trespasses, in particular those committed by a newly deceased person, but also those who might have caused his death. They were addressed and physically conveyed to heaven, earth, and water. They were meant to be a vehicle of redemption for the deceased but also, more importantly, for the living. So, too, are the *San dao xing shu,* but for society as a whole rather than for a particular family or group of people. The perusal and distribution of these texts—and this, we must add, means the implementation of what they say—is in the Celestial Master's view bound to go along with great peace (TPJ 127.319; 132.362; 136.381; 152.420). They belong to the Master's own texts as indicated by the expression *tian shi san dao xing shu* 天師三道行書 (The Celestial Master's threefold writings) (TPJ 127.312; 317).

23. This translation is tentative. The passage deals with the frequently discussed topic (see above, section 43, and the passage from section 79 just quoted) of the need to maintain a flow of information from the grassroots to higher levels, while guaranteeing the safety of the informant.

24. The two missing characters are read as "*zhi. Jin*" 之. 今.

25. As Qing Xitai (1979) points out, during the last period of the Han Dynasty there was a lot of criticism of the way in which officials were chosen and promoted. While much of this criticism came from the erudites and from certain families whose members were traditionally employed as officials, the argument was widespread. Xiang Kai, who propagated a *taiping* text at Emperor Huan's court, belonged to the group, or "party,"

who called themselves "clean," as opposed to empresses' relatives and eunuchs who had supposedly assumed political power in a corrupt fashion.

26. The people's will represents heaven's will; see, for instance, TPJ 132.354. The Master makes use of "the people" as it suits his argument. Their "heart" is reliable, or so it seems, but their judgment is not.

27. Long (2000: 312) corrects *fang* 放 to *xiao* 效.

28. With Yu (2001a: 132), I read *ling* 令 for *jin* 今.

29. Yu (2001a: 132) points out that the meaning of the character for *ba* 八 (eight) is seen as "to divide" (see *Shuo wen jie zi*, p. 109b). According to Gui Fu's (1736–1805) notes on *ba* 捌, this character was originally written with the character for "eight" (*Shuo wen jie zi*, p. 337a).

30. The phonetic element of *jiu* 究 (to inspect) is *jiu* 九 (nine).

31. The character *hai* 亥 is the phonetic element of *he* 核 (seed). Rao Zongyi (1972) points out that the Celestial Master speculates about the character *hai* from a pictographic (cf. also section 53, note 13, above) as well as a phonetic perspective, and that both approaches have parallels in earlier and contemporary writings (see *Shuo wen jie zi*, p. 1312a, and *Huangdi neijing suwen* 70 "*Wu chang zheng da lun*" 五常政大論, p. 20b). In the passage at hand phonetic considerations also prevail in the following sentence that links *shi* 十 (ten) with *shi* 實 (fruit) (cf. Petersen 1990c: 140). Sound glosses were quite popular among second-century C.E. scholars (see Bodman 1954).

32. This passage leads back to the original question of proper government and the need to address issues in autumn and winter. As the yields are investigated during the harvest season, so too should the performance of officials, "the amount of good and bad," be evaluated. The terms used for this latter process are identical to those applied to the gathering and distribution of the harvest.

The gist of the argument is that cooperation between the leadership, the administration, and the people is based on regular and public performance records, and that such records are to be kept mainly at the lower end of the administrative hierarchy, which will thus inspire self-control.

33. With Long (2000: 312), I read *yao* 繇 as *yao* 遙 (distant).

34. For *shan* 善 (good) as a Daoist rank, see section 41.

35. This passage gives voice to one of the Celestial Master's most original propositions: the moral force of the subordinate equals that of his superior, and influence travels both ways. Although this is the conclusion one can draw from the social reforms envisaged throughout the TPJ, it is here stated with unusual theoretical rigidity. It is matched by the idea that heaven does as men should do, that is, it shuns people who don't have children, for instance (see TPJ 208.658f.).

36. This passage makes *tian* (heaven) look unusually omniscient and powerful. The course of nature is its tool, as are the words uttered by men. That the spoken word is in-

tegrated in the system of correlations is merely a logical conclusion, hardly thematized, as opposed to the frequency with which texts are mentioned.

37. This is expressed by *tian di shi li* 天地事立, which is probably erroneous for *tian di li shi* 立事, as in line 9 of this page and which also occurs TPJ 79, p. 200.

38. Three characters are here in the position of a verbal predicate: *fen bie jie* 分別解.

39. With Yu (2001a: 134), I correct *tian wen* 天文 to *da wen* 大文. Given the Master's interest in collecting texts, this statement is problematic, but it is repeated elsewhere—see TPJ 136.382; 139.393; 157.445—using the term *da wen*. These passages warn against the writing of new texts, not against collating material already in existence, and these new texts are the TPJ, or a text similar to the received TPJ, rather than reports about natural calamities and other celestial warnings.

40. The summary says:

This section deals with embracing primordial *qi* and what is as it is; [with the fact that] three must join forces and be of the same mind in all matters, in heaven and on earth; and with heaven's bright contract and the reign of majestic peace.

On the Need to
Study What Is True

This section does not have much to say that is new. We hear about the chance for great peace to arrive and the necessary preparations, and learn that without moral reform this chance will be missed. The word "good," which throughout the text is applied to *taiping* believers, is here defined as adhering to "*dao,* virtue, and benevolence." The Master stresses that a moral person will not only be of benefit to the world, but he will also himself thrive by obtaining cosmic support for all his endeavors. He is thus assured of living a long life and being successful in it.

With such promises the Master asserts that it is profitable to learn from him. Throughout the section he seems to promote his own training of students rather than any social or political cause. The disciple facilitates this by establishing the topic as "teaching and learning." When Master and disciple speak of learning, they use the term in the sense in which a scholar of the *Lun yu* would view the studies through which he hopes to become not only educated but also good and benevolent. Learning is described as an activity that takes up all one's time and energy. It must not be postponed or interrupted.

In explaining what is to be learned, the Master mentions what he calls experience and what we might call psychological considerations. He claims that the process of becoming good is hampered by human insufficiency, which prevents most human beings from reaching their aim. For this reason, he advises the adept to take a radical approach to moral improvement. He should aim at immortality, for instance, if he wants to avoid dying young. With this advice the Celestial Master modifies the longevity expectations set forth in the *Lie xian zhuan* and elsewhere, and also the utopian elements of the TPJ's social and political reform agenda. We might put it thus: learning must focus on ideals. The study of lesser objects is said to lead to moral depravity. Students are advised to aim for the impossible in order to achieve what is necessary for their own and the world's survival. If aims are set high enough, all men who are engaged in learning are bound to profit from it, regardless of their talent.

The high standards for what is to be learned contrasts with the Master's realistic expectations regarding the students' aptitude and the process of learning. Also, despite his encouraging description of what a successful student can achieve, the Master argues against what he calls empty promises and distances himself from the carelessness of other teachers. Much of this section is concerned with the Master's attacks on others and their wrong attitudes toward teaching and learning rather than with what the Master himself thinks right. His main target is the well-established project of following "the classics" and their norms of benevolent conduct. He suggests that these norms must have been taught poorly or else men would not behave as they do.

As the Celestial Master sees it, one subject of proper learning must be "auspicious conduct," which is opposed to the fascination with mortuary rituals that, he argues, holds sway at present. Finally, the disciple refers to the Master's accusation that good people are few nowadays and asks how does he know? The Master's answer seems to imply that the movement he has created is small. He complains that good people find few friends, which, he says, can only mean that the majority do not cherish goodness.

·   ·   ·

(66.157) Perfected, step forward. Since *qi* of honesty and harmony is now about to arrive in full measure, men should give up duties and tasks and let their spirit roam about. But how can they become enlightened and straighten out their hearts and their intentions?

For a start they should refrain from doing evil and then gradually learn to like doing good, until they don't know how to do without it. This will allow emperors and kings to lay down their official insignia, since there is nothing that will need to be governed;[1] men of outstanding goodness will flock to the court, and plenty of loyal, trustworthy, and filial gentlemen will reside there.

But how is this to be achieved? Your heart, Perfected, loves the good by nature (*tian xing* 天性). You never cease to worry about heaven's way. Concentrate your mind and explain it all.

Well, we must urgently instruct men in true dao, *true virtue, and true benevolence.*[2]

Why should we teach them true *dao?*

Well, nothing is more appropriate than dao *to make them convert* (dao hua 道 化). *To love life has no equal. "To possess true* dao" *is the name for supreme goodness. But "without* dao" *is the word for someone utterly wicked, wretched, disastrous, and deadly.*

What you have just said is truly good. I have nothing to add. Why should we instruct men in true virtue?

"Man with true virtue" is the name for someone who can embrace and nurture what is without limit.[3] *"Without virtue" is a small-minded man, who is utterly deficient and weary.*

Fine, what you have said. Again, I have nothing to add. It is all quite true. Why should we make them study the way *(dao)* of benevolence?

Because a benevolent man is generous and loving, his embrace reaches everything. (66.158) The word "benevolent" is used only for someone who likes to give without end and limit. But the nonbenevolent likes to get [things],[4] *hating to pledge and give them away. The word means someone greedy and vile whose wants are as those of animals; he can't distinguish between them and himself.*

What you have said is excellent. Again, I have nothing to add. Now after you have explained these three cases, leaving me nothing to add, [can we say that] nowadays men must study to be good?

They must study hard to be good.

Doesn't "to be good" apply to something specific?

I don't understand what you mean. Please explain.

Well, if someone is good his actions agree with heaven's will and don't go against the intentions of men. This is what we call being good. A good person is not surpassed by anybody. His name is on a par with *dao;* he is loved by heaven, nurtured by earth, and engaged by emperors and kings, and the men who serve a ruler are bound to be of the same heart and join forces with him. A wicked person acts contrary to heaven's will and forever offends men's intentions. In opposition to heaven's way, he doesn't attend to the four seasons, so the spirits of heaven and of earth hate him. Men dislike the sight of him. He causes father and mother great harm. The ruler suffers bitterly from [his actions]. ["Wicked"] is the name for the world's most[5] rotten, disastrous, ruinous thing.

So a man's conduct becomes disastrous as soon as it is no longer auspicious and becomes auspicious when it turns away from disaster. Take someone who is auspicious one moment and disastrous the next, good now and wicked a moment later— we would not see him as a pure-hearted and attentive person. You understand, don't you?

Yes, I do.

Now in your opinion, what should a man's conduct be like?

Well, if he were not to study dao *with diligence he would at once become ignorant of it and be "a man without* dao*." But such a man is a most wicked and disastrous [creature].*

Now anyone who does not earnestly study virtue becomes at once ignorant of it. But such a man likes to inflict harm and injuries. He is a token of disaster and ruin. Should a man not study benevolence he will end up without it, walking the same road as animals do and sharing their feelings. This is indeed little better than being dead. Now a man who doesn't try hard day and night to learn how to be good forgets the good and becomes wicked. Death and disaster come about through wickedness. Therefore, once the common people don't try hard to learn auspicious conduct, they meet with disaster. "Disaster" is the word for this world's wickedness.

Good. Some time ago you already entered true *dao* and have never returned to wickedness. Now you have long harbored all this knowledge, yet still you pretend to be a fool. How come?

I would not dare do that.

All right. Luckily, you have been able to explain it all. I am quite happy with what you have said. (66.159) Now that you have managed to achieve this, you have heard all I have to say. Should I give up and stop here?

Oh, no. When I listen to your warnings I come to the conclusion that I am not good enough. I would not dare to do all the talking.

What you have said is fine, modest as always.

That I am now able to go all the way to the true gate[6] *is only because you have shown me what I lack.*

Well. All you have just said is correct. Thus were the great wise men and Three Majestic Rulers of antiquity always engaged from morning to night in the study of the true doctrine. We call someone who does not like this study a man without *dao*. Now such a person's conduct is outrageous (*wu shu* 無數). Again and again, this fills heaven with great resentment. Truly, heaven does not wish to cover such a man, nor earth to carry him; neither spirits, nor numinous and vital beings, nor even demons wish to render support. The whole world suffers bitterly from this. The wise, the worthies, and all gentlemen greatly detest such a man. Therefore, during the reign of rulers of highest majesty in antiquity, everyone studied how to be pure and quiet. They understood profoundly the innermost conditions of heaven and earth. Therefore, we must all study the true doctrine *(dao)* before we can reach an understanding of what heaven and earth want.

We call a man who doesn't undertake a diligent study of virtue man without virtue. Heaven doesn't love such a man, nor does earth rejoice in him; men don't wish to be friendly with him or close to him. His conduct is such that his acts are never virtuous. He brings harm to the king and calamities to the gentleman. Heaven instructs demons and spirits to no longer support [his] affairs. That is why the worthy, wise, and great learned of old would not talk to a man who lacked virtue if they came upon him.

Anyone who does not study benevolence all day long will neglect affairs and be unkind. So I would say that a man without benevolence runs counter to everything, hurts men's feelings, and disagrees with heaven's intentions. He is more like an animal. That is why the wise and worthy of the past would have nothing to do with him.

Now anyone who doesn't learn goodness from a teacher remains a fool and stays dumb. He is ignorant of how to be a good person,[7] giving reign to his own stupidity instead and making light of being wicked. Now a wicked man is utterly foolish, stupid, and dumb. His actions don't follow the way of heaven and earth. If a ruler were to employ him, he would bring disgrace on his father and mother and cause his ancestors and relatives grief. Since his conduct doesn't follow [heaven's] example, demons and spirits, being commissioned by the heart of heaven, dislike him. The harm done is so big that even by [antiquity's lenient] three models[8] he is found guilty. The wise and worthy of old strongly resented [such conduct], (66.160) and therefore the ancients investigated their own learning. Was it in line with heaven's intentions? Did their activities promote nothing but *dao,* virtue, benevolence, and goodness? Conduct must agree with the intentions of heaven and earth and not entail frivolous and superficial words and acts, as these ignore heaven's model. Ignore it and you run into disaster, shorten your life, and perhaps even harm later generations.

Heaven's way doesn't go wrong; it has rules and model. Not to study teachings *(dao)* that are auspicious but instead to neglect affairs and make light of oneself is bound to lead to disaster. Now disaster is what heaven, earth, men, and the ten thousand beings and things all detest, and no disaster must be permitted to last long. Otherwise, it might become the root of great harm and the entrance gate to bad luck.

If someone is caught up in it by mistake, he might die before he has had a chance to repent his wrongdoings and make them undone. Everyone [who lives] in this world knows this. But certain low-ranking scholars act like great fools and continue to make fun of *dao*.[9] They don't know how to preserve it and how to prevent the onset of disaster and harm. They continue to transmit their foolish ideas, which are thus received and passed on from one to the other. [In consequence,] latter-born generations are even more foolish and dumb than their ancestors. Thus, true *dao* is blocked and can't get through, with the result that men make light of themselves and cannot finish the years heaven [has destined] for them. What we have just been talking about must bear a great burden of blame for this. On seeing my book, Perfected, you must thoroughly take note of it. Be careful not to lock it away but let worthy, learned, and bright men have it so that they can study and understand what it says.

So teachings *(dao)* from former times transmit heaven's wishes and adhere to earth's intentions. Since we have the model of the great and true *dao* of early antiquity, we must always teach the study of *dao*, virtue, longevity, goodness, attentiveness, auspicious conduct, antiquity, balance *(ping)*, and the prolongation of life. By documenting what goodness is, [the firmament of] heaven sets the model that keeps the gate to *dao* open; earth establishes the model that always opens the door to virtue. The model set by the wise and worthy of old continues to clear the road to benevolence. Thus the wise and worthy of old shared heaven's wishes and earth's intentions. In the process of prolonging life, they nourished the twelve thousand plants and beings. They continued to transmit the idea of *dao*, virtue, and benevolence, and thus made the ten thousand beings thrive. If someone were to transmit disastrous and wicked ideas, all beings would fall into decline. Thus by holding unto *dao*, virtue, and benevolence the population grows and enjoys being good. When these things are given up, numbers dwindle and a reign becomes poor and miserable.

This is the example set by heaven and earth that has been proclaimed as law. Only with a heart of perfect *dao*, bright virtue, benevolence, and goodness does [man] respond to heaven's constellations. Then spirits and other numinous beings enlighten his actions. So the wise and worthy of old never ceased to think of doing good, until they had no energy left.[10] They would not have dared to have wicked thoughts and take the road to disaster. However, the hearts of certain very foolish men are blocked. They really lack insight. (66.161) One must not continue to willfully mislead them on that wicked road to disaster and decay. Left to themselves they won't know how much they have departed from heaven's way. Since following in one another's footsteps, they have made wicked [conduct] their constant practice and can't turn away from it on their own. So, obeying heaven's wish, I show them the written instructions I have respectfully received from heaven. They open wide the road to great peace as it prevailed in early antiquity and let men enjoy goodness while unlearning the arts of evil conduct.

The men [who live in] this world always aim high, but what they achieve is necessarily inferior and can't match what they had originally wanted and thought of. Thus when a superior scholar is ardent in his hatred of death and his joy in life and intends to learn how to become a transcendent, he will barely manage to live for a long time. This holds true for a superior scholar of first-rate ambition. While a scholar of medium rank with some ambition who regrets that his ancestors have died young might be ardent in the search for *dao* and the study of longevity, he will barely be able to finish the years destined for him by heaven.[11] This is as far as a scholar whose ambition is as firm as it can be gets. Next comes someone who is frequently ill and whose health is below average. If he is ardent in his study he will put a stop [to being ill], but he will barely be able to go back to its cause. If illness worries him but little, he might conceive of bringing it to a halt by studying while he is ill, at a point where his illness has already become serious. The next instance is of someone who is seriously ill who might search for *dao* and ways of treatment to save his life when he is dying. For this reason, my writings attempt to instruct men in heaven's life-prolonging model. Work hard at it, day and night. Only then will your life be of average length. The common people have met with disaster because they have studied nothing but an average model.

A foolish person doesn't understand the ambition of the ordinary people of the world.[12] They always think of what is best but can't achieve their aim. Thus only by raising their goal as high as reaching transcendence might they be able to live out the years that heaven has destined for them. Great worthies who fulfill all their ambitions are bound to conform to what I have written about *dao*. A worthy of medium rank might want all but will stop in between and achieve only half of what he wants. A small-minded man might have an aim in the morning, but when evening comes he will have forgotten what it was. Thus by setting high goals we make it possible for everyone, whether they are of superior, average, or inferior ability, to obtain their aims.

Nowadays the men of late antiquity, great fools that they are, have sent the true doctrine *(dao)* off into the distance. Only through an intense study of heaven's standard patterns and models[13] can they avoid being misled by deceit. To instruct them with average texts is to deceive them. Great fraud, jealousy, and cunning arise from the study of ordinary texts and well-assembled words. Heaven considers emperors and kings to be its children and hates subordinates who deceive their superiors.

(66.162) Because inferiors are often evil and false, the lord up above with *dao,* virtue, and benevolence has nobody to trust and, down below, the people have nobody to whom they would devote their lives.

The true doctrine, and nothing else, must be studied from morning to night.[14] [Only] through a diligent study of good teachings *(dao)* can we acquire average teachings. Learning average teachings, one ends up with frivolous and superficial [knowledge]. When the common people acquire such knowledge they become confused and their circumstances grow difficult. It is the road to great disaster and wickedness, bringing emperors and kings bitter suffering and causing the people to be uncontrollable. As proof, take a family's kind father and mother. They teach their children every day to be good and to endure hardship and go without food and clothing in order to nourish their elders. [The children], however, stick stubbornly to their wickedness. How much more does this apply to ordinary people who teach each other frivolous and superficial texts because they don't believe in my writings! If we were to make them look at my writings, they could judge for themselves what they are missing.

Since middle antiquity, men with valuable teachings *(dao)*[15] taught them to each other in secret. They were not willing to share them with their disciples. Instead, they taught their disciples frivolous, superficial, faked texts. Since this has been going on for a long time, the way of heaven of today is soiled by great disorder. So it is to be expected that natural calamities and anomalies happen by the ten thousand–fold in heaven and on earth. The worthy and learned should thoroughly examine this problem.[16] Well. This is something I clearly understand, although at present I don't mix from morning to night with the common people. Since [this disorder] causes the world much suffering, let us publish this text to make it known. I have reasons for what I say. You must be even more careful, or heaven might find fault with you.

Yes, I wouldn't dare [not be careful]! I am always full of concern when I hear you speak. You have said this well, so heaven is quite pleased and happy. It won't harm you.

Yes!

Ordinary men achieve nothing but average virtue, even though they might diligently and persistently study true virtue. Should they study average virtue they find only evil and fake virtue. If they study such virtue they turn into fools, beyond all measure (*shu* 數).[17] To be without true virtue and do as one chooses is alien to the pure conduct of a gentleman.

Only through diligent study of supreme benevolence does anyone achieve medium benevolence. Let him study hard to be moderately benevolent and he will only learn to act in an average manner, without benevolence. Should he study without regard for benevolence he will turn into a fool and end up as bandit. Without knowing [what he is doing], he will kill or injure [others], without all proper measure. Heaven resents anyone acting as it suits them without concern for the proper order of things (*dao li* 道理); earth opposes it as well and it is quite alien to humankind.

Only through diligent and ongoing study of the way *(dao)* to great good luck can anyone achieve moderately good luck. He will have little luck if he should study what is moderately auspicious. (66.163) If he studies how to behave in a slightly auspicious manner, he will be on the way *(dao)* to disaster. Let him study the way that leads to disaster and he is beyond rescue. Dumb and stupid men who don't understand a single thing think that what heaven's *dao* says is not true but is full of deceit and betrayal. They have complete faith in their own foolish hearts and careless words. Up above, they offend heaven's patterns; down below, they ruin earth's structures. They bring natural calamities upon the hundred families. That is why what I have written about *dao* is meant to teach everyone. Someone who studies a lot of it will rank with perfected and transcendents. Should he not get that far he might achieve a state of peace and security and give the virtuous lord no cause for worries. You must think deeply about my words. Then you will never again find fault with them.

Yes, indeed.

At present, I speak on behalf of heaven. We must dissolve the mass of inherited and transmitted [evil] that has been piled up since the division between heaven and earth. If we can't lead men on by the patterns of great *dao* and great virtue, the techniques of supreme longevity, and the road to outstanding goodness they will go astray in their dumbness and stupidity. The sincere and long-lasting belief in their own foolish and beclouded hearts makes them wicked. If we can't stop this, we don't stand a chance of resolving inherited and transmitted [evil] and the accusations made by heaven and earth. You had better comprehend what I say, hadn't you?

Yes, certainly.

The wise man, the worthy, and the superior scholar will certainly agree with my book once they see and peruse the texts. Then they won't go wrong by the width of a single hair. A scholar of medium rank who is willing to go half the way will understand half of what it says. Should scholars of low rank apply themselves they will just about manage not to ignore the proper model.[18] For this reason they will all be promoted to a place among heaven's people.[19] Common men, as long as they like the whole of this book and don't ignore the proper model, will find the standard way (zheng dao 正道) and look after their own person. They won't dare take things lightly and give [others] cause to worry greatly. Once a superior scholar accepts my teachings and studies without interruption, he might become an honest official and after a long time fulfill his main wish, that is, transcend the world and never again debate issues or covet authority. Upon learning my teachings a scholar of medium rank will become an honest and good clerk and finish the years destined for him by heaven. Once small-minded people study my teachings, they will manage to become quite attentive. They will be a kind father, a loving mother, a filial son, an older brother who is able to lead, or a younger brother who is willing to obey. Living as husband and wife they will plan jointly, won't offend and harm each other, and throughout their life feel no resentment. Placed belowground as demons and spirits they will still carry on in a state of leisure[20] and never will they be accused of having been wicked. None of their children will die young, before its time.

Now at the time when primordial qi and heaven were originally created, in antiquity, all men liked to learn.[21] They hoped to become transcendent. Yet they did not manage to live long lives. They escaped criminal punishment out of fear of death, that's all. (66.164) Men of late antiquity, great fools that they are, recite and teach frivolous and superficial material and learn skills that don't lead to longevity. Although their lives might end all of a sudden, they talk about themselves as if they were immortal. Teaching others to be unconcerned and careless, they promote ominous activities. They do more for their dead than they do for the living, although the living belong to heaven and the dead to earth. It is damaging to serve earth more than heaven. I predict from this conduct that they will become even more foolish.

They don't know a single thing. Once ominous activities flourish, demons thrive. They pester and murder men so that they can't finish the years destined for them by heaven. Now even someone who diligently studies true teachings might learn only what is false; working hard to learn true virtue, he might only find its false version. How much more is this the case for men of outgoing antiquity who have moved far away from dao and are teaching frivolous and superficial material? When they are in dire circumstances and no longer able to restrain each other, they even teach how to promulgate laws and statutes and how to debate about issues of diplomacy.[22] One has been teaching others a path not really leading to benevolence when, the teaching finished, one must grieve about a lack of benevolent behavior.

Heaven has set up a model for men to follow and its own name is "great dao." Earth is "virtue." Since this is so, heaven and earth are [like] father and mother to the ten thousand beings. They take the lead in all activities and so they always guide men to goodness. They would not dare mislead them by setting them on a path to disaster and wickedness. How much more should this be the case for men [teaching men]! They are heaven's children and must act in resemblance to heaven. Nowadays, men are difficult to control because they ignore the proper model. Once we educate a man through *dao* and virtue, we let him know how to value, take care of, cherish, and control himself. If we were instead to show him the penal code, we would make him realize that death can come suddenly. So, out of a feeling of bravery, he would make light of himself. Therefore, if he were to control others, he would do so by force, and then there would be even more robbers and murderers who would make others suffer bitterly. So the men who live in this world would show no concern for each other. There is much in this to blame. Do you understand? Heed it.

Yes, I will.

It must be deplored that men still don't show any benevolence, even after some diligent instruction. In late antiquity, since the propagation of speculative arts,[23] men have become very shallow. Their mutual hatred and resentment never ceases. Having learned auspicious ways of conduct, they are still, sorry to say, unlucky. In late antiquity they have promoted the study of mourning rituals; they prepare for such an ominous event as if they were waiting for it. By the time they die they have not lived as long as was destined for them, they have almost ruined their family, and still they don't understand what they have done wrong. When their time comes, they shout to heaven, wail to earth, and call themselves maltreated: "The king's reign is not at peace, so I have to die early." They have brought this upon themselves through their own private affairs. They are foolish men, disregarding their own roots. (66.165) Once their crime has been identified they might repent, but to little avail, since they are not attentive enough. Upon their death, they might cry aloud, but this won't save them.[24]

This is why I am now trying to admonish you. One can reach the steps that lead to longevity by following the constant path *(dao)* of the great transcendents. Only by educating a man in virtuous conduct will one make him benevolent. Only by educating him in benevolence will one make him behave decently and maintain his character. Then he won't dare deceive others and deprive them of their property. Teach him to be decent and he will ignore the proper model. Teach him the model and he will ignore it and murder and rob people. Teach him murder and robbery and he will start a great war. Once this happens even innocent people will cheat [others] and become robbers and bandits in dire circumstances. For this reason I promote the model that is presented by heaven's way. It unlocks the gate to all-prevailing good luck, closes the road to disaster and wickedness, and [helps us to] reach the steps leading to heaven's great peace. Each man must recite it for himself. Moreover, since everyone will be attentive, there will be no further need for governmental control.[25] Men will let the seasons of the year follow each other and be happy to see their king at his leisure go on long spiritual journeys.

Therefore, my writings examine the root and origin of all activities so that we can grasp their central point. Once we have examined the center, we can understand the outcome. Educate a fool in the outcome and great disorder will arise. If at present, in the days of late antiquity, emperors and kings had as much *dao*, virtue, and benevolence as ten thousand times ten thousand men, and if they tried to fulfill heaven's will, they would still be unable to halt disaster. Instead, the numerous calamities and disturbances that are being received and transmitted would increase. Although [rulers] might think of it with personal distress and sorrow and wish to bring order to it all, they are faced with natural disasters and with robbers and bandits in large numbers. Barbarians plot against China. It is not only the ruler's responsibility that former kings made mistakes. We must thoroughly examine its root.

That is why heaven has sent me to publish writings that deliver emperors and kings from the evils that are received and transmitted. Should you, Perfected, be of the opinion that my teachings don't match heaven, just try to act according to my text: you will set things up in complete response [to heaven], and not one fraction amiss. This proves my text is right. If we don't try hard to overcome the grief we are stricken with, why should heaven's way in its silence, without having been stimulated, respond to us?[26]

How can a fool become worthy without study? Where would his harvest come from if a poor man didn't till the soil? Worthiness comes from study as harvesting comes from tilling the soil. Practice what my writings say and you will indeed be harvesting.[27] This I can guarantee. Without study you won't become worthy; without tilling you won't harvest. You know this, don't you?

Yes, I do.

The true doctrine makes [everyone] upright, great virtue brings prosperity, and with benevolence everyone is at the right place. (66.166) We may say that such a regime will bring peace about, necessarily.[28] Do you understand? If you wish to repay heaven and earth and thus live for a long time you must never allow your belief in *dao* to lie idle.

Yes, indeed. I would now like to ask something else. I don't dare stop talking.

Go ahead.

Now how do you know that so many men lack dao, *virtue, and benevolence?*

You have put this well. I watch what they do and what they say.

I would like to hear about it.

Well, when a man notices *dao* but opposes it with hatred, I know that he is completely without it. When someone notices virtue but detests it, I know him to be greatly lacking in virtue. I know that a man who sees benevolence but takes a dislike to it is wicked and unkind. I know that a man who dislikes the sight of good and attentive behavior is a disrespectful and evil person. It is natural for [men] to love others who share their interest and hate those who don't. A good man detests the wicked, just as a wicked person dislikes the good. Is this clear to you?

Yes, it is.

When the wise and worthy of old met someone, they did not talk to him right away but looked at him thoroughly in order to know his good and bad points.[29] When they used this method to mirror someone's conduct they didn't fail once.

Excellent!

Now [it is as if] *dao* had the same bone structure (*gu fa* 骨法) and blood vessels as majestic heaven. So it is heaven's way to detest men who are prone to murdering others. For this reason, heaven repeatedly resents such men. Earth shares bone structure and blood vessels with virtue, and for this reason hates men who cause injury and harm. Earth sees such men as a great nuisance. Benevolence and the wise and worthy have identical bone structure and blood vessels, so the wise and worthy like benevolent action and hate the use of force. Thus, benevolence befriends wise men. That is why the wise and worthy of old had a profound knowledge of how the three dispensations were arranged. When they made laws, they did not dare offend against or depart from true *dao*, virtue, and benevolence. Heaven acts jointly with the four seasons. Since they both put *qi* in motion, with the same intention, heaven resents someone who runs counter to the four seasons. Earth is of the same heart as the five phases and cooperates with them. Together they nourish all beings, and earth greatly deplores that something should be injured and damaged before it is destined to die. The wise and worthy feel and act in unison with benevolence. For this reason, wherever they are, they always venerate *dao*, treasure virtue, and rely on benevolence. They resent as companions men who are prone to using force and doing without benevolence.

So the phase of fire [dominates the] heart. The heart is [the seat of] wisdom.[30] Fire relies on wood for its existence. Benevolence is the characteristic virtue (heart, *xin*) of wood. Fire shines, so it can [help to] distinguish right and wrong, just as the heart is wise and intelligent. (66.167) For this reason the great wise and worthy of old relied on benevolence and intelligence and turned to a lord with *dao*, virtue, and benevolence. So I warn you strictly to give my writings to a lord who knows *dao* and who is virtuous, benevolent, and intelligent. He will certainly take delight in my teachings, arrive at a thorough understanding of their meaning, and publicize them in an edited version. [It all works] as spirits might do. I don't want to brag to you. Put it into practice and [what you do] will correspond [to heaven], as if you had used a pair of compasses and a carpenter's square. In future times, the men of late antiquity will remember my words.

Yes, indeed.

Go now. Study hard. Be diligent in learning *dao*, virtue, and benevolence. You won't achieve anything without them. Make these writings public; don't just store them.

Yes![31]

NOTES

1. As in *Lieʐi* 4 "*Zhong ni*" 仲尼, p. 121, and as below in this section (p. 337), *ʐhi* in *wu ke ʐhi* 無可治 means not "to order," but tedious and oppressive control (see also *Shiji* 87.2561, in the biography of Li Si). Elsewhere in the TPJ, *wu ke ʐhi* means that government can't take place, as is the case without people; see TPJ 65.151.

2. Benevolence *(ren)* is stressed throughout this section, as it is elsewhere (TPJ 41.32) when a program of moral reform is contrasted with the application of a penal code.

3. "Limitless" (*wu ji* 無極) is here used as in *Laoʐi* 28.

4. With Yu (2001a: 135), I correct *de* (virtue) to *de* (to obtain).

5. The character *dong* in *juedong* 絕洞 (most), as above in *juedong wu shang* 絕洞無上 (unsurpassed by anybody), is here mistakenly written as *diao* 涸 (exhausted).

6. "True gate" (*ʐhen men* 真門) does not seem to be found elsewhere in the TPJ or other Daoist material. It probably means the origin of everything, similar to the *miao ʐhi men* 妙之門 of *Laoʐi* 1, which also occurs TPJ 168.472, layer C. "Gate" is used in a similar way in the *Huainan ʐi* 1 "*Yuan dao*" 原道, p. 14a.

7. This passage shows the limitation of the text's ethical thinking. Morality is to be learned for a purpose, that is, to guarantee well-being and long life. It is not a need in itself. Because morality is the result of learning, moral depravity, its opposite, can be identified with stupidity, which is in the first instance evident from not choosing the right teacher.

8. The wording of this passage is doubtful. I understand *san fa* 三法 (three models) in the sense in which it is used in Jia Gongyan's 賈公彥 (seventh-century) commen-

tary to the *Zhou li* (*"Qiu guan, si ci"* 秋官司刺, p. 880c) to describe methods of government used in the past, which did not alienate the population. Elsewhere in the TPJ, the term is used similarly to *tian fa* (heaven's model), in the sense of "the models of heaven and earth, Yin and Yang, and of their intercourse" (TPJ p. 695, *Chao,* part 8). Yu (2001a: 137) argues that "three" stands here, as in so many other cases, for heaven, earth, and man. The problem with this is that *fa* used in this sense is never said to proclaim or implement punishment, as suggested in the passage at hand.

The word *shi* 士 (scholar) is used here and throughout the text as broadly as in other Han dynasty material (see Ch'ü 1972: 101) and refers to all men who were literate and played a role as teachers, students, and advisors to local magnates, and also played a role in official service.

9. This refers to *Laozi* 41, which in Waley's (1934: 193) translation reads: "When the man of highest capacities (*shang shi* 上士) hears Tao he does his best to put it into practice. When the man of middling capacity (*zhong shi* 中士) hears Tao he is in two minds about it. When the man of low capacity (*xia shi* 下士) hears Tao he laughs loudly at it. If he did not laugh, it would not be worth the name of Tao."

10. *Yi* (through) is here and frequently in this section read as *yi* (already), with Yu (2001a: 138).

11. With Yu (2001a: 138), I read *er* as *neng,* and throughout the passage I understand *qin* 勤 (diligent) as *jin* 僅 (barely).

12. There is a strong psychological element throughout this passage. Here the text's utopian quality is explained as being caused by the gap between aim and achievement in the average person. The Celestial Master argues that his doctrine takes this into consideration by raising behavioral norms to the highest possible level.

13. The expression *tian zheng wen fa,* which is used only here, combines heaven's "standard patterns" (TPJ 48.58) and "standard models" (TPJ 132.359).

14. Yu (2001a: 139) suggests that the passage is corrupt. He suggests the addition of *cai de zhong shan* 纔得中善: "Only through a diligent study of the true doctrine will someone learn to be of average goodness." As the text stands, much stress is laid on the final particle *er* 耳.

15. *Shan dao* 善道 is occasionally used as if it were another term for *zhen dao* 真道: "Preserve the valuable teachings and you cut off the road to disaster" (TPJ 134.374). What is *shan* (good), however, is worth less than what is *zhen,* as can be seen from the modifications of *shan:* the true cannot exist in high, medium, and lower forms, as can the good.

16. The two missing characters are read as *zhi yi* 之矣.

17. "Without measure" *(wu shu)* is here and in the following intensified to *wu fu shu* 無復數, an expression that is characteristic of this section.

18. For "ignore the model" (*shi fa* 失法) as used in this section, cf. the expression *shi fa du* in section 58.

19. "The people of heaven" are *taiping* adherents; see above, section 61.

20. Forced labor was one of the punishments meted out in the world below.

21. *Xue* (study) is the general remedy:

> Well, if this is the fate heaven has destined for you, you will leave the world far behind once you take up the study [of *dao*]. When a person of medium worth studies it, he can live a very long time, and when a foolish person does so, he can still live a long time. If you want to see some proof of this, take the way in which people in general study. Through study a person of great worth can become a high official, a person of medium worth can become an official of medium rank, and a foolish person can become a petty official who, compared to the masses, is a figure of some impact. This means that one must study hard. (TPJ 108.289)

22. *Zhang duan* 長短 (the long and the short) was a Warring States political and rhetorical skill: see Tian Dan's biography in the *Shi ji* (94.2649, in Sima Qian's evaluation) and the *Wen xin diao long* 18 *"Lun shuo,"* p. 27a.

23. The expression *shu shu* 數書 is understood as referring to the books listed in the *shu shu* 數術 division of the bibliographical chapter of the *Han shu*. These books deal with the theory and practice of divination (cf. Kalinoswki 2003:11). In disparaging this material the Celestial Master attacks an important element of Han dynasty scholarship.

24. Throughout the text it becomes clear that the Celestial Master does not think highly of rituals; cf. Harper's (2004: 264f.) discussion and his translation of TPJ 201.620, layer B. But this does not mean that the culprit must give up all hope of redemption. The following passage belongs to a section full of polemics against certain "heterodox," and perhaps Buddhist, practices:

> Someone about to be exterminated by heaven might still say, full of confidence, that he will live a long time. Once heaven is in the process of killing him he might cry to heaven and wail to earth and call himself maltreated (*yuan* 冤). He still won't understand what he did wrong. Then heaven will interrogate him and banish him. He will be put somewhere unpleasant and wild, to make him think of himself. If you want to understand how this works, this is just as when an enlightened ruler examines a person's crime but does not have him killed. Depending on the size of his crime, he is being sentenced, more severely for a big crime, and less so for a petty crime. This should make him submissive. If he dies knowing himself, he will be without hatred and not say a word. If he does not give up talking but calls himself maltreated, he will die full of hate, just as the subjects of the Five Hegemons died with great hatred in their hearts. (TPJ 208.663; cf. Masaaki 2002: 47)

This passage leaves unclear whether the culprit's address to heaven is actually of much use to him. The view expressed in layer B is more clear-cut and practical:

> What people nowadays do is foolish and shallow. When they become ill and are on the brink of death they don't turn to heaven to acknowledge their mistakes and bow to it. All the members of a family must help each other to seek forgiveness. After a number of days, heaven might pardon [the culprit] and let him recover and live for a while.

Should he trespass again, it would be of no avail to bow to heaven. (TPJ 201.621; cf. Masaaki 2002: 46; Espesset 2002b: 42f.)

Timing is an important aspect of redemption. Confession, regret, and reform must come at the right time, as the passage at hand stresses.

25. The section contrasts governmental control with spiritual self-discipline. The gist is that proper education makes government virtually superfluous. In its detail, the argument does not follow quietist principles, as, for instance, expressed in the *Laozi*, but rather moral philosophers like Xunzi, who contrasts virtuous and thus responsible conduct with behavior that needs to be restrained by penalties.

26. This is another example of heaven's almost divine way of action. It extends active support when it sees and esteems a human being's serious effort; see also TPJ 63.134, where it is proposed that the son, exhausted by his efforts on behalf of his parents' longevity, will get celestial support.

27. The two missing characters are read as *you shou* 有收.

28. With Yu (2001a: 142), I read *wan* 萬 (ten thousand) for *mo* 莫 (none).

29. The sage King Wen is said to have shown an interest in this question. The *Da Dai Li ji* (chap. 10 *"Wen wang guan ren"* 文王官人, pp. 169–72) contains a section on the criteria he thought appropriate for choosing officials.

30. The sixth-century *Wu xing dayi* 3.54 discusses the problem that, during the Han, the heart was identified with fire by some—for example, the *Shuo wen jie zi* author Xu Shen (ca. 55–ca.149)—and with earth by Zheng Xuan (127–200) and others (see Kalinowski 1991: 287 and 520f.). The tradition of the Monthly Ordinances (see, for instance, *Huainan zi* 5 *"Shi ze"* 時則, p. 8a) associates the heart with earth. As the leading body organ, the heart had to belong to the phase that was seen as leading, as earth was until the outgoing first century B.C.E. In contrast to this, the TPJ coherently identifies heart with fire: see TPJ 212.678 and:

> Heart is the most spiritlike and most honored of the bodily organs. It is spiritlike, wise, and pure and is Yang. [It belongs to] the phase of fire. Fire is what moves upward and shines like heaven. Thus the sun reigns through fire and creates heaven's standard (*zheng* 正) so that everything becomes clear. (TPJ 153.426)

31. The summary says:

> This section enlightens the heart of the worthy again in order to do away with foolish and dumb writings. If you are in doubt, use it for instruction.

· Appendix

THE COMPOSITION OF THE TPJ

The transmitted text of the TPJ goes back to Upper Clarity adherents in the sixth century who, with imperial support, edited and published an old *taiping* scripture. Despite all we know about these editors, we do not know who the authors of the original material were. It is important to realize, however, that the TPJ was by no means the only "old" Daoist text to emerge in the sixth century. Although it was older than the rest, and it differed from virtually all the other texts in its style and message, we may assume that it was given treatment similar to that of other edited materials, which were indeed as old as their editors claimed and were left largely in their original shape.[1] Tao Hongjing's *Declaration of the Perfected (Zhen'gao)* consists to a large extent of carefully edited fourth-century material. Since earlier or parallel sources of *taiping* material are not available, it is hard to estimate the exact input of Upper Clarity editors. As far as we know, *taiping* material has been transmitted only in the TPJ. This makes it difficult to specify editorial methods. However, if we look at the way in which the *Taiping jing chao* (hereafter *Chao*) edits the old text, we can get an idea of what can be done. The *Chao* cuts out small talk, repetitions, tedious and clumsy passages, and inelegant or unclear expressions. The received text of the TPJ, or at least the Celestial Master dialogues, shows no traces of such editorial censorship. We must assume that its editors were more faithful to their material. It may be added that the stylistic peculiarity of layer A makes imitation rather difficult, as can be seen from one obvious and very poorly executed attempt to do so.[2] All this allows us to assume that the sixth-century text was indeed edited rather than written. However, controversy remains over the extent to which the editors rearranged the material. Ōfuchi Ninji,[3] for instance, has argued for a high level of correspondence between the old text and its reedited version, while Yoshioka Yoshitoyo[4] has stressed the intensity of sixth-century editorial activity. He has proposed that the sixth-century text was derived from two sources. First, and providing the material for the Celestial Master dialogues of layer A, there was a *Dongji zhi jing* 洞極之經 in 144 *juan,* which he suggests went back to Zhang Daoling; second, and only as a supplement, there was the 170-*juan* TPJ, which he identified with Gan Ji's *Taiping qing ling shu.* The main source for supposing there to have been two old *taiping* texts—that is, one in 170 and another in 144 *juan*—is the "Seven Divisions" section in *Yunji qiqian,* chapter 6. After quoting passages from the TPJ, the "Seven Divisions" says:

> The number of chapters is perhaps not identical [in different editions?].
> Nowadays an edition in ten divisions, *jia, yi,* etc., in 170 *juan* is in circulation.
> According to the *Zhengyi jing* a *Taiping dongji zhi jing* exists in 144 *juan.* Today
> this scripture is almost entirely lost. Both scriptures provide a comprehensive
> explanation of the proper way of governing, evident causes, long-term effects,
> prohibitions and techniques, etc. According to the [now lost] *Zhengyi jing,* the
> Greatest and Highest [that is, Laozi] gave the *Dongji zhi jing* in 140 *juan*[5] to the
> Celestial Master [that is, Zhang Daoling] in the year 142 C.E.[6]

The passage continues with a quotation from the *Preface to the 180 Precepts,* which explains the origin of the 170-*juan* version: it was supposed to have been handed to Gan Ji.[7] A *Dongji zhi jing* was identified with the TPJ because the received text of the TPJ contains the term *dongji* (complete pervasion) and even refers to a *Dongji zhi jing.*[8] The "Seven Divisions" passage seems to tell us that there were two versions of the text, one going back to Zhang Daoling, the other to Gan Ji, and that in the Sui period, that is, after Zhou Zhixiang's edition of what became the received text, most of the old *Dongji jing* was lost.[9] The *Zhengyi jing,* of which we only have the isolated fragments that are quoted in other works, is a crucial source for this information. Ōfuchi doubts its reliability because he sees it as nothing more than the propagandistic effort of a more northern-oriented group of Celestial Master adherents to increase the status of Zhang Daoling.[10] Without the two texts to lean on, Yoshioka's complicated construction of a multilayered editing process is hard to sustain, which would leave Ōfuchi to argue that the sixth-century text is more or less the original *Taiping qing ling shu.*

There are other references, however, that point to two separate texts. Yamada uses the fact that the *Baopu zi* bibliography mentions two texts, that is, the 50-*juan Taiping jing* and the 170-*juan Jiayi jing*, to support Yoshioka's thesis of a twofold transmission of the old text. He further reminds us that Upper Clarity Daoists had a tradition of collating texts from different sources.[11] This is a valid point. We can add to this that the suggestion of separate sources, at least for layer A and layer B, as will be pointed out in the following, makes sense. The sixth-century editors do not convey details of their sources; the reason for this might be that the TPJ contains hardly any material that could be represented as revealed in the sense in which passages in the *Zhen'gao* are said to have originated directly with divine figures.

A major editorial addition to the old material is a table of contents, which lists titles for all 366 sections, mainly as "methods" (*fa* 法) and "instructions" (*jue* 訣), with a few interspersed "precepts" (*jie* 戒). With good reason, this table was published separately, as can be seen from Dunhuang fragment S 4226. It is an impressive list of topics for anyone interested in the Daoist worldview and style of life, and it is a testament to the wide range of the old text, from the first section's "The method for distinguishing between right and wrong by divination" and "The method for guarding oneself against misfortune" to more general topics such as "The method for distinguishing between good and evil in human actions." Other topics are more concerned with matters of cultural and political practice, as reflecting in the sections "The method for revising old writings" and "The method for a king to be carefree." For those parts of the text that have been transmitted and for which comparison is possible, the titles are appropriate more often than not. They tend to select one of several points dealt with in a section, but usually this selection is in line with the main theme of a section. The Daoist canon edition has section titles—there are no chapter titles—which are in general identical with the titles given in S 4226. As if to provide the reader with some guidance, sections in the Daoist canon edition are as a rule followed by brief one-line summaries.[12] As Wang Ming points out, titles in "old books"[13] were customarily given at the end, since readers would open a scripture by rolling it up from the back. We may assume, therefore, that the titles placed at the opening of each section go back to the sixth-century editors of the 366-section version of the text, while the summaries are of a different and necessarily earlier origin. They have been transmitted in particularly bad shape and are often corrupt beyond any hope of emendation. They do not add up to 366, and one summary can cover two or more sections.[14] We may assume, therefore, that the division into 366 sections arose with the sixth-century editors, and that the material they used consisted of a smaller number of subdivisions.[15] That there were subdivisions holds true for all layers, even for the talismans of layer C, which contains the following summary: "To the right is advice on reduplicated characters that promote what is supreme and reduce harmful influences."[16] Often such a summary repeats or varies a section's title, or, to put it correctly, the authors of the title seem to make use of what is said in the summary. Although summaries do not exist for material available only in the *Chao*, they cover virtually the whole of the transmitted text. Titles and summaries are useful organizational tools, especially since it is not easy to make out any general rule that would guide the sequence of sections. While they form clusters, so that several consecutive sections deal with various aspects of one specific topic, the sequence of these clusters does not seem be of any doctrinal relevance.[17]

The external appearance of the TPJ conforms to what we can conjecture about its origin. The originality of the text's message is in many parts matched by a use of language that has no parallels in the written tradition. Words are newly created, characters are used in a mistaken or at least an unusual way, and structural components are given new functions. In this, some similarities to Han dynasty epigraphical material can be detected,[18] and there are certain parallels to the language used in early Buddhist translations.[19]

The TPJ corpus consists of different sets, the most important of which is the textus receptus, which has been transmitted in the Daoist canon. There is also the table of contents of the sixth-century text that was found among the Dunhuang manuscripts (S 4226). Of particular importance is the *Chao*, a digest version of the original text. The *Chao* consists of excerpts of the TPJ, organized in ten parts like the scripture itself, and it follows more or less the TPJ's order of chapters and sections. It has been attributed to Lüqiu Fangyuan (d. 902), who lived a hermit's life, wrote several texts, and took, as we are told, an interest in "guarding the one," which is one of the TPJ's main topics.[20]

This additional material helps us go beyond the corruption and curtailment of the received text to restore an image of its original sixth-century version. Espesset gives a careful account of the stages by which parts of the original sixth-century text were lost. From the sixth century onward, the TPJ's fate was linked to the general destiny of Daoist scriptures, and in particular to the different editions of the Daoist canon through the Song and Ming dynasties. The original text had 170 chapters, while the present-day text, while still long, has only 57.

One might call today's text overorganized, but so was the original sixth-century text. It consisted of ten parts, 170 chapters, and 366 sections. The received text contains a passage that explains the symbolic value of the figure 170. We are told that

170 represents a combination of the "one," where everything begins, and "hundred," where it ends, supported by "seven," which is the number of stars in the Dipper.[21] The symbolic value of "ten," representing the ten celestial stems, and of "366" for the days of the year is evident. The size and structure of the scripture are unusual, as a cursory glance at the tables of contents of other lengthy ancient and medieval scriptures will affirm. However, there are reasons for this. One is the almost divine position attributed to heaven throughout most of the text. It therefore makes sense to represent heaven's structure visibly in the celestial scripture it is supposed to have authorized. The other is the argumentative and stylistic weakness of the textual material. Chapters and sections are often badly presented; they do not consist of the neatly composed individual essays that make up the great Han dynasty texts. Internal links and sequence are weak. From an editor's point of view, it is a reasonable endeavor to mend this by an outside structure of some rigidity.

The organization of the text remains superficial. The seventeen chapters of one identical part have little in common, and the same often holds true for the sections that make up one chapter. Sections are the text's smallest units, and they deal in general with one topic only, or at least with interconnected topics. The text's first two parts, in which one chapter contains only one section, are neatly organized. The number of sections per chapter differs widely in the rest of the text, depending on the size of the sections and on the style in which they are written, and varies from one to twelve. When sections are written in a compact style, without dialogues, more of them are assembled into a single chapter. Since the scripture's contents are organized in sections, the present translation is also divided into sections.

The inherent disorder of the text relates not only to its content, but also to the way it is written. Distinctly different styles of writing can be made out. Xiong Deji was the first to analyze this,[22] and Hachiya and Takahashi have slightly modified his division of the text according to these styles.[23] Much of this modification has to do with differences within style B material and does not force us to assume the existence of another style. Style A, or layer A, material looks as if it were based on transcriptions of the discussions taking place between a Daoist master and a select group of disciples. The suggestions made above in the Introduction about the text's origin are mainly based on evidence derived from this part of the TPJ. Layer B material is far less colloquial, although it also contains some passages in direct speech. Disparate though they are, we may categorize all passages that do not belong to either layer A or layer B as layer C material. Layer C includes an illustration showing a "house of emptiness and nothingness" that resembles the picture of a small building in the Upper Clarity text *Shangqing qusu jueci lu*.[24] Layer C also contains talismans; such talismans accompanied many Daoist scriptures.[25] *Taiping* talismans were known before the sixth-century TPJ, as mentioned in Ge Hong's *Neipian* under the title *Li'er taiping fu* 李耳太平符.[26] We must assume that all of this material assembled in today's text was part of the sixth-century text. The only later additions to layer C are four sets of drawings of Daoist adepts and their spiritual counterparts, which seem to be of Ming dynasty origin and to be replacing a set of original illustrations. There is no reason to doubt the age of the written text accompanying them, and the S 4226 table of contents lists the respective sections as "illustrations" 圖.

It is appropriate to refer to the stylistically different materials of the text as "layers" since the difference in style is to some extent accompanied by a difference in topic. The program of social reform that is expected to prepare for and facilitate the arrival of great peace is a specialty of layer A. The search for transcendence, for becoming a *xian* 仙, and for joining the ranks of celestial figures is more pronounced in layer B. Layer C comprises material that does not contain dialogues, has little to say that cannot be found elsewhere, and shows no trace of missionary activity.

Most of the text belongs to layer A, that is, it consists of dialogues between a Celestial Master and his disciple or disciples. They interact as if they were real people, asking questions of each other and responding in turn. At times the Master criticizes the disciple's answers, or the disciple demands a more detailed reply. As far as can be determined, the discussion is always between two parties. A disciple always addresses the Master, never another disciple. We do not know whether the Master is speaking to an individual disciple or to a group of disciples, except in the rare instance when he addresses a Perfected called Chun 純.[27] When the Master talks to a group, its members are called the "six disciples" or the "disciples of the six directions." We may assume that the two names refer to the same group and that the terms are used as shorthand for the "disciples who have come from everywhere."[28] Dialogues generally begin with one of two scenarios. The Celestial Master might issue an invitation to an individual student, addressed as "Perfected," to step forward and discuss matters with him, or a disciple might approach the Master with a question. The two forms are used without any noticeable distinction. They both involve an introductory interchange of short remarks. Once the disciple's misunderstanding has been clarified and the topic of interest has been pinpointed, the Master then embarks on a longish lecture, with only occasional interruptions. Throughout the dialogues he shows a personal concern for the disciples. He is pleased or angry with his audience, and praises and admonishes them. The disciples are eager and attentive, fearful and curious. Their straightforward, often self-interested, approach demands the reader's attention and even sympathy. The disciples are not very bright. Often—and sometimes repeatedly—they fall into an intellectual trap laid for them by the Master. They are also worldly and filled with human weakness, while the Master's views tend to be strict and fundamentalist.

It is not difficult to distinguish layer A from layer B since their stylistic characteristics and general language use are different enough. It is possible, moreover, to approach the rest of the text from the assumption that it resembles either layer A or layer B material. Most of the text that shows no clear characteristic of either layer A or layer B contains traces of layer A. This is obvious for sections 68 to 77 and for section 83, for example, which are close to layer A. The topics dealt with are all in the range of layer A topics: writings, prognostics, the healing powers of plants and animals, the cosmic order, moxibustion, acupuncture, tombs, and music.[29] The language has certain layer A peculiarities: "my writings" (*wo shu* 我 書) and "my teachings" (*wu dao* 吾 道) do not occur in layer B material;[30] "emperors and kings" (*di wang* 帝 王), which is used in these sections, occurs continuously in layer A material but is very rare in layer B;[31] and the phrase *wan bu shi yi* 萬 不 失 一, which is used frequently in layer A material, does not occur in layer B sections. Other sections include the posing of questions in addition to the use of layer A vocabulary and deal with topics that fall within the range of layer A. This range is wide but is principally concerned with the political and social effects of the Master's doctrine. I see such sections as shortened and stylistically improved versions of the lectures that are central to most of layer A. They are therefore rewritten or alternative written versions of original layer A sections. This material does not amount to an independent layer. It is termed layer A' in the following.

The term "Celestial Master" does not occur in layer A'. It is also avoided in the *Chao* and in most of the quotations from the TPJ.[32] The reason for this is probably that at a certain stage in the development of the religion the title "Celestial Master" had become identified with specific historical figures: Zhang Daoling, for instance, or Kou Qianzhi.

It may be argued that the long-winded, space-consuming layer A style of writing encouraged the production of résumés, that is, of layer A' material. Some of this layer A' material may well go back to the original note taking. Individual note takers might have chosen to provide synopses rather than full transcriptions of the whole session. The original sixth-century text may have contained more of such digest passages. This would explain why the few early quotations from the text that have been transmitted do not contain colloquial elements.[33] It is easy to see why résumés would have been more widely distributed than the full text.

The TPJ contains far less layer B than layer A material. Part 7 consists mainly of layer B material; part 9 contains two chapters with six sections of layer B material, according to my reading of the *Chao;* and there are possibly a couple of sections of layer B material in part 4. The use of language in the Layer B material represents a conservative writing style and follows the standards customary in literary Chinese. Clusters are avoided, parallel sentences structure the flow of the text, and there are sequences of short, four-character sentences. The difference between the styles of expression of layers A and B is striking. To give an example, in layer A, the Celestial Master uses the following words to demand that his disciples distribute his material:

So I warn you strictly to give my writings to a lord who knows *dao* and who is virtuous, benevolent, and intelligent. He will certainly take delight in my teachings, arrive at a thorough understanding of their meaning, and publicize them in an edited version.[34]

In layer B, a similar message is expressed in two brief four-character sentences: "This text must be distributed; it must not be intercepted."[35] Layer B praises the men of old in the following words:

In early antiquity, men were knowledgeable and never dared act against the commandments. They improved and corrected themselves in fear of going astray.[36]

In layer A, these men are usually "the wise and worthy of old" and their "knowledge" is outlined in much detail:

This is why the wise and worthy of old withdrew day and night from business in order to think deeply. They never dared ignore what heaven felt. So they were able to serve majestic heaven as their father and majestic earth as their mother, the sun as their older and the moon as their younger brother. They kept the firmament (*tian wen* 天文) in correct shape and the five phases stable. They followed the four seasons. They observed their coming and going. Through self-reflection, they corrected their own conduct. By understanding [things] thoroughly they knew about gain and loss. Their essential *dao* was simply [the way in which] heaven and earth maintained themselves. They took heaven's support, expressed in Yellow River maps and Luo writings, as their mandate. For this reason all their actions were in correspondence, as if they were spirits. Only by these means did they thoroughly fulfill heaven's wishes. Their words were a precise fit, as if compasses and carpenter's square had been applied. So spirits and other numinous beings were busy on their behalf.[37]

Layer A is verbose and circuitous, whereas layer B is brief and to the point. This difference cannot be put down to the use of direct speech in layer A; the dialogues interspersed in layer B material do not differ in language use or content from the rest of this layer.[38] In layer B, the Celestial Lord (*tian jun* 天君), Great Spirit (*da shen* 大神), Disciple (*sheng* 生), and Wise Man (*sheng ren* 聖人) speak literary Chinese, as do discussants in the *Zhen'gao*.[39] The Celestial Lord is not "heaven," but through the spirits, whom he employs, he knows all, so we may call him omniscient.[40] He has an impact on the length of a human being's life, in contrast to the Celestial Master, who does not. Therefore, the Celestial Lord's authority resembles that of heaven more closely than does that of the Celestial Master. The main speaker is the Great Spirit. He is teacher of the Disciple and the Wise Man, and himself a subordinate and disciple of the Celestial Lord, who takes an interest in the Disciple through the Great Spirit's mediation. The scenario of these conversations resembles the situation depicted in the first chapter of the *Zhen'gao*. Whether the disciple, when meeting with transcendents, is on a spiritual journey is not expressed clearly, but given that he meets with a figure as spiritual as the Celestial Lord, we must expect that it is so. In contrast, the Celestial Master meets his disciples in a worldly, school-like environment.

Certain sections of the text where these figures are not mentioned may still be seen as layer B material. An introductory *wei* 惟 [41] characterizes this style. The character is used as if by editorial design, to announce that the following comes from one source rather than from another.

The content of layer B is distinct, at least in parts. The main concern is longevity, which is seen as an individual problem. Although the date of a person's birth has some impact on the length of his life, he won't live long if he does not adhere to moral rules. A good person believes in heaven, does as heaven bids, and respects all the generally established rules of good conduct. He does not lie, cheat, or rob, is a good son, and does not ruin his family by drinking.[42] However, in layer B the more specific reforms suggested in layer A are not referred to, and the definition of good and bad conduct is conservative. Filial piety, for instance, is seen as an important condition for living a long life,[43] and it is said to consist largely of performing the appropriate sacrifices and other rituals in honor of one's ancestors.[44] The Celestial Master of layer A, on the other hand, stresses the need for a filial son to prolong the life of his parents.[45] There is no mention in layer B of an approaching apocalypse, and consequently no need for mass conversion and government-induced social reform. However, good conduct does not automatically guarantee a long life. The text envisages a dual-track system. On one side is the disciple's lifestyle and personal background. On the other is a bureaucratic process of submitting petitions to the right figures in the celestial bureaucracy in the hope of influencing examinations and high-level decisions so that the applicant's good qualities are taken into proper consideration. Words pertaining to bookkeeping abound.[46] The administration of heaven, its bureaucracy, its archives, and the form of its publications are of great interest to the authors of layer B. The attraction of this topic is enhanced by the fact that the celestial bureaucracy is not a closed shop, something that is hinted at in layer A and further described throughout layer B. Deserving individuals can look forward to positions in the celestial world. The textus receptus also contains a few modified layer B passages, similar to layer A' passages.[47]

There are two reasons that I read layer A and layer B material under the assumption that layer A material was produced before layer B and that it was known to the author or authors of layer B. First, specific TPJ terms like "inheriting and transmitting [evil]" (*cheng fu* 承 負) and "twelve thousand beings and objects" (*wan er qian wu* 萬 二 千 物) are used but not explained in layer B, as if readers were expected to know their meaning.[48] Second, we might call the layer A vision of sociopolitical renewal empire-oriented. It is easier to place it in the environment of the Han empire than in the period during or after its breakdown, that is, after the "apocalypse" had in some sense taken place. For layer A, a world that deserved saving and could be saved still existed. For layer B material, the individual's main contact is with a celestial bureaucracy. He must learn to understand its rules, regulations, and archives for the sake of his own earthly and post-earthly well-being. The controller of destiny is frequently mentioned throughout layer B material, and so too is the "broad daylight" (*bai ri* 白 日) in which the fortunate adept will rise to heaven. This term does not occur at all in layer A material. Still, the two layers share a number of features. Stylistically, in the first instance, both contain dialogues between adepts and their superiors that involve elements of direct speech and, in particular, frequent exhortations. "Be careful to . . . " (*shen zhi* 慎 之) is a constant feature of both layers. In terms of content, both layers state that attending to moral norms is the basis for human happiness. Layer B material shows traces of a missionary project.[49] The promise of a great peace bound to arrive pervades the text. The misery of the poor is deplored.[50]

Clearly, what has been presented here is not a thorough method of dividing the text. The main problem with this division is the assumption that the use of language in layers A and B of the received text provides the full picture, and that it is thus permissible to define a combination of characters as "characteristic of layer A" if they are frequent in the layer A material of the textus receptus and are not used in layer B. Moreover, an argument based on certain isolated language elements cannot replace a full-fledged linguistic analysis. In the meantime, however, I consider the results of this division sound enough to suggest reducing the amount of layer C material to a few isolated chapters and sections, and calling the rest either layer A' or layer B'. A similar approach is taken to the large amount of text that is available only in the form of the *Chao*. Here again we find traces of either layer A or layer B expressions, and of specific terminology. No joint characteristics can be established for layer C. The common feature of these materials is the scripture's sixth-century editors.[51]

With all of this, it must be kept in mind that until its sixth-century edition the transmission of *taiping*-related material was open to loss, additions, and changes. We are told that it was practiced "in private."[52] Going back to the very beginnings of Daoism, it was not protected by any school or movement. It has been suggested that at some stage the Du 杜 family, with its long background of Daoist commitment, felt responsible for the text.[53] However, this is hard to verify, and in any case it would not amount to a continuous tradition. Material was therefore added, as, for instance, section 51, which is rendered suspect by the fact that it has virtually nothing to say and contains a direct appeal to the editors regarding where it should be placed.

A rough overview of the received text might clarify some of what has been said here. It follows Wang Ming's division of the text supported by Yu Liming's corrections. Espesset's thorough and meticulous account of the whole text has been consulted continuously, in particular for those parts for which the *Chao* is our only source.[54] I have marked the points where my division of the text into sections differs from his. According to my list, a number of *Chao* passages cannot be attributed to an S 4226 section title. This is not surprising when we consider that some TPJ section titles are not entirely appropriate and that some *Chao* quotations are quite short. The attribution to layers is my own.[55] Since, according to S 4226, none of the first seventeen chapters is subdivided into sections, we must assume that part 1 was relatively short to begin with. From the evidence of the textus receptus, we know that the *Chao* skips sections and that it changes their sequence. This must be kept in mind when attempting to sketch the original text according to the *Chao*. In the following list italics are used for those parts, chapters, and sections that are not in the transmitted text of the TPJ; "ch." stands for "chapter," "s." for "section," and "p." for page number, and the number following the page number is the line number.

PART 1 (CHAO ONLY)

ch. 1	A?[56]	(p. 718.7–720.11)
ch. 2	?[57]	(p. 720.12–722.4)
ch. 3	?[58]	(p. 722.5–723.2)
ch. 4	?	(p. 723.2–8)
ch. 5	?	(p. 724.4–7)
ch. 6	?	(p. 724.8–725.5)
ch. 7	A?[59]	(p. 725.6–726.1)
ch. 8	?	(p. 726.1–4)
ch. 9	A?[60]	(p. 726.5–12)
ch. 10	?	(p. 727.1–11)
ch. 11	?	(p. 728.1–5)
ch. 12	?	(p. 728.6–12)
ch. 13	?	(p. 729.1–730.2)
ch. 14	?	(p. 730.3–11)
ch. 15	?	(p. 723.9–724.3)
ch. 16	?	(p. 730.12–731.9)
ch. 17	A?[61]	(p. 731.10–732.6)

PART 2 (CHAO ONLY)[62]

ch. 18	?[63]	(p. 11.3–8)
ch. 19	?	(p. 12.1–10)
ch. 21	A?[64]	(p. 12.11–13.7)
ch. 22	A?[65]	(p. 13.8–15.1)
ch. 24?	?[66]	(p. 15.1–4)
ch. 26	A?[67]	(p. 15.5–9)
ch. 27	?[68]	(p. 15.10–16.11)
ch. 29	A?[69]	(p. 16.12–17.6)
ch. 30	?	(p. 17.7–18.10)
ch. 31	A[70]	(p. 18.11–20.6)
ch. 32	A?[71]	(p. 20.7–21.11)

ch. 33	*s. 33*	*A?*[72]	*(p. 21.12–22.3)*
ch. 34	*s. ?*	*A*[73]	*(p. 24.10–27.8)*
	s. 40	*A*[74]	*(p. 22.4–24.9)*

PART 3[75]

ch. 35	s. 41	A; the second half is linked to section 42.
	s. 42	A
	s. 43	A
ch. 36	s. 44	A
	s. 45	A; this section is close to section 44.
	s. 46	A
ch. 37	s. 47	A; the second half is linked to section 48.
	s. 48	A
ch. 38[76]		
ch. 39	s. 50	A
	s. 51	A; this very short section is linked to section 50.
ch. 40	s. 52	A
	s. 53	A
ch. 41	s. 54	A; this section records two dialogues; the second half is poorly transmitted.
	s. 55	A
ch. 42	s. 56	A; there is no introduction.
	s. 57	A; the introduction is unusual.
	s. 58	A
ch. 43	s. 59	A
ch. 44	s. 60	A; Chun is mentioned.
ch. 45	s. 61	A; this section records two dialogues (rupture p. 122?); the content is coherent.
ch. 46	s. 62	A
ch. 47	s. 63	A
	s. 64	A
ch. 48	s. 65	A
ch. 49	s. 66	A

ch. 50	s. 67	A; Chun is mentioned; there are no dialogue elements toward the end.
	s. 68	A'?[77] This and the next sections of this chapter are very short.
	s. 69	?
	s. 70	?
	s. 71	?
	s. 72	A'?[78]
	s. 73	?
	s. 74	?
	s. 75	?
	s. 76	?
	s. 77	A[79]
ch. 51	s. 78	A; Chun is mentioned.

PART 4

ch. 52	s. 79	? (Chao *only*)[80]	
ch. 53	s. 80	A	
ch. 54	s. 81	A	
ch. 55	s. 82	A	
	s. 83	?	
ch. 56	s. 84	B?[81]	*(p. 212.3–12)*
ch. 57	s. 88	B?[82]	*(p. 212.12–214.6)*
	s. 89	A?[83]	*(p. 214.8–215.6)*
ch. 58	s. 90	A?[84]	*(p. 216.6–217.7)*
ch. 59	s. 91	A[85]	*(p. 217.9–219.2)*
ch. 60	s. 94	A[86]	*(p. 219.4–5)*
ch. 61	s. 95	A?[87]	*(p. 219.6–220.7)*
ch. 62	s. 96?	A?[88]	*(p. 220.9–222.8)*
ch. 64	s. 98?	A[89]	*(p. 222.13–323.3)*
ch. 65	s. 99	A; Chun and the "six Perfected" are mentioned.	
	s. 100	A; the topic is close to sections 99 and 101; the "six Perfected" are mentioned.	

s. 101   A; the topic is close to sections 100 and 102; the "six Per-
        fected" are mentioned.

ch. 66 s. 102   A; linked to section 101; a short second session is dealt with at
        the end (p. 239.7).

ch. 67 s. 103   A; this section is very long and consists of four dialogues.[90]

ch. 68 s. 104   A; the "six Perfected" are mentioned.

PART 5

ch. 69 s. 105   A

ch. 70 s. 106   A; there are dialogue elements only at the beginning.

ch. 71 s. 107   A

        s. 108   A'; the dialogue between the Perfected and Spiritlike Man is
        recorded in *Chao* style.[91]

ch. 72 s. 109   A ; the "Perfected from all six directions" are mentioned.

        s. 110   A

        s. 111   A

ch. 73 *s. 112* *A*[92]   *(p. 309.2–310.2)* (Chao *only*)

ch. 74 *s. 115?* *A?*[93]   *(p. 301.4–302.13)*[94] (Chao *only*)

ch. 77 *s. 118* *A?*[95]   *(p. 303.2–304.3)* (Chao *only*)

ch 79 *s. 120* *A*[96]   *(p. 304.3–305.3)* (Chao *only*)

ch. 80 *s. 121* *?*[97]   *(p. 305.3–306.3)* (Chao *only*)

ch. 81 *s. 122* *A'?*[98]   *(p. 306.5–307.9)* (Chao *only*)

ch. 82 *s. 123* *?*   *(p. 310.4–311.8)* (Chao *only*)

ch. 83 *s. 124* *?*   *(p. 307.11–308.7)* (Chao *only*)

PART 6

ch. 86 s. 127   A; the "six disciples" are mentioned; several dialogues are
        reported.[99]

ch. 87 *s. 128* *A?*[100]   *(p. 330.3–7)* (Chao *only*)

ch. 88 s. 129   A; "Perfected from all six directions" are mentioned; two
        dialogues are reported.[101]

ch. 89 s. 130   A'?[102]

ch. 90 s. 131   A

ch. 91 s. 132   A

ch. 92	s. 133	A; the topic of this section is close to that of sections 134 and 135.
	s. 134	A[103]
	s. 135	A
	s. 136	A
ch. 93	s. 137	A
	s. 138	A
	s. 139	A; "six Perfected"; two dialogues are reported.[104]
	s. 140	A
	s. 141	A: there is no introductory passage.
ch. 94	*s. 143*	*?[105]*	*(p. 464.3–8)* (Chao *only*)
	s. 144	*?*	*(p. 464.8–465.11)* (Chao *only*)
	s. 145	*A?[106]*	*(p. 465.11–466.11)* (Chao *only*)
	s. 146	*?*	*(p. 467.12–468.1)* (Chao *only*)
ch. 95	*s. 148*	*A?[107]*	*(p. 468.1–7)* (Chao *only*)
	s. 149	*A[108]*	*(p. 466.12–467.10)* (Chao *only*)
ch. 96	s. 151	A; "six Perfected"; the discussion is continued in section 152.
	s. 152	A;[109] there is no introductory passage.
	s. 153	A[110]
ch. 97	s. 154	A
	s. 155	A
ch. 98	s. 156	A
	s. 157	A; there is no introductory passage.
	s. 158	A
	s. 159	A; this section is very short.
	s. 160	A; this section is linked to section 159.
	s. 161	A
ch. 99	s. 162	This section consists of illustrations.
ch. 100	s. 163	C and illustrations.[111]
ch. 101	s. 164	C and illustration.
ch. 102	s. 165	A; there is no introductory passage.
	s. 166	A

s. 167 A'?;[112] this section is very short and has no dialogue elements.

ch. 103 s. 168 C and illustrations.[113]

ch. 104 s. 169 C; sections 169 to 172 consist of *fu* talismans.

ch. 105 s. 170 C

ch. 106 s. 171 C

ch. 107 s. 172 C

ch. 108 s. 173 A'?; this consists of only 19 practical instructions and has no dialogue elements.[114]

s. 174 A; this and the following two sections are very short.

s. 175 A

s. 176 A

ch. 109 s. 177 A

s. 178 A

ch. 110 s. 179 B

ch. 111 s. 180 B

s. 181 B

s. 182 B

s. 183 B

s. 184 B

ch. 112 s. 185 B?[115]

s. 186 B?[116]

s. 187 B?[117]

s. 188 ?[118]

s. 189 B?[119]

s. 190 B

ch. 113 s. 191 A

ch. 114 s. 192 B?[120]

s. 193 B

s. 194 B

s. 195 B

	s. 196	B
	s. 197	B
	s. 198	B
	s. 199	B
	s. 200	B
	s. 201	B
	s. 202	B
	s. 203	B

ch. 115   s. 204 A[121]   *(p. 647.1–2)* (Chao *only*)

s. 205 A[122]   *(p. 647.4–651.13)* (Chao *only*)

ch. 116   s. 206   A; there is no introductory dialogue.[123]

ch. 117   s. 207   A

s. 208   A; this section deals with attacks against "heterodox," perhaps Buddhist, practices.

ch. 118   s. 209   A; this section is linked to s. 210.

s. 210   A

s. 211   A; there are few dialogue elements and some links to sections 209 and 210.

ch. 119   s. 212   A; this section quotes section 50.

s. 213   A

PART 8 (CHAO *ONLY*)[124]

ch. 120   *s. 214* A[125]   *(p. 684.3–685.2)*

ch. 121   *s. 215*   *?*   *(p. 685.3–686.4)*

ch. 122   *s. 216* A[126]   *(p. 686.5–13)*

ch. 123   *s. 217* A[127]   *(p. 686.13–687.10)*

ch. 124   *s. 218*   *?*[128]   *(p. 687.10–688.2)*

ch. 125   *s. 219* A[129]   *(p. 688.2–688.8)*

ch. 126   *s. 220* $A?$[130]   *(p. 688.8–691.1)*

ch. 127   *s. 221* A[131]   *(p. 691.4–13)*

s. 222 $A?$[132]   *(p. 692.1–7)*

ch. 128   *s. 224* A[133]   *(p. 691.2–4)*

ch. 129   *s. 225* A[134]   *(p. 692.8–694.6)*

	s. 226?	?[135]	(p. 694.7–11)
	s. 227	?	(p. 694.12–695.1)
ch. 130	s. 230	A[136]	(p. 695.1–6)
	s. 231	A[137]	(p. 695.7–12)
ch. 131	s. 234	A[138]	(p. 695.13–696.10)
ch. 132	s. 239	A?[139]	(p. 696.11–14)
ch. 133	s. 245	?	(p. 697.1–9)
	s. 246	?[140]	(p. 697.10–11)
	s. 247	A[141]	(p. 697.12–698.1)
ch. 134	s. 251	?	(p. 698.2–698.8)
ch. 135	s. 253	A[142]	(p. 698.9–13)
ch. 136	s. 257	A[143]	(p. 699.10–11)
	s. 258	A[144]	(p. 698.12–699.9)

PART 9 (CHAO ONLY)

ch. 137	s. 262	?	(p. 701.3–10)
	s. 263	A[145]	(p. 702.1–10)
ch. 138	s. 266	A[146]	(p. 702.11–703.2)
ch. 139	s. 270	A?[147]	(p. 704.9–14)
	s. 272	A[148]	(p. 704.14–706.5)
ch. 140	s. 273	?[149]	(p. 709.11–710.2)
	s. 274	?	(p. 706.5–9)
ch. 141	s. 276	A[150]	(p. 703.7–12)
	s. 277	A[151]	(p. 703.13–704.9)
ch. 142	s. 278	A?[152]	(p. 706.10–707.6)
ch. 143	s. 281	?	(p. 703.3–6)
	s. 282	A[153]	(p. 707.7–12)
	s. 283	A'	(p. 707.13–708.5)
	s. 284	A'	(p. 708.6–11)
ch. 144	s. 286	A[154]	(p. 708.12–709.10)
ch. 146	s. 290	B[155]	(p. 710.2–711.4)
	s. 291	B	(p. 711.4–6)
	s. 292	B	(p. 711.6–8)

	s. 293	B	(p. 711.8–11)
	s. 294	B	(p. 711.11–12)
	s. 295	B	(p. 711.11–712.1)
	s. 296	B	(p. 712.1–4)
ch. 147	s. 297	A[156]	(p. 712.5–8)
	s. 298	A[157]	(p. 712.9–11)
ch. 148	s. 299	B[158]	(p. 715.4–8)
ch. 150	s. 304	A[159]	(p. 715.9–716.1)
ch. 151	s. 309	A[160]	(p. 716.2–5)
ch. 153	s. 315	A[161]	(p. 716.6–12)

PART 10 (CHAO LOST; S 4226 LIST OF TITLES ONLY)

NOTES

1. Cf. Robinet 1984, Strickmann 1981, and Bokenkamp (1997: 278–81).
2. See TPJ pp. 1–8, *Chao*.
3. See Ōfuchi 1941: 145f. and cf. Mansvelt Beck 1980: 170f.
4. See Yoshioka 1970: 104, whose proposal has been influential and was again upheld by Yamada Toshiaki in 1993 (reprinted in Yamada 1999). Maeda queried it in 1994, and in a further round these queries were taken up by Ōfuchi (1997: 533–39), who questions the attribution of such a dominant role to the rather spurious *Dongji zhi jing*, insisting on one identical old *taiping* text as the major source for the received text. Although Ōfuchi argues that Yoshioka's description of the text's reedition is tantamount to an admission that the editors faked the old text, this was not what Yoshioka meant. His effort to involve Zhang Daoling, who from all we know was active in Sichuan, in the transmission of a text that has been closely linked to the Langye region in China's east does indeed seem far-fetched and difficult to sustain. But to argue that the material assembled in the received text stemmed entirely from one single line of transmission is also problematic.
5. The character *shi* (ten) is perhaps erroneous, based on a misreading of the sign (or "ditto" mark) for repeating "four," so that the number of *juan* would be 144.
6. In the first year of *han'an*, during the reign of Emperor Shun (r. 125–44); see *Yunji qiqian* 6.15b–16a; cf. *Daojiao yishu* 2.7b–14a; according to Yoshioka (1970: 67), the passage is based on the *Xuanmen dayi*.
7. See *Laojun shuo yibai bashi jie*, as in *Yunji qiqian* 39:1a–b. The date of the *Preface to the 180 Precepts* is not clear. Yoshioka (1970: 70) argues for the middle of the sixth century, but it could be earlier (cf. Hendrischke and Penny 1996: 17). The way it is used in

the process of promoting the newly edited TPJ could, in itself, provide an argument for an earlier date.

8. See TPJ 188.576 (probably layer A): "Formerly the *Scripture on Complete Pervasion* with the title 'Great Peace' was bestowed"; cf. also TPJ 41.87, "Thus it was called 'government of all-pervading heaven,'" and 129.331; 132.361; 136.378, all layer A.

9. This last observation regarding the *Dongji zhi jing* is not included in the *Daojiao yishu* (2.9b) version of the passage, which seems to slightly reduce the reliability of what is said.

10. The *Zhengyi jing* argued that all four of the later Daoist canon's "support" sections had been given to Zhang Daoling in the first instance; see Ōfuchi (1997: 533f.), who has a point when he argues that what the *Zhengyi jing* seems to say is not backed up by any other evidence; compare, for instance, *Wushang biyao* 84.10b on Zhang Daoling's reception of the *Zhengyi mengwei*.

11. See Yamada 1999: 136–39.

12. In some cases one summary covers several sections (TPJ p. 402 for sections 140 and 141; p. 449 for sections 158 and 159; p. 452 for sections 160 and 161) or all sections of a chapter (TPJ p. 300 for chap. 72; p. 382 for chap. 92; p. 516 for chap. 108; p. 627 for chap. 114; p. 667 for chap. 117; p. 674 for chap. 118; p. 683 for chap. 119), although the linkage is sometimes difficult to recognize (TPJ p. 186 for chap. 50; p. 522 for chap. 109; p. 562 for chap. 111). There are also cases where a summary seems to be missing (sections 99–101 and 151–52) or does not seem to fit the section (section 213).

13. See TPJ p. 754.

14. See Petersen 1990a: 209. Wang Ming (TPJ pp. 755–57) argues that the *Chao* makes use of a text not divided into 366 sections. He shows that the *Chao* takes summaries—which the transmitted text has at the end of chapters 92 and 111, dealing with all the separate sections in each chapter—as the titles for its own digest of each chapter as if there had been no sections. In pursuing his argument, Wang Ming does not consider S 4226. He has a point, however. There are many instances where the *Chao* does not follow the sequence of sections and chapters of the textus receptus. While we can say that it includes more or less the material contained in the S 4226 TPJ, we cannot be sure whether the text it followed was structured in exactly the same way as the S 4226 table of contents suggests.

15. This brings to mind the number of 170 *juan* mentioned in Ge Hong's bibliography. The TPJ (74.179) itself gives the figure of 360 for the number of days in a year. In a similar vein, the *Taiping jing fuwen xu* (TPJ p. 744), that is, the *Preface to the Double Character Talismans of the Scripture on Great Peace*, written after the production of the sixth-century text, states, erroneously we must assume, that the text had 360 *zhang* 章. S 4226 gives the figure as "366 *pian* 篇" (Yoshioka 1970: 59).

16. See TPJ 169.482.

17. We cannot exclude the possibility that the original text might have looked more or-

ganized than it does today. The loss of the first of its ten divisions might have deprived us of some means of understanding its structure, although the table of contents does not indicate this. However, S 4226 seems to quote mainly from this first division, as if it were basic to the rest.

18. See section 48, above, and compare Yu (1997 and 1999) for the TPJ's unusual use of characters.

19. See Zuercher 1977 and "Introduction," above.

20. See *Xu xian zhuan* 3.5a.

21. TPJ pp. 708f., *Chao*, part 9.

22. See Xiong Deji 1962.

23. See Hachiya 1983 and Takahashi 1988.

24. See TPJ 168.470; as Isabelle Robinet (1984: 436f.) points out, this building is meant to represent a star in the Northern Dipper.

25. As pointed out by Despeux 2000: 508f.

26. See *Baopu zi neipian* 17.89; cf. Yoshioka 1966: 349. Liu Zhongyu (1994) refers to the TPJ talismans as an example of the way in which talismans in general were built from individual characters. Wang Yucheng (1991: 46f.) quotes the complaints expressed in the *Baopu zi* (*Neipian* 19.97) about the lack of perspicuity in recently produced talismans and sees the TPJ talismans as relatively clear and "understandable."

27. Chun (the pure one) is the only disciple mentioned by name (TPJ 65.146; 78.187; 79.195; 99.224). His status differs slightly from that of the others.

28. The six are mentioned in TPJ 77.168; section 99 (*liu fang zhen ren* 六方真人 at the opening of the session, *liu zi* 六子 and *liu zhen ren* in the following); 101.231 (*liu zi*); 104.258 and passim (*zi liu ren*); 109.291 (*liu fang zhen ren*); section 127 (*liu fang zhen ren* at the opening of the session, and *liu zhen ren* and *liu zi* later on); section 129 (*liu fang zhen ren* at the opening followed by *liu zhen ren* on p. 333); 151.408.

29. For writings, see sections 67, 68, 69, 72, 75; for prognostics, see section 68; for plants and animals, see sections 70 and 71; for cosmic order, see sections 73 and 83; for acupuncture, see section 74; for tombs, see section 76; for music, see section 77.

30. See TPJ 72.176; 77.184 and 185. This does not mean that in layer B believers are not expected to distribute texts and admonish others to implement what they say, but different words are used. For example, it is said that heaven has sent "good texts and good men *(shan wen shan ren)* to keep records written on silk and bamboo" to convey the message to future generations: "this text must be adhered to 當法此書" (see TPJ 114.627).

31. See TPJ 68.171; 75.181. For layer B the two characters occur only in TPJ 190.582 and 203.627.

32. A remarkable exception is Li Xian's (651–84) quotation of a TPJ passage to annotate Xiang Kai's *Hou Han shu* biography (see TPJ p. 733). The fact that Li Xian was not a practicing Daoist might have made the term less problematic for him than for writers whose works were transmitted in the Daoist canon.

33. Hachiya Kunio 1983: 37 has commented on this problem.

34. See above, TPJ 66.167.

35. See TPJ 187.573.

36. See TPJ 179.528.

37. See above, TPJ 59.101f.

38. Takahashi (1988: 265–81) argues that they do.

39. See, for instance, *Zhen'gao* 6.74.

40. Espesset (2002b) gives a good description of this figure and his bureaucratic rule over what Espesset calls a pantheon of deities. Since they are all spirits active in heaven's interest, this term is perhaps a little misleading.

41. Also written *wei* 唯; see TPJ 182.555.

42. See sections 192 and 194.

43. See TPJ 192.592–594.

44. See TPJ 196.605f.

45. See above, section 46.

46. As, for instance, compounds including *ji* 藉 or *bu* 簿; cf. Espesset 2002b.

47. Hachiya (1983) gives an excellent short account of the notions stressed in the two different layers in his analysis of "dialogue style" and "prose and conversation style." He mentions the notion of community stressed in the one, as opposed to the individual stressed in the other, and all that this entails for the project of salvation, which is an aim common to both layers; cf. also Espesset's (2002b) account of layer B bureaucratic procedures.

48. *Cheng fu* occurs in layer B in TPJ 179.534; 182.550; 184.561; 197.608; the twelve thousand beings and objects are mentioned in TPJ 200.615.

49. See, for instance, the end of section 189 on the need to make the truth known.

50. See section 200.

51. The expressions *jin que* 金闕 (golden gate) and *shou ziran* (guard what is as it is) used in layer C passages (TPJ 168.471 and 472) occur nowhere else in the text. "Golden gate" points to the Latter Sage of the Golden Gate. This sage played a role in sixth-century Daoism and, as shown above, was associated with the TPJ to add to the text's authority. The *Chao* in its transmitted form has a passage that tells how the sage instigated the production of a Scripture on Great Peace. However, judging by the S 4226 table of contents, this passage was added to the text of the *Chao* at a later stage, certainly before the compilation of the Ming dynasty Daoist canon, to replace a part that had been lost.

52. As set forth in the first part of S 4226; see Yoshioka 1970: 18.

53. See Maeda 1994: 172, and cf. Strickmann 1977: 17f.

54. See Espesset 2002a.

55. In this respect, I am not quite clear on the criteria Espesset uses for his own attribution.

56. I cannot place anywhere the first four lines (TPJ p. 718) that precede what Wang Ming has correctly identified as the title of chapter 1. The topic is *da shun zhi dao* 大順

之道 (the way of great prosperity), which men are reminded to approach through the production of texts. The argument is spurious and unclear. The title of S 4226 section 39 in part 2, *Zaozuo jing shu fa* 造作經書法 (The method of creating scriptures), would cover the passage, but the author of the *Chao* tends to keep material from each part of the TPJ separate and place it in the relevant parts of the *Chao*.

For the first chapter, the use of *fu hua* 浮華 (frivolous and superficial) and *shou ben* 守本 (guard the root) (p. 720) point to layer A, where both expressions are frequent; they do not occur in layer B material. The use of the isolated phrase *he ye* 何也 (what does it mean, or what do you mean) (p. 719, twice) is typical of layer A dialogues.

57. Yu (2001a: 3) corrects Wang Ming's reading. The phrase *yi zi fang* 以自防 belongs to the end of chapter 1, and chapter 2 starts with *que* 卻, as does its title in the S 4226 rendering.

58. This is followed by chapter 4 in the rendering of Wang Ming, who adheres to Yoshioka's identification (1970: 20). If we reduced the chapter title given in the *Chao* to the second half—*Zi xiao qing shen xing fa* 自消清身行法 (The method to achieve dissolving the self and purifying the body)—and left the first half—*fenbie xingrong xie* 分別形容邪—at the end of chapter 3, this chapter title would correspond to S 4226 chapter 15, *Qing shen shou yi fa* 清身守一法 (The method to purify the body and guard the one). The relevant *Chao* passage discusses the concept of *shou yi* (TPJ p. 724).

59. The use of *di wang* (emperors and kings) and *yi di* (barbarians) (p. 725) points to layer A.

60. The expression *bai xing* 百姓 (the hundred surnames), p. 726, does not occur in layer B. Layer A typically uses *wuyou* 無憂 (untroubled), as used here to describe the state of mind of a ruler who implements great peace reforms: see sections 61 and 62.

61. The use of *di wang* (p. 732) points to layer A.

62. Those chapters and sections for which the *Chao* does not provide any material are not listed. S 4226 shows that the last two chapters of this part were subdivided into sections.

63. The *Chao*'s rendering of this and the following chapter is rhetorically more impressive than usual. The sentence structure is regular, with marked parallelism, and there are rhymed passages.

64. The passage has *tian di kaibi* 天地開闢 (p. 12), a phrase that occurs only in layer A.

65. The passage has *di wang* (p. 14), which occurs only in layer A. Several lines (p. 14.4–10) of the rendition of this chapter make up the *Chao* version of chap. 33 (p. 22.1–3). We cannot tell whether this is based on an error of the *Chao* or on the wording of the original TPJ text.

66. A discussion of good and bad, as suggested by the S 4226 title of chapter 24, starts with *wan wu jie ban hao ban e* 萬物皆半好半惡.

67. The passage deals with spirits, a topic of both chapters 25 and 26, according to S 4226. It contains *di wang* and *wu* (me).

68. The phrase *ke bu shen zai* 可不慎哉 used in this passage occurs in TPJ 60.111 and 81.204, both of which belong to layer A material. However, it also occurs in TPJ 185.566 in material that is difficult to attribute. *Shen* (be careful), on the other hand, is used frequently in layer B material; cf. section 179, where it is used throughout.

69. The expression *di wang* occurs twice on p. 17.

70. The phrase *zhen ren wen shen ren* 真人問神人 points to layer A.

71. The use of *fu hua* (frivolous and superficial) (p. 21) points to layer A.

72. For this chapter, the *Chao* gives the chapter heading and three lines, which repeat what was said for chapter 22.

73. Wang and Yu divide this material into two sections, but more divisions are possible. The question that is raised on p. 26, line 11—"How do we know a doctrine's efficacy"—seems to start a new section. S 4226 has six sections for this chapter. Only the title for section 40—"How to explain reception and transmission"—occurs in the *Chao*. Moreover, the *Chao* material does not match the titles for any of the chapter 34 sections as transmitted in S 4226. It consists of dialogues between the Perfected and Spiritlike Man.

74. This section contains enough Celestial Master–type dialogue elements to attribute it with certainty to layer A. Also, for the first part, the phrase *wu zhi tian yi bu qi zi* 吾知天意不欺子 (I know that heaven does not intend to betray you) (p. 23) and the occurrence of *di wang* (p. 22) and *tian di kaibi* (pp. 22 and 23) point to layer A.

75. The Daoist canon textus receptus does not mention the TPJ's ten parts but has chapters as the largest unit. The S 4226 table of contents organizes chapters and sections in ten parts. The fact that the received text starts with section 35, that is, with the first section of part 3, and ends with chapter 119, that is, the last chapter of part 7, attests to the text being transmitted as divided into parts.

76. Wang Ming sees the *Master's Declaration* as chapter 38. S 4226 has the title "The method of guarding the one" *(shou yi fa)* and *Master's Declaration* as the title for chapter and section 20; see above, section 50, for more details.

77. The term *di wang* occurs in this passage.

78. The terms *fu hua* and *di wang* point to layer A material.

79. The passage has *wu dao* and *wu shu,* which do not occur in layer B material.

80. The *Chao* starts part 4 with a section title and quotations that are close to the title given in S 4226 for section 79. The Daoist canon lacks chapter 52 (53 follows after 51) and section 80 (79 is followed by 81). This confusion at the beginning of part 4 confirms that at one stage the division of the text into parts was more prominent than it is in the present edition of the Daoist canon; cf. above, note 75.

81. The term Celestial Lord *(tian jun)* points to layer B, although it also occurs in section 63 (p. 295) understood as "heaven" and "lord."

82. The Celestial Lord is mentioned several times. The topic is the accounts kept in heaven.

83. The passage contains the expressions *di wang* and *wuyou* (untroubled); it deals with the prohibition of wine.

84. The expression *di wang* points to layer A material.

85. The expression *he wei ye* 何 謂 也 (What do you mean?) points to layer A.

86. The expression *wu shu* occurs only in layer A.

87. The expression *di wang* points to layer A.

88. The expression *di wang* points to layer A; the passage deals with different ranks of moral perfection, one of the Celestial Master's favorite topics.

89. The expression *qing wen* occurs in layer A only.

90. There are breaks at p. 252, line 8, p. 253, line 13, and p. 254, line 10. The last session returns to the "six crimes." The third dialogue, starting p. 253, deals with *shi fa* 十 法, here "ten methods to rule a country." The term is otherwise used for the ten Mahayana rules for thinking and living (Soothill 1972: 51).

91. Toward the beginning of the section, there are more colloquial elements than is customary in the *Chao*.

92. The expression *wu zhi shu* 吾 之 書 points to layer A.

93. The expression *di wang* points to layer A; the section deals with the ancient ways of governing.

94. On p. 301 there is some confusion in regard to the allocation of *Chao* passages. Lines 3–4 belong to the *Chao* account of section 108.

95. The phrase *di wang* points to layer A.

96. The phrase *yuan wen* 願 聞 (I would like to know . . .) points to layer A.

97. From p. 305, line 10 until the end of the passage the text consists mainly of rhymed seven-character phrases.

98. The passage has the expression *di wang*. There are rhymed seven-character phrases starting with p. 306, line 12, and the four-character phrases at the beginning of the passage are regular.

99. This section is long; the phrase *xing qu* 行 去 (You may go now) occurs on pp. 322 and 326. The six disciples are mentioned pp. 314, 318, 319, and 323.

100. The use of *zi* (you)—"If you ignore what is as it is you can't live long"—in an admonitory phrase points to layer A.

101. The break is p. 334, line 7.

102. The use of *zi* (you)—"If you guard *dao*, where should disorder come from?"—points to layer A.

103. There are perhaps two dialogues. The topic is modified on p. 380, line 4.

104. The six are mentioned on pp. 394, 395, and 397; there is a break on p. 394, line 11, and another, which remains only rhetorical, on p. 395, line 9.

105. The phrase *yu zhi daxiao* 欲 知 大 效 (If you want to see the proof of this . . .) occurs frequently in layer A material. However, the section deals with the units of life *suan* 算, which is a layer B topic.

106. The use of *zi* (you)—"I would now like to explain to you something else"—points to layer A.

107. The expression *di wang* occurs twice.

108. The expression *di wang* is used on p. 467.

109. The editor of the sixth-century text has made a mistake here. The section continues the session started in section 151, probably p. 408, line 8, where, in reply to the disciple's demand for instruction, the Celestial Master starts to talk about guarding the one. Section 152 lacks all introductory elements because it continues this discussion.

110. The section (on p. 426) has the unusual editorial phrase "The Perfected says" *(zhen ren yue)*.

111. The text accompanying this and the following illustration has certain colloquial elements reminiscent of the dialogues in layer A (*duoduo* 咄 咄 occurs only in layer A material) and layer B (*shen zhi* 慎 之 is frequent in layers A and B).

112. The phrase *wu shu* (my book) points to layer A material.

113. The passage mentions the "golden gate" *(jin que)*. It contains on p. 472 a sequence of ten seven-character lines that are rhymed, as has been pointed out by Wu Weimin (1989).

114. With regard to content, this section belongs to layer A. It mentions the prohibition of female infanticide, the need to allow women to earn a living, and the nine ranks of men.

115. The expression *luji* 錄籍 (registers) points to layer B; it occurs in layer A material only in section 213 (p. 681).

116. The same as for section 185; moreover, there are the expressions *suan* (units of life), *jinji* 禁忌 (proscriptions), and, repeatedly, *bu* 簿 (registers).

117. The same as for section 185; there is also the term *zhu shen* 諸神 (all the spirits), which is much more frequent in layer B material.

118. The phrase *zhen ren ji yi ci wen fu you de zhi guo* 真人急以此文付有德之國 (Perfected, give this text quickly to a ruler [*guo* here in the meaning of *guo jun*, which is unusual for the TPJ] with virtue) (p. 575) is typical of layer A material. It does not occur in layer B. The section also contains several layer B expressions: *luji* (registers), *zhu shen* (all the spirits), Celestial Lord (578.2), and *cao* 曹 (bureau) (579.10), which is frequently used in layer B (cf. Espesset 2002b) and does not occur in layer A. I assume, therefore, that the section consists of two parts, and that the layer B part starts at 576.5 with *chang yan* 常言.

119. Expressions like *mingbu* (registers of life) and *yusuan* 餘算 (remaining units of life) point to layer B. The section deals with details of proper moral conduct, and toward the end it is said that publication of this text will remove all doubts.

120. There are no manifest layer A elements, but a few dialogue elements; "registers" and "all the spirits" are mentioned.

121. Chapter 115, which is supposed to contain sections 204 and 205, is missing in the

received text. There are passages in the *Chao* that deal with topics of S 4226 headings for sections 204 and 205. In Wang Ming's edition they are placed after the long "chapter 116, section 204" (pp. 629–46). The *Chao* version of section 204 (TPJ p. 647) repeats lines from the *Chao* version of section 94 (TPJ p. 219); it has the expressions *wu shu* and *wu dao*.

122. The passage contains several layer A dialogue elements, such as *qing wen* and *yu sheng* 愚生 (this foolish pupil).

123. The section number, which is given as 204 in the received text, is changed to 206. The section is of unusual length and diversity. Its main topic is music, as suggested by the S 4226 section title.

124. For part 8, Wang Ming does not attempt to link *Chao* material to the section titles transmitted in S 4226, but Luo (1996) and Yu (2001a) do, and in most cases quite convincingly. We may assume that the *Chao* deals with these chapters and sections of the TPJ in the same way as with the chapters and sections that have been transmitted in the textus receptus. The amount of material quoted is about the same as for parts 1, 2, 4, and 5 but is twice as much for parts 3, 6, and 7, which is based on the fact that these parts are about twice as long as parts 4 and 5. Therefore, we may assume that, in length, parts 8 and 9 resembled parts 4 and 5 rather than the longer parts.

125. The phrase *qing wen* that is used in this passage occurs only in layer A.

126. The passage contains the phrase "I personally advise and command you the Perfected to make the writings public."

127. The passage contains the expression *di wang*.

128. The topic is order and hierarchy within the body.

129. The passage contains the phrase "What a good question!" (*shan ʒai ʒi ʒhi wen ye* 善哉子之問也).

130. The passage contains the expression *di wang* (p. 689).

131. The passage contains the expressions "Now does the Perfected understand this?" and "my true text."

132. The passage contains the expression *di wang*.

133. The passage is introduced by *qing wen*.

134. The passage has *wu* (me) and in particular the formula "Remember what my book says and make use of it."

135. It is possible but not necessary to link this passage with the title that S 4226 attributes to section 226; cf. Yu (2001a: 516f.) and Luo (1996: 1154).

136. The passage contains *he ye* (What do you mean?).

137. The passage contains *wu* (me): "Now someone who conducts himself well, in line with my writings, will have the units [that make up his life] *(suan)* increased, up in heaven as well as down below." Concern about "units of life" is much more pronounced in layer B. However, the passage at hand also has the expression *du shi* 度世 (to transcend), which hardly occurs in layer B material.

138. The passage contains *he ye* (What do you mean?).

139. The *da shen* who figures in this passage is not the Great Spirit who acts as a discussant in layer B material, but someone superior to small and medium spirits, and on the same level of achievement as *da dao* 大道. There is the expression *du shi*.

140. This short passage must have proven irresistible to the author of the *Chao*, which is not only a digest but also a florilegium:

> The teachings *(dao)* of great peace—their text is attested to, the country [where they prevail] is rich. They are heaven's decree and a person's treasure. They come forth from the heart and encircle the world. Do as they tell you and you can make the world secure and your family rich.

This is phrased in short three- and four-character phrases, very different from the way in which the Celestial Master expresses himself.

141. This has the expression *di wang*.

142. The passage is introduced by *qing wen*.

143. The short passage following the quotation from section 258 is introduced by *qing wen*.

144. The passage is introduced by the phrase "If you want to make sure that later generations will always be attentive and faithful, then look after yourself and cherish yourself."

145. The passage is introduced by *qing wen*.

146. The passage is introduced by *qing wen* and has the phrase "This will free emperors and kings from trouble (*wuyou* 無憂) and let them live long."

147. The expression *di wang* occurs twice.

148. The expressions *di wang* and *wu* (me) point to layer A. There are dialogue elements.

149. This short passage deals with the need for introspection, as does the title of S 4226 section 273. Its position in the *Chao* links it to the S 4226 section 288, "The eight [types of] men who can follow the three ways of eating," for which Yu (2001a: 541) rightly refers to a *Sandong zhunang* quotation of the TPJ: see TPJ pp. 716f.

150. The passage is introduced by *qing wen*; *shen ren* (spiritlike man) acts as a partner in the dialogue; the phrase *he zai* 何哉 (What do you mean?) also occurs.

151. The passage is introduced by *qing wen* and features a spiritlike man, who says "I (*wu*) have received these writings from the spirits (*zhu shen*) in heaven."

152. The expression *di wang* is used twice.

153. The passage is introduced by the phrase *wen yue* 問曰, which is found frequently only in the *Chao* rendition of part 9—see sections 282–284, 286—and, to the extent to which they figure in the *Chao*, sections 297–315. Passages thus introduced show several layer A characteristics. Elsewhere in the TPJ the phrase occurs in section 108, which depicts a talk between Perfected and *shen ren*, as is common in *Chao* representations of layer A passages. Wang Xuanhe (fl. 683) uses the phrase in his *Sandong zhunang* when quoting a layer A dialogue (TPJ 61.122), and Zhu Faman (d. 720) uses the phrase twice in

the *Yaoxiu keyi jielü chao* (TPJ pp. 215 and 309) when quoting talks between Celestial Master, termed *shen ren*, as in the *Chao*, and disciple. For part 9 of the *Chao* we may assume that the figure who raises a question is meant to be the Perfected. Judging from the quotations referred to above, *wen yue* was a common rendering of the peculiar and circumstantial way in which Celestial Master dialogues were begun. We may also conclude that for part 9 the *Chao* was based on an original text whose condensed format differed from the main part of layer A (A' is used to indicate this material). In this respect one can draw a parallel to chapter 50 (sections 67–77) at the end of part 3, whose content resembles layer A, with which it also shares certain expressions while being written in regular and brief literary prose.

154.   As above; the question raised in this section is "What does it mean that the *Taiping jing* has 170 chapters (*Taiping jing he yibai qishi juan wei yi* 太平經何以百七十卷為意)?" This adds to the observation that in part 9 there are more traces of intermediate editing than in earlier parts.

155.   This passage is introduced by the particle *wei*. It deals with the Celestial Lord, the Great Spirit, the Hall of Light, and other aspects of the celestial bureaucracy. Sections 291 to 296 follow suit.

156.   The passage is introduced by *wen yue*. It contains dialogue elements.

157.   The passage is introduced by *wen yue*. It reads like a summary of a certain layer A view of history, but is too well written and too compact to really be part of it:

> The following question was raised: [Although] in ancient times there were no writings, the way of heaven was without disorder.
>
> [The answer:] At that time heaven's contract *quanwen* 券文 [cf. *zhen quan* as used in section 51] had not yet appeared, but a spiritlike man of supreme majesty (*shang huang shen ren* 上皇神人) [also in section 290, layer B] was in control who investigated the root of things, keeping in view the ancestors [and their proceedings]. With the division from majestic heaven, the distance from heaven's way gradually increased and in sorrow and disorder heaven's intentions were no longer understood. So heaven issued a contract, made a wise man write it out, and had a teacher distribute it. Since the wise man is not always around, it must be properly recorded for later generations. When this is done, heaven's way will be in order when *qi* of great peace arrives.

158.   The passage deals with the Celestial Lord and with *tianshang zhi shi* 天上之士, a "celestial gentleman" who is powerful like an heir apparent.

159.   This passage is introduced by *wen yue*. It proposes a two-tier approach (west and east, man and woman, Yin and Yang) instead of stressing the three, as is common in the TPJ.

160.   The passage is introduced by *wen yue*; *wu* (me) occurs: "Now I can provide long-lasting protection against the recurrence of disasters."

161.   The passage is introduced by *wen yue*. It deals with guarding the one.

BIBLIOGRAPHY

ABBREVIATIONS

Chao   Refers to the *Taiping jing chao,* a late Tang dynasty digest of the TPJ.
It is quoted according to Wang Ming's *Taiping jing hejiao.*

DZ   Refers to texts in the Daoist canon by the number assigned to them in
*Dao zang zi mu yinde. Harvard-Yenching Institute Sinological Index Series
No. 25.* Taipei: Chinese Materials and Research Aids Center, 1966.

TPJ   Refers to the received text of the *Taiping jing* in general, and, when
followed by a page number, refers to the *Taiping jing* and other texts in
the corpus of *taiping* material as they have been edited by Wang Ming
in *Taiping jing hejiao.*

CRITICAL EDITIONS OF, TRANSLATIONS OF,
AND INTERNET RESOURCES FOR THE *TAIPING JING*

Academia Sinica

Han ji dianzi wenxian. Electronic version of Wang Ming's edition.
See www.sinica.edu.tw/ftms-bin/ftmsw3.

Liu Dianjue

2000. *Taiping jing zhuzi suoyin.* Hong Kong: Shangwu yinshuguan.

Long Hui et al.

2000. *Taiping jing quanyi.* Guiyang: Guizhou renmin chubanshe.

Luo Chi

1996. *Taiping jing zhuyi.* Chongqing: Xinan shifan daxue chubanshe.

Wang Ming

1979. *Taiping jing hejiao*. Beijing: Zhonghua shuju.

Yang Jilin

1994. *Taiping jing shidu*. In *Zhonghua Daoxue tongdian*, ed. Wu Feng and Song Yifu, pp. 267–656. Haikou: Nanhai chuban gongsi.

2002. *Taiping jing jinzhu jinyi*. Shijiazhuang: Hebei renmin chubanshe.

Yu Liming

2001a. *Taiping jing zhengdu*. Chengdu: Ba Shu shushe.

PRIMARY SOURCES

Bai hu tong shuzheng. Ed. Chen Li. Beijing: Zhonghua shuju, 1994.

Baopu zi. In *Zhuzi jicheng*.

Chu ci buzhu. In *Siku quanshu huiyao*.

Chun qiu fan lu yizheng. Ed. Su Yu. Beijing: Zhonghua shuju, 1992.

Da Dai Li ji. In *Congshu jicheng*.

Da zhong song zhang. See *Chisong zi zhang li*. DZ 615.

Daodian lun. DZ 1122.

Daojiao yishu. DZ 1121.

Daoyao lingqi shengui pin jing. DZ 1192.

Dengzhen yinjue. DZ 421.

Dongxuan lingbao zhen ling weiye tu. DZ 167.

Gong yang zhuan. In *Shisan jing zhushu*. Beijing: Zhonghua shuju, 1980.

Gu liang zhuan. In *Shisan jing zhushu*. Beijing: Zhonghua shuju, 1980.

Guanzi. In *Zhuzi jicheng*.

Guo yu. In *Congshu jicheng*.

Han Feizi suoyin. Ed. Zhou Zhongling et al. Beijing: Zhonghua shuju, 1982.

Han shi wai zhuan. In *Han Wei congshu*.

Han shu. Beijing: Zhonghua shuju, 1962.

Hong ming ji. In *Taishō shinshū daizōkyō*, vol. 52.

Hou Han ji. Taipei: Taiwan shangwu yinshuguan, 1971.

Hou Han shu. Beijing: Zhonghua shuju, 1963.

Hou qing lu. In *Congshu jicheng*.

Huainan zi. Ed. Liu Wendian. Taipei: Taiwan shangwu yinshuguan, 1970.

Huangdi neijing suwen. In *Siku quanshu huiyao*.

Huayang Tao yinju neizhuan. DZ 300.

Hunyuan sheng ji. DZ 769.

Jin shu. Beijing: Zhonghua zhuju, 1974.

Jing fa. Ed. Mawangdui han mu boshu zhengli xiaozu. Beijing: Wenwu chubanshe, 1976.

Jinlou zi. In *Congshu jicheng*.

Kong Congzi. In *Congshu jicheng*.

Laojun shuo yibai bashi jie. See *Yunji qiqian*. DZ 1026.

Laojun yinsong jie jing. DZ 784.

Laozi jiaoshi. Ed. Zhu Qianzhi. Beijing: Zhonghua shuju, 1987.

Li ji. In *Shisan jing zhushu*. Beijing: Zhonghua shuju, 1980.

Liang shu. Beijing: Zhonghua shuju, 1987.

Lie nü zhuan. In *Guoxue jiben congshu*.

Liezi jishi. Ed. Yang Bojun. Beijing: Zhonghua shuju, 1979.

Ling xian. In *Yuhan shan fang ji shi shu* (Xiangyuan tang edition).

Lishi zhen xian tidao tongjian. DZ 296.

Lü shi chun qiu jiaoshi. Ed. Chen Qiyou. Shanghai: Xue lin chubanshe, 1984.

Lun heng jiaoshi. Ed. Huang Hui. Beijing: Zhonghua shuju, 1996.

Lun yu yinde. Shanghai: Guji chubanshe, 1986.

Mao shan zhi. DZ 304.

Mengzi yinde. Shanghai: Guji chubanshe, 1986.

Nan Qi shu. Beijing: Zhonghua shuju, 1983.

Nan shi. Beijing: Zhonghua shuju, 1983.

Qi jia Hou Han shu. Ed. Wang Wentai. Taipei: Wenhai chubanshe, 1972.

Qian fu lun jian. Ed. Peng Duo. Beijing: Zhonghua shuju, 1979.

Quan Shanggu Sandai Qin Han Sanguo Liuchao wen. Ed. Yan Kejun. Beijing: Zhonghua shuju, 1985.

San guo zhi. Beijing: Zhonghua shuju, 1995.

Sandong zhunang. DZ 1131.

Shang shu da zhuan. In *Congshu jicheng*.

Shangqing daolei shixiang. DZ 1132.

Shangqing housheng daojun lieji. DZ 442.

Shangqing qusu jueci lu. DZ 1381.

Shen jian. In *Zhuzi jicheng*.

Shenxian zhuan. In *Longwei mishu*.

Shi ji. Beijing: Zhonghua shuju, 1959.

Shi jing. In *Shisan jing zhushu*. Beijing: Zhonghua shuju, 1980.

Shi shuo xin yu. In *Zhuzi jicheng*.

Shuo wen jie zi yizheng. Ed. Gui Fu. Shanghai: Guji chubanshe, 1987.

Shuo yuan. In *Congshu jicheng*.

Sui shu. Beijing: Zhonghua shuju, 1959.

Taiping yulan. Shanghai: Zhonghua shuju, 1960.

Wei shu. Beijing: Zhonghua shuju, 1959.

Wen xin diao long. In *Congshu jicheng*.

Wenzi shuyi. Ed. Wang Liqi. Beijing: Zhonghua shuju, 2000.

Wu xing dayi. In *Congshu jicheng*.

Wushang biyao. DZ 1130.

Xiang'er. In Mugitani Kunio, *Rōshi Sōjichū sakuin*. Kyoto: Hōyū shoten, 1985.

Xin shu. In *Congshu jicheng*.

Xu xian zhuan. In *Longwei mishu*.

Xunzi yinde. Shanghai: Guji chubanshe, 1986.

Yan shi jia xun jijie. Ed. Wang Liqi. Beijing: Zhonghua shuju, 1993.

Yan tie lun. In *Zhuzi jicheng*.

Yanzi chun qiu. In *Zhuzi jicheng*.

Yaoxiu keyi jielü chao. DZ 463.

Yi jing. See *Zhou yi yinde*.

Yuanshi wulao chishu yu pian zhenwen tianshu jing. DZ 22.

Yunji qiqian. DZ 1026.

Zhen'gao. In *Congshu jicheng*.

Zhong shuo. In *Siku quanshu huiyao*.

Zhou li. In *Shisan jing zhushu*. Beijing: Zhonghua shuju, 1980.

Zhou yi yinde. Taipei: Chinese Materials and Research Aids Service Center, 1966.

Zhuangzi yinde. Shanghai: Guji chubanshe, 1986.

Zi zhi tong jian. Beijing: Guji chubanshe, 1956.

Ziyang zhenren neizhuan. DZ 303.

Zuo zhuan. In *Shisan jing zhushu*. Beijing: Zhonghua shuju, 1980.

SECONDARY SOURCES IN CHINESE AND JAPANESE

Asano Yūichi

1982. "*Taihei kyō* ni okeru kyūkyoku sha." *Tōhō shūkyō* 60:1–22.

Chen Guofu

1963. *Dao zang yuanliu kao*. Beijing: Zhonghua shuju.

Fang Shiming

1993. "Huangjin qiyi xianqu yu wu ji yuanshi Daojiao de guanxi." *Lishi yanjiu* 3:3–13.

Fukui Kojun

1952. *Dōkyō no kisoteki kenkyū.* Tokyo: Shoseki bumbutsu ryūtsūkai.

Gong Pengcheng

1991. *Daojiao xin lun.* Taipei: Taiwan xuesheng shuju.

Hachiya Kunio

1983. "*Taihei kyō* ni okeru genji bunsho: kyō, shū, tsū no shisō." *Tōyō bunka kenkyūjo kiyō* 92:35–81.

Hanyu da cidian bianji weiyuanhui

1994. *Hanyu da cidian.* Shanghai: *Hanyu da cidian* chubanshe.

Harada Jirō

1984. "*Taihei kyō* no seimei kan, 'chōsei setsu' ni tsuite." *Nihon chūgoku gakkai hō* 36:71–83.

Hayashi Minao

1989. *Kandai no kamigami.* Kyoto: Rinsen shoten.

Hou Wailu

1959. "Zhongguo fengjian shehui qianhouqi de nongmin zhanzheng ji qi gangling kouhao de fazhan." *Lishi yanjiu* 4:45–59.

Hu Chirui

2002. Lun heng *yu Dong Han fodian ciyu bijiao yanjiu.* Chengdu: Ba Shu shushe.

Jin Chunfeng

1997. *Handai sixiang shi.* Beijing: Zhongguo shehui kexue chubanshe.

Ju Zan

1995. *Ju Zan ji.* Beijing: Zhongguo shehui kexue chubanshe.

Kalinowski, Marc

1995. "Mawangdui boshu *xing de* shitan." In *Hua xue*, ed. Rao Zongyi, 1:82–110. Guangdong: Zhongshan daxue chubanshe.

Kamitsuka Yoshiko

1999. *Rikuchō dōkyō shisō no kenkyū.* Tokyo: Sōbunsha.

Koyanagi Shikita

1942. *Tōyō shisō no kenkyū.* Tokyo: Shinhoku shoten.

Kusuyama Haruki

1992. "Tonkō isho *Taihei bu kan daini* ni tsuite." In Kusuyama Haruki, *Dōka shisō to dōkyō*, pp. 205–22. Tokyo: Hirakawa.

Lai Chi Tim

　2000. "Cong *Taiping jing* de 'zhong he' sixiang kan ren yu ziran de guanxi: tian di jibing yu ren de zeren." In *Daojiao wenhua de jinghua: dier jie haixia liang'an daojiao xueshu yantaohui lunwen ji*, ed. Zheng Zhiming, 1:49–75. Dalin: Nanhua daxue zongjiao wenhua yanjiu zhongxin.

Li Jiayan

　1984. "*Taiping jing* de 'yuan qi' lun." *Zhongguo zhexue shi yanjiu* 15.2:52–58.

Lian Shaoming

　2002. "Yunmeng Qin jian *jie* bian kaoshu." *Kaogu xuebao* 1:23–38.

Lin Fushi

　1993. "Shilun *Taiping jing* de jibing guannian." *Lishi yuyan yanjiusuo jikan* 62.2:225–63.

　1998. "Shilun *Taiping jing* de zhuzhi yu xingzhi." *Lishi yuyan yanjiusuo jikan* 69.2:205–44.

Liu Zhaorui

　1992. "*Taiping jing* yu kaogu faxian de Dong Han zhenmu wen." *Shijie zongjiao yanjiu* 4:111–19.

　1996. "Lun Huangshen Yuezhang." *Lishi yanjiu* 1:125–32.

Liu Zhongyu

　1994. "Dao fu su yuan." *Shijie zongjiao yanjiu* 1:1–10.

Maeda Shigeki

　1994. "Saishuppon *Taihei kyō* ni tsuite." In *Dōkyō bunka e no tenbō*, ed. Dōkyō bunka kenkyūkai, pp. 153–79. Tokyo: Hirakawa.

Miyakawa Hisayuki

　1964. *Rikuchō shi kenkyū: shūkyō hen*. Kyoto: Heirakuji shoten.

　1983. *Chūgoku shūkyōshi kenkyū*. Kyoto: Dōhōsha.

Morohashi Tetsuji

　1985. *Dai Kan Wa jiten*. Tokyo: Taishūkan.

Ōfuchi Ninji

　1940. "*Taihei kyō* no raireki ni tsuite." *Tōyō gakuhō* 27.2:100–124.

　1941. "*Taihei kyō* no shisō ni tsuite." *Tōyō gakuhō* 28.4:145–68.

　1979a. *Tonkō dōkyō: toroku hen*. Tokyo: Fukutake shoten.

　1997. *Dōkyō to sono kyōten. Dōkyōshi no kenkyū, sono ni*. Tokyo: Sōbunsha.

Ōfuchi Ninji and Ishii Masako, eds.

　1988. *Rikuchō Tō Sō no kobunken shoin: Dōkyō tenseki mokuroku: sakuin*. Tokyo: Kokusho kankōkai.

Qi Chongtian

　1992. "'Chou' zi de youlai ji qi benyi." *Wen shi zhishi* 10:103–6.

Qin Jiang

2005. "Chu Boyu yu *Taiping jing*." *Zongjiao xue yanjiu* 66.1:15–19 and 49.

Qing Xitai

1979. "*Taiping jing* de zhiren shanren sixiang qianxi." *Sixiang zhanxian* 2:43–47.

Rao Zongyi

1956. Laozi Xiang'er *zhu jiaojian*. Hong Kong: Tong Nam.

1972. "*Taiping jing* yu *Shuo wen jie zi*." *Dalu zazhi* 45.6:39–41.

1996. "Zhongwen daxue Wenwuguan cang Jianchu sinian 'Xuning bingjian' yu 'Baoshan jian'. Lun Zhanguo, Qin, Han jieji daoci zhi zhushen yu gushi renwu." In *Hua Xia wenming yu chuanshi cangshu: Zhongguo guoji Hanxue yantaohui lunwenji*, ed. Zhongguo shehui kexueyuan lishi yanjiusuo, pp. 662–72. Beijing: Zhongguo shehui kexue chubanshe.

Ren Jiyu and Zhong Zhaopeng

1991. *Daozang tiyao*. Beijing: Zhongguo shehui kexue chubanshe.

Takahashi Tadahiko

1984. "*Taihei kyō* no shisō kōzō." *Tōyō bunka kenkyūjo kiyō* 95:295–336.

1986. "*Taihei kyō* no shisō no shakaiteki sokumen." *Tōyō bunka kenkyūjo kiyō* 100:249–84.

1988. "*Taihei kyō* no kaiwatai no seikaku ni tsuite." *Tōyō bunka kenkyūjo kiyō* 105:243–81.

Tanaka Fumio

1984. "*Taihei kyō* no 'kan shin hō' ni tsuite." In *Chūgoku no shūkyō, shisō to kagaku*, ed. Makio Ryōkai hakushi shōju kinen ronshu kankōkai, pp. 291–303. Tokyo: Kokusho kankōkai.

Tang Yijie

1984. "Guanyu *Taiping jing* chengshu wenti." *Zhongguo wenhua yanjiu jikan* 1:168–86.

Tang Yongtong

1938. *Han Wei liang Jin Nanbei chao fojiao shi*. Shanghai: Shangwu yinshuguan.

Wakae Kenzo

1982. "Kandai no *fudō* tsumi ni tsuite." In *Rekishi ni okeru minshū to bunka*, ed. Sakai Tadao sensei koki shukuga kinen no kai, pp. 27–40. Tokyo: Kokusho kankōkai.

Wang Ming

1948. "Lun *Taiping jing chao* 'jia bu' zhi wei." *Lishi yuyan yanjiusuo jikan* 18:375–84.

Wang Yucheng

1991. "Dong Han Dao fu shili." *Kaogu xuebao* 1:45–56.

1996. "Wenwu suo jian Zhongguo gudai Dao fu shulun." In *Daojia wenhua yanjiu*, ed. Chen Guying, 9:267–301. Shanghai: Guji chubanshe.

Watanabe Yoshihiro
  2001. "'Kan ji' kara 'mo sei' e." *Tōhō gaku* 102:20–33.
Wu Rongzeng
  1981. "Zhenmuwen zhong suo jiandao de Dong Han Dao wu guanxi." *Wen wu*
    3:56–63.
Wu Weimin
  1989. "*Taiping jing* he qiyanshi de chuxing." *Shanghai Daojiao* 3–4:34–35 and 40.
Xiong Deji
  1962. "*Taiping jing* de zhuozhe he sixiang ji qi yu Huangjin he Tianshidao de
    guanxi." *Lishi yanjiu* 2:8–25.
Yamada Toshiaki
  1999. *Rikuchō Dōkyō girei no kenkyū.* Tokyo: Tōhō shoten.
Yang Kuan
  1959. "Lun *Taiping jing:* wo guo di yi bu nongmin geming de lilun zhuzuo." *Xueshu
    yuekan* 9:26–34.
Yasui Kōzan and Nakamura Shōhachi, eds.
  1971–92. *Chōshū isho shūsei.* Tokyo: Meitoku shuppansha.
Yoshioka Yoshitoyo
  1965. "Dōkyō shumin shisō no shūkyōteki seikaku." *Shūkan tōyō gaku* 13:1–18.
  1966. *Dōkyō kyōten shiron.* Tokyo: Dōkyō kankōkai.
  1967. "*Taihei kyō* no shuitsu shisō." In *Tōyō shigaku ronshū*, ed. Yamazaki sensei
    taikan kinenkai, pp. 491–500. Tokyo: Yamazaki sensei taikan kinenkai.
  1970. *Dōkyō to Bukkyō*, vol. 2. Tokyo: Toshima shobo.
Yu Liming
  1997. "Daojiao dianji *Taiping jing* zhong de Han dai zili he ziyi." *Zongjiaoxue yan-
    jiu* 34.1:49–53.
  1999. "*Taiping jing* zhong de xingjin zi zhengwu." *Zongjiaoxue yanjiu* 45.4:13–15
    and 28.
  2000. "*Taiping jing* zhong fei zhuangyu diwei de foudingci 'bu'." *Zhongguo yuwen*
    276.3:212–14.
  2001. "*Taiping jing* zhong fei zhuangyu diwei de foudingci 'bu' he fanfu wenju."
    Zhongguo yuwen 284.5:466–70.
Zhang Gong, ed.
  1992. *Dunhuang Manuscripts in British Collections*, vol. 6. Chengdu: Sichuan ren-
    min chubanshe.

SECONDARY SOURCES IN WESTERN LANGUAGES

Akahori, Akira

1989. "Drug Taking and Immortality." In *Taoist Meditation and Longevity Techniques*, ed. L. Kohn, pp. 73–98. Ann Arbor, Mich.: Center for Chinese Studies, The University of Michigan Press.

Andersen, Poul

1980. *The Method of Holding the Three Ones: A Taoist Manual of Meditation of the Fourth Century A.D.* London: Curzon Press.

Ariel, Yoav

1989. *K'ung-ts'ung-tzu: The K'ung Family Masters' Anthology*. Princeton, N.J.: Princeton University Press.

Balazs, Étienne

1954. *Le Traité Juridique du "Souei-chou."* Leiden: E. J. Brill.

1964. *Chinese Civilization and Bureaucracy.* New Haven: Yale University Press.

Bauer, Wolfgang

1976. *China and the Search for Happiness.* New York: Seabury Press.

Benn, Charles

2000. "Daoist Ordination and *Zhai* Rituals." In Kohn (2000):309–39.

Bielenstein, Hans

1980. *The Bureaucracy of Han Times.* Cambridge: Cambridge University Press.

1984. "Han Portents and Prognostication." Bulletin of the Museum of Far Eastern Antiquities 56:97–110.

1986. "Wang Mang, the Restoration of the Han Dynasty, and Later Han." In Twitchett and Loewe (1986):223–90.

Birrell, Anne

1988. *Popular Songs and Ballads of Han China.* London: Unwin Hyman 1988.

Bodde, Derk

1981. *Essays on Chinese Civilization*, ed. Charles leBlanc and Dorothy Borei. Princeton, N.J.: Princeton University Press.

Bodham, Nicholas Cleaveland

1954. *A Linguistic Study of the Shih Ming.* Cambridge, Mass.: Harvard University Press.

Bokenkamp, Stephen

1993. "Traces of Early Celestial Master Physiological Practice in the *Xiang'er* Commentary." *Taoist Resources* 4.2:37–51.

1994. "Time after Time: Taoist Apocalyptic History and the Founding of the T'ang Dynasty." *Asia Major* 7.1:59–88.

1996. "Answering a Summons." In *Religions of China in Practice*, ed. D. S. Lopez, pp. 188–202. Princeton, N.J.: Princeton University Press.

1997. *Early Daoist Scriptures*. Berkeley: University of California Press.

Brashier, K. E.

1996. "Han Thanatology and the Division of 'Souls'." *Early China* 21:125–58.

Bumbacher, Stephan

2000. *The Fragments of the Daoxue ţhuan*. Frankfurt/Main: Peter Lang.

Cahill, Suzanne

1993. *Transcendence and Divine Passion: The Queen Mother of the West in Medieval China*. Stanford, Calif.: Stanford University Press.

Callicott, J. Baird, and Roger T. Ames, eds.

1989. *Nature in Asian Traditions of Thought*. Albany, N.Y.: State University of New York Press.

Campany, Robert Ford

2002. *To Live as Long as Heaven and Earth*. Berkeley: University of California Press.

Cao, Guangshu, and Hsiao-jung Yu

2000. "The Influence of Translated Later Han Buddhist Sutras on the Development of the Chinese Disposal Construction," *Cahiers de Linguistique—Asie Orientale* 29.2:151–77.

Cedzich, Ursula-Angelika

1987. *Das Ritual der Himmelsmeister im Spiegel früher Quellen: Übersetzung und Untersuchung des liturgischen Materials im dritten chüan des Teng-chen yin-chüeh*. Dissertation, Julius-Maximilians-Universität, Würzburg.

1993. "Ghosts and Demons, Law and Order: Grave Quelling Texts and Early Taoist Liturgy." *Taoist Resources* 4.2:23–35.

Cheng, Anne

1985. *Étude sur le Confucianisme Han*. Paris: Collège de France.

2001. "What Did It Mean to Be a *Ru* in Han Times?" *Asia Major* 14.2:101–18.

Ch'ü T'ung-tsu

1972. *Han Social Structure*. Seattle: University of Washington Press.

Cohn, Norman

1970. *The Pursuit of the Millennium*. New York: Oxford University Press.

de Crespigny, Rafe

1969. *The Last of the Han: Being the Chronicle of the Years 181–220 A.D. as Recorded in Chapter 58–68 of the Tzu-chih t'ung-chien of Ssu-ma Kuang*. Canberra: Faculty of Asian Studies.

1975. "The Harem of Emperor Huan: A Study of Court Politics in Later Han." *Papers on Far Eastern History* 12:1–42.

1976. *Portents of Protest in the Later Han Dynasty: The Memorials of Hsiang K'ai to Emperor Huan*. Canberra: Faculty of Asian Studies.

1980. "Politics and Philosophy under the Government of Emperor Huan 159–168 A.D." *T'oung Pao* 66.1–3:41–83.

Despeux, Catherine

2000 "Talismans and Sacred Diagrams." In Kohn (2000):498–540.

DeWoskin, Kenneth

1983. *Doctors, Diviners, and Magicians of Ancient China: Biographies of* Fang-shih. New York: Columbia University Press.

Dubs, Homer

1938/1955. *The History of the Former Han Dynasty*, vols. 1–3. Baltimore, Md.: Waverly Press.

Eberhard, Wolfram

1970. *Sternkunde und Weltbild im Alten China*. Taipei: Chinese Materials and Research Aids Service Center.

Ebrey, Patricia

1980. "Later Han Stone Inscriptions." *Harvard Journal of Asiatic Studies* 40:325–53.

1986. "The Economic and Social History of Later Han." In Twitchett and Loewe (1986):608–48.

Eichhorn, Werner

1955. "Bemerkungen zum Aufstand des Chang Chio und zum Staate des Chang Lu." *Mitteilungen des Instituts für Orientforschung* 3:291–327.

1957. "T'ai-p'ing and T'ai-p'ing Religion." *Mitteilungen des Instituts für Orientforschung* 5:113–40.

1973. *Die Religionen Chinas*. Stuttgart: Kohlhammer.

Eskildsen, Stephen

1998. *Asceticism in Early Taoist Religion*. Albany, N.Y.: State University of New York Press.

Espesset, Grégoire

2002a. "Cosmologie et trifonctionnalité dans l'idéologie du *Livre de la Grande paix*." Dissertation, Université Paris 7, Paris.

2002b. "Criminalized Abnormality, Moral Etiology, and Redemptive Suffering in the Secondary Strata of the *Taiping jing*." *Asia Major* 15.2:1–50.

2002c. "Revelation between Orality and Writing in Early Imperial China: The Epistemology of the *Taiping jing*." *Bulletin of the Museum of Far Eastern Antiquities* 74:66–100.

Fang Shiming

1995. "The Forerunner of the Yellow Turban Uprising and its Relationship with Shamanism and Primitive Daoism." *Social Sciences in China* 1:142–52.

Forke, Alfred

1962. *Lun-Heng*. New York: Paragon Book Gallery.

Fung Yu-lan

1952/1953. *A History of Chinese Philosophy*. Trans. Derk Bodde. Princeton, N.J.: Princeton University Press.

Giles, Lionel

1957. *Descriptive Catalogue of the Chinese Manuscripts from Tunhuang in the British Museum*. London: Trustees of the British Museum.

Graham, A. C.

1981. *Chuang-tzu: The Seven Inner Chapters and Other Writings from the Book Chuang-tzu*. London: Allen and Unwin.

1989. *Disputers of the Tao*. La Salle, Ill.: Open Court.

1991. *The Book of Lieh-tzu*. London: Mandala.

Harper, Donald

1987. "The Sexual Arts of Ancient China as Described in a Manuscript of the Second Century B.C." *Harvard Journal of Asiatic Studies* 47:539–93.

1999. "Warring States Natural Philosophy and Occult Thought." In *The Cambridge History of Ancient China*, ed. Michael Loewe and Edward Shaughnessy, pp. 813–84. Cambridge: Cambridge University Press.

2004. "Contracts with the Spirit World in Han Common Religion: The Xuning Prayer and Sacrifice Documents of A.D. 79." *Cahiers d'Extrême Asie* 14:227–67.

Hawkes, David

1959. *Ch'u Tz'u: The Songs of the South*. Oxford: Oxford University Press.

Hendrischke, Barbara

1991. "The Concept of Inherited Evil in the *Taiping jing*." *East Asian History* 2:1–30.

1992. "The Taoist Utopia of Great Peace." *Oriens Extremus* 35:61–91.

Hendrischke, Barbara, and Benjamin Penny

1996. "The 180 Precepts Spoken by Lord Lao." *Taoist Resources* 6.2:17–29.

Henricks, Robert G.

1990. *Lao-tzu: Te-Tao Ching*. London: The Bodley Head.

Hsiao, Kung-chuan

1979. *A History of Chinese Political Thought*, trans. F. W. Mote. Princeton, N.J.: Princeton University Press.

Hsu, Cho-yun

1980. *Han Agriculture*. Seattle: University of Washington Press.

1988. "The Roles of the Literati and of Regionalism in the Fall of the Han Dynasty." In *The Collapse of Ancient States and Civilizations*, ed. N. Yoffee and G. L. Cowgill, pp. 176–95. Tucson: University of Arizona Press.

Hulsewe, A. F. P.
1955. *Remnants of Han Law. Volume 1*. Leiden: E. J. Brill.

Kalinowski, Marc
1991. *Cosmologie et Divination dans la Chine Ancienne*. Paris: École Française d'Extrême-Orient.

Kalinowski, Marc, ed.
2003. *Divination et société dans la Chine médiévale*. Paris: Bibliothèque nationale de France.

Kaltenmark, Max
1979. "The Ideology of the *T'ai-p'ing ching*." In Welch and Seidel (1979):19–52.
1987. *Le Lie-Sien Tchouan*. Paris: Collège de France.

Kandel, Barbara
1979. *Taiping jing: The Origin and Transmission of the "Scripture on General Welfare."* Hamburg: Mitteilungen der Gesellschaft für Natur- und Völkerkunde Ostasiens 75.

Karlgren, Bernhard
1950. *The Book of Odes*. Stockholm: Museum of Far Eastern Antiquities.
1972. *Grammata Serica Recensa*. Stockholm: Museum of Far Eastern Antiquities.

Keenan, John P.
1994. *How Master Mou Removes Our Doubts*. Albany: State University of New York Press.

Kinney, Anne Behnke
1993. "Infant Abandonment in Early China." *Early China* 18:107–37.

Kleeman, Terry F.
1998. *Great Perfection: Religion and Ethnicity in a Chinese Millennial Kingdom*. Honolulu: University of Hawai'i Press.

Knoblock, John
1988. *Xunzi: A Translation and Study of the Complete Works*. Vol. 1. Stanford, Calif.: Stanford University Press.

Kohn, Livia
1989. "Guarding the One: Concentrative Meditation in Taoism". In *Taoist Meditation and Longevity Techniques*, ed. L. Kohn, pp. 125–58. Ann Arbor, Mich.: Center for Chinese Studies, The University of Michigan Press.
1993. *The Taoist Experience: An Anthology*. Albany: State University of New York Press.

1995. *Laughing at the Tao: Debates among Buddhists and Taoists in Medieval China.* Princeton, N.J.: Princeton University Press.

Kohn, Livia, ed.

2000. *Daoism Handbook.* Leiden: Brill.

Kroll, Paul

1985. "In the Halls of the Azure Lad." *Journal of the American Oriental Society* 105.1:75–89.

Lagerwey, John

1981. *Wu-shang pi-yao: Somme taoiste du VIe siècle.* Paris: École Française d'Extrême-Orient.

Lau, D. C.

1970. *Mencius.* Harmondsworth: Penguin.

1979. *The Analects.* Harmondsworth: Penguin.

Legge, James

1960. *The Chinese Classics.* Hong Kong: Hong Kong University Press.

Lewis, Marc

1999. *Writing and Authority in Early China.* Albany: State University of New York Press.

Loewe, Michael

1967. *Records of Han Administration.* Cambridge: Cambridge University Press.

1974. *Crisis and Conflict in Han China.* London: George Allen and Unwin.

1981. "China." In *Oracles and Divination*, ed. Michael Loewe and Carmen Blacker, pp. 38–62. London: Allen and Unwin.

1982. *Chinese Ideas of Life and Death: Faith, Myth and Reason in the Han Period.* London: Allen and Unwin.

1986. "The Concept of Sovereignty." In Twitchett and Loewe (1986):726–46.

Maeda Shigeki

2006. "Between Karmic Retribution and Entwining Infusion: Is the Karma of the Parent Visited upon the Child?" In *Daoism in History: Essays in Honour of Liu Ts'un-yan*, ed. Benjamin Penny, pp. 101–120. London: Routledge.

Major, John

1987. "The Meaning of Hsing-te." In *Chinese Ideas about Nature and Society: Studies in Honour of Derk Bodde*, ed. Charles LeBlanc and Susan Blader, pp. 281–91. Hong Kong: Hong Kong University Press.

1993. *Heaven and Earth in Early Han Thought.* Albany: State University of New York Press.

Mansvelt Beck, B. J.

1980. "The Date of the *Taiping jing*." *T'oung Pao* 67:149–82.

1986. "The Fall of Han." In Twitchett and Loewe (1986):317–76.

Marney, John

　　1976. *Liang Chien-wen Ti.* Boston: Twayne.

Masaaki, Tsuchiya

　　2002. "Confession of Sins and Awareness of Self in the *Taiping jing.*" In *Daoist Identity: History, Lineage and Ritual,* ed. L. Kohn and H. Roth, pp. 39–57. Honolulu: University of Hawai'i Press.

Maspero, Henri

　　1981. *Taoism and Chinese Religion,* trans. Frank A. Kierman Jr. Amherst: University of Massachusetts Press.

Mather, Richard

　　1976. *Shih-shuo hsin-yu: A New Account of Tales of the World.* Minneapolis: University of Minnesota Press.

　　1979. "K'ou Ch'ien-chih and the Taoist Theocracy at the Northern Wei Court 425–451." In Welch and Seidel (1979):103–22.

Michaud, Paul

　　1958. "The Yellow Turbans." *Monumenta Serica* 17:47–127.

Naundorf, G., K.-H. Pohl, and H.-H. Schmidt, eds.

　　1985. *Religion und Philosophie in Ostasien.* Würzburg: Königshausen und Neumann.

Needham, Joseph

　　1956. *Science and Civilisation in China,* vol. 2. Cambridge: Cambridge University Press.

　　1959. *Science and Civilisation in China,* vol. 3. Cambridge: Cambridge University Press.

　　1962. *Science and Civilisation in China,* vol. 4.1. Cambridge: Cambridge University Press.

　　1971. *Science and Civilisation in China,* vol. 4.3. Cambridge: Cambridge University Press.

Ngo Van Xuet

　　1976. *Divination, magie et politique dans la Chine ancienne.* Paris: Presses Universitaires de France.

Nickerson, Peter

　　1997. "The Great Petition for Sepulchral Plaints." In Bokenkamp (1997):230–74.

　　2000. "The Southern Celestial Masters." In Kohn (2000):256–82.

Ōfuchi Ninji

　　1979b. "The Formation of the Taoist Canon." In Welch and Seidel (1979):253–67.

Pearson, Margaret

　　1989. *Wang Fu and the* Comments of a Recluse. Tempe: Center for Asian Studies, Arizona State University.

Peerenboom, R. P.

    1993. *Law and Morality in Ancient China*. Albany: State University of New York Press.

Penny, Benjamin

    1990. "A System of Fate Calculation in the *Taiping jing*." *Papers on Far Eastern History* 41:1–8.

    1996. "The Text and Authorship of *Shenxian zhuan*." *Journal of Oriental Studies* 34.2:165–209.

Petersen, J. O.

    1989. "The Early Traditions Relating to the Han Dynasty Transmission of the *Taiping jing*." Part 1, *Acta Orientalia* 50:133–71.

    1990a. "The Early Traditions Relating to the Han Dynasty Transmission of the *Taiping jing*." Part 2, *Acta Orientalia* 51:173–216.

    1990b. "The Anti-Messianism of the *Taiping jing*." *Journal of the Seminar for Buddhist Studies* 3:1–36.

    1990c. "The *Taiping jing* and the *Shuowen jiezi*." In *The Master said: To Study and . . . To Soren Egerod on the Occasion of His Sixty-Seventh Birthday*, ed. B. Arendrup, S. B. Heilesen and J. O. Petersen, pp. 139–49. Copenhagen: East Asia Institute, University of Copenhagen.

    1992. 'The *Taiping jing* and the A.D. 102 Clepsydra Reform." *Acta Orientalia* 53:122–58.

Pines, Yuri

    1997. "Intellectual Change in the Chunqiu Period: The Reliability of the Speeches in the *Zuozhuan* as the Sources of Chunqiu Intellectual History." *Early China* 22:78–132.

Pokora, Timoteus

    1975. *Hsin-lun (New Treatise) and Other Writings by Huan T'an (43 B.C.–28 A.D.)*. Ann Arbor: Center for Chinese Studies, University of Michigan.

Poo, Mu-chou

    1990. "Ideas Concerning Death and Burial in Pre-Han and Han China." *Asia Major* 2:25–62.

Powers, Martin

    1991. *Art and Political Expression in Early China*. New Haven: Yale University Press.

Puett, Michael

    2001. *The Ambivalence of Creation: Debates Concerning Innovation and Artifice in Early China*. Stanford, Calif.: Stanford University Press.

    2002. *To Become a God: Cosmology, Sacrifice and Self-Divinization in Early China*. Cambridge, Mass.: Harvard Yenching Institute Monograph Series 57.

2004. "Forming Spirits for the Way: The Cosmology of the *Xiang'er* Commentary to the *Laoʐi.*" *Journal of Chinese Religions* 32:1–27.

Reiter, Florian

1990. *Der Perlenbeutel aus den drei Höhlen: San-tung chu-nang.* Wiesbaden: Harrassowitz.

1992. *Kategorien und Realien im Shang-Ch'ing Taoismus.* Wiesbaden: Harrassowitz.

Rickett, W. Allyn

1965. *Kuan-tʐu.* Hong Kong: Hong Kong University Press.

1985. *Guanʐi: Political, Economic, and Philosophical Essays from Early China: A Study and Translation,* vol. 1. Princeton, N.J.: Princeton University Press.

Robinet, Isabelle

1977. *Les commentaires du Tao To King jusqu'au VIIe siècle.* Paris: Collège de France, Institut des Hautes Études Chinoises.

1984. *La révélation de Shangqing dans l'histoire du taoisme.* Paris: École Française d'Extrême-Orient.

1997. *Taoism: Growth of a Religion,* trans. P. Brooks. Stanford, Calif.: Stanford University Press.

Schaberg, David

2001. *A Patterned Past: Form and Thought in Early Chinese Historiography.* Cambridge, Mass.: Harvard University Press.

Schipper, Kristofer

1975. *Concordance du Tao-Tsang.* Paris: École Française d'Extrême-Orient.

1979. "Millenarismes et Messianismes dans la Chine Ancienne." In *Understanding Modern China: Problems and Methods,* ed. L. Lanciotti and P. Corradini, pp. 31–49. Rome: IsMEO.

1996. *The Taoist Body.* Selangur Darul Ehsan: Pelanduk.

Schmidt-Glintzer, Helwig

1990. *Geschichte der chinesischen Literatur.* Bern: Scherz.

Schuessler, Axel

1987. *A Dictionary of Early Zhou Chinese.* Honolulu: University of Hawai'i Press.

Seidel, Anna

1969. *La Divinisation de Lao Tseu dans le Taoism des Han.* Paris: École Française d'Extrême-Orient.

1969/1970. "The Image of the Perfect Ruler in Early Daoist Messianism." *History of Religions* 9:216–47.

1983. "Imperial Treasures and Taoist Sacraments—Taoist Roots in the Apocrypha." In *Tantric and Taoist Studies,* ed. M. Strickmann, vol. 2, pp. 291–371. Bruxelles: Institut Belge des Hautes Études Chinoises.

1985. "Geleitbrief an die Unterwelt: Jenseitsvorstellungen in den Graburkunden der Späteren Han Zeit." In Naundorf et al. (1985):161–83.

Serruys, Paul

1984. "On the System of the Pu Shou in the *Shuo-wen chieh-tzu*." *Lishi yuyan yanjiusuo jikan* 55.4:651–754.

Sommer, Deborah

1995. *Chinese Religion: An Anthology of Sources*. New York: Oxford University Press.

Soothill, W. E.

1972. *Chinese Buddhist Terms*. Taipei: Ch'eng wen.

Stein, Rolf

1963. "Remarques sur les movements du Taoisme politico-religieux au IIe siècle ap. J. C." *T'oung Pao* 50:1–78.

1979. "Religious Taoism and Popular Religion from the Second to Seventh Century." In Welch and Seidel (1979):53–81.

Strickmann, Michel

1977. "The Maoshan Revelations. Taoism and the Aristocracy." *T'oung Pao* 63:1–64.

1978. "A Taoist Confirmation of Liang Wu Ti's Suppression of Taoism." *Journal of the American Oriental Society* 98.4:467–75.

1979. "On the Alchemy of T'ao Hung-ching." In Welch and Seidel (1979):123–92.

1981. *Le Taoisme du Mao chan: Chronique d'une révélation*. Paris: Collège de France.

1985. "Therapeutische Rituale und das Problem des Bösen im frühen Taoismus." In Naundorf et al. (1985):185–200.

2002. *Chinese Magical Medicine*, ed. Bernard Faure. Stanford, Calif.: Stanford University Press.

Swann, Nancy Lee

1950. *Food and Money in Ancient China*. Princeton, N.J.: Princeton University Press.

Teng Ssu-yu

1968. *Family Instructions for the Yen Clan (Yen-shih chia-hsun)*. Leiden: Brill.

Teng Ssu-yu and Knight Biggerstaff

1971. *An Annotated Bibliography of Selected Chinese Reference Works*, 3rd edition. Cambridge, Mass.: Harvard University Press.

Tjan, Tjoe Som

1949/52. *Po hu t'ung: The Comprehensive Discussions in the White Tiger Hall*. Leiden: Brill.

Twitchett, Denis, and Michael Loewe, eds.

1986. *The Cambridge History of China*. Vol. 1: *The Ch'in and Han Empires*. Cambridge: Cambridge University Press.

Waley, Arthur

1934. *The Way and its Power*. London: George Allen and Unwin.

Ware, James R.

1966. *Alchemy, Medicine, and Religion in the China of A.D. 320: The Nei P'ien of Ko Hung (Pao-p'u tzu)*. Cambridge, Mass.: M.I.T. Press.

Watson, Burton

1964. *Han Fei Tzu: Basic Writings*. New York: Columbia University Press.

Welch, Holmes, and Anna Seidel, eds.

1979. *Facets of Taoism*. New Haven, Conn.: Yale University Press.

Wechsler, Howard J.

1985. *Offerings of Jade and Silk*. New Haven: Yale University Press.

Wilhelm, Richard

1972. *I Ging: Das Buch der Wandlungen*. Düsseldorf: Diederichs.

1989. *I Ching or Book of Changes*. Trans. Cary F. Baynes. Harmondsworth: Penguin (Arkana).

Yü Ying-shi

1964. "Life and Immortality in the Mind of Han China." *Harvard Journal of Asiatic Studies* 25:80–122.

Zuercher, Erik

1959. *The Buddhist Conquest of China*. Leiden: Brill.

1977. "Late Han Vernacular Elements in the Earliest Buddhist Translations." *Journal of the Chinese Language Teachers' Association* 12:177–203.

1980. "Buddhist Influences on Early Taoism." *T'oung Pao* 66:84–147.

1982. "Prince Moonlight." *T'oung Pao* 68:1–75.

1991. "A New Look at the Earliest Chinese Buddhist Texts." In *From Benares to Beijing: Essays on Buddhism and Chinese Religions in Honour of Prof. Jan Yün-Hua*, ed. Koichi Shinohara and G. Schopen, pp. 277–304. Oakville, Ontario: Mosaic Press.

1996. "Vernacular Elements in Early Buddhist Texts: An Attempt to Define the Optimal Source Materials." *Sino-Platonic Papers* 71:1–31.

INDEX

cipher. See *shu*

clothes: as a need, 74–75, 93n47, 116, 258, 288, 313; of dark and yellow silk, 116, 123; as reward, 292

commandments: in the Celestial Master community, 31; in the TPJ, 3, 52, 93n47, 201n3; of the TPJ's Celestial Lord, 41; in the *Xiang'er*, 29

Commands and Admonitions of the Families of the Great Dao (Da dao jia lingjie), 213n7

confession, 26, 166n31, 230n22, 239n17, 341–42n24

Confucius: and arrival of great peace, 10; on control of spirits, 133n13; on family life, 177n4; and his disciples, 147n3; on neglecting the need for food, 113; on self-cultivation, 7, 206; on serving parents, 132n4; subtle sayings, 81n19; and the TPJ's Celestial Master, 11. See also *Lun yu*

constancy in human conduct *(chang)*, 222–24, 229n16, 304, 305n5

Controller of Fate *(si ming)*, 73, 90n39

Controller of Time *(si hou)*, 90n39

cooperation: between man, heaven and earth, 181; between social strata, 206, 208–10, 214n16; of both hands, 98n3, 307–8; of three, 308, 311–13

cosmogony: congealing of three *qi*, 311, 321n10, 322n14; one is the beginning, 145, 181; relationship between *dao* and heaven, 71, 84n24; role of *ziran*, 118n7

county *(xian)*: head, 90n39, 107–8, 109n4, 112n17; office, 111n9, 143, 151n10, 284, 291–92, 315

crimes *(guo, zui*; offences): against heaven and earth *(zui)*, 76, 97, 259, 268; against heaven and earth *(guo)*, 129, 134n19, 264; committed by demons *(zui)*, 130, 323n22; considered so by the people *(da guo)*, 290; in the legal sense *(zui)*, 285, 288; treatment

within Celestial Master movement, 27, 31

Cui Shi, 66n186, 127, 242, 299–300n36

cycles: cosmic, 15, 31, 162n14, 203n12, 281–82n13, 306n5; of inherited evil, 141, 150n10

Da dongji tian zhi zhengshi (Great All-Pervading Reign of Heaven), 201, 205n21

dao: in Celestial Master movement, 29–30; corruption of, 68, 115, 224; devoid of *(wu dao)*, 75, 91n43, 298n22, 328–29; essential *(yao)*, 240n23; great, 122, 291, 335; and heaven, 71, 84n24, 338; intentions of, 190, 192n2, 223; man of, 211–12n6, 218, 268; and primordial *qi*, 213n7, 322n14; safeguarding *(shou dao)*, 133n13, 174, 209, 285; in the TPJ, 31, 41; true, 225, 240n23, 328–29, 331 *(see also* teachings)

dao and virtue *(de;* morality), 160; and benevolence (humaneness), 71, 326, 331, 338; rule by, 70, 246, 289, 304; safeguarding, 248

Daode jing, 6. See also *Laozi*

Daodian lun, 62n150

Daoism: elementary stage, 39; eschatological beliefs in, 31, 36, 37–38, 41; and *fang shi*, 23, 154; and the notion of great peace, 26, 35, 62n150; pantheon, 23, 38, 365n40; and the TPJ, 30, 39–41, 47, 102n4, 154, 353, 365n51

Daoist canon *(Dao zang)*, 35; 346, 363n9; *Lingbao* cavern of, 60n136; *Taiping* section of, 35, 60n135

Daojiao yishu, 184n5, 203n8, 363n9

dao li (proper order), 75, 258, 259, 334

daolu (the right way), 45, 223–24

Daoxue zhuan, 61n140, 188n21

Daoyao lingqi shengui pin jing, 229n16

daping (great peace), 8, 54n11

Da Qin ("Roman Empire"), 59n107

dark chamber *(you shi)*, 70, 80–81n15, 124, 155, 248. *See also* meditation

datong (great unity), 10

daughters, 50, 68, 73–75, 92n47

Da zhong song zhang, 79n9

de. See virtue

death: caused by crimes against heaven, 259, 292, 329, 336; and earth, 134n21, 249; hatred of, 18, 133n12, 332; penalty, 189, 190–91; as rupture, 15, 103n8; transcendence of, 29, 183,212, 229n17, 291

deceitfulness: as cause of illness, 158; as mode of government, 302–3; in texts, 185n7, 219, 293, 332; in texts as in society, 199, 205n18, 225; towards superiors, 117, 129, 143, 318

de Crespigny, Rafe, 59n112, 242

demons *(gui)*: in early Daoist movements, 23, 28, 58n87; good, 183, 299n28; hungry, 80n12; at leisure, 175, 183, 335; mischievous, 126, 128, 256–57; wicked, 175

demon soldiers *(gui zui)*, 58–59n106; *Dengzhen yinjue*, 79n9

disaster analysis, 231, 282n13

disasters: causes of, 71, 91n45, 96, 108, 114, 223, 329; ending of, 200, 234, 258; and government, 131, 247, 274, 313, 333; increasing, 139, 145, 160, 199; sent by heaven, 40, 112n17, 136, 257; as sign of earth's anger, 73

disciples: of the Great Spirit, 84n23, 351; of Zhang Jue, 19; of Zhang Ling, 25

disciples of the TPJ's Celestial Master, 30, 35, 291, 329; argumentative role of, 42, 138, 142–43, 265–66; attitude towards speaking, 114, 168n42; careers, 42, 174, 191, 219, 165, 279n2, 294; and the common people, 127, 243, 261, 285–86, 302; from the six directions, 278, 348, 364n28; and heaven, 191,

196; must not say thank you, 182–83, 187n16; and note taking, 42, 89–90n38

dispensation *(tong)*, 13, 74, 90–91n40, 96

divination: limited number of attempts, 180, 181–82, 186n9; material on, 341n23; as raising questions, 309. *See also* knowledge; prognostication

dongji (all pervading), 199, 203n12, 205n21, 305n5, 314

Dongji zhi jing (Scripture That Pervades All), 35, 204n12, 344, 362n4; and nourishing the vital principle, 140n4

dongming (brightness), 224, 228n11

Dongxian zhuan, 167n38

Dongxuan lingbao zhen ling weiye tu, 63n154

Dong Zhongshu, 6; on cyclical development, 15; on great peace, 10; on the unity of three, 65n182. See also *Chun qiu fan lu*

dragon, 88n30, 102n4, 157, 165n20, 213n6, 298n27, 306n7

Dunhuang fragment S 4226: and the *Chao*, 353, 363n14; dating, 62n151; on guarding the one, 149n9, 161n1; on origin of the TPJ, 63n157; and TPJ table of contents, 37, 202n5, 211n6, 345–46, 348, 367n75

earth: angry, 73, 160, 259; as model, 191, 224; as mother, 128, 131, 263; offended, 75–76, 258–62; as a phase, 17; and virtue *(de)*, 338. *See also* heaven and earth

Ebrey, Patricia, 12

educated (learned; *ru*), 111n9, 214n12, 299n33

education: replaced by conversion, 27, 51; within the reform process, 187n17, 208, 234, 342; for Wang Fu, 11. *See also* learning

Eichhorn, Werner, 1, 55n20, 55n28

eight directions, 277, 296, 322n18

food: for the dead, 80n12, 127, 130, 284; need for, 113, 115, 122; provision of, 75, 258, 292; replaced by *qi*, 209; scarcity of, 17, 74, 92n47, 333

foreign tribes. *See* barbarian tribes

four: directions, 107, 182; modes of conduct, 222; oceans and four borders, 205n22

four seasons: in disorder, 233, 235; in men, 76, 175; transformative power of, 156, 159, 207, 226, 257; of the year, 241, 258, 311, 316–17, 338

frivolous and superficial *(fu hua)*: in activities, 116, 130; how to discard, 166n25; in teachings, 137, 162n10, 185n7; in texts, 158, 219

fu (again): in adverbial compounds, 44, 65n177; as ornamental particle, 64n168

funerary rituals, 127, 129, 336

fu ze (encumbered by debt), 151n10

gai tian theory, 88n29

Gan Ji (Han dynasty *fang shi*; Yu Ji), 32–33, 39, 161n1, 297n20

Gaozu (Tang dynasty emperor), 62n150

Ge Hong, 34, 35, 60n131, 177n2, 230n21, 283. See also *Baopu zi*

gentleman *(junzi)*, 84n23, 246, 250

geomancy *(fengshui)*, 135n21

Ge Xuan, library of, 34–35

gong (together), in adverbial compounds, 44, 65n177

Gong Chong (Han dynasty *fang shi*), 32, 34

good *(shan)*, 71, 283; men are scarce, 101n4, 327; men in government, 292; men resemble seed people, 83–84n23, 273n46; officials, 286–87, 292, 313; people, 28, 106, 209, 273n47, 313; teachings *(dao)*, 19, 333; things *(wu*; harvest), 70, 79–80n11; wife, 276, 313. *See also* valuable *(shan)*

good and bad: as auspicious and inaus-

picious, 222–24, 227n2, 227n3; defined in early Daoist movements, 31; as true and false, 201–2n4; as willed by heaven, 328. *See also* knowledge

good deeds: in early Celestial Master Daoism, 28; in governing, 200–201, 317; rewards for, 27, 79n10, 173–75, 177n2, 177–78n7

good fortune and misfortune, 122, 125n7, 221–23, 228n8, 236n3

government: achieving great peace, 6, 11, 96, 268, 277; losing authority, 131, 145; ranks of, 84–85n25, 302–3, 313–14, 318–19; reduction of, 113–14, 181, 286, 327; resembling heaven, 189–90, 247

gradualism, 217–18

Grand One *(Tai yi)*, 23

Grand One of the Center and of Yellow *(Zhong huang tai yi)*, 23

grass hut, 209

graves, 255, 263, 271n23, 132n4, 134n21; securing writs, 22, 58n87, 63n165, 151n10, 167n32

great contrariness *(da ni)*, 75, 91n43, 93n47, 96, 290, 298n22

great peace *(taiping)*, in Han dynasty and later Chinese thought: and Confucius, 10–11; historical dimensions of, 9–10; ideal of, 6–9; reign period, 37; of yellow heaven, 22–24

great peace *(taiping)*, in the TPJ: arrival of, 98–100n3, 105, 108, 162–63n14; and becoming transcendent, 158; geographic extension of, 10, 88n29, 276; and guarding the root, 184n5; inclusiveness of, 131, 134n17, 203n12, 248; the Master's linguistic analysis, 310; obstructing the arrival of, 268, 304; and protection of life, 191; *qi* of, 319–20n2; and salvation, 16, 22, 40–41, 47, 53–54, 265, 365n47; Son of Heaven of, 62n150; supreme majestic

Laozi zhongjing, 237n6

late antiquity *(xia gu)*, 119n14. *See also* historical stages

Latter Sage of the Golden Gate (Jin que hou sheng dijun), 37–38, 47, 62n153, 63n154, 365n51

learning: content, 281n12, 326–27, 330–31, 333–34, 339n7; and salvation, 218; and social mobility, 187n19, 211–13n6; and teaching, 183

lei (subject, topic), 197–98; *leishu* (anthology), 196, 201n1, 203n8

leisure, 73, 288, 289, 337

Lewis, Mark, 9

Li (family name), 38, 63n154

Liang Ji, 19

Liang Shang, 127

libationers *(jijiu)*, 26, 27

Li'er taiping fu, 348

Liezi, 178n10, 252n9

life: constraints, 113, 173–74; danger to, 16, 40, 73, 103n8; and death, 18, 89n33, 246, 281n13; esteem for, 15, 93n50, 113, 126, 190–91, 242; human, 73, 121, 256, 303; strengthening of, 28, 31, 38, 136, 206; units of *(suan)*, 370n137

Li Hong, 38

Ling (Han dynasty emperor), 33, 280n7

Lishi zhen xian tidao tongjian, 161n1

Liu An, 13, 253n13

Liu Bei, 25

Liu Shaorui, 151n10

Liu Xiang, 27

Liu Zhang (warlord of the late Han dynasty), 25

living and the dead, the, 129–30, 227n2, 335

Li Xian, 62n150, 63n157, 104n16, 162n14, 364n32

Li Xun (Han dynasty astronomer), 33–34, 165n25

longevity: and Celestial Master movement, 25; and Huang-Lao, 20, 59n111

longevity, in the TPJ, 41, 53; finishing the years destined by heaven, 157, 175; given to others, 286; and good deeds, 66n187, 175, 177–78n7, 292–93; practices, 136, 150n10, 298n27, 351–52; ranking of, 322n22

Lun heng: agrees with the TPJ, 134n16, 134n20, 135n22, 237n8, 237n9, 253n17; comparison of language use, 43, 253n23; disagrees with the TPJ, 86n29, 118n7, 270n13

Lun yu: on good men, 84n23; on master and disciples, 46, 147n3, 166n25, 326, 272n38, 326; on proper behavior, 296n4; on the ruler's integrity, 13; on substance and decorum, 124n4; in the TPJ, 63n161. *See also* Confucius

Luoyang, 20, 32, 39, 63n160, 167n32

Lüqiu Fangyuan (ninth-century Daoist), 161n1, 346

Lü shi chun qiu, 15, 117n6

Lu Xiujing, 60n136

majestic *(huang)*, 310, 319–20n2; numinous *(huang ling)*, 309, 320n3

Mansvelt Beck, B. J., 19

Mao shan zhi (Report on the Mao Range), 36, 61n140, 61n147

Maspero, Henri, 140n4

Ma Yuanyi (Yellow Turban general), 20

meat, consumption of, 31

meditation: and governing, 49, 70, 81n16, 125n8, 206, 286; self-cultivation, 29, 38, 139n4, 142; special room for, 24, 80–81n15, 155; stages of, 188n21, 211n5, 228n11; women practicing, 103n11. *See also* one, guarding the; oratory; *qi*

memorials, 204n12, 293, 308, 314–16

men: equality in producing texts, 202–3n7; and heaven and earth, 96–97; 134n19, 257–59; insufficiency, 72, 106; ranking of, 107, 111n9, 162n5,

Zhang Jue (Yellow Turban leader), 19–23, 57n70; conducting human sacrifices, 58n90; and Huang-Lao, 28; as a missionary, 31; and a scripture on great peace, 33; trusting *shen* and *ling* spirits, 59n106. *See also* yellow; Yellow Turban rebellion

Zhang Ling (Celestial Master), 24–26, 42, 344, 362n4, 363n10; and Laozi, 30

Zhang Lu (Celestial Master), 23, 25, 41; controlling men with the help of spirits, 28, 58–59n106; and the *Laozi*, 28; mother of, 25; and the *Xiang'er*, 29

Zhang Mancheng (Yellow Turban rebel), 22, 64n166

Zhang Rong, 271n24

Zhang Xiu, 25

Zhen'gao, 62n153, 62n154, 345

Zhengyi fawen taishang wai lu yi, 212n6

Zhengyi jing, 60n135, 344, 363n10

Zheng Yin, library of, 34

zhen men (true gate), 329

zhen ren. See perfected

zhong fu (heavy load), 151n10

zhonghe (harmony between), 82–83n22,

321n12; and heaven and earth, 257; and Yin and Yang, 223, 264, 303, 312

Zhongshan yugui fuqi jing, 210n5

Zhou Zhixiang (sixth-century Daoist), 36–37, 61–62n147

Zhuangzi: on great peace, 8; on heaven's subjects, 273n46; on the man of heaven, 161–62n5; on the perfected, 18; on transformation, 214n10

ziran (what is as it is): as cosmogonic force, 84n24, 90n40, 117–18n7, 124; guarding *(shou ziran)*, 365n51; interacting with primordial *qi* and with Yin and Yang, 311; method, 115, 218, 258; model, 250, 314

Zi xu yuan jun neizhuan, 125n5

Zong Qing (official of the late Han dynasty), 92–93n47

Zou Yan, 86–88n29, 253n17

Zuercher, Erik, 43–44

Zuo Ci (*fang shi* of the late Han dynasty), 60n131

Zuo zhuan: on recompense, 58n104, 133n12; on spirits, 177n4, 214n8

Text: 10.25/14 Fournier
Display: Fournier
Compositor: Integrated Composition Systems